Our Endangered Children

Also by Vance Packard

The Hidden Persuaders
The Status Seekers
The Waste Makers
The Pyramid Climbers
The Naked Society
The Sexual Wilderness
A Nation of Strangers
The People Shapers

VANCE PACKARD

Our Endangered Children

Growing Up in a Changing World

Little, Brown and Company —

Boston — Toronto

Library of Congress Cataloging in Publication Data

Packard, Vance Oakley, 1914–
   Our endangered children.

   Includes bibliographical references and index.
   1. Children — United States — Social conditions.
2. Child rearing — United States. 3. Family — United States. 4. Child psychology. I. Title.
HQ792.U5P29   1983   649′.1′0973   83-9438
ISBN 0-316-68751-0

VB
Designed by Patricia Girvin Dunbar

*Published simultaneously in Canada
by Little, Brown & Company (Canada) Limited*

PRINTED IN THE UNITED STATES OF AMERICA

To my grandchildren
Amanda, Kendra, Matthew and Ned

"We should take a tough look at the modern form of damnation that confronts our children."

— William Kessen, Chairman, Department of Psychology, Yale University

Contents

Part 5. Some Concluding Thoughts

Introduction:
Children at Risk

Mismanagement in raising children did not begin in the late twentieth century — only a new and dangerous kind of mismanagement. Other societies have been harsh, neglectful or misguided with children, particularly when they, like us, were facing novel difficulties under turbulent social conditions or new ideologies.

It wasn't until recent times that the concept of childhood, as a state different from adulthood, even existed. Previously, children in Western societies were treated as miniature adults.

In medieval societies as well as primitive ones, by the age of seven children began sharing the work and play of adults. Philip Aries, a leading historian of children, said that soon after weaning "the child became the natural companion of the adult." Even when adult play got a little voluptuous under the influence of drink, as depicted in some of Brueghel's sixteenth-century paintings, the children were right there having their own kind of fun.

The lack of distinction between child and adult also applied to clothing. Whether at work or play or at dress-up parties the children dressed pretty much as adults did. I have before me six American folk paintings of children or children with adults. All the children are dressed as adults. A painting of a "Schoolmaster and Two Boys" painted around 1815 shows all three in identical garb.

Only in nineteenth-century America did a general trend develop to dress adults and children differently. Boys were put in short pants or sailor suits; girls in pigtails. In short, childhood came to be recognized as something apart. It coincided with the growing separation of children from adults which was brought about primarily by the rise of schooling.

Still there was little celebration of children as the Western World broke into modern times. This was particularly true from the mid-seventeenth century to the mid-nineteenth century. The upheavals created by the harsh beginnings of industrialism, the sweeping up of people into vast cities, and the stern notions of the hell-fire Calvinists all tended to be bad news for children.

In many European cities during the eighteenth century it was then the vogue for mothers to "put out" their infants to live with some local wet nurse. Commonly the infant was sent to a wet nurse in the countryside. At one point the great majority of Paris-born infants were thus put out in the country.

Callous and selfish? In many cases yes, although the infant still had the advantage of a single caretaker. But consider the circumstances. Rapid urbanization had undermined much of the sense of family and community life and had made life considerably more hazardous for small children.

Cities were exploding. London, for example, by 1700 had swollen to a vast filthy metropolis of 750,000 people. Garbage and piles of horse manure attracted rats, fleas, and flies bearing germs that caused typhus and infantile diarrhea.

Most children born in new urban areas died before their sixth birthday. Under such odds parents of newborn babies may well have held back from developing any intense attachment to their infants and toddlers. Historians suggest that a kind of "tenderness taboo" existed in the seventeenth century regarding small children.

Or consider child labor. Children in traditional societies are given early responsibilities. Six-year-olds are given responsibility for younger brothers or sisters and carry them around in slings.

Before Western societies began industrializing it was common for families to send all but the oldest son out of the home to be apprentices to other masters. This usually occurred when the children were between seven and nine years old. The masters trained the child in a trade, often were obligated to teach the child reading and writing, and could discipline the child. The practice had some logic at the time. Free public schooling was rarely available.

Child labor in the early days of the Industrial Revolution, however, was something quite brutally different. Some of the exploitation of children was more appalling than I ever imagined before I began this exploration.

There were few regulations regarding employment. Factory and mine owners exploited the cheap labor of children. They cited the Puritan Ethic, which defended child labor as a natural blessing; and they benefited from the then-popular economic theory exalting laissez-faire capitalism.

In New England cotton mills children often worked at machines fourteen hours a day. In a "reformation" of 1842 the working hours of a child under twelve were reduced to ten hours a day.[1]

Apparently the worst exploitation was in the early-nineteenth-century coal mines of England and Scotland. The meager laws regarding child labor in factories did not apply to mines. The evidence of what went on was laid out coolly with many specifics in a presentation made to the House of Commons in 1842 by the seventh earl of Shaftesbury.[2]

The earl detailed the sending of young boys *and* girls into the pits. In Derbyshire children could be sent down into the mines at the age of five. Near Oldham they began work as young as four years old.

The children worked in the mines fourteen to sixteen hours a day. Most of the boys and girls were used as beasts of burden in the narrow tunnels. They were down on their hands and knees hauling carts. The boys were typically naked, the girls stripped to the waist. In this character-building work they had a girdle strapped around their waist. A chain led back between their legs to the cart and often scraped the flesh in the crotch. They went for hours without being able to straighten their backs. Their lungs were fouled by coal dust. If they complained, the bosses usually would beat them.

A clergyman of Tranent complained that children who went into the mines with amiable tempers soon developed "hellish dispositions."

Another cause of painful childhood experience during the seventeenth and eighteenth centuries was religion. Many children raised in the home of dedicated evangelical Protestants — particularly Calvinists — were viewed as carrying the burden of Original Sin. They had to be cured of their satanic will in order to achieve salvation and escape Hell's fires.

It was the Christian duty of their parents — and the new breed of schoolmasters — to do the purging of sin with sternness and whippings when indicated. Playfulness in children was considered ominous. Any signs that a child had erred by wetting his bed might result in the child's being required to drink a pint of piss.[3]

In evangelical homes it was held that children could learn to obey God only by first learning to obey their parents. The noted clergyman John Wesley admonished parents: "Break their wills that you may save their souls."

The widely held view that young children were inherently evil and needed stern treatment was challenged most effectively by two of the leading philosophers of the era. The great naturalist Rousseau scorned the idea that children were inherently evil. He advocated that children were intrinsically natural and the laws of Nature would assure healthy growth. Childhood was an important time in life. He urged affectionate ties between parent and child. And the highly regarded humanist John Locke urged parents to love their children. To gain the respect of a son, he said, the parent must respect that son.

The notions of Rousseau and Locke were particularly well received in America where members of families were dependent upon one another for survival on the frontiers and where servants were scarce. American youngsters were quicker than those in Europe to lose their awe of elders.

During the century leading up to 1965 Americans generally experienced a pattern of family living combining affection and discipline and community-centered living that was congenial for the development of most of their children.

The notion still persists that America is a uniquely child-centered country. Look at some of the indicators:

- North Americans spend twice as much per inhabitant on educating their youngsters as Europeans do.
- The nation has more than three million teachers; and of these about 67,000 are public school guidance counselors.
- The American Medical Association reported that at the beginning of 1981 U.S. children were watched over by 3,271 child psychiatrists and 28,342 pediatricians.

• Dozens of books and thousands of articles offering counsel on child care are published each year.

Still, a deep malaise has rather swiftly come over child-raising in the U.S.A. To some extent it is also afflicting other technologically advanced societies. This condition is starting to be sensed in America. In 1982 the findings of a survey by the noted polling firm Louis Harris and Associates was released. About two thousand persons were questioned. Three-quarters were family adults, but there were also teenagers, corporate and labor leaders, leaders of women's groups. The conclusion:

"Clearly, the perception of deterioration in the overall quality of parenting is widespread."

What's happening?

To me it seems clear that our society is seriously malfunctioning in its role of preparing children for adulthood. The upheaval and disarray we are seeing in childrearing patterns are unprecedented in modern times.

We make pronouncements about building a better life, making progress and meeting tomorrow's challenges. But those prospects for tomorrow will be crucially affected by how well we bring up today's children. Insistently we should be asking: But what about the children?

Our Western World has millions of marvelous, well-developed children. They are raised in supportive, stimulating communities by thoughtful, loving parents. I have met many of them and have felt rewarded by the encounters. The larger fact, however, is that the whole tilt of our society, our institutions and, yes, our family functioning is toward blighting our youngsters and burdening them with pain, anxiety, and discouraging problems. Many of these pains and problems threaten to create a permanent warping of a large segment of our coming generation. All this is occurring at a time when we are seeing a demographic upsurge of young couples moving into the normal child-rearing stage.

Child-raising is becoming a bigger puzzle for parents and potential parents — and a greater challenge. Many feel less in command of their family prospects. Parents often feel, justifiably, that both our institutions and our social attitudes are stacked against them. Our basic social unit, the family, is under significant assault.

A few years ago one of America's leading authorities on child-rearing, Urie Bronfenbrenner, Professor of Human Development and Family Studies, Cornell University, warned that the radical changes occurring in the family have consequences for the young that were "approaching the calamitous."

What are the radical changes?

I believe they relate particularly to three areas of change in our society.

1. Unwittingly we have developed an anti-child culture that confronts children with a cool, hard world outside their home.

2. We have failed to come to grips with one of the more momentous phenomena of this century, the surge of married women — including millions of mothers — into jobs outside the home.

3. We are witnessing a very great increase in the splitting up of parents and are just starting to perceive the reverberating impact on the millions of children involved.

These factors, I believe, contribute greatly to the "modern forms of damnation that confront our children," to use Professor William Kessen's marvelously perceptive phrase. This book, in essence, will take a close look at what seem to me to be some of these forms of damnation, and suggest what we can do about them.

In exploring the world of "children" I will be focusing on the young who range in age from infancy to fourteen, or early adolescence. They comprise more than fifty million individuals. The emphasis will not be on those who are delinquents, severely deprived, disturbed or battered children, adoptees, or those unfortunates caught in the toils of our legal system. Rather, the focus will be on typical children coming from increasingly typical families — the millions of families trying to cope with the increasingly perplexing and challenging world in which children currently are being reared.

My exploration has convinced me that youngsters are tougher and more adaptable than I had originally assumed. They can take quite a few hard knocks early in life, and even thrive from them, if certain other factors are present. At the same time we are seeing an increase in patterns of living and of child-raising that can often inflict lasting damage on children.

One fortunate development is that we have recently seen a considerable advance in scientific findings on how to raise very well developed children. The findings often carry over to children reared under very difficult circumstances.

Acknowledgments

I am indebted to numerous investigators of various aspects of child life and modern life styles who took the time to supply me with insights in various areas of my interest. Many will be cited in the text, but here are some I wish to single out for an expression of thanks:

Leonard Bachelis, Caroline Bird, Paul Bohannan, Sarah Broman, Urie Bronfenbrenner, Richard Chasin, John Clausen, Amitai Etzioni, Harold Feldman, Paul Glick, Carole Goldman, George Grebner, Louise Guerney, Joan Gussow, Muriel Hirt, Seymour Gold, Mavis Hetherington, Sidney Johnson III, William Kessen, Alan Levy, Jeannette Lofas, Helen Maley, Gwen Morgan, Alice Rossi, Meredith Ringler-White, Michael Rutter, Richard Schnell, Harold Shane, Lora Tessman, Nancy Weston, Judith Wallerstein, Thomas Weisner, Robert Weiss, Daniel Yankelovich, Nicholas Zill.

I am particularly indebted to Marian Edelman and the Children's Defense Fund which she directs.

I received important assistance from lawyers involved in interesting legal battles concerning children, particularly Eugene Gratz, Marcia Robinson Lowry, Harriet Pilpel, Arlan Preblud, Marion Robinson, Jesse Rothman, Stephen Wolfson; and from San Francisco court counselor Jeanne Ames.

Here are some others from whom I received important guidance or help:

- Eight officials of the Massachusetts Office for Children.

- Many knowledgeable people involved in providing substitute child care, including Robert Benson and Perry Mendel, directors of day-care chains; Michelle Seltzer of Wellesley College's School Age Child Care Project; Bess Emanuel of the Child Care Resource Center, Cambridge, Massachusetts; officials of the Day Care and Child Development Council of America; and officials of several day care centers.

- Seven members of Parents Without Partners.

- Officials of Catalyst, the organization to promote the interests of women in business and professional life.

- Officials working with children at Co-Op City, New York City, particularly Fran Gordon and Myra Weinstein.

- School officials in Lexington, Massachusetts, and Lomita Park, California.

- Steve Gaskin of The Farm commune in Tennessee.

- Peggy Charren of Action for Children's Television.

- Scott Thomson of the National Association of Secondary School Principals; John Ourth, 1981–82 president of the National Association of Elementary School Principals; Dorothy Rich, president of The Home and School Institute.

- Dozens of federal and state officials, including especially Joseph Coates and S. P. Hersh.

- Many exceptional parents including Holly Righter, John Lama, Mrs. Robert Alto, Judy Nathanson, and Helen Miller.

- Dora Ashford, who spent a day giving me a tour of the apartment houses in Southern California that were then banning children.

This book would have taken me at least a year longer to complete if at various phases of assembling and processing research materials I had not had the help of Peter X. Tierney and Lynn Hickey Schultz (both with advanced training in child development), my daughter Cynthia Packard Richmond, my son Randall and his wife Carolyn, and my daughter-in-law Bonnie Smith (a child custody master).

1

Growing Up in Our Anti-Child Culture

1

What It Means
to Be Young Today

"Children are now running behind automobiles as a
consumer preference."

— *Headline*, Behavior Today

Children today are confronting, as indicated, some modern forms of damnation. What are the forms? Who are the children?

Millions of children are barely involved at all. They are being well raised in stimulating, concerned communities. Perhaps they have stresses, lots of them. But they enjoy their parents. Life is an engrossing, frequently delightful experience.

For more millions, however, life in much of the Western World provides a scarcity of delights for youngsters and many blighting and bruising experiences. For the *majority* of today's children, being young may mean, among other things:

Wondering if your parents are going to split — or, if they have, living in a one-parent home The rise in the break-up of homes in the past dozen years has been stunningly swift by historical standards. Largely as a result, nearly half the children born in the last few years will spend a portion of their lives living in a one-parent household before reaching age eighteen, according to projections based on U.S. Bureau of Census figures. That assumes present trends in marital disruption (and illegitimacy) continue.

At many U.S. elementary schools more than 40 percent of the students come from disrupted homes. In such situations a youngster, after listening to classmates from such homes, may start wondering and worrying, even though his or her own mom and dad seem to be getting along okay.

A girl at a Lexington, Massachusetts, school recalled what it was like as the split-up of her parents began: "You hear your parents fighting about you all the time. I had to watch my parents fight over the dumbest little things. It makes you feel really guilty. It makes you feel bad, very small and inferior."

Approximately a third of all U.S. youngsters no longer live with both their natural parents. Historian Christopher Lasch suggests that "the absence of the father impresses many observers as the most striking fact about the contemporary family."

Being lonely a lot of the time   There are many indicators of a new loneliness among children. The new sprawling metropolitan areas tend to be anti-child. It is hard to find decent places to play; the child learns: You have to be wary of strangers. You are likely to be alone a lot at home or feel alone at school (vast school facilities discourage intimacy; if you live in a high-rise, fewer friends visit you; if you are one of the twelve million youngsters who now move every year, you have to wait for overtures of friendship from new neighbors and classmates who are appraising you).

I have met children of corporate nomads who by the age of eleven have moved nine times, often to distant places. A mother in Darien, Connecticut, where many corporate families move in and out every year, told me of the traumatic effect their latest move had on their shy fourteen-year-old daughter. She had reached the age where being in a peer group and dating had suddenly become very important. This girl went to the refrigerator and gained forty pounds within a year. An assistant school principal in Darien commented: "We often see a newcomer looking lonely and miserable."

Seeing a lot of "No Children" signs on apartment houses while on your way to school   Nationwide, a large majority of all apartment house owners now put restrictions of some kind on tenants who have children.

Often it is an outright ban. In several major cities children are banned from almost all the nice new apartment complexes being built. Youngsters are learning early how it feels to be a liability to their parents.

Some of the signs on apartment buildings indicate that pets are acceptable but not children. Many children sent away to boarding school know that one reason is that it was the only way their parents could keep their home in an apartment or condominium.

If you are small, there is a strong possibility of being left every weekday with some kind of caretaker (or caretakers), usually outside your home   A large number of preschool children today have mothers who at some point will take outside jobs. Presently, at least a fourth of America's infants and toddlers under age three have mothers who hold down some sort of an outside job; among all preschoolers, the mothers of almost half have jobs.

As mothers have surged into the labor force — a 200 percent increase in twelve years — U.S. society is still fumbling with the challenge of assuring good care for their children. Only beginnings are being made by employers to provide flexible arrangements to ease the new difficulties of parenting. There are no licensed facilities available for three-quarters of the children whose mothers work.

The result is that quite a few million children today are being shortchanged on good care in their early years. Many, in fact, are placed in what are essentially warehouses for children — from eight to ten hours a day.

Being home a lot in an empty house   It is estimated that about twenty thousand small children under the age of six stay in the home all day alone, usually with a television set left on. Their desperate working mothers haven't been able to make any other arrangement. A Chicago boy, age three, was found making his own lunch. The main problem was climbing up on chairs to get to cabinet doors.

After school, the number of young school-age children home alone soars. In the U.S. there are by conservative estimates two million "latchkey" children. The Y.M.C.A. puts the figure closer to ten million. Most let themselves into empty homes with their own key, sometimes hung around their necks. Many hate it.

In State College, Pennsylvania, a community organization became concerned because increasing numbers of elementary school children had to fend for themselves in an empty house after school. The group set up a "Phone Friend" service to act as a mother's assistant in providing information and advice. It receives about thirty to forty calls a week from children. The overwhelming proportion of the calls, according to Penn State University Professor Louise Guerney, are "because of loneliness and fear — usually from noises or because parents, sitters, older sibs fail to arrive home when expected."

Another Penn State specialist in human development, James Garbarino, says we have been seeing "a general emptying of the social environment of children."

Having little real contact with adults   Most of the adults on a child's block go away to a kind of work he or she only vaguely understands. There is little chance to work alongside interesting adults on interesting projects.

A study by Herbert Wright and associates at the University of Kansas found that children growing up where there is a real community, as in a small town, get to know *well* a considerably greater number of adults in various walks of life than do their urban agemates. And they are more apt to be active participants in the adult settings.

Children today even have less interactive contact with their own parents who, on average, spend less time in the home area than they did previously. One study of fathers found they typically spent less than a minute a day in warm, close interaction with their infant children.

Feeling you are a burden and being given few ways to make yourself useful   A youngster knows that the reason for living in a crummy neighborhood is so that he and his sister can each have a separate bedroom. In most of urban America the cost of a three-bedroom home in a good neighborhood is beyond the means of the typical family. Youngsters wonder if they will be able to go to college because already it would cost nearly a third of the family income. In many millions of families the only way offered for youngsters to demonstrate responsibility is to do nonproductive maintenance chores around the house.

More traditional societies have usually viewed children as treasured assets.

Living in a neighborhood that makes you apprehensive   The Foundation for Child Development, in a nationwide survey of 2,300 youngsters aged seven to eleven, reported that its "most disturbing discovery" was the high level of apprehensiveness among the children.[1] More than two-thirds said they felt afraid "that somebody might get into their home." And a quarter of the children said "yes" to the question "When you go outside are you afraid someone might hurt you?"

Some of the apprehension might be based on a generalized anxiety about life, aggravated in many cases by watching too much violence on television. But most of the youngsters could report disturbing experiences. About a fourth of them lived in areas where crime was commonplace or where "undesirable" people were likely to be on the streets or in the parks and playgrounds.

Adjusting to newcomers in your home   If Mom has gone through divorce, it means that in a matter of months new men will probably be coming into the house. One who becomes special may leave around dawn, or stay for breakfast. In most cases both parents will eventually remarry. About one youngster in eight now has a parent who is not a biological parent. For a child, the parent's remarrying can become confusing. Rutgers behaviorist Lionel Tiger vividly put it this way:

"Many people are married to people who have been married to other people who are now married to still others to whom the first partners may not have been married but to whom somebody has likely been married."

In that scramble, where are the child's two natural parents? We have been seeing a breaking up and regrouping of parental affiliations unprecedented in history.

Eating a lot of food that has been left for you — or food you must go out and get at some fast-food place   Eating together has been called the oldest human ritual. The tradition of families eating their meals at home together around a table and discussing the triumphs and problems of the day is a long one in many countries. Now such family dining is becoming a fading custom in America.

First the family lunch disappeared as members began traveling beyond their neighborhood for work or school. Then the family breakfast disappeared as everyone including mother became in a hurry to depart on differing schedules. Now only a minority of families eat a supper together around a table at home. About half of all parents who still eat supper with their children do so in a darkened room eating off trays grouped around the television set, according to a communications study made at the University of Pennsylvania. The food has often been brought in from nearby fast-food outlets in paper containers. If family members arrive home at different hours, the child may eat his food alone, often in front of the TV set in his or her own room.

Most of the talk you hear coming from machines rather than from people you know   In one generation the circumstances of growing up in America have been profoundly changed by television and radio.

Millions of young children are put down in front of television, the great babysitter/pacifier, and left there for hours at a stretch. Mary Jo Bane, a Harvard authority on children, states: "Television is by far the most important new child-care arrangement of this century." Pre-school children — most of them unable to distinguish commercials from programming — listen to the TV voices nearly four hours a day. Older youngsters, despite time spent at school, spend almost as many hours watching TV. In addition, those over ten years old hear, for about two hours a day, voices — often throbbing or raucous voices — coming from their radios or tape decks. Often these voices are coming at them as they do homework.

Often coping with parents who are pretty self-absorbed, or uncertain about their proper role in life   The noted polling firm headed by Daniel Yankelovich made a study of the changing American family. Its principal finding was that a "new breed" of parent was emerging, much less family-oriented than traditionally. It found 43 percent of the parents surveyed to be of this new breed. They put self-fulfillment over worldly success and duty to self over duty to others, including their own children. In effect they say to their children: "I want to be free, so why shouldn't you children be free? We will not sacrifice for you because we have our own life to lead. But when you are grown, you owe us nothing."

Many employed mothers of small children relish the work experience. And both parents appreciate the extra income. Still, many such mothers are torn emotionally. They wonder if they are short-changing their children on nurturance. Many young fathers, too, are confused about their changing role. They know that with their wife working they should be pitching in as a partner in child and household care. They espouse the egalitarian ideal, but often do more talking than acting.

I have noted in a dozen different ways what it is likely to mean to be young today. And I could go on.

These meanings add up to a new kind of adversity for millions of children. They promote a sense of insecurity that may lie behind a seemingly cheerful countenance. They often add up to a poor foundation for adult life.

Many of these new kinds of stresses and possible blighting factors can be counteracted by wise parenting and good community situations. But these meanings of being young today do present a challenge to parents and to our society.

2

Symptoms of a Society
in Trouble with Its Children

"We have not yet found a cure for children whose
nightmares are real."

— *Selma Fraiberg, Department of Psychoanalysis,
University of Michigan, Ann Arbor*

During the past decade the problem of so-called runaway children has
become a considerably increased cause for concern. In the United States
it has reached "epidemic proportions."[1] A Senate committee estimated
the number at more than one million a year.

An interesting aspect is that the age of the youngsters has been declining, until it presently averages about thirteen and a half. Those who
run away come from all social backgrounds, including wealthy suburbs.
Commonly girls are impelled to escape from what they perceive as harsh
parental control; boys from slack, normless parental controls. Often,
one of the natural parents is missing. Or the parents are in deep conflict.

America is not alone in becoming concerned about the phenomenon
of runaways. They are a problem, for example, in Germany and England also. When I was last in England the country seemed convulsed
with collective guilt over the death of a little boy who had been unknown outside his town. An eight-year-old runaway, he had frozen to
death at night trying to cross a swamp to reach another village. Almost

every newspaper ran lamenting banners for days. *The Daily Express* called it "a tragedy of our times."

The boy was "Lonely Lester," son of a divorcée. He had been in public care until she had remarried and resumed custody. Lester stayed to himself, having been frequently smacked and bruised by his step-father, who was bewildered by Lester's lack of respect. Little Lester had tried to run away four times in two months, but the police had always brought him home.

Many of the runaway children of the Western World are not really runaways but "throwaways," kicked-out kids. They've become too much of a bother. Or they are sassy or sullen. Girls may refuse to wear bras. Boys refuse to accept hours to be home at night. Violent quarrels erupt, and out the youngsters go by the hundreds of thousands. "Throw-aways" tend to be more depressed and helpless than youngsters who leave on their own.

In the U.S. if the runaway-throwaways do not return home within a few weeks, they are likely to be in a desperate fix. Some are caught up in the sexploitation network: they slip into prostitution, or they may earn money posing for pictures for the several hundred magazines and films that have been showing children in sexual acts.

A National Runaway Switchboard centered in Chicago now offers toll-free, twenty-four-hour service to runaways. It gives advice and as-sistance to about fifty thousand kids a year. Virtually every major U.S. city has set up runaway houses. They have organized into a national network.

I visited a large runaway house west of Broadway in New York City. Open twenty-four hours a day, it was in one of the city's toughest neighborhoods. Drug-pushing, pornography, and prostitution all flourished in the area. Most involved recent runaways. To get into this shelter, you faced a guard in a protected booth. This was to keep out pimps and other undesirables. The guard would push a buzzer after es-tablishing that you had a justifiable reason for entering.

I was there around four o'clock in the afternoon. Many youngsters were sprawled out asleep on couches or heavy cushions on the floor. Others, half asleep, were watching a TV in the corner.

At night the girls slept on one floor, the boys on another. The overflow slept in a nearby room. If there was still an overflow, latecom-ers were taken on a minibus to affiliated shelters. Hot food is served at this "crisis center" three times a day upstairs at a long table.

Many of the youngsters have been raped or forcibly sodomized, and many have tried to earn money as male or female prostitutes. An official explained: "You don't find any happy hookers here."

A thirteen-year-old runaway prostitute turned up lugging a baby. A ten-year-old runaway boy came in with an armful of toys; he had been used as a prostitute by a homosexual who had paid him in toys, legally a safer payment than cash.

Of the thousands of youngsters who pass through the center each year, two thousand are under fifteen years of age. When questioned, most of them mention rotten fathers as a chief complaint.

The center insists that a parent of each youngster be telephoned to let the parent know the youngster is "safe." The calls often establish that the youngsters are throwaways, not runaways. An official told me: "We call and say we've got your son here. They reply, 'Fine. Keep him.' "

He adds: "They are basically good kids, but every institution in their lives, including their family and school, have failed them." In only a small proportion of the cases can arrangements be made for an immediate return home. The center tries to get them jobs such as selling hot dogs or refers them to longer term rehabilitation centers.

A broader view of the malaise in U.S. homes has been uncovered by a nearby research center, the Foundation for Child Development. It has made a nationwide survey of 2301 youngsters between the ages of seven and eleven. Eight out of ten of the children said they worry about their families. Less than a half of the youngsters lived in a home where both biological parents were still together and judged by the youngsters to be happily married. Yet when asked to pick a face indicating how they feel about their families, nine out of ten picked a happy face. We will see more about the level of anxiety of these youngsters later.

The increasing loneliness or rootlessness of youths emerges from a number of reports. In the U.S. at least two million children (as indicated) are left alone at home much of the day.[2] Tens of thousands are under the age of six. In Detroit, studies have indicated that such home-alone children are a significant cause of residential fires.

A grandmother in San Diego, Mrs. Carol Baras, was so struck by the number of lonely children she encountered or read about that she began recording inspirational messages that children could hear by dialing her number. About 200,000 calls, she reported, came in from children of the area during 1980.

The Survey Research Center at the University of Michigan has reported on two samplings of people's moods which were made two decades apart: in 1956 and again in 1976. Two thousand people were questioned in each. The most dramatic finding was that in the 1976 group — particularly younger people who had grown to adulthood during the two decades between the surveys — seemed to be having much greater difficulty "in connecting to their roles and relationships in society." There were striking increases in symptoms of anxiety in the more recent sample among the younger people, symptoms such as upset stomach, insomnia, and nervousness.[3]

Childhood depression is becoming an increased concern of mental health authorities. Fifteen years ago it wasn't even being seriously explored as a mental health problem (though of course childhood depression is not something recently "invented"). Now many clinics are being set up for that specific malady. And childhood depression is not the only concern.

Child behavior researcher Robert J. Thompson of Duke University lists these behaviors as indicators that a child may have serious emotional problems: too much activity, aggressiveness, being demanding, anxiety, anger, sadness, being very withdrawn.

A long-term family research project involving a study by eight behavioral scientists was made of 1,034 children drawn from a cross-section of Manhattan households. The children were measured on eighteen types of behavior. Some of the more serious were regressive anxiety (such as often waking up in a panic), mentation problems (such as mixing up words), repetitive motor behavior (such as banging head). The project found that about one-third of the youngsters were psychologically or mentally impaired and one in eight was diagnosed by psychiatrists as so severely impaired that they required immediate attention.[4] Even if you argue that the therapy community may overinterpret the behaviors noted, the statistics are still staggering and cannot be dismissed.

KIDS OUT OF CONTROL

"Parents have loosened the reins and kids are kind of floundering," suggests a New York State mental health official. Whatever the causes — and certainly parents are not the only ones — a sharply rising number of youngsters have been breaking out of control.

School behavior as an indicator   The National Association of Secondary School Principals reports that our schools are coping with a new breed of pupil. A top official, Scott D. Thomson, told me: "In some ways the adolescents of our culture are beyond the constraints normally required by adults of young people in general."

There is rampant stealing. According to one study, a pupil in a typical secondary school has a one-in-nine chance of being a victim of theft during any given school month. That, if true, certainly would tend to cause the victim to start building a lifetime distrust toward his or her fellow man.

There has been a widespread slacking off in scholastic effort, a refusal to take schooling seriously. In some areas so many students skip classes that they are now being offered bribes of Frisbees and T-shirts or yo-yos for simply attending classes. The slacking off cuts across all segments of society. Perhaps much of the blame is with the home environment, the quality of the schools, too much TV viewing. Whatever the cause, the facts involved are depressing.

During a period from the early 1960s to the late 1970s — at a time when spending for public school education soared 400 percent and many new education technologies were introduced — student ability to use language, as measured by SAT scores, dropped 10 percent. In five recent years, whether you measure at the nine-year-old level, the thirteen-year-old level or the seventeen-year-old level, there has been a dropping off in problem-solving scores. One-eighth of all students approaching their final year in high school in the late 1970s were still functionally illiterate. In 1981 the federally funded National Assessment of Educational Progress reported that in the 1970s there had been a drop in reasoning ability among thirteen- and seventeen-year-olds. The public alarm about all these diving indicators brought clamor for tougher standards and better techniques for motivating students, which may now be ending the skid.

Lawbreaking as an indicator   Crime in America has increasingly become a problem that involves youths. In West Germany, crime by the young is being called a "social catastrophe."

The offenders there, as in the U.S., are getting younger. In 1982 California officials found themselves trying to cope with a seven-year-old boy charged with being involved in seventeen acts of arson or vandalism resulting in $40,000 worth of destruction. For the nation as a whole, half of all burglars pulled in are youngsters under eighteen. In several countries more and more girls are involved in criminal activity. The arrest rate of young females in the U.S. is rising three times faster than that of young males. Youthful crimes often are mindlessly brutal, such as beating up elderly people after robbing them.

The Federal Bureau of Investigation reports that arrests of children as criminals rose three times as fast as that for adults in fifteen recent years ending in 1977. Arrests of children for serious crimes rose 200 percent in that period.[5] By 1981 the FBI reported the crime rate was starting to level off because there were now fewer teenagers in the total population.

Sexual behavior as an indicator   In the U.S. the *average* age of first intercourse for girls has dropped in the past two decades from the late teens to close to age fifteen. A fifth of all youngsters are sexually experienced within a year of entering puberty.

Two professors at Johns Hopkins University, Melvin Zelnik and John F. Kanter, found in a series of studies that the proportion of sexually experienced teenage girls doubled in less than a decade.

Even though teenagers are starting to use contraceptives on a fairly large scale, early teen pregnancies are still very high. Four hundred thousand girls under the age of fifteen become pregnant each year. The Alan Guttmacher Institute in New York estimated in 1981 that about 40 percent of girls then age fourteen would become pregnant at least once during their teenage years.

In many areas there has been a decrease in the stigma attached to having an illegitimate child. (Some early teenagers, lonely, confess they went ahead and bore their child because they wanted to have a kind of cuddly living doll to play with.) *Time* quoted a pregnant fourteen-year-old girl as saying she was going to dress her baby up "real warm in little clothes and things like that." Another pregnant early teenager having a baby out of wedlock said, "I guess everyone wants a baby. Probably to fill in their life. They feel so bored. They got nothing to do with this life."

The trend of teenage girls having babies but electing not to marry has risen substantially in the past two decades, according to the chief of fertility statistics at the Census Bureau. About a quarter-million new babies born to unwed mothers between ages twelve and nineteen are added to the U.S. population each year.

In cities such as Phoenix, Arizona, the biggest growth in pregnancies has been among children twelve to fourteen years old. A lot of the newborns, in short, are children of children and will spend their most formative years being raised by child-mothers. The Director of the Catholic Social Service of Fort Wayne, Indiana, said that the phenomenom of young unwed girls choosing to try to rear their babies has become a major issue for the agency and is becoming a potentially disastrous development for society.

Venereal disease among early adolescents also has been soaring. Adolescents in general now account for one-fourth of all cases reported.[6]

Drug use as an indicator   Once again the term "epidemic" is frequently used by health officials. In fifteen years the arrest of youngsters for use or trafficking in drugs rose 4600 percent. Marijuana and cocaine have been among the most popular; also "angel dust," which is more likely to trigger freaky violence.

A decade ago the college crowd was the principal user of marijuana. Then it became the high school crowd, until it started experimenting with speed pills and cocaine. More recently the big growth in marijuana use has been among the junior high crowd. A common reason given for the upsurge in drug use by youngsters is boredom. Another is loneliness.

Meanwhile, the pot available has become at least five times more potent than that used in the early 1970s by the college crowd. The National Institute of Drug Abuse warns that the marijuana now available "impairs classroom learning" and is now an unquestioned health hazard.

Alcohol use as an indicator   Youngsters are drinking harder and starting earlier. The National Institute on Alcohol Abuse and Alcoholism reports that the U.S. has 1,300,000 youngsters between twelve and seventeen who have serious drinking problems, serious enough to have run-ins with cops or school personnel. The Institute reports the *average* youngster now has his or her first drink by the age of twelve, a year younger than in the 1960s. Alcoholics Anonymous now has a special brochure for the young. One typical confession (which AA requires) begins: "My name is Diane. I am fourteen and I am an alcoholic." She began drinking heavily out of loneliness when her parents moved to a distant town. That was when she was in fourth grade.

America is not alone in concern about child drinkers. The Associated Press reports many Europeans are deeply worried about the ravages of alcohol on young people. In Britain, teenage convictions for drunkenness have doubled in twelve years. In the Soviet Union officials have admitted their concern about heavy teenage drinking. A long-term observer of Russian life, George Feiffer, reports "drunken sprees" by school children under twelve have become common.

PARENTS OUT OF CONTROL

Each complaining group has its own definition of "child abuse." Many include any form of laying a hand or switch on a child. Others include "neglect" and "psychological abuse." Such abuses do abound. Some certainly are not unique to our time.

Sweden has recently passed a national law outlawing spanking. It is primarily a statement of an ideal: only flagrant child-beaters are prosecuted.

But true child abuse, where the parent flies out of control in a fury of random violence, is apparently growing. The child is often battered and sometimes killed. The parent is the problem, not the child. The National Center on Child Abuse and Neglect reported in 1982 that in the previous year at least 625,000 U.S. children had been abused or neglected to the point that they suffered demonstrable signs of physical or mental harm.

The child is a convenient target for the parent's frustrations, resentments, or neuroses. In 1979 an international investigation involving three years of interviews in twenty-five countries, mostly European, found a worldwide trend toward increased violence against children.[7]

One of the best studies of parents losing control with their children was a report by Richard J. Gelles in *The American Journal of Orthopsychiatry*.[8] His study was of 2,143 intact families chosen from a national probability sample. The children ranged in age from three to seventeen. He did not include infants and toddlers, who are often targets of violence, nor did he include one-parent households where violence is believed to be more common.

He found "an astoundingly large number of children who were kicked, bitten, punched, beaten up, threatened with a gun or knife or had a gun or knife actually used on them." Close to a fourth of the children had received such violent, out-of-control treatment during the preceding year. Projecting nationally, he estimated that nearly two million children were in serious danger of injury from parents.

The number of truly battered children — those so seriously injured that they require hospital treatment — is estimated to be around 40,000 each year in the U.S. At least 700 U.S. children die each year as a result of parental assaults. Gelles's report included an estimate made to a congressional subcommittee on children and youth that the death rate from parental assault could grow to 5,000 a year during the 1980s.

As for infants, Graham Blaine, Jr. reported a case that came to the attention of the Harvard medical clinic that involved a graduate student. The student was working on his thesis and tending the baby while his wife made money by working as a waitress. Neighbors became concerned about the frequent screaming of the baby and wondered if it was alone. When the child was admitted to the clinic with a broken leg, the young father explained that the baby had caught his foot inside the rails of the crib. Later he admitted to his wife that he could not stand the crying. He had struck the baby in anger, he had hit its leg with a hammer. He had held the baby under water until it stopped crying. Blaine said that in almost all such cases the family backgrounds of both parents have been disturbed ones. In this case the wife grew up in a home where the father had deserted the family. The husband grew up in a military household; his father was "harsh and incapable of expressing any feelings other than anger."[9]

Other reports indicate that the severe child abusers tend to be:

- young parents living on tight budgets;
- parents who have an unsatisfactory sex life;
- parents who feel children exist to satisfy parental needs, not vice-versa;
- parents who were on bad terms with their own parents;
- parents who refer to their child as a monster;
- mothers who tend to be low on motherliness.

Investigators at the Colorado General Hospital were able to build a profile on mothers likely to become serious abusers just by watching the way the newborn baby was treated at the hospital. Did she smile at the baby a lot and look into its eyes? Or did she seem depressed, or disappointed with the sex of the baby, or make disparaging remarks, or to be bothered by its cries and to show no real affection? Such mothers were termed high-potential abusers. The investigators identified one hundred mothers as high-potential abusers. After two years, twenty-five were chosen at random and evaluated. Five children in this group had been hospitalized for serious injuries that were believed to have been inflicted by parents. In a comparable low-potential group of parents there had been no injuries.

With both youngsters and parents manifesting significant difficulties in maintaining control of their behavior, society would seem indeed to be floundering in its normal function of maintaining reasonable social control.

3

The Rise of Sentiment against Children

"The decision to have a child is met with perhaps less enthusiasm than at any time in our history except possibly the Depression years."

— *Joseph Featherstone, Harvard University*

The idea of having children is far from a universal dream among young people today. Consider, for example, these comments:

A married Oregon bookkeeper: "Sure, I have motherly instincts. But I'd rather raise horses."

A Little Rock husband who designs sprinkler systems: "Children are the worst things that can happen to a marriage."[1]

A young woman at a Tulane University panel discussion on alternative life-styles tentatively asked: "I just want to get married and have children. Is that still okay?"

One of the more profound changes occurring in Western society in the late twentieth century is this change in attitudes toward family formation.

Having a child has changed from being a part of the natural flow of life to an apprehensive act — or an act of courage.

This new coolness toward child-raising is coming at the time when, as indicated, there is a great upsurge of people entering the prime child-bearing period of life. In sheer numbers there are more people thinking about having babies today than ever before in U.S. history. The young women currently pondering parenthood were mostly born in the 1950s when there was an incredible increase of 9,000,000 babies born in one decade. Immediately after the 1950s baby boom, a baby bust began that still continues. In 1958 women in their reproductive years were having more than three children. Now the rate hovers at around 1.9 children. But today there are about 6,000,000 more women in the prime child-bearing years of twenty-five to thirty-five than there were a decade ago.

Countries such as Germany, Sweden, Denmark, and England have reported approximately the same very low rate of reproduction. In the U.S., while the actual number of children born rose between 1980 and 1981, the U.S. birth *rate* reflected by family size declined a couple of percent.

The Joint Center for Urban Studies analyzed the attitude of young married couples born in the 1950s period. It concluded that 40 percent of the young women expect to have either one child or no child at all. The younger people born after 1960 who are just thinking about marriage seem to be in a more pro-baby mood. But perhaps this is because it is not an immediate question.

We do know that:

- Married women in America who are having children at all are doing so at a much later age. Childlessness seems to be rising. In a recent fifteen-year period, childlessness doubled among women in their twenties.[2]
- The percentage of U.S. married couples who expect *never* to have a baby is near the highest point in a century, census figures indicate. At least a fourth of all married women presently in the child-bearing age range may never have children.
- The intention to remain childless is particularly conspicuous among young college-trained career women.[3]
- In the U.S. fecundity has become more conspicuous only where it is accidental and the parents, usually teenagers, are unmarried.

For the long term, behavioral scientist George Masnick of Harvard sees a hazard for children in the fact that more and more households will include no children at all. Proportionately there will be fewer voters and taxpayers with any direct stake in children.

America had a fairly rapid population growth in the 1950s, which was a cause of rejoicing by marketers of consumer goods. More people meant more customers. The U.S. advertising industry put on billboards a picture of a stork with the caption, "This bird means business." The possibility of overpopulation briefly became a matter of serious concern because of the drain on resources and living space that rapid growth implied.

I can recall forecasts in the 1950s that the American population would reach 350,000,000 by 1980. The figure turned out to be wrong by more than 100,000,000 on the high side. What happened? Shortly after 1960 we had a long slide in average family size. This was due to a convergence of forces — improved contraception, the surge of women into the work force, many more millions of people living in more cramped quarters in apartments and mobile homes, the counterculture with its scorn for traditional family life patterns, women's liberation. By the time the cry of zero population went up, primarily in the 1970s, overpopulation was not a seriously relevant problem for Western nations. Their populations were growing, if at all, very slowly.

It was among the three-quarters of the world's population in the poorest, least developed countries that a threat to our globe's populace — with rapidly shrinking resources — was posed and is still posed.

Demographers at the Rockefeller Foundation have forecast that between the years 1980 and 2000 populations in Africa will grow by 75 percent, in Latin America by 65 percent, and in North America, at most, by 17 percent. Currently the U.S. birth rate hovers around replacement level.

THE PRO AND CON VIEWPOINTS

So what do we make of this emerging pattern in the Western world of a low level of child-creation and the evidence of family planning?

The pattern with married people is probably cause for celebration. We are entering the Era of the Wanted Child. This has been the long-time dream held by many.

Effective contraceptives, sterilization, and legalized abortion have made the choice of child-creation and its timing a realistic option (and a hot political issue). This is the first generation in history in which married couples have such a choice.

What is worrisome is that this long-dreamed-of option is coming at a time when there is so much wariness about having children. The whole idea of creating children has been downgraded. As the noted George Washington University sociologist Amitai Etzioni put it: "More and more Americans are ceasing to view motherhood as a highly valued or legitimate 'career.' "

The new mood toward children is perhaps unwittingly reflected in the new vocabulary that has started appearing in some of the writings of professionals who deal with marriage and the family in their effort to reflect new viewpoints. For example:

- "Childless" couples are becoming "childfree" couples. One author in a national child study journal divided married couples into "childfree couples" and "childed couples." People in favor of having children are now being given the ideological label of "pronatalists" in some family journals.
- Mothers who are traditional homemakers are now occasionally referred to as "unemployed mothers" (as distinguished from "working mothers"; homemakers don't "work" because there is no pay).
- Parents are sometimes referred to in paired references as being either "bioparents" or "stepparents."
- The time a homemaker spends with her children is often referred to as "quantity time," implying a custodial sort of care. "Quality time" is what conscientious job-holding mothers spend with their children after a hard day's work at the office.

There is even confusion as to what constitutes a family. *UNICEF News* still uses the definition that "Families everywhere consist of men, women and children united by ties of kinship and mutual obligation." Some modernists, however, count as families any two or more people living together on a fairly permanent basis. They can be same sex or different sexed, and children may or may not be present.

A White House Conference on the Family was postponed mainly because of haggling by the planners on what constitutes a family today. I lean toward the UNICEF view that you don't have a family until you have children involved. Sociologist Alice Rossi of the University of Massachusetts, a pioneering feminist two decades ago, accepts that view. She says the new ways of referring to the "family" neglect "the central biological fact that the core function of any family system is human continuity through reproduction and child-rearing."

The new reservations about child-creation have caused many to stop being defensive about being without children or unmarried. Some have taken the offensive. They proclaim a loathing for children. Or they hail childlessness as the "ultimate liberation."[4]

Carlos Castaneda has written a series of best-selling books, purportedly based on Mexican Indian lore, that have been enormously popular with counterculture people. In *The Second Ring of Power* he cites the wisdom of a native woman named La Gorda. She reveals that "A complete person is one who has never had children . . . when one has a child that child takes the edge off our spirit." People who become parents, she asserts, "have lost the edge."

Philosopher Michael Novak has tried to diagnose the aggressiveness of the anti-family sentiments.[5] He says: "To marry, to have children is to make a political statement hostile to what passes for 'liberation' today. It is a statement of flesh, intelligence and courage."

He adds that we seem to be dividing into "individual people" who find happiness by focusing on themselves and "family people" who identify themselves primarily with a kinship group.

"Many people," he says, "now refer to children as piranhas, eels, brats, snots."

The anti-child mood may have peaked when the vast number of young people born in the "baby boom" were imposing their adolescent tastes and views on the rest of us before they passed into adulthood in the late 1970s. But there still is plenty of anti-child sentiment around. Organized movements have emerged to glorify or justify childlessness.

In England a National Association of the Childless has sprung up. And in the U.S., a national lobbying organization promoting the child-free life emerged. At first it called itself forthrightly the National Organization of Non-Parents, with headquarters in Baltimore. Now it has the less provocative name of the National Alliance for Optional Childhood.

Its executive secretary advised me that its main goals have been to provide a "support system" for nonparents and "to try to begin to counter the pronatalist biases of our culture."

This organization provides speakers, sets up chapters, advertises in *Bride's Magazine,* and has broadcast hundreds of TV ads and radio spots. It puts high priority on getting into schools with a teen project "Are You Kidding Yourself?" This provides literature encouraging students to consider as an option the "childfree lifestyle." It objects to children's books that have a pronatalist bias. It even objects to airlines and hotels that offer special rates for families with children.

The organization published an interview with Los Angeles psychologist Nathaniel Branden, who was asked: "Would you agree that parenthood really should be regarded as a specialized occupation?"

Answer: "Emphatically yes. . . . We must get rid of the notion of having children as a 'normal' part of every couple's destiny."

The journal *Alternate Lifestyles* interviewed forty-four "childfree" couples, many of them members of the organization just cited. What techniques did they employ to counter pronatalist pressures in their lives? The four favorite cited were:

1. Defense of the childfree life-style.
2. Devaluation of the parenthood status.
3. Denigration of parents.
4. Avoidance of pronatalist company in their socializing.

To some of the more ardent women's liberationists children loomed as the big stumbling blocks of progress. Some of the far-out radicals in fact have seen being childfree as "woman's ultimate liberation."

It has been asserted, for example, that having babies turned a woman's brain to mush. The whole process of being a brood mare was disgusting. A true-blue homemaker is a kind of parasite and legalized prostitute. One of the more emphatic feminist revolutionaries who took to book writing was Shulamith Firestone, author of *The Dialectic of Sex*. "The heart of woman's oppression is her child-bearing and child-rearing roles," she said. Mothers are *expected* to make motherhood a central focus of their lives, with the child as the only substitute for all that she has been denied in "the larger world."

Pregnancy itself she said is "barbaric." She cited a new mother as saying that the so-called exalting experience of having a baby is like "shitting a pumpkin." Women should be freed as far as possible "from the tyranny of their reproductive biology."

Firestone accepted the proposition that some children should continue to be born, not for "ego" reasons but for species propagation. Some women might want to continue their lives in "reproductive social structures." Marriage should be phased out in favor of licensed "households" of perhaps a dozen people. The household would have a limited-time contract of say seven years. At first children might be created by volunteer couples or by injection of sperm into a volunteer woman. The created child would love people of its own choosing rather than the "decreed" mother and father. After the children had developed stable personalities they could be diffused out to society at large — including men — for rearing.

Her long-term hope, however, was that "artificial reproduction," apparently in incubators, could take over human gestation.

Other highly liberationist-oriented thinkers have suggested that the breeding of children should be taken over by a select minority of professional child-bearers. They have proposed the best technologies for multiple births, high quality seed banks, embryo transfers, etc. Such professional breeders could in their fifteen prime years command high incomes comparable with athletic stars.

Brooklyn College sociologist Judith Lorber suggested in a family-life journal that the whole business of child-breeding could be handled neatly by buying children from over-populated countries.[6] We would have to guarantee them an education to avoid the appearance of exploitation.

These, as indicated, are extreme views, but the fact that they are not dismissed out of hand says something about society's current uncertain views on child-creation and child-rearing.

Fundamental changes in life patterns, life-styles, and job opportunities lie behind the new wariness about children. Here are what appear to be the major causes of the changes in feeling.

CHILDREN SEEN AS OBSTACLES TO "FULFILLMENT"

Californians are now said to have more cars per family than children. This results partially from new priorities on what is essential for the good life. Cars promise freedom and mobility; young children don't.

Social Casework carried a report citing an assortment of reasons why childlessness seems to make sense to a lot of married couples these days.[7] It reported findings of one research team that childless couples believe that child-bearing would interfere with careers, education, and other goals. For these people, it said, parenthood is a "static and sterile way of life that restricts 'individual life and development.' "

The article reported a sampling of married nonparents. The "overwhelming consensus" was that "freedom was by far the best part of being a non-parent." One woman explained: "I have the time to see who I am, what I am, what I want, and where I want to go. I never could have done this with children. I would have felt trapped." Parenthood clearly makes demands on time and patience. It means, for example, seeing to the changing of at least thirty-five hundred diapers during a child's earliest years.

In the 1970s the national mood in America showed an upthrust toward emphasis on individualism and self-fulfillment. Much of this new mood came out of the counterculture period. The mood led some enthusiasts to espouse less cherished values. There has been a strong emphasis on a quest for sensations, wanderlust, doing your own thing. It was this me-first focus that caused Christopher Lasch to write a whole book about the new cult of narcissism. The cult, he suggests, is symptomatic of a society "that has lost interest in the future." This preoccupation with self that became conspicuous in the past decade is not something dreamed up by social observers. Daniel Yankelovich, head of the well-known U.S. polling firm, says flatly that all national surveys looking into the matter "showed an increase in preoccupation with self."

Many of these individualists and self-fulfillers of the sixties and seventies are now into parenthood. How do they work out as child-raisers? I have mentioned briefly the analysis of the self-fulfillers in marriage made by analysis of Yankelovich's firm as a part of a study on the changing American family.[8]

Questions were directed to 1,230 families having children ages one through twelve. Yankelovich found that a small majority were still "Traditional Parents." That is, they were glad to sacrifice for their children. They thought discipline was important. They shared traditional family values.

As indicated, however, nearly half of the sample struck Yankelovich as a "new breed" of parent, who push freedom on their children with the quid pro quo that the children not expect much sacrifice from the parents. That is indeed a novel kind of large-scale social contract between parents and children. The Yankelovich report added: "New Breed children feel less pressure from their parents to excel in school, to be popular or to be outstanding in other ways among their peers."

For growing youngsters, is that a relief or a let-down? Are such children prone to be low in motivation? Further, some psychologists and attorneys who deal regularly with middle-class juvenile delinquents suggest they are morally adrift because of their parents' failure to provide a moral framework. That in turn can create children without the ability "to feel remorse."[9]

Psychologist Henry Smith, long with Michigan State University commented to me: "You can't do your own thing, search for your identity, and raise children at the same time."

He probably has a point.

CHILDREN AS OBSTACLES TO A CAREER

A host of factors have converged in the past two decades to cause many more young women of reproductive age to think about careers outside the home. For example:

- the great increase in young women with occupational skills as a result of higher education;
- the dramatic shift in the Western World from national economies based primarily on production to economies providing services, where women are in great demand;
- the great rise in young mothers who are single or divorced and urgently need income;
- the growth of the women's liberation movement, whose main thrust has been toward the woman's right to be a person herself, free of dependency on men and free to pursue her own paycheck.

In the United States in the 1970s there was an increase of four million families in which both husband and wife worked, according to the *U.S. News and World Report*. The dilemma is that children can often be a seriously complicating factor for women who need to work or want to plan a career.

Author and feminist Caroline Bird offers a viewpoint on this factor. She contends that no matter how much energy a young mother has, babies are still a distraction for the serious careerist when she is getting started. Generally speaking, she says, early babies "have been career disasters. They interfere with the investment that career-bound parents should be making in themselves." She suggests that such women make decisions about babies later on. Efficient contraception has made it feasible for the young woman to map out how she will invest her energy during the years ahead.

A recent survey of three thousand students at eastern colleges by investigators working through Brown University found that among the career oriented coeds, a substantial majority claimed that they were also pro-family. They felt that when babies arrived they should take a few years off to be with their small children. The director of the study wondered if they were not being "naive," given present employment and job opportunity patterns. But as children of the Baby Bust, perhaps they were reflecting the generally more optimistic view about life of their group, which is small and therefore in demand. That at least is in line with a theory of Richard Easterlin, University of Pennsylvania authority on demography.

The pioneering feminist Betty Friedan now is calling for recognition that modern feminism after two decades has taken a new turn.[10] She has given a label to it in her 1981 book *Second Stage*. The idea that women should go their own way and liberate themselves from the family, she says, is a lonely road. Women now should do their pioneering within the family context.

She says women are finding that "it's not so easy to live with — or without — men and children solely on the basis of the first feminist agenda. The great challenge of the 1980s is to frame a new agenda that makes it possible for women to be able to work and love in equality with men — and to choose, if they so desire, to have children . . . the choices we have sought in the Seventies are not as simple as they once seemed." She added that the measure of equality already achieved "is not secure until we face the unanticipated conflicts between the demands of the workplace and professional success on the one hand and the demands of the family on the other." The profound human impulse to have children, she now agrees, is more than just a "mystique." And women who have become too "obsessive" about careers can suffer from pretty heavy stresses.

In short, she seems to be saying, the challenge facing modern women is more profound than first assumed. However, some on the liberationist battlefront such as Bella Abzug seem wary of embracing a "second stage."

CHILDREN AS AN ECONOMIC BURDEN

In simpler societies and in pre-1930 America, children have been viewed as assets. A man with many children considered himself as a rich man. This is still true in primitive societies, which makes population control so frustrating to those seeking to moderate the global population explosion. The family in those primitive societies is still the basic productive economic unit. And when there are no pensions, children are a form of old-age insurance. Typically, by the age of six children in such societies are productive, which makes their presence welcome. And the children's contributions usually foster their own sense of well-being.

I was raised, until the age of nine, on a farm in northern Pennsylvania in the early part of this century, and my experience was fairly typical. By the age of eight I was milking cows every morning and herding them out to pasture, before catching the kid-hack to school. I contributed to family income by tending our skunk traps. I was in charge of cleaning the hen house and gathering the eggs. And I often had to hitch up our horse Nell to a cultivator and plowed a field. By age ten I held down a full salaried job during the summer running a horse-drawn water wagon. The pay: $6 a week. And I was pretty pleased to receive it.

Today, offspring within our system are officially classified as "dependents" — even late teenagers — and usually are. With the growth of technology and urbanization, the family economy has disappeared. Father goes away to work. Children mostly do nonproductive chores around the house. In high school, some may be able to pick up part-time jobs, but most employers are reluctant to consider most teenagers for a regular full-time job.[11]

Deciding to have children is as big an economic decision as deciding to buy a house. And you can always sell the house, but not the child. At the beginning of the 1980s the Urban Institute in Washington, D.C., estimated that it would cost a middle-income family about $85,000 to bear a child and raise it through four years at a public university. Thus the average annual cost from birth would be about $4,000. *Parents Magazine* puts the cost much higher by adding inflation and the possible loss of income during preschool years by a mother who otherwise might have had an outside job.

CHILDREN SEEN AS IMPEDIMENTS TO MARITAL HAPPINESS

Recently it has been frequently asserted that childless couples have happier marriages. They can reportedly focus more on their own relationship and have more freedom as a couple to enjoy the outside world.

The contention might seem plausible in view of the changing nature of marriage. In the new life-style, both partners in a childless marriage are capable of being reasonably self-sufficient. And both tend to place a high value on freedom from bothersome details of life.

The data from studies comparing the "marital satisfaction" of parents and nonparents, however, are not so clearly favorable to the childless couples. A half-dozen comparisons, mostly with small samples, do present a pro-childless edge. Almost all have been criticized by colleagues for methodological limitations. They don't clarify whether the childless couples they studied were childless by choice, childless for physiological reasons, or simply couples who plan to have children but haven't had them yet.

The two most comprehensive studies of children and marital satisfaction — both national in scope — offer very little support for the idea that childless couples are happier. One was a study of "The Quality of American Life" made by a team led by Angus Campbell.[12] The other was an analysis of a survey by the National Opinion Research Council made by the hardly traditionalist Harvard professor Mary Jo Bane.[13]

The Campbell group specifically rejected a 1972 finding that "childless couples that survive tend to be happier than marriages with children." The Campbell group noted a 20 percent drop in "life satisfaction" of childless couples after they passed age thirty. (But their satisfaction was still roughly comparable to that of same-age parents.)

The Bane analysis of the NORC study separated married couples into eight life-cycle stages and noted how many reported their marriages to be "very happy." There may have been a general tendency of respondents in such a "general social survey" to overstate their "happiness." But in any case the group labeled "childless couples, no children expected" ranked lowest of the eight groups in reporting being "very happy" — 48 percent. Childless couples "with children expected" provided a score of 84 percent. Families with teenage children provided a score of 73 percent.

A few conclusions seem warranted from the whole body of study findings:

- Couples under thirty who still have not had a baby tend to rank high in marriage satisfaction. Even at later ages many childless couples report high levels of marital satisfaction.
- Marital satisfaction drops significantly, particularly for the wife, during the first few years after the first child arrives. New stresses beset such couples.
- Marital satisfaction rises with the age of children and is highest when the youngsters launch out on their own.

The impact of children on a marriage relationship is, of course, only one way to assess the individual or social payoff in creating new humans.

A point can be made that a husband and wife do a lot of growing up when they have their first wanted child. Jean Macfarlane directed a long-term study that followed the lives of more than 150 individuals from babyhood to the age of thirty.[14]

One of her conclusions was that "parenthood turns out to be a very important period for consolidating identity and for expanding maturity." Even among boys who had been hostile and rebellious she found that the responsibility for nurturing others "induced new feelings of self worth which liberated potentials for other adult tasks."

Erik Erikson, the noted professor of human development, emeritus, Harvard, has delineated eight stages of psychological development people go through in the process of growing (if they do grow up). Stage seven is Generativity, a drive to nurture, to procreate, to be concerned about helping establish and guide the next generation. In 1979, he warned an international conference of psychoanalysts that the present widespread trend to have fewer children or none at all represented a new and dangerous kind of repression comparable to sexual repression in Victorian days. He has suggested that people who do not or cannot have children of their own should involve themselves, for their own well-being, with other people's children in the community or in the world.

Another "pronatalist" point is that often parenthood brings out the better sides of people. One finding of the survey of 2,300 youngsters and their mothers made by the Foundation for Child Development was that a very large majority of the mothers felt that having children "made them better people." It could be a rationalization, but it also could be a fact.

At any rate — still being argumentative — parenthood, while being painful at times, can be an enormously rewarding role for many people. I was talking with a female psychologist who did not have a baby until her late thirties. It was a boy. She recalled: "I thought of calling him Jonah because having him has been a rebirth for me."

The late author John Cheever, famed for his sophisticated, hard-edged fiction, was often asked in interviews, "What has been the most exciting thing that has ever happened to you?" His invariable answer was, "The birth of my children." He added, "The amount of richness that children can bring into lives of their parents is indescribable."

Generally speaking however our culture increasingly finds child-bearing a bother.

Youngsters are not dummies. They can readily sense that they have become big-ticket items — and hardly stylish ones today.

THE GUILT-RIDDEN FULL-TIME HOMEMAKER

The housewife-mother who used to look down on, feel sorry for, or deplore mothers who took jobs now is more likely to feel she is one of the deplored. A new type of mother is emerging as a predominant force. She has an outside position. Today a shrinking minority of families with children living at home have a full-time homemaker-mother.

One such housewife-mother, Terry Martin Hekker, wrote an hilarious article about her embarrassments nowadays when she has to explain that her occupation is that of a housewife-mother.[15] She is the wife of a small-town judge in New York State, has five children and a rather large house to take care of. She calls herself one of an endangered species. Constantly she is being asked when she is going to "work." Her own son, she wrote, lied about her occupation (housewife) in filling out his college application. She identified herself as one of a type that is now considered to be an unproductive parasite. As a type, she said, she is viewed as having nothing better to do than fetch other women's children after they have thrown up in the school lunchroom. These "other women" have careers. In the new assigning of status the only "work worth doing is that for which you get paid." At parties when the talk gets to what people do, she said, she finds herself viewed as more lowly than a hooker. When one woman asked her who she was, she said she was "Jack Hekker's wife." The woman took her hand and asked if that was all she thought of herself, being just someone's wife. She mentioned she had five children. That did not bring much of a reaction beyond sympathy. Then on a whim, "I told her they weren't mine, that they belonged to my dead sister. And then I basked in the glow of her warm approval."

4

The Harsh Entry into Life

"Agony . . . is given in strange ways to children."
— *Flannery O'Connor*

Many modern children are being born to adversity, and not only because of poverty. In the finest family circles pregnant women are often unwittingly affecting the life chances of their infant-to-be by their own habits of life.

In the past twenty years the amount of cigarette smoking by young women and teenage girls has soared. Young women now are more likely to be active smokers than young men. Fifty years ago women rarely smoked. In the single decade ending in 1976 the amount of *heavy* smoking by women in their major reproductive years increased by 20 percent. And their rate of heavy smoking today is still at around the 1976 level.

The general health hazards of smoking are well known but recently scientific findings point to a new victim of cigarette smoking, the fetus inside the mother who smokes. The nicotine inhaled by a mother can reduce fetal breathing movements, and the carbon monoxide inhaled can reduce the amount of oxygen that the mother's blood delivers to the fetus.

The two effects have the potential for blighting the infant. Dozens of studies — some of them massive — have now been made that bear on the effect of maternal smoking on the child.[1] The U.S. Surgeon General in his 1979 report *Smoking and Health* reviewed the evidence and concluded, "Cigarette smoking during pregnancy has a significant and adverse effect upon the well-being of the fetus, the health of the newborn baby and the future development of the infant and child." Effects have been noted in some children up to the age of twelve.

Here are some of his specific conclusions:

- Cigarette smoking increases the chance of premature birth.
- It tends to reduce the size of babies that are born. On average they weigh less, are shorter, and have smaller head circumference.
- There is "suggestive evidence" of long-term impairments in physical growth, diminished intellectual function, and deficiencies in behavioral development. It appears that children of mothers who smoke regularly do not catch up with the offspring of nonsmoking mothers in a number of phases of development.
- The more a mother smokes during pregnancy, the greater the reduction in weight of the baby at birth.
- A child of a mother who smoked during pregnancy has a greater chance of being hyperactive.

Others have recently reported finding an association between maternal smoking and the possibility of respiratory illnesses and congenital malformations in the children. And since the Surgeon General's report the massive U.S.-funded Collaborative Perinatal Project has found that heavy smoking by a woman increases the chance that the placenta will be attached low in the womb, thus creating a greater probability of complications during labor and birth.

Recently it also has become dramatically clear that tippling during pregnancy can blight the growing fetus. The fetus shares its mother's blood. If there is alcohol in the blood it passes freely through the placental and brain barriers of the growing fetus.

Meanwhile, in the past two decades drinking by young women and girls has risen. The most dramatic rise for girls came between the mid 1960s and the mid 1970s when there was a 300 percent increase in high school girls drinking to the point of drunkenness in the U.S. These were the girls soon to enter the prime years for child-bearing.[2] They were getting drunk just as often as their male classmates. Similar but less dramatic increases in drinking by females have been reported in Europe.

It was not until 1968, beginning with the findings of a French investigator, P. Lemoine, that persuasive scientific evidence began appearing on the effect of heavy drinking by pregnant mothers on their offspring. By 1973 a team of Seattle investigators had detailed the "fetal alcohol syndrome" in infants, associated with women who drank heavily during pregnancy.[3] Infants with this full syndrome, as it has been further refined, have a somewhat flattened face. There is also shortness of body length, abnormalities of the joints and palms of the hands, cardiac defects, and, most disturbing, some mental retardation.[4] Those children who often showed the full range of symptoms had mothers who consumed at least three ounces of absolute alcohol a day. That's about six drinks. But even social drinking during pregnancy, say a drink or two a day, is also under suspicion. The National Institute on Alcohol Abuse and Alcoholism hypothesizes that there should be a tendency for subtle effects to appear at low alcoholic dosages. It has cautioned that the pregnant mother who has two drinks of hard liquor a day can be flirting with trouble. Some authorities are concluding that even one drink a day can have some effect on the fetus, and that abstinence is the safest of all courses.

Federal investigators now believe there may be critical periods when heavy drinking can be especially harmful. The most critical period, apparently, is the first month or so of pregnancy, with the final month also suspected as being a period of above-average vulnerability for the fetus.

Use of various mood-changing drugs, including marijuana, by young women also has been dramatically on the rise in the Western world in the past two decades. Women who are abusers of hard drugs during pregnancy tend to have children who lag in development and are prone to have serious behavioral problems. Even marijuana poses a problem. Its mind-altering chemical, THC, can cross the placenta and, being soluble, can remain in the fetus up to a week. Animal studies indicate that marijuana can kill fetuses, so presumably it has the potential for injuring human fetuses.

And how about junk foods? Pregnant women tend to snack. A psychologist at the University of Minnesota has surmised, on the basis of animal studies, that a pregnant mother can create ill effects in her child by regularly eating so-called junk foods. Such consumption has soared in the younger population. Junk foods commonly are high in sugar, fat, and salt and commonly are low in essential nutrients.

A 1981 report in *The Journal of the Canadian Medical Association* said a mother's poor eating patterns may result in greater deprivation of the fetus than had previously been believed. But little specifically is known beyond surmise about the impact of so-called modern junk foods on unborn humans. A 1977 report in *Science* stated that the common food additive monosodium glutamate, a crystalline salt used to enhance the flavor of foods such as meat and soup, has produced bodily deficits in animals.

Analysis of the data on fetuses, assembled in the Collaborative Perinatal Project, also puts in question certain working patterns of pregnant women. Those who have a job that requires them to stand up for long hours at a stretch will in the ninth month of pregnancy be seriously restricting flow of blood to the fetus. Such expectant mothers have an increased chance of giving birth to an infant of reduced weight.

OUR INHOSPITABLE BIRTHING SYSTEM

Muriel Sugarman, of the Harvard Medical School, has observed: "The mother in our society gives birth under the most artificial conditions imaginable, in a strange place, among strangers, often without a voice in decisions affecting her labor and birth and the subsequent handling of her infant." Almost all these "most artificial conditions imaginable" promote the convenience of the professional medical staff. Professor Sugarman's charge was made as recently as 1977.

Such convenience for the mass production of babies is what scientific birthing innovations in the U.S. have been largely about.

At the time of a child's birth it is the doctor, with his machines and chemicals, who becomes the star performer in the high drama of the infant's entry. The mother is supposed to be out flat, passive, sometimes nearly unconscious. And family members, often, must not be near, where they might possibly get in the way of the doctors and aides.

The only doctor in an upstate New York county who still performed home deliveries in 1981 found his license suspended because of alleged deficiencies in his practice. Many mothers he had attended rushed to his defense. He contended that his practice was depriving local hospitals of about $250,000 a year in lost revenues. The board that recommended his removal was headed by a hospital administrator. A State Supreme Court justice ruled the suspension unreasonable and arbitrary.

The U.S. medical professional made childbirth into a kind of mysterious illness and has just recently been persuaded to change some of its ways. The mother's "sickness," it was felt, could be coped with only by high technology, preferably on a nine-to-five schedule. *Medical World News* in 1970 reported approvingly on the injection of the hormone oxytocin into expectant mothers.[5] It triggers contractions of the mother's uterus, which permits the obstetrical staff to schedule births at evenly spaced daytime periods and to get a good night's sleep. A full decade later, in 1980, the annual meeting of the American Association for the Advancement of Science heard a report that oxytocin is associated with "psychomotor deficit" in children and later on with "lower achievement test scores."

Psychologists analyzing follow-up data from the huge U.S.-funded Collaborative Perinatal Project find that the use of anesthetics and the heavy use of sedatives can have long-term subtle effects on children. The drugs evidently reach the brain of the baby about to be born.

In the Project's follow-up study of 3,500 "normal births," it was found that babies whose mothers were heavily sedated during the long hours of labor were substantially more likely to be slow to sit up or to crawl. They often kept crying long after they had been comforted. Some differences in babies of mothers who had been heavily sedated were apparent in children at the age of seven, particularly when the mothers had been given inhalant anesthesia. With inhaled anesthetics "significant associations with adverse outcomes" showed up in 41 percent of the tests.[6]

A grim summary of the analysis of 1,944 of the full-term babies in the Collaborative Perinatal Project was stated in May 1980 in these medically precise words:

The results suggest that inhalants are associated with deficits in psychomotor and neuromotor functioning in the first year, and that oxytocin is also associated with psychomotor deficit. Scopolamine and secobarbital are related to respiratory difficulties in the newborn, and inhalants, scopolamine and secobarbital are associated with palpable liver at four months. At older ages, scopolamine is associated with slightly lower scores on some cognitive tasks, and oxytocin is associated with lower achievement test scores.[7]

Obstetricians have recently become less inclined to employ inhalants.

Other reports indicate that heavy medication impairs the new mother's ability to breast-feed for several days. These are the days when special proteins in the colostrum are coming in the first milk from the mother's breast to protect against infection. They are far more abundant at this point than at any later time.

HIGH TECHNOLOGY'S DELIVERY METHODS

A fairly recent innovation in many areas is for a number of obstetricians to function on a group basis. It promotes convenience for the doctors. Whichever one is on call and not busy handles the case when the mother rushes to the hospital. While this may promote efficiency as well as let the doctors get their regular sleep, it can create anxiety in an already anxious expectant mother.

My daughter Cindy, before she had her last baby in Connecticut, mentioned to me her concern about who she was going to "get" for the delivery. It turned out to be the doctor she liked least of those in her group. The doctor she had assumed to be "hers" in some special way, because she had been assigned to him at her first office visit, came into her double room the day following delivery with chart in hand. He looked confused and said, "Who am I looking for?" Cindy said, "Me, I guess. You are the one who told me I was pregnant."

Mothers in societies where little has changed for centuries have their babies with relative ease and swiftness when compared with mothers in modern hospitals. During labor the woman in such societies stands and walks around so that the force of gravity will help bring the infant's head down into the expulsion position.

When the time for birth approaches she semi-sits, squats, or kneels, still drawing upon the force of gravity. Friends encourage her in these moments of birthing which can have mystical meaning for her.

Civilized man starting with the Greeks introduced a chair with a crescent-shaped opening. The lady sat, but still had gravity working for her. And through the centuries these chairs became more elaborate. It was only two centuries ago, when doctors began taking over the assistance of birthing from midwives, that birthing mothers were put into beds, flat on the back, like sick patients.

More recently, still on their backs, the expectant mothers have been hooked up to a machine and told to be careful about moving.

Now still at a typical hospital when birth approaches, the mother is moved to a delivery table where she is again placed on her back. Further, as Muriel Sugarman described in 1977, the mother's legs are elevated "and spread widely apart so that the obstetrician can see easily and work comfortably." She added that in this position the infant is significantly endangered. The pressure of its weight on the large abdominal blood vessels "impedes circulation and produces a serious drop in blood pressure, depriving the placenta and the new born of blood and oxygen."[8]

In some more enlightened hospitals a compromise is being struck. The mother at birthing is seated in a plastic motorized chair that can be raised and tilted as the doctor prefers. (Something like the dentist chair, which has been around for decades.) This mobile chair cuts second stage delivery time in half.

One doctor using the chair, Warner Nash of New York's Lenox Hill Hospital, says: "It's embarrassing for us doctors in 1981 to finally learn what nature told us many years ago. Most of womankind will give birth in the vertical position if there's no interfering doctor to make them lie down."[9]

The startled, newly born infant has been typically hung upside down and slapped on the bottom. This has been done not to open the lungs, as widely assumed, but to clear out mucus. It can be done and now frequently is done effectively with a suction device.

The newly arrived baby has emerged from the warm darkness of mother's ninety-eight-degree womb into a bright, relatively frigid room of about sixty-eight degrees — a temperature that doctors like to work in. To add to the infant's misery, stinging silver nitrate drops are added to its eyes. This adding of eyedrops can be postponed.

AFTER THE ARRIVAL

With the mother often still drowsy, the pattern for decades has been to take her furious, panic-stricken infant into a room with twenty other howling infants. Frequently it has been twelve to sixteen hours before the infant has been formally introduced to its mother and permitted to snuggle and suck happily on her warm breast and to hear the long-familiar beat of her heart.

Hospitals have tended to assume that their nurses in the baby rooms are more expert at mothering than the mothers, especially first mothers. But nurses don't have the heightened hormonal levels, that promote nurture and attachment, which new mothers have after birth. The mother is in a high arousal state that seems to make her extraordinarily responsive to her infant. There is speculation that the first two hours after birth can be important to the baby's future.

If so, then critical get-acquainted hours may be lost under the hospital routine that has long prevailed in maternity wards. Under that routine, mothers, after the first, often long-delayed meeting, have been permitted to have their babies every four hours for a half-hour feeding time. During the mother's whole hospital stay, in short, she has her infant with her for less than one-twelfth of the time.

When there is more immediate and frequent contact, the chance of sustained, successful breast-feeding seems to be improved, according to three studies cited by Information Sheet 20 (January 1978) of the La Leche League International. Further there is substantial evidence that the mother's identification with the infant becomes deeper. And there is some evidence that the infants develop more rapidly.

Investigators at Case Western Reserve University, particularly Marshall Klaus and John Kennell, carried out an interesting series of studies on the impact of hospital procedures on the attachment behavior of the mother. They compared a group of mothers given typical hospital exposure to their infants with a group given considerably enhanced exposure.

The enhanced-exposure mothers were given their naked newborn infants for the entire first hour after birth. And during the hospital stay the mothers were permitted to have their babies with them several hours a day.

After a month all the mothers of both groups were assessed as to the depth of attachment to their infants by expert observers who did not know from which group the mothers came. Mothers from the enhanced-exposure group clearly showed more concern about their babies during the assessment sessions, were more soothing, did more fondling, and enjoyed gazing at their infants more.

The initial studies did not clarify what aspects of the enhanced exposure were particularly important, so a larger study in a different culture (Guatemala) was conducted. This time the enhanced-exposure group was divided into two. About half the babies were placed with their mothers for forty-five minutes immediately after birth, the others were not given the forty-five-minute session with the mothers until twelve hours after birth.

The difference was reported to be startling. Only the mothers given their babies immediately after birth showed the great increase in affectionate behavior. The delayed-enhanced-exposure-group mothers acted pretty much like the control-group mothers. The investigators concluded that the "maternal sensitivity period is less than twelve hours in length."

Others are still cautious about such a generalization. It should be pointed out that the interest of the investigators was on the mother. Deep infant attachment to the mother is widely believed to come much later. Urie Bronfenbrenner, while commending the study, expressed a wish that the infants' attachment behavior had been assessed, and not just the mothers'.

In a quite separate series of observations, Michael Daly, as chief of obstetrics at Temple University, concluded that infants who spent forty-five minutes with their mothers during the first two hours after birth performed better. They gained weight better and had a larger vocabulary at the age of two than children given the usual hospital separation treatment after delivery.

A revolt against the high-technology approach of hospital staffs to childbirthing has been gathering force for several years. The pro-natural mood of young parents coming out of the counterculture has played a part; as has gradual public awareness of scientific findings about the importance of early mother-infant contact. Many more young mothers are now asking for natural childbirth with the husband present.

As recently as thirteen years ago most hospitals banned fathers from the delivery rooms. Now it is finally widely recognized that fathers as well as mothers develop a long-lasting sense of emotional involvement with a child by being able to greet the newborn. There is now a clear trend for mothers to want to greet their babies immediately and to be able to spend more time with the newborn child. And a new interest is being shown by some of the bolder pro-naturalists in using midwives if they have quick access to medical clinics and no complications are evident. A few baby doctors are adding midwives to their personal staffs. Also a number of maternity centers run by midwives have been appearing.

A doctor in Danbury, Connecticut, whose clientele of pregnant mothers is mostly college-educated, reports 80 percent are asking for natural childbirth if the pregnancy seems normal.

Belatedly, quite a few hospitals are starting to give thought to family success as well as staff convenience. With the decline in family size, many hospitals now are competing for business by catering to the consumer-parents.

About one hospital in six in America now offers the option of a birthing room. It is decorated like a family room. The mother can walk around during labor. She has her baby in any position on the bed she wishes. The husband is typically present. Emergency equipment is within a few feet, but out of sight. The newborn stays in the same room with the mother. Curious young siblings of the infant are permitted brief visits. In Great Britain for some years it has been common for the baby to stay on a cot by its mother's bed.

Several French obstetricians created wide interest and replication by trying to make the baby's entrance into the world a soothing one rather than a wrenching experience. The lights were dim. The attendants spoke softly. Immediately upon birth the baby, instead of being slapped, washed, and stung with eyedrops, was placed on the mother's belly. As the baby began to breathe the cord was cut and the baby was placed at its mother's breast and over her heart. Frederick Lebouyer of France even began putting the newborn babies in water the same temperature as the womb fluid they had left.

5

The Banning of Children

"When you think of the good life, think of OAKWOOD
GARDEN APARTMENTS . . . Sorry, no children."

— *From an ad in a West Coast newspaper, 1978*

Oakwood Gardens is no small-fry landlord. It has more than 19,000 apartment units in the United States, with the biggest concentration in the West. Children have been banned from living in many of the units. In California the parent company has now modified its "adults only" policy. A new state law prohibits such banning of children there.

And Oakwood has been far from being alone. U.S. landlords by the thousands, large and small, have been banning or severely restricting the presence of children.

Finding a home for one's children has suddenly escalated into a major national problem in the U.S.A. In just four years ending in 1980 there was a 53 percent increase in the number of rental apartments across the U.S.A. where children were flatly banned. A fourth of all apartment-owners in the land now forbid children; and in some cities the figure reaches more than 60 percent of all units. Nationwide a large majority of *all* apartment-owners now are putting restrictions of some kind on tenants with children.

The anti-child movement is not restricted to apartment-owners. In many areas if you have children you can't even buy a home if the home is a condominium. Rules in condominiums are set by an association of owners.

Why the upsurge of anti-child discrimination in housing? Partly it reflects a shrinkage of the vacancy rate of available housing of any kind. This shrinkage, alas, has developed just at a time when that enormous group of people born in the post-World War II baby boom are hitting the family-formation stage. The shrinkage of available housing is due to the high mortgage interest rates and soaring building costs. Most of the apartment units being built in many cities are one-bedroom or studio apartments aimed at the singles and childless couple market. And rental space available is being further shrunk by the widespread conversion of apartments to condominiums which must be bought. The idea of owning one's own house is a fading dream for most young families in U.S. metropolitan areas.

Apartment vacancy rates in many cities are now under 3 percent, which permits landlords to be extremely arbitrary.

The upsurge in discrimination also is a reflection of the rise in anti-child attitudes. Reports of widespread discrimination against children in housing have come in recent years from such widely separated cities as Dallas, Houston, Atlanta, and Denver.

A federal official noted in 1979 that all four of the newest major housing complexes in Atlanta excluded children. In Denver a major builder estimated that 90 percent of the new buildings were strictly for adults. A builder in Houston conceded that virtually all new housing complexes either excluded children or restricted them to certain buildings. A survey of 197 privately owned apartment buildings in Cincinnati revealed that children were excluded from about 70 percent of the apartment buildings and subject to restrictions, such as age or number of children, in most of the rest.

THE BANS COMBATTED IN ONE STATE

In the past few years, Californians have seen some of the nation's nastiest quarrels over landlord bans on children. Some angry parents finally prevailed against the bans, at least in court. Children were not welcome in about three-quarters of the rental housing in many California cities in the late 1970s. Early in my research I went out to look around. En route from the Los Angeles airport to Santa Monica I passed a giant apartment complex. A sign in large letters read: "Apartments for Men and Women." I read it aloud to the cab driver, who seemed to be a fine-looking young man of about twenty-seven. He responded: "I don't like that a bit. I'm getting married in a few months and want to start having children in about a year. The people who want to isolate themselves from children don't seem to me like good citizens. I think they are acting kind of childish themselves."

The person I was traveling to see was Dora Ashford. She is a soft-spoken, handsome young divorcée with a cute daughter, Alisa, then aged eleven. Ms. Ashford had held a variety of jobs but in recent years she had been out on the ramparts in the fight against child discrimination while studying for a law degree.

Her battle started partly because of her own personal fury. She spent several months searching for a home and was turned down by at least fifty landlords before finding someone willing to take her and her daughter.

Out of her anger Dora Ashford helped set up, and became director of, the Fair Housing for Children Coalition. (Nonprofit and tax-exempt. P.O. Box 5877, Santa Monica, CA 90405.) It has always had a shoe-string budget but it has had considerable impact not only in Southern California but elsewhere in the U.S. in making child discrimination more difficult.

Soon after we met we were touring the western part of Greater Los Angeles. We passed a high-rise complex on Ocean Avenue. She said, "It doesn't say so on its sign or in the ads, but it doesn't take children. I called and they said no."

I suggested we ask them. She pulled in under a rather swanky entry-way and asked the doorman if the place took children.

Doorman: (Pause) "Yeah . . . but you would have to talk to the leasing agent about a thing like that. You may have to talk him into it."

Ms. Ashford said thanks and drove away. "Sometimes places that have a few extra-expensive or extra-dingy apartments they can't rent will take children in them."

We passed many buildings that had signs indicating children were not wanted. Then we passed a school in Brentwood. Several children were playing outside. A few hundred feet away, facing the schoolyard, was a large apartment building. The sign read, "Adults only."

As we rode and noted signs, Dora Ashford began discussing some of the desperate parents her group had tried to help. She said: "A man and his three children had been living in his car. They just parked in the streets and kept moving. He seemed to have a job and money but said no one would rent to him because of his children.

"We had another family with five children who couldn't find anyone who would rent to them. They lived in a station wagon. For several summer months they parked it in a public parking place on a public pier. They used the public facilities. He had a job. They seemed like a nice family, but the wife was very thin and tired looking. The police finally forced them to leave the pier.

"This family spent about a year living out of a car. They had moved so much during the search that they pretty much gave up trying to keep their children in school."

Ms. Ashford said she had encountered quite a few families who in desperation turned to motel living, even though it was expensive. Motels are one place you can check in with any number of children.

When Dora Ashford's group have tried to nail down landlords on the reasons for their aversion to children, the landlords sometimes cite noise. She said: "It seems there is something about the sound of children that annoys some adults much more than the sound of each other's stereos or of airplanes or motorcycles. Many people I know have to put up with incredible noise in all-adult neighborhoods caused by couples tangling in marital fights."

A 1980 national survey by the Institute for Social Research of the University of Michigan found that a higher proportion of landlords think children bother tenants than did the tenants who were questioned.

Another common rationale for bans on children is that they cause damage. Surveys show this is mentioned far more by landlords who ban children than by those who accept them. The major insurance companies make no distinction between all-adult and family housing.

Since the bans are encountered most often in middle- to low-priced rental housing, the bans fall heavily upon households headed by a woman and upon minority families.

Some landlords have selective bans based on the age and sex of the children. The Flowers family in San Diego, with two boys and two girls, was evicted because the landlord had decided that his hundred-unit complex didn't want boys over five years of age. Girls were okay. A judge upheld the landlord's right to select his tenants.

The number of children you have can also be a decisive factor in many areas. People with three or more children in California were often told to go to public housing. But most urban housing authorities had long waiting lists. The national survey by the Institute of Social Research found that families with three or more children would be banned from 60 percent of the nation's rental units.

Some of the more vast complexes with five or six buildings may set aside a remote building for families with children.

Divorced fathers with an apartment in an adult-only complex can run into problems when their own children come to visit overnight.

Ms. Ashford said: "Some managers permit children as visitors. Others don't want children around at all."

Under pressure from angry parents some California cities began banning discrimination against children, but wide areas of the state remained without any legal protection.

A FAMILY THAT FOUGHT BACK

In Los Angeles County, outside the Los Angeles city limits, one of the tightest concentrations of no-children housing has been at Marina del Rey on the Pacific Coast, well below Santa Monica. There are about six thousand apartment units, split up among various managements, in this area. One check showed that about one hundred children were permitted to live in the entire area.

The flagrancy of this situation is heightened by the fact that the marina area, originally a swamp, was created by federal, state, and county funds. And the land on which the thousands of apartments sit is still owned by the county! In short, this fierce anti-child enclave has largely been created by funds drawn from public taxes, and sits on land owned by the general public.

One of the most-watched legal cases to test discrimination against children in American rental housing began here at Marina del Rey. The family of Stephen and Lois Wolfson and their young son Adam was evicted from one of the complexes. The Wolfsons were both schoolteachers at the time of the eviction. He specialized in problem children and was studying law at night. Since the eviction he has qualified as a lawyer.

The Fair Housing for Children Coalition along with the Legal Aid Foundation of Los Angeles helped them out by supplying attorneys and research. The major work on the suit has been handled by a young constitutional lawyer, Eugene Gratz, largely on a volunteer basis. Gratz moved from New York to California to take on the case. Recently Wolfson and Gratz have set up their own law office. The tour that Dora

Ashford gave me of housing in Greater L.A. ended up at the office of these two men. Over lunch we talked about the case.

The particular complex at Marina del Rey where the Wolfsons lived used to permit children, Wolfson said. In fact, it had a special children's pool. Around the mid 1970s the management began to cultivate a singles image. Children were not wanted.

While Lois Wolfson was pregnant the management announced a policy excluding children *and pregnant females*. At the Wolfsons' complex of 680 units the Wolfsons were one of seven tenants with live-in children. The complex was large, and no one raised an objection to baby Adam. In fact, workmen at the complex brought Adam presents. And later the neighbors came to the Wolfsons' defense. Still, the Wolfsons were a bit anxious and took pains to keep Adam quiet.

Eugene Gratz explains: "It's like the Anne Frank syndrome." One day there was an incident. Lois Wolfson was coming home. She had the toddler in one arm and a bag of groceries in the other. As she struggled to open the door, the manager, a very authoritative type who had apparently been trailing her, stepped up and said, "Is that your kid?" and Lois said, "No."

I asked: "Why did she say no?"

Gratz: "She doesn't know. She was frightened. She was lying to protect her child and her home."

The manager obviously didn't believe her. A few days later the Wolfsons received an eviction notice.

The Wolfsons, with the help of Gratz, stalled the eviction for a year by seeking an injunction. They lost, and the Wolfsons began searching for a new home. They finally bought a condominium in Culver City that permitted children. Their two-bedroom unit was really a converted apartment. The monthly mortgage payment was more than twice what they had been paying in rent at Marina Point, Ltd.

The Wolfsons' suit against the management charges it with being in violation of the thrust of the California Civil Rights Act, the California Fair Housing Act, and the Fourteenth Amendment of the U.S. Constitution. They lost at the municipal court. However, the Los Angeles Superior Court, on appeal, ruled in their favor, at least as far as general apartment buildings were concerned. This favorable decision was reversed by the California Court of Appeals. Again the Wolfsons appealed. Finally in 1982, after five years of legal struggle, the Supreme Court of California held in their favor. And in late 1982 the U.S. Supreme Court left the California court's decision intact. However, since the case was based on California laws, the U.S. Supreme Court's decision is not binding in other states. The complex from which the Wolfsons were evicted now accepts children.

At least a dozen other lawsuits have challenged discrimination against children in housing in the U.S. Most have not gotten very far.

The U.S. Supreme Court, in interpreting the Fourteenth Amendment, has held that people have a fundamental right to beget and bear children. The Fourteenth Amendment, however, requires that a state action be involved. In the Wolfson case there was a clear involvement of the state since the state, federal, and county government had made Marina del Rey possible.

Because of the Wolfson decision, the "No Children" signs have been coming down all over the state. Parents in California are not yet free of problems, however. Enforcement is still left up to the victim except in a few cities such as Santa Monica and San Francisco. And because of a tight housing situation very few vacant apartments are, at this writing, available.

WAYS OF FIGHTING BACK

People angered by discrimination against children in housing areas other than Southern California have been jolting landlords in a variety of ways. For example:

Local action   In Howard County, Maryland, housing complexes with more than three hundred units must now make at least 80 percent of them available to families.

State action   At least ten states, as well as the District of Columbia, now have statutes that prohibit discrimination against children. Those are New York, New Jersey, Delaware, Illinois, Michigan, Massachusetts, Arizona, Montana, Connecticut, Minnesota.

Some of the statutes are ancient, and most are deficient in terms of enforcement by specifying only nominal fines. Violations abound in most of the states.

At a dinner party recently I was talking with a handsome young man from Illinois who said he managed an apartment complex near Barrington, outside Chicago. I asked if there were children in the complex. Response:

"Not if I can help it. They're vicious. They get cookie crumbs on the hall carpets. They take fire extinguishers off the wall." Out of curiosity I mentioned the Illinois law and he abruptly became cautious. He said: "We just don't say no or anything like that. We take them if we have to." Some Illinois landlords cope with the law by charging higher prices for an apartment if children will be living in it.

Arizona seems to have the toughest law, although there is some question about how well it is enforced. In Arizona, violators can be both fined and imprisoned for repeat offenses. Sentences must increase with repeat offenses. And discriminatory advertising is prohibited.[1]

Federal government action   The federal government seems to have done more to validate discrimination against children than to protect children. Its laws providing special programs for the elderly encourage the idea that certain groups of people deserve to be spared from living near children.

The one area where children are explicitly protected from housing discrimination is where the landlord has accepted FHA insurance mortgage loans for rental housing. But there are a number of exceptions, and an enforcement administrator of the program claimed he had not heard of a violation in seventeen years!

Apparently the clearest opportunity for effective federal action would be for Congress to add one word to the Title VIII of the Civil Rights Act of 1978, which relates to housing discrimination. It prohibits discrimination in the rental, sales, or financing of almost all housing, public or private, for reasons of race, color, religion, sex, or national origin. The word that should be added is "age." Or if there is a desire to protect rights of the elderly to engage in self-segregation, the phrase "children in the family" could be substituted for age.

Tenant action   Many landlords do not like being depicted as scrooges with children. In West Covina, California, a manager took over a building and sent eviction notices to twenty-eight families. The families began picketing the site and called in news reporters. The landlord came out and said he didn't realize there were so many children there because the building looked so nice. He had assumed that if there were children the places would look a wreck. The eviction notices were rescinded.

Some small progress is starting to be made against the anti-child forces in housing. But the continued widespread toleration of this discrimination throughout urban America adds up to degenerative social policy. Trouble looms when one generation tries to insist that the succeeding generation should go someplace else.

6

Growing Up Isolated

"Mommy, what is a hometown?"

— *Young son of a highly mobile Detroit executive after hearing classmates use the term*

Fragmentation of families and fragmentation of communities because of the high mobility of the American populace are just two reasons why youngsters are growing up with an increased sense of isolation and unconnectedness.

Of the more than twelve million U.S. youngsters who move to a different house in a given year, about seven million also move to a different school system. American youngsters move twice as frequently as European youngsters.

Surveyers for Louis Harris and Associates found that 65 percent of the 1,503 U.S. family members questioned agreed with the statement: "People who expect to get ahead in their careers or jobs should be willing to relocate their families."

Telephone company records for disconnected residential telephones indicate that movement by Americans soared in the three decades starting around World War II, especially long-distance moves. For an urban child under ten, a move of even ten blocks throws the child into a totally strange environment.

About a fifth of all families now move every year. The rate is much higher for families with young children. Movement is not new to Americans. In the middle of the nineteenth century when waves of immigrants were hitting eastern port cities such as Boston, there are records of very high transience in specific frontier towns.

Most of the nineteenth-century movement, however, was for short distances to places where there were relatives. The longer moves were typically by wagon train. A group of people banded together, got to know each other intimately on the trail, and tended frequently to settle in the same small frontier towns.

This was far less disruptive than the modern movement of a parent who relocates, or is relocated, hundreds of miles away because of job.

I took an informal survey of thirty-six corporate wives who had recently been moved to Darien, Connecticut. They were asked how often they had moved. On the average, they had moved every two and a half years since marriage. The record was a wife who had relocated twenty-two times in her thirty-five years of marriage. Another, younger, wife had moved sixteen times in her twenty-one years of marriage. She shrugged and said, "I feel it is the wife's duty to go where the paycheck is." Of her husband she said, "To get ahead in his company means moving."

Such corporate nomads usually find themselves far from relatives or any long-term friends. Loneliness becomes a problem. Mothers of young children in the missile base town of Great Falls, Montana, complained to me that a major problem was finding playmates for their children.

If you take the U.S. as a whole there is a fairly precise correlation between an area's rate of family mobility and its divorce rate. Both mobility and divorce are lowest in the Northeast and highest in the Southwest. For example, the marital disruption rates in Dallas, Fort Worth, and Houston are all three times as high as in Boston, and two and a half times as high as Philadelphia and Pittsburgh. Mobility, as indicated by residential telephone disconnection rates, show Texans more than twice as mobile as Pennsylvanians.

There is some evidence that the frenzy of people-moving caused by bureaucratic transfer policies in the past decade is moderating. For one thing, high mortgage rates and the shortage of decent housing makes some people reluctant to accept moves even if they look like promotions. Cost-of-living variations — and variances in cost of housing — also may make people wary of being moved. An Oklahoman being promoted to New England may find living costs 15 percent higher.

The great surge of college-educated wives with well-paying careers where the family has been living has become another deterrent. One study involving thirty-six dual-career couples found that transfer had generated serious marital conflict for a third of the couples.[1]

When transfers are made, the organizations doing the transferring — and communities receiving the newcomers — should start recognizing that they are transferring a whole family, not just an employee. The company should see that every member of an incoming family is welcomed and shown around by same-age people. Teachers should stage welcoming ceremonies for newcomers and appoint a classmate to serve as a buddy to each newcomer in getting her or him involved with classmates and neighborhood activities.

WHAT HAPPENS TO CHILDREN WHO MOVE A LOT?

For kids, the experience of moving — for whatever reason — requires them to cope with a new environment. They need to adjust to a new neighborhood, new folkways, new schools, and finding new friends. For many children between the ages of seven and twelve, family moves can contribute to character growth and to their prospects of success in life. The challenge of adaptation to a new environment serves as a stimulus and broadens their horizons — if the moves are a few years apart and are made in the summer when school is out of session. But they do miss their old friends. For infants and toddlers, a move has little meaning except perhaps movement away from loved ones or a caretaker who has become important to them.

For children in the three-to-four-year range, a move can be very upsetting because they have an unusual need for stability in their lives, according to the noted child development specialist Louise Bates Ames. They like everything to be familiar. For youngsters in their early to middle teens, she added, a move can be shattering because they already are going through rapid physiological changes and because dating and acceptance by peer groups (being in the *right* set) can be enormously important to them. A move means they have to start over in gaining social acceptance. Also they are at a stage where they are starting to break from parental dependence. Any additional turbulence in their lives at this time, she has reported, complicates their problem of making the transition to personal autonomy.

A father working for Sperry Rand, who was being transferred from Connecticut to Italy, had a hard time selling the house because the "For

Sale'' sign kept disappearing. He thought it was vandals or neighbors. It turned out the culprits were his own teenage sons, who were pained by the thought of another move.

At all ages youngsters lose their credentials every time they move. Just as they are developing self-esteem from respect they have earned for special talents or appealing personality they find themselves, after a move, back to square one. A mother in Darien, Connecticut, who called the ninth- and tenth-grade years the "murderous ones" for newcomers, said it was in those years that children from high-mobile families tended, under the pressure to attain popularity, to get on the "fast track" and to get "too far out in their behavior."

For a great many children, a move can be more unsettling than stimulating. Some become depressed. While I was visiting the home of a man who had moved to Maryland from Roslyn, Long Island, he described in glowing terms the fine features of their new community. His family had been there more than a year. While we talked his nine-year-old daughter walked in. I asked her how she liked her new hometown. She frowned, paused, then said, "It's okay, I guess. But I miss my friends back in Roslyn very much."

What happens to the schoolwork of children who keep changing schools every two or three years? Many children reach the age of ten without ever having finished a grade in the same school. A Darien mother said her fourteen-year-old son had been in three school systems in one year. She added: "This is the price we pay for progress."

For the reasonably good student, a move, if not made during the school year, may not affect his or her school grades significantly. A principal in a school with many high-mobile children, in Great Falls, Montana, commented, however, that for the average or below-average student moving to a new school could cause his or her performance to drop. Schools vary in what they teach at different grade levels. A student struggling to cope with academic problems may end up being emotionally upset. Perhaps his new class is "ahead" of his former class — or so far behind it he becomes frustrated by boredom.

For the families that move frequently, one major study shows, grades are likely to be affected for good students and poor students alike. This study was made in the Denver school system. Test scores of elementary school students in the city's twenty-three schools with the most stable student populations were compared with the scores of those in the twenty-three schools with the most mobile populations (not counting desegregation movement). Students in the schools with highly stable student populations scored much higher than both the national and local averages. Students at the schools where there was high mobility had much lower test scores and were below the national average, according to the Denver system's supervisor of development and evaluation.

A friend tells me her eight-year-old grandson, in Oklahoma City, already is being treated for stomach ulcers! He has been in five different school systems in three years. In a Fort Worth school he had gotten outstanding grades. By the time he settled in the Oklahoma City schools he was threatened with being held back a year. Grading was apparently tougher there, and the seemingly calm youngster was distressed by adjustment problems. The father, a military man, has asked that another pending career transfer be postponed for his son's sake.

A systematic federal study shows that violence tends to be higher in schools with high turnover.[2] That seems plausible. Already-established students tend to test any newcomer, at least male, by some sort of combat. Also, it is easier to steal from strangers than from classmates you know personally.

By their teens, youngsters who move a lot have a greater than average chance of developing one of three behavioral patterns, I concluded from talking with many U.S. school officials and troubled parents:

1.   they become supercool; or
2.   they become far-out in their behavior to attract attention; or
3.   they become lonely recluses.

The high-mobile youngsters, I learned, seem to have more than average difficulty in developing really close friendships. They have been hurt by being uprooted from friendships which were immensely important to them, and apparently they don't want to get hurt again.

Along with this is an identity problem for many youngsters. They can't answer to where they are "from." They're from a lot of places.

High-mobile families tend to congregate in the same neighborhoods. They tend to stay away from the old, established section of town. Realtors advise me that the high-mobiles tend to prefer standardized houses because they are easier to sell than those with unique designs. The high-transient-neighborhood people tend to develop many mechanisms for building instant friendships. So youngsters are thrown in mainly with youngsters as uprooted as they are.

Another point: High mobility makes it more difficult to be good parents. At a forum I conducted with members of the Darien Newcomers'

Club, one mother raised an interesting point. She asked: "How do parents who are new in a town help their children evaluate their friends? How can parents counsel wisely when they don't know what kind of parents these friends of their children have? Do these newcoming parents feel they are less in touch with their children — and thus losing their relevance?"

That woman, I thought, put her finger on a lot of emerging problems, such as an eroding of the traditional critical role of parents in socializing their children. Perhaps she was suggesting why the generation gap has become such a disturbing thing. The network of both parental and community guidance that has traditionally helped orient youngsters in the transition to adulthood was coming apart. She suggested that many youngsters new in a community are hurting themselves by falling in with poor company at an important stage in their growth. They may be too eager for friendship from anyone.

A move to a quite different environment in terms of mores and moral expectations — say, from Orrville, Ohio, to Los Angeles — can also undercut parents as authority figures for a youngster.

A point might be made that married couples with children should think long and hard about accepting a transfer if they have a shaky marriage. The kids are probably already anxious about the family situation and a move might well tip them into more serious trouble. The least hazardous moves are made by families who have a good home life. Such families can handle an occasional move as an interesting challenge.

RAISING CHILDREN IN NEIGHBORHOODS OF FEAR

Distrust of fellow man starts early in modern America. The Foundation of Child Development, as noted, stated that the "most disturbing" discovery it uncovered in its massive survey of children's attitudes and feelings involved their high degree of apprehension. This survey was drawn from a cross-section of America. The eleven-year-olds were just as apprehensive as the seven-year-olds. Girls were somewhat more prone to admit fearfulness about going outside than boys. Youngsters from low-income families were more apprehensive than the norm.

We seem to be talking about a society where community cohesion, individual morality, and child-rearing patterns all are in such disarray that simple safety has become a significant concern.

In general, violent crimes against Americans tripled between 1960 and 1976. Many attributed the rise of the young criminals to the sheer numbers of teenagers in the population because of the "baby boom" generation. And there was a slight easing as that group passed out of the teens. But in 1979 the rate of violent crimes turned sharply up again.

It is not just an inner-city problem, such as the terror of child killings in Atlanta. Many suburbs and rural towns, such as Friendship, Wisconsin, report sharp rises in crimes. In rural areas the crimes are mostly against property, not crimes of violence. Titusville, Pennsylvania (population 7,000), had only one reported crime of violence in 1981.

One big reason for the increase of U.S. crime is the frustration of minority youngsters in urban areas. Here are some other possible explanations:

- the pervasiveness of violence on television;
- the fact that a hundred million guns are owned by U.S. civilians;
- the high level of transience of the population;
- the fact that whole neighborhoods are almost emptied of adults during the daytime in this era of the two-paycheck family;
- the disenchantment of many young people because of a lack of challenging roles for them while still in their teens.

One of the saddest aspects of the violent nature of our society is the preying of young barbarians on elderly people. Traditional societies respect, often revere, elders. Any ongoing society needs a sense of continuity between generations. Occasionally we see it. An elementary school class in Florida visits a nursing home every week and both the youngsters and oldsters have come to look forward to the visits.

In America in the 1980s in hundreds of urban areas, however, the elderly people leave the parks and their senior citizen centers when school lets out and retreat behind bolted doors. A survey by a Penn State parks administration professor, Geoffrey Godbey, of two thousand older people found that nine out of ten of them fear teenagers so greatly that they often cross the street or change direction to avoid young people.

REARING CHILDREN IN GLASS TOWERS

The Journal of Architectural Research carried a report by Clare Cooper Marcus that "The high-rise building is an essentially anti-child environment [requiring] a type of behavior which is . . . the antithesis of childhood.''

Many of the more desirable rental and condominium complexes from which children are banned are the two- and three-story "garden" structures. More and more city children in America and in Europe have been pushed into high-rise buildings in the last two decades.

Paris and Rome rather suddenly have become rimmed by towering residential buildings. As more and more Americans have begun living in vast metropolitan areas, the living space of many U.S. cities has been moving upward. New York City children for a century have been living in walk-up apartment buildings and are used to stoop living. Living in high-rise buildings where one's home can be reached only by elevator, however, is something quite recent and presents novel problems in adjustment.

In the U.S. at least a million youngsters live from four to thirty stories above ground. More than 200,000 live above the twelfth floor. For younger children in particular, living in glass towers is inhibiting, in not only obvious but subtle ways.

French critics such as psychiatrist Ménie Grégoire have called the vast high-rise housing "estates" in France, particularly outside Paris, modern concentration camps for children. "Everywhere I went," Grégoire related, "I found the authorities had forgotten the children." She said that at one such estate where children had been raised in "apartment slabs" she asked the young children to draw a house. "Without exception they each drew a small cottage with two windows and smoke curling up from a chimney roof." To Grégoire the implication seemed clear: the children longed for more homelike living arrangements of some sort. She cited a statement written by a ten-year-old girl named Olga living in a high-rise structure: "Here there is no place to walk to. There are only apartment buildings. Our project has 350 families but even the parents don't see each other. Many would like other children to visit us but no one wants to come because they are with their families. . . . I would really like to live in a small house where I could have a dog or a cat and where I could plant flowers and watch them grow and also play ball."

High-rise living does not have to be a burden for youngsters. The problem is that so few developers — including public housing builders — have given much thought to creating an environment that is convenient and congenial to children.

The British did most of the pioneering research on the impact of high-rise living on children. I was able to find only a few relevant U.S. studies before 1980.

British researchers were documenting the effect of high-rise living on children more than a decade ago. In the mid 1960s a British doctor, D. M. Fanning, was finding, in a study of British military families stationed in Germany, that children living in apartments were far more likely to suffer from psychoneurotic ailments as well as respiratory ones. And the higher they lived above ground, the more likely they were to have problems.[3]

Another early British study of more than 250 families living above the third floor was emphatic in its conclusions that living in high "flats" was "damaging" to children because of the loneliness and isolation. A study of life in high-rise flats in Glasgow concluded that children in high-rises suffered from not being able to engage in "doorstep play," with all the chances to mix with other children such play normally affords. Teachers from a school attended by many children from the high flats described the children in general as "reluctant talkers" and "oddly incurious about each other." The teachers also reported that the children, when they did talk, said a good deal about their mothers being cross.[4]

At least three early British studies show that children in high-rise flats play outside less than children reared near ground level.

In 1974 the New York State Urban Development Corporation received a cautionary report that children in high-rise developments had only about half as many friends visit them at home as children in low-rise buildings.[5]

Why high-rise living bothers children   There seem to be a number of reasons why children on high floors lead an abnormal, constricted life. The compacting of people into high-rise buildings — if no amenities for easy, natural interaction are provided — causes people to draw barriers around themselves. They tend to see neighbors as potential nuisances. Children absorb the feeling. More troublesome is the problem of finding a place where young children can safely engage in active play with other children. In city row houses this is no problem. The mother can continue her work while keeping an eye on her child in the backyard or on the front step. For the high-rise mother it means interrupting work and making a special trip, usually to some playground.

Psychologist Leonard Bachelis, director of the Behavior Therapy Center of New York, has given a lot of thought to the impact of high-rise living on children. In addition to handling children at his center he has raised his own youngster in a high-rise building on the East Side.

In his chat with me he stressed the unnaturalness of such living for children: "They don't get much sense of the change of weather or seasons. They don't get a chance to shovel snow. They have few chances to demonstrate resourcefulness by planting a tree or digging a trench."

Youngsters in high-rise buildings, he said, may have difficulty developing adequate large motor skills that come from running, climbing trees, or playing cops and robbers. The tendency to muscular inadequacy emerged in a 1971 research report.[6]

As recently as 1978 a U.S. family-life journal carried a complaint that researchers had paid little attention to the impact of housing on children. A year later, in January 1979, a New York expert on obesity, Chhaya Chakrabarti, noted in Today's Child that overweight had become a big problem among children living in city apartments. He suggested that eating becomes one of the few unobtrusive activities left to bored, frustrated kids who feel confined and are expected to be quiet.

Another problem is the anonymity of high-rise living. In these violent times there is a real basis for fear of being mugged in the elevator or in a bleak, twentieth-floor corridor.

A fascinating study of this hazard was made by Oscar Newman of New York, who studied crime prevention through urban design.[7] He compared life in apartment complexes near each other that were similar in many ways. The complexes were public housing projects in the five boroughs of New York. But they were conspicuously different in the number of stories. Some were walk-up complexes and others rose up more than sixteen stories. A second way the high-rises were different was that some were in vast complexes of more than a thousand units and some were in small complexes.

Approximately two and a half times more felonies were committed in the high-rise complexes than in the walk-up complexes. As for robberies alone, there were four and a half times more muggings in the high-rises than in the walk-ups. Furthermore there was more crime at the higher floors of the vast high-rise complexes than in the smaller complexes.

Newman concluded that "larger projects encourage crime by fostering feelings of anonymity, isolation, irresponsibility, lack of identity with surroundings." Even among high buildings, the higher the building, the more likely residents were to be victims of felonies, particularly muggings. For example, muggings were four times as likely to occur in a nineteen-story building as in a six-story building.

The evidence suggested that in big complexes and on the high floors thieves could prowl around and not be noticed because of the anonymity there. If someone becomes suspicious in the high buildings the thieves have more opportunities to hide or escape, or slip to another floor by the many stairs. Rescue takes longer. The vastness of big high-rise buildings also promotes more generalized wariness of strangers. A friend told me that as a boy in an Iowa town on Halloween night he covered more than a square mile of streets knocking on doors. When his family moved to a Chicago apartment, people were so reluctant to open doors that he confined his door-knocking to people in his own building. Most recognized him, at least vaguely. When his family later moved to a much larger apartment building, he found that children were expected to knock on doors only on their own floor. And even then they might find some people uncivil.

In walk-up complexes by contrast only a few people share accessways so that all the residents are known to each other. As neighbors they are much more likely to spot prowlers. In such a setting people too are more likely to be neighborly and thoughtful toward each other. And their children play on the front steps together.

During the national Bicentennial celebration of July 4, 1976, the major networks focused a great deal of their coverage on small-town America. In Seward, Nebraska, an eleven-year-old boy picked from the crowd was asked what life was like in Seward. He pondered a moment and said:

"It's an unwritten law in Seward that you do what is right."

It is difficult to imagine a lad pulled from a crowd in front of a high-rise complex making the same remark.

Obviously we can't go back to small-town living in any major way. But we can do a lot within big cities to bring youngsters and adults back into communion and to reduce for youngsters the frustrations and impersonality of big city living.

CONTRASTING CHILD WORLDS IN CITIES

Aside from the high-rises, children have been adapting to large city life — with its walk-up apartments, row houses and tiny plot homes — for centuries. Whether the children thrive or not depends to a very large extent upon the character of their immediate area. If their area is run down or disorganized or turbulent, only strong parenting can usually pull them through unscarred. But many cities have numerous islands of authentic neighborhoods that typically provide a good environment for growing up.

The degree of any particular urban area's sense of community and continuity largely determines, I have concluded, whether it is a good or bad place to raise kids. A few years ago two New York newspapers ran reports on the mood and life-styles of nearly a score of neighborhoods within that vast city. The mood of the people was distinctly negative in eight of these areas, distinctly positive in five.

One of the emphatically positive-mood neighborhoods was what *The New York Times* called "Safe, Proud Maspeth." A mixed ethnic middle- and lower-middle-class neighborhood with many active churches and other community organizations, Maspeth is located near the geographic heart of New York City. It is in Queens, bordering Brooklyn. Crime there was dropping at a time it was soaring elsewhere in the city. Multitudes of children played football or roller-skate hockey on clean, tree-lined streets periodically set aside for play. Neighbors chatted on the stoops. One mother said, "In Maspeth, children are kept stricter." There were heavy turnouts for parades. A sixty-three-year-old butcher said, "When the kids go to school in the morning they stick their heads in and say, 'Hello.' "

Not far away in middle-class Jackson Heights the pervading mood was one of tension. There was a strong feeling that things were changing too fast. Increasingly, young people were leaving the area and few children were visible. There was widespread apprehension and there were steel gates on many dozens of stores.

THE SHRINKAGE OF GOOD PLACES TO PLAY

If children had their choice, they would prefer to play in gravel pits and abandoned lumberyards or to play by walking on barn beams. Alas, with urbanization transforming the U.S. landscape, such places are disappearing. And the playgrounds available in most greater metropolitan areas strike active, imaginative kids as being straight out of Dullsville. The city youngsters invent ways to play that would never occur to adults and may be dangerous, such as crawling over cars. Even younger children lose interest within a half hour in the usual array of public playground slides, swings, seesaws and climbing bars, all on blacktop.

As for youngsters in high-rise apartment complexes, they must do much of their playing in lobbies, elevators, and parking lots. They are ordered to stay off any grassy areas. So they often end up loitering.

The play areas of America's cities — I was advised by Seymour Gold, of the University of California, Davis, who has won wide respect for his work on play environments — "are a national scandal when compared with those of other countries." Our neglect, he contends, contributes to vandalism, environmental stress, lack of civic pride, high levels of violence, and lack of identity, as well as low levels of physical fitness.

A recreational expert in San Diego said that kids in Tijuana slums across the border had more stimulating play opportunities than San Diego youngsters. The Mexican youths play in areas filled with rubble. They create their own play.

Play is an extremely serious business to kids. For them, opportunities for stimulating play are crucial to personality development. By imaginative play the youngster learns where he ends and the outer world begins. He or she learns to initiate independent activity, which builds confidence. Play is a bridge to relating to others. By arguing and learning to share with other children a youngster moves out of aloneness. Fantasy play gives the child a sense of power as he conceives, constructs, and flies spaceships or furnishes castles, and it helps the child to work out his anxieties.

Several authorities on child development have stressed the importance of play in helping youngsters develop social and conversational skills. Children who are constricted in play opportunities with others may well in later life have problems with expression.[8]

Most of the efforts to improve U.S. playgrounds have gone in the direction of pleasing adults, rather than children. The hot new so-called contemporary playground has aesthetically pleasing, novel forms and textures and playful-looking figures. It may have a tunnel to crawl through. Slides have bumps in them. There are cement turtles to ride. Everything usually has a sculptured look. Parents think they are charming. Officials of insurance companies have approved them, and the playground maintenance people like them. They may be an improvement, but from the reactions of youngsters, not much of one. Such playgrounds are still pretty static, unchallenging places that mainly offer a chance for some exercise.

The playgrounds that kids stand in line to get into, and stay at all day, are called "adventure playgrounds" by some. They are often so unsightly that they are surrounded by a high board fence. Inside may be a vacant lot, an old quarry, or a pond or an unusable gully. But whatever the locale it will probably contain a number of hand-made shanties, some two-stories high, rickety forts, rope-walks across water, mud slides. There may be individual flower or vegetable plots being tended by youngsters and a crude grill for cooking hot dogs. Typically each youngster is assigned a small plot of land on which he can do whatever he pleases. There is usually just one adult present, more as a safety watcher than a supervisor.

A Danish landscape architect, C. T. Sorenson, apparently invented the first adventure playground in the 1930s after he noticed one weekend an oddity in kid behavior. He had built many conventional playgrounds and was in the process of building another. Many of the slides, seesaws, and so on were already in place and a few children were already playing on them. But in one corner of the playground were piles of work materials and scraps the workmen had left. In overwhelming numbers the children were playing with this debris of workmen rather than the already-built play equipment.

Adventure playgrounds spread first in Scandinavia and then after World War II in countries such as Great Britain, where by unfortunate accident many marvelous sites had become available — the bombed-out areas of cities.

In 1950 the first U.S. adventure playground on the European model was built in Minneapolis as a demonstration project sponsored by a women's magazine. It was an immediate success. Local contractors supplied scraps of material. Local union members built the fence.

Since then adventure playgrounds have become popular in several California cities and in a few other U.S. cities. The biggest obstacle to faster growth seems to be the American fetish for cleanliness and for things that look like progress. Adventure playgrounds don't offer either — only a lot of excitement for the six-to-thirteen crowd.

Alternative ideas for exciting, creative play which are less down-to-earth are also being developed. For example, at the Children's Museum of Boston children can obtain all sorts of strange, interesting materials created by a recycling center. They can get material, from eyeglass frames to foam rubber. They can get buttons or lenses. Best of all they can obtain cutting tools, glue, and so forth and can invent on the spot whatever they wish as long as they clean up after themselves.

TROUBLES IN SUBURBIA

Another innovation in environment which affects even more children than high-rises is urban sprawl. Most U.S. children now live in our "greater" metropolitan areas, which embrace both the central cities and their fast-spreading outlying areas, including satellite cities and suburbs. Some of the latter can reasonably be called "slurbs."

Demographers often divide up the U.S. population neatly into urban, suburban, and rural. Conceptually such a division has merit, but it often fits the facts only loosely as we move toward what demographer Philip Hauser called a "mass society."

In Southern California a number of suburbs are islands within the city of Los Angeles. Paramus, New Jersey, is technically a suburb of New York City. Once it was a truck-gardening hamlet about ten miles west of the George Washington Bridge. Today it is a jungle of housing tracts surrounding two of the world's largest shopping centers and is sliced by intersecting superhighways. It has no downtown in any conventional sense. The town hall is off one of the superhighways, near a giant motel.

East and south of Pittsburgh are two other enormous malls, both built by the same developer. Surrounding them is a sea of development housing tracts and apartment complexes that have engulfed and almost obliterated the authentic communities that used to lie in these hills.

Such malls are the new downtowns in many dozens of suburban areas. But they are private property. Even presidential candidates need a proprietor's permission to give a speech on the parking lots of these places, where it is easy to assemble crowds. Kids are tolerated as long as they are shopping. But the managers don't want them hanging around or playing.

In one of these malls south of Pittsburgh the management built a community room and made it available to youths at certain hours. Later, the management changed its mind. It said too many of the young were creating confusion among customers in corridors and using the community room as a place just to hang out.

A strong critic of the management's action was a young Presbyterian minister. He spoke sharply to what I feel is an important point:

"These are suburban kids, whose fathers have often been moved around the country by their companies. These youngsters don't know anything else but the shopping center as a gathering place. Even if you don't do anything for them here they will come anyway. I don't think the developers have any moral right to turn away the kids when they are pushing so hard to get their parents in here to spend their money."

Urie Bronfenbrenner, the noted child specialist, has expressed his worry about the impact of the lonely and constricted world of "shifting suburbia.'' His concern was with the sameness and dullness as far as children are concerned. Tract developers tend to single out one economic or ethnic group as the focus of their sales appeals, whereas a true town has a diversity of people and settings. Bronfenbrenner said, ''Now for millions of American children the neighborhood is nothing but row upon row of buildings inhabited by strangers. One house or apartment is much like another, and so are the people. . . .''

Many of the suburbs that actually resemble physically an old-fashioned town also by necessity have a sameness. Their houses are so sought after that only the well-to-do can usually afford to live there (unless there is subsidized housing). In a number of such suburbs in Fairfield County, Connecticut, the cleaning women and most of the firemen, teachers, and police commute in from somewhere else. In Darien, Connecticut, for example, a youngster rarely sees a man carrying a lunch-bucket. Almost all of the few members of minority racial groups seen by children are employed in some serving role.

Elsewhere handsome, prosperous suburban towns, in the late 1970s, were running into increased problems with their youths. Under the heading ''Suburbs Seeking to Deal with Restive Youth,'' *The New York Times* cited as typical of what was happening in Westchester County towns the situation in the idyllic-looking suburban village with the marvelous name of Pleasantville, New York. Pleasantville had found itself grappling with an embarrassing problem that threatened to hurt the village's image as a fine place to buy a high-priced home. The town's youngsters were increasingly getting out of hand, with one mass confrontation with the police. Even with suspected underreporting of offenses, this village of 7,100 had witnessed more than six hundred juvenile arrests in one year for vandalism, ''loitering,'' trouble-making, etc. Boredom may have been a factor. The village was up in arms. Some residents blamed the troubles on poor family relationships, more empty homes because mothers were working. Efforts were made to hold parents responsible. The village set aside a ''free area'' near the railroad station where youngsters could hang out.

Several efforts have been made to measure differences in youngsters on the urban-suburban-rural dimension. Here are a few of the more interesting findings:

Loneliness and apprehension   The Foundation for Child Development in its study of 2,301 youngsters aged seven to eleven sought a national sample. The surveyers expected to find the most loneliness in rural settings but that was not the case. Kids in poor sections of inner cities were twice as likely to say they felt lonely "a lot." About one in seven said it. Rural kids were the least likely to report fear-inducing experiences of being threatened or hurt.

Delinquency and drug use   The commission of unlawful acts by juveniles has been rising in all settings, but evidence is still skimpy on differences between rural, suburban, and urban areas. Kathleen Natalino at Bowling Green State University in Ohio studied the responses of 660 white teenagers in a Midwestern metropolis with those of 514 white teenagers in rural high schools. She found plenty of hell-raising in both but said, "Findings support the traditional view of urban delinquency as generally more serious than rural delinquency." Some sociologists speculate that it takes an urban setting to develop the "critical mass" for gang-type delinquency. On the other hand an investigator in rural Oregon concluded that run-ins with the law there were as frequent as in Philadelphia.[9]

As for drug use, some studies have indicated rates vary by degree of urbanization. The New York State Drug Abuse Control Commission made a self-reporting survey of 4,000 rural and 2,700 suburban high school students. The suburban youths were about 27 percent more likely to use one or more drugs for "highs."[10]

Precocious sex   Much of the indication here has to be inferred from the reported behavior of late adolescents who have reached college age. A group, for example, headed by Thomas Abernathy of the University of British Columbia compared the reported behavior of 295 white students based on whether they came from rural, suburban, or urban homes.[11] Urban males were twice as likely to report having experienced sexual intercourse as were rural males, with suburbanites falling in between. Among females the suburbanites reported being most experienced sexually. They were slightly more experienced than urban females and four times as likely to report having experienced intercourse as the rural females.

Several years ago I conducted a study of sexual behavior and attitudes among 2,200 students at twenty-one U.S. colleges and universities and five foreign universities (as a part of my research on *The Sexual Wilderness*). One finding was of possible relevance here. Five of the U.S. schools were located in rural settings at least thirty miles from any major metropolitan area. For both males and females the reported coital rate of these schools was about 10 percent lower than the average of all twenty-one schools.

THE DECLINE IN ADULT CONTACT

Authentic small-town communities often are not as romantic as many of us like to imagine. There can be feuding and slighting and dullness. But they have one great plus: in them youngsters by the age of eleven are interacting every day with adults and learning fast how to behave like adults themselves. Families are mostly old acquaintances.

One of the nation's leading authorities on children, Yale psychologist Edward Zigler, has stated that children need adults in their lives. They really don't want a Huck Finn existence and often feel they are being deprived of something important.

Yet adults and youth today in general tend to live in different worlds. Adults go away to do a kind of work that youngsters only vaguely comprehend. Children are taken off to huge consolidated schools. Apprentice systems for teenagers have virtually been abolished. Grandparents often have moved off to retirement areas and other adult relatives who normally would be supportive often are now dozens or hundreds of miles away.

Adult cocktail parties, which in effect exclude children, have replaced family get-togethers.

The most visible decline in contact between fathers and the children seems to occur in the suburban "bedroom" towns where the father leaves to commute around dawn, often is gone overnight on trips or returns at night in time for a fast drink while saying good night to his children. Darien, Connecticut, as indicated, is such a town. A junior high school official there told me: "If the father works nearby and the commuting hours are moderate, the father commands a great deal more authority with his children. Many problems at school stem from the fact the parents are not home. The male image is lacking and ought to be there."

A Darien mother active in community affairs observed: "I've been watching a whole generation grow up here. The local doctors and lawyers and merchants have yet to turn up a serious problem youngster that I have seen. Almost all the problems come out of families where the father commutes or travels a lot — or where the family is split. It's unbelievable how sharp the difference is, especially if there is no local grandfather."

Even contact between children and adults inside the home is in sharp decline, not only in the U.S. but in countries such as Germany. The National Academy of Sciences' Advisory Committee on Child Development in 1976 called for a new national policy toward children.[12] It cited a twenty-five-year study by Urie Bronfenbrenner of Cornell which revealed a clear decline in interaction between parents and children. Bronfenbrenner said the decline in contact of children with middle-income fathers had been particularly abrupt, and he felt it was a factor in the origin of alienation. He reported a study in which such fathers told interviewers they spent an average of fifteen to twenty minutes a day playing with their infant children. But he said another study indicated that even that was probably an exaggeration. In the latter study a microphone was attached to the crawling infant's shirt. Analysis of the recordings indicated that as far as warm voice interaction, such as laughing and cooing, was concerned, the daily average father-child contact was thirty-seven *seconds*.[13]

The declining contact of typical American family members is perhaps best illustrated by eating patterns.

I was commenting to my wife Virginia about the marvelous family life that a neighboring family seemed to have. The father is a postal employee; the mother runs a cleaning service. There are three teenagers. The family has just completed most of the work, part time, of building a summer home. Virginia commented:

"They always eat supper together."

In the homes of many Western countries the dining room is replaced by an alcove. Partly this is because the home size is shrinking, partly it is because an area is needed for TV viewing.

In most areas of the U.S., the extended family with relatives in the home or nearby is long gone. New York child psychiatrist Arthur Kornhaber reports that only 5 percent of U.S. children see a grandparent regularly. And that is a shame, he contends, because grandparents are natural allies of children. When they are in regular contact they are an extra source of love and companionship. They can extend their love unconditionally whereas parents often unwittingly tend to make it conditional on acceptable behavior.

At the same time there has been a decisive rise in the dependency of youngsters of all ages on agemates, as ever-increasing millions of homes become empty of adults during the day. (And in this century there has also been a spectacular decline in adults other than parents living in the typical home.) As a result peer groups often become a kind of substitute family.

Do youngsters heavily involved in peer-group affiliation differ from children who are more family oriented? Definitely yes. They tend to have a negative view of themselves, a dim view of the world, and are more prone to aggressiveness and other antisocial behavior. High school students who report they have a low affiliation with their family are *five* times more likely to get caught up in the drug or heavy drinking scene than high school students who report having a close affiliation with their family, according to a study of 8,553 public school students in 102 schools in New York State.[14]

An analysis was made by John Condry and Michael Siman of the differences between ninth-graders who were classified as being either adult-oriented or peer-oriented. The peer-oriented children reported having said and done things which hurt others significantly more than the adult-oriented children. The adult-oriented kids tested out as being significantly higher in self-esteem.

An alternative pattern for youngsters feeling passive neglect in the home is to fall into a state of loneliness, which can do even more damage. A lonely child is apt to become socially inept. He does not, as we assume, reach out for warmth. He usually withdraws and develops a cold personality. Child specialist Helen Maley told of dealing with such cold, unresponsive children. She said often they act as if they were "dead already."

A question about any bad effect of low parent-child contact and high peer contact might seem to arise from the experience of children of Israeli kibbutzim. They have been raised largely in communal children's houses. Most investigators, including the noted Bruno Bettelheim, University of Chicago psychologist, have agreed that children there seemed to thrive in growing up. At these collectives parent-child relations are more like those of grandparents enjoying their children without the difficulties parents often experience. However a kibbutz is not like an American bedroom town. It is like a small village where the children are often in contact with adults, watched carefully by adults, and become involved early with adults in economic activities. Their parents are always within calling distance. Babies are usually breast-fed by their mothers. The children typically spend time with their parents every afternoon after work and on weekends. By most accounts there is a great deal of affection between the parents and their children reared in separate houses. The parents seem more adversely affected by their low responsibility, according to a view reached by New York psychologist Howard Halpern, by having all the fun of parenting and none of the anguish. His point was that parenting ideally expands people's capacity for giving, sacrificing, protecting, and loving.

In September 1981 *The Journal of Family Issues* carried a report that family life within the kibbutz is enjoying a great revival. It was even forecast that within twenty-five years the kibbutz family would be close to the Western family system.

LIFE WITH STATE-APPOINTED PARENTS

In 1979 the National Commission for Children in Need of Parents reported that "A surer system for harming children and wasting money could hardly be invented than what passes for a foster care system" as it has been functioning recently.

The story of a Louisiana boy called Joey illustrates how muddled the state can become in taking charge of a young human. The case was tracked down by the Children's Defense Fund.

Joey was surrendered to the welfare people for foster care by his mother for what she thought would be a brief period. Joey was age three. She had gone through a divorce and was having a very hard time making ends meet.

For the next two years Joey was in three different Louisiana foster homes. His mother visited him repeatedly but he became a "difficult" child. Louisiana sent him off to a New York State facility for five years. His father, in nearby New Jersey, attempted to visit Joey but was refused permission.

New York welfare officials wrote Louisiana officials stating that they thought Joey should go back to his mother. Louisiana officials claimed they couldn't locate her, even though she had written asking for information about him and asking for his return to her. Louisiana instead sent him to a facility in Texas for two years. His mother finally got Joey back after an absence of ten years as a result of a class action lawsuit (*Gary W.* v. *Louisiana*). It was brought on behalf of 591 Louisiana children in Texas facilities. Joey is now in public school.

Joey's story of course is an extreme case in terms of movement. But it is also untypical because he finally did get back to a natural parent. The majority of foster children do not.

The number of U.S. children removed from their family and put into foster care has been soaring: in 1961 the number was less than 200,000; by 1977 it was more than 500,000.

In September 1981 *Marriage and Divorce Today,* under the heading "Foster Care — Big Business," carried the statement that "Official removal of children from their natural parents is one of the fastest growing industries in the country." It reported cases of children who had been moved as many as eighteen times.

Children end up in foster homes — or other "out-of-home" facilities — because the parents have serious problems such as drinking, emotional disturbance, or because they are so strapped financially that they can't seem to cope with a crisis condition or because of child abuse or neglect. (Sometimes the foster home is also abusive or neglectful.) Or perhaps the child has a serious problem requiring special services. The welfare agency takes over legal custody as a part of providing the services. Some children are taken from homes by court order, some are voluntarily turned over to authorities by desperate parents.

Foster parents are paid about $4,000 a year, on average, for taking on the child. Funding ends if the child is adopted, or is returned to its parents.

Many foster parents learn to love the child and provide the child with a stable home and good substitute parenting. In some states they are prevented by law from adopting a child they have come to love.

The foster home was invented as a temporary response to a family in crisis. In recent years it has come close to providing a semipermanent way of life for children. These children are commonly shifted from one strange household to another and live in a kind of limbo for several years.

The agencies are supposed to work to return the children to their home; or if that remains impractical to work to get them adopted. Years often go by while neither happens, due to the forces of governmental red tape, court delays, and agency inertia.

In New York City kids put into foster homes stay there on the average for seven critical years of their life. A state commissioner said he was led to wonder whether the program's primary goal was to perpetuate the foster-care system.

Federal money goes to the states to help support out-of-home care for children. One reason states have been quick to take over custody of children of troubled families is that until recently it was very difficult to get federal funding if they didn't take the child out of its home.

Perhaps the most serious criticism of America's foster-care system is its anti-family bias. The system typically has been quick to take a child away from its parents; and to contend, year after year, that the child is better off in foster care than it would be in its own home. This has happened even when the family is fighting to regain the child.

In an experiment in a California county (Alameda) the agency people in charge of one group of foster youngsters were strongly reminded that their goal was to seek actively a permanent arrangement for the children. Agency people in charge of another group of foster children were not given this forceful reminder and proceeded on normal course. At the end of two years, according to a 1979 report in *Children Today,* a check was made. Four-fifths of the children in the experimental group were back in a permanent home setting of some sort. Sixty percent of the kids in the "as usual" group were still in the limbo of foster care.

The impact of prolonged care in a series of foster homes need not necessarily wreck a youngster's life if he or she is resilient and has emotional resources to start with, and some good luck with foster parents.

For many children, according to the Children's Defense Fund, out-of-home care with strangers can be "psychologically devastating."

This conclusion came after the Fund took a long, penetrating look at the system. Investigators for the Fund analyzed the foster-care situation in 140 counties in many states. Its report, *Children Without Homes,* startled many Congressmen. Some of its major conclusions:

- Families get short shrift when the child welfare people move in. "At every point in the placement process children and their natural parents are isolated from one another." Parents are often restricted in their efforts to visit their children. These visits may be restricted to "special occasions" or "once a month" or "in a courtroom." The parents are usually not given any kind of regular report on how the children are progressing. "Sometimes they are not even informed when the children are moved." Strangers are usually preferred over relatives as possible substitute parents.

- Children in out-of-home care frequently are shuttled considerable distances. We noted the travels of Joey. In San Francisco 40 percent of all child placements in a recent year were sent to some other county. At the time of the Children's Defense Fund study, at least ten thousand foster youngsters were known to be in some state other than their original home. In these other states they were in foster homes or group residences, or special facilities, many of them profit-making operations. Texas seems to be running a kind of processing mill for children with problems. It was receiving children from thirty-two states.

- Child welfare officials seem to find it easier to solve a difficult family situation by sending the child away rather than offering support to the family. By support I mean such alternatives as paying for homemaker visits, specialized day treatment, day-care, or helping the family with a housing problem. The CDF report stated: "Funds for removal are available; adequate funds for alternatives are not." This is the situation even though the alternatives would usually cost less — often much less — than foster or institutional care. The latter, with all the overhead, runs near $8,000 a year per child nationally, closer to $30,000 in some large cities. Government child welfare bureaus often turn the children over to private social agencies for placement and supervision in foster homes. (These agencies may develop a vested interest in keeping foster children on their rolls and may be reluctant to report children in bad foster home situations.)

- Child welfare people too often do not get to know the children in their care. Most officials surveyed didn't know how long a child in their care had been away from home. A fifteen-year-old girl named Thelma was quoted in a newspaper as saying: "I have an allocations worker, I have a caseworker, and I have a caseworker's supervisor. None of them have ever met me."

In situations of adversity children urgently need a feeling of belonging to a reliable and loving adult. Ideally — no matter how bad things look on the surface — those adults should include their own natural parents. Many foster-care officials have the notions that visits from natural parents just upset the child. There is now persuasive evidence to the contrary — that maintaining contact with natural parents is enormously important to foster children. This came out of a five-year study of 624 children in foster care by two New York professors of social work, David Fanshel and Eugene B. Shinn.[15]

Fanshel and Shinn found that foster children who were visited by their natural parents made "significantly greater gains" in intelligence and emotional adjustment than those unvisited. The unvisited apparently feel their sense of identity profoundly insulted if they are old enough to know they have natural parents somewhere else. The investigators found these gains held even if the visiting by natural parents was irregular. Further, those visited by their natural parents during their first year were more than twice as likely to be back in their own homes within the period of study.

Much needs to be done at the state levels to require semiannual reviews of how much progress is being made toward getting each child into a permanent home setting.

In California — the frequent policy innovator among U.S. states —a notable advance was made when the state passed the Family Protection Act. The primary aim was to finance pilot studies in two counties on better ways to handle foster children. A major goal is to provide help that will keep the child in its natural home. Communities are establishing "parental stress hotlines." Family caseworkers, according to the plan, will come into the home for short-term help on a twenty-four-hour basis. If the situation is so bad that the child is placed outside the home, then the case is to be assigned immediately to "family re-unifications planning" in which an attempt is made to make a contract with the natural parent or parents on what needs to be done to restore the child to the home. The program seems to be cutting costs.

Another promising new development is that in several cities such as Dallas, St. Louis, and Detroit the courts appoint volunteers to monitor the handling of specific children placed in foster care. The aim is to assure that the children are established in a permanent home as soon as possible.

In my view officials should not be permitted to propose foster care until all alternatives for helping to keep the child in the home have been explored (unless child abuse by the parent is charged). The government should intrude in family affairs only in crisis situations; and the intervention should be directed toward preservation of the families. If the decision is finally made that this is not feasible, then the interveners should work actively to establish the child in a permanent home setting.

7

Schools That Upset Children

"By lashing out, kids are trying to tell us something
and we aren't listening."

— *Jane Mace, teacher in a Milwaukee high school with
2,800 students*

One of the more glorious of political actions in the nineteenth century
was to introduce free, universal public schooling. In the U.S. this action
was intended to thrust us into being a more enlightened, competent, and
democratic society. Well into the twentieth century public schools were
community monuments, and schoolteachers were rated very high in
public esteem. They represented wisdom and progress. Even in their
private lives teachers were watched with sharp interest because they
were believed to be playing a substantial role in shaping not only the
minds but the character and morals of our youth. I witnessed the esteem
and the scrutiny: my mother, my sister, and my fiancée-turned-wife were
public schoolteachers at one time.

There are still a host of dedicated, talented public schoolteachers, and
many are greatly esteemed. Many U.S. public schools with good community support are doing fine, imaginative jobs in helping prepare children for promising lives in adulthood, and making the preparation an
exhilarating experience for the youngster.

In this chapter, however, we will be talking about the growth experience now provided for children by the more typical public school and the more typical modern teacher. The schools and their personnel are affected not only by giantism, urbanization, community fragmentation, ethnic shifts, union rules, and a decline in parental involvement — but by a tendency of our society to push more child-care and child-socialization roles upon the schools.

In 1982 Amitai Etzioni, director of the Center for Policy Research, estimated that roughly a third of U.S. schools actually inflict psychic harm on pupils.

Schools today are expected to feed 25,000,000 youngsters lunch, despite sharply constricted budgets. At the same time schools are expected to perform an unspoken but valued function: keeping older youths out of the home, off the street, and out of the full-time job market.

In recent years public schools have had a mandate to provide equal access to educational opportunity. Implementing this in residential areas of cities where there is sharp racial stratification has gotten many schools into mandatory transport of students to distant neighborhoods. There have been gains toward the goal of equal education. But all the forced balancing has inevitably created stress and problems of self-esteem for the children being shuffled about.

Also, when disadvantaged children are mingled in large numbers with children who have plenty of advantages, a major concern of the parents of advantaged children may be whether the disadvantaged children will absorb a disproportionate amount of the conscientious teacher's time to the neglect of their children. They start thinking of private schools.

In 1981 the U.S. Education Department released a startling finding: students at the typically hard-pressed private and parochial schools of America were producing higher academic achievers on average than were the public schools. The study was supervised by the noted educational sociologist James S. Coleman, University of Chicago, and was controlled for family background factors. In some respects, the study showed private schools were more integrated in terms of minorities than the public schools.

The report understandably provoked denunciations from some public school educators. Coleman attributed the better results being achieved at the private and parochial schools primarily to two factors:

- They make greater academic demands.
- They provide a higher level of discipline and consequently a more ordered environment for learning.

He might have added that the non-public schools have a built-in advantage: they can accept or reject applications and they can throw out troublemakers without fear of a legal hassle. Also a parent must make an active commitment to get a youngster into a private school and keep him there, and thus may have a special motive to pay close attention to how the youngster is doing in school.

Perhaps the main reason the public schools are in trouble — and they are in trouble — is that they more truly reflect problems afflicting society at large.

Urie Bronfenbrenner has called the American school system ''a major breeding ground of alienation.'' He puts much of the blame on the fact that schools are often located a considerable distance from most of the families they serve.

Let's note some of the major problem areas of the typical school system.

THE BIGNESS

In urban America Bronfenbrenner's ''remoteness'' means that the school will be large. Economies of scale are eating the heart out of U.S. schools. At the end of World War II the average local school system had less than 250 students. Today it has more than 2,500. Civic pride in bigness as well as educators' concepts of efficiency have contributed to the trend to giantism. In a sprawling structure teachers often do not recognize most of the pupils they are trying to herd through the corridors.

Even in a school building of 500 students, younger pupils are often troubled by anonymity, powerlessness, and passiveness. This is at a time when they need a school setting intimate enough for them to develop self-esteem through class achievements, friendship, or participation in activities.

There is an abundance of evidence that at larger schools violence and vandalism soar. Medford, Massachusetts, a middle-class suburb of Boston, built a magnificent high school complex to handle 3,800 students and soon found it was spending about as much to repair damage due to vandalism as it was for textbooks.

THE CALIBER AND MOTIVATION OF TYPICAL TEACHERS

Today the *average* public schoolteacher can no longer be assumed to be wise or even competent to teach basic skills. This deficiency in the people who by law control our children for at least ten years merits concern in many U.S. areas.

There is, for our contemplation, the steady fifteen-year decline in test scores of students. The caliber and motivation of teachers is certainly one cause.

Another indicator of problems in the quality of schooling is that in recent tests 13 percent of eleventh-graders tested were still functionally illiterate. Why were they permitted to get that far — within one year of a high school diploma? Recently we have had a rash of state laws requiring minimum competency tests to reduce this embarrassment.

The problem regarding caliber of teachers starts at the teacher-training institutions. The U.S. has notable exceptions, such as Stanford, Ohio State, Indiana University and the Columbia Teachers College, but by and large the nation's institutions for teacher training offer many snap courses. They often put more focus on methods of teaching than mastering the subjects to be taught. Also, these institutions attract fewer of the bright, high-striving high school graduates than in former decades. An educational researcher at Boston University has found that high school graduates planning to enter teachers' colleges were thirty-four points below the average of high school graduates entering colleges in verbal skills and a whopping forty-three points below average in math.[1]

Many parents, after noticing misspellings in messages they receive from teachers, have begun demanding that teachers, too, pass minimum competency tests to enter the profession. Many school boards agree. Quite a few states, mostly in the South, now are starting to require competency testing.

In Dallas, Texas, several hundred first-year teachers were given a classification test. About half of them scored unacceptably low. The same test was given to junior and senior high school students at a local parochial high school. The students scored well above the public school teachers.[2] At about the time Texas newspapers were publicizing these results, a national association of teachers was holding its annual meeting in Dallas. It passed a resolution condemning the competency testing of teachers.

Under a new law prospective teachers in Texas, starting in 1984, will have to pass a test demonstrating competence at least in the subject they will be teaching.

One long-term study of declining competence of young people who become teachers in North Carolina came up with a surprise. Researchers

Phillip Schlechty and Victor Vance analyzed the National Teacher Examination scores of all 32,000 persons taking jobs in the state's schools between 1973 and 1980. There was indeed a steady seven-year decline. But the decline was confined to white females, who make up two-thirds of the public schoolteachers.

There was no similar decline among white males or among black male or female teachers. This suggested to the investigators that the great opening up of career opportunities for women has caused many of the brighter white women, at least, to look elsewhere for jobs that may offer greater prestige, money, or fulfillment.

Educational administrators have complained to me it has been particularly hard to recruit or keep outstanding math and science teachers because they are in considerable demand in the new high technology industries offering high-paying, year-round jobs.

Another problem is that at many schools the teachers will not stay after school to confer with students for more than one hour per week. They frequently require extra pay if they are asked to supervise any student activities. Some believe that reviewing student homework by handling it as their own homework is passé.

But there are others to blame beyond the school systems. Willard Wirtz, who headed a special panel appointed to assess the decline in test scores, cited as a cause "the family's declining participation in the learning process in this country."

THE RISE IN PANDEMONIUM

A general rise in pandemonium is the most conspicuous change that has occurred in our public schools, especially urban schools, in the past two decades. Many teachers report that violence, mass disobedience, or resistance in the classroom are problems. An official of the National Association of Secondary School Principals told me:

"Teachers today are simply exhausted from the amount of energy demanded to just keep a decent level of order in the classroom."

Children sense they are in alien territory as they see frequent evidence of vandalism. One federal report put the annual school vandalism cost at close to a half-billion dollars.

Along with vandalism there are on many large school grounds fellow students peddling drugs to classmates.

And then there is the sheer violence in schools, which has been running in unprecedented levels for several years. During the past decade just about every category of violence and disruption in the nation's schools soared. In the late 1970s the *NEA Reporter* summed the situation up this way:

"Last year American school children committed 100 murders, 12,000 armed robberies, 9,000 rapes, 204,000 aggravated assaults. . . . They were responsible for 270,000 school burglaries."

The bigger the school and the bigger the community, the higher the level of violence and destruction is likely to be. Uncontrolled violence apparently is worst at the junior high school level, where the students, going through puberty, are most prone to have problems controlling their behavior. A 1978 report of the National Institute of Education made the harsh assertion that students feel safer on city streets than they do in school buildings.

A novel suit has been brought in California to force Los Angeles to provide safe schools for children required to attend them. Nearly a fourth of all secondary students try to avoid use of restrooms out of anxiety, according to a national study mandated by Congress.[3] This has given rise to what is called the "bladder syndrome." Children are so frightened that they fight to maintain bladder control rather than use the restroom. Some urinate in crannies of the corridor.

The same report pointed to a solution of all the disorder. It said: "The more support a school gets from parents, community agencies, police, the board of education and other sources, the lower the school crime rate will be." There is for example a clear correlation between PTA participation by parents and good schools. Really good schools have lots of parent volunteers and parents attending sessions on how they can help their children do better in school.

Some schools get such support and thrive. But a great many do not get broad community support, except from the police.

Security guards carrying walkie-talkies may lock classroom doors after classes begin. Many teachers have panic buttons to signal the central office when trouble starts. In a few school systems teachers are even starting to wear a kind of wrist polygraph that automatically emits a radio signal to the office when the teacher's body signals fright.

In Prince Georges County, Maryland, where violence prevailed in many schools, a significant reduction was achieved by inviting students to enlist in a school "security council." They wear armbands and are required to report disorders. More than a thousand students in twenty schools volunteered. An official said: "There are many students in any school who really want to have a hand in making their school better."

At the prepuberty level, school administrations in hundreds of schools have tried to cope with restlessness among students by encouraging parents to put pupils labeled "hyperactive" on drug tranquilizers. The subjects overwhelmingly are young boys. And the pills of choice, oddly, are the "speed" pills that grown-ups take — amphetamines and Ritalin — to get a high charge. For prepubescent boys the pills often have an opposite effect. The typical pattern is that parents of a troublesome child are advised by a teacher, nurse, or administrator that Johnny is causing problems by his restlessness. Parents are advised that one of the cited drugs might help. Doctors have typically written the prescriptions with little inquiry.

Since the 1970s at least a million school youngsters have been given such drugs. The drugs while often making a boy less fidgety have a number of possible bad side effects. Some parents have claimed they were pressured by school officials into complying and that their children suffered cramps, crying spells, listlessness, etc.

Some children have an actual identifiable physiological basis for their restlessness, perhaps a deficiency of a brain neurotransmitter such as dopamine. But others are hyperactive because they consume too many sweets, or too much artificial food coloring, or because they are hungry, or because their parents are fighting, or because they are watching too much TV. Or they feel ignored and are bored.

TEACHERS UNDER ASSAULT

Typical teachers, far from being held in awe by older students, have been frequent victims of school violence, especially in inner cities. At least 65,000 teachers are victims of assault of some sort each year. Urban high school teachers are nine times more likely to be threatened than rural high school teachers. Some examples of assaults:

- In New York City a student who was denied permission to leave the room came at his teacher with a chain.
- In Los Angeles a husky male teacher, who intervened when students were assaulting a female teacher, was knocked down and kicked in the head until unconscious. His hearing was seriously affected. The assaulters were arrested but no action was taken.
- Also in Los Angeles a teacher who was handing out report cards was assaulted by female students who didn't like her reports on

them. They set her hair on fire. When she tried to report the matter to the principal, he criticized her for leaving the classroom and not maintaining order. She underwent psychiatric treatment. A psychiatrist has reported that many inner-city teachers exhibit symptoms comparable to combat neurosis.

- In Norfolk, Virginia, a high school student bit off a third of a teacher's ear.

- New York City teachers are admonished to stay out of empty rooms and to leave the school building directly after dismissing the final class.

CURBS ON ENFORCING DISCIPLINE

Often the teacher in cities and suburbs is only verbally attacked. In Prince Georges County, Maryland, a junior high school student retorted to his female teacher, "Fuck you, bitch." She sent him to the principal. By the end of the school day the boy still had not been sent home. Others in the class noted this. The teacher felt her control had been undermined.

School administrators have been increasingly reluctant to back up teachers by issuing suspensions, unless the offense involves something that would be illegal off school grounds, such as carrying a concealed weapon or rape.

In 1969 the U.S. Supreme Court held that students do not shed their constitutional rights "at the schoolhouse gate." Later the Court upheld the right to due process for students. This raised an interesting dilemma. If we require students to attend school then we are required to let them attend, no matter how unscholarly they are. Suspended students have been suing schools for violation of their constitutional rights. The result, as a federal document put it, was that "increasingly disruptive behavior became tolerated in the schools."[4]

As it is today, if a student assaults someone on school grounds seriously enough to require a doctor's attention the chances are about one in three that the assault will be reported to the police.

One threatened teacher who got involved in a legal action brought by a suspended student made three court appearances over a nine-month period. In each instance the case was continued without testimony. The teacher's life was threatened. Finally he gave up his tenured job for a position in another school system. Result: "The teachers simply do not want to get involved legally with the students,'' an official of the National Association of Secondary School Principals told me.

Some big-city school systems such as Denver's go for years without suspending a single student. Suspension is becoming a last resort.

Courts stress the right and responsibility of schools to maintain an orderly school climate, and leave it to the schools to figure out how to do it legally. The most commonly used technique is to send a letter home.

Some schools have invented ''suspension rooms'' within the school compound. Others condemn serious offenders to work on school beautification projects.

POT IN THE SCHOOLS

An entirely new problem in school life has developed in the past eight years: widespread use of marijuana by youngsters during school hours.

This vogue to use pot, which peaked in the colleges in the early 1970s, seemingly has been peaking among junior high school students just in the past few years.

Youngsters often become dealers to cover the costs of obtaining marijuana for themselves, and to make some big change besides. They sell joints at school bus stops, and during lunch hour, and on school grounds. A U.S. government report in 1977 put the number of youngsters aged twelve to seventeen who were current users of marijuana at four million.

Most youngsters are convinced it won't ''hurt'' them because that was widely asserted in the 1970s, when the stuff used was far milder. At the least, steady use impedes the learning process of young people, according to a 1981 report in *Behavior Today* (November 2) entitled ''High Human Price of Pot Smoking Starting to Show.''

Regular users tend to be notably inattentive in class. They feel placidly passive and drowsy. Grades go down. An NBC News Report team interviewed a sixteen-year-old who regularly used marijuana. In school, he explained, ''When you smoke you just don't feel like doing work right then. You don't feel like getting into it at all, listening or nothing. It makes it seem like a drag.''

In 1982 the Institute of Medicine of the National Academy of Sciences reported that marijuana slows learning, interferes with memory, and distorts judgment.

Youth who regularly smoke pot are also missing out on important tasks of growing up, such as learning to control stress and anxiety.

Further, they are developing a mental attitude of being an outlaw since they are dealing with an illegal substance.

THE FLIGHT FROM HOMEWORK

Historically — at least since young Abe Lincoln read his lessons by flickering firelight — homework has been considered a critical part of educating a youngster. It was believed to be valuable in helping a pupil stimulate his thought processes through writing. It trained him in self-discipline and initiative in undertaking projects. Students typically have six or seven free hours after school, or theoretically around thirty-five hours a week, plus weekends. The National Center for Education Statistics found that most seventeen-year-olds in the U.S. in 1978 were doing less than five hours of homework a week. The less-than-five-hour-a-week students did much more poorly on assessment tests than students who did more than ten hours of homework a week.

A New York panel trying to understand the prolonged decline in students' test scores found that during a decade of this decline the assigning of homework had been cut in half.

What is behind the many reports of a decline in assignment of homework? Teachers blame it on permissive parents who don't enforce home study habits, and working parents too busy or tired to keep close watch on how well their children do their homework. They say pupils spend the logical hours for such study watching television or getting blasts of rock from their headsets. Teacher organizations claim that at least 20 percent of students flatly refuse to complete homework assignments. Many students have learned that nothing happens when they fail to turn in homework assignments.

The Home and School Institute, in studying how schools should relate to the New Family, concluded that "the family continues to be the most significant educational institution in children's lives." The Institute is waging a national campaign to get parents more involved by making the home a place of learning. For example a game is made of finding letters and numbers on cereal boxes and soup cans.

There is more than a suspicion that teachers have also been thinking of themselves in cutting back on homework. Some New York City teachers have been reported collecting homework but just filing it away instead of correcting it. They blame the teaching workload.

The school board in Montgomery County outside Washington, D.C., became involved in a prolonged battle over homework. One board member found so little homework being assigned that she proposed making homework assignments mandatory. Her proposal drew fire from teacher organizations as an intrusion into their professional expertise as educators. The board finally backed off but endorsed a general commendation of homework as vital to the learning process.

THE PROLONGED DEPENDENCE OF YOUNGSTERS

Perhaps the most distressing problem with the giant run-of-the-mill secondary schools is their frequent failure to provide teenagers with a sense that they are growing up, moving toward adulthood. Yet at present, they are society's primary formal institution for promoting this transition.

A newsletter of the National Association of Secondary School Principals expresses concern that "prolonged adolescent dependence" causes disruptive students. "Older youth today remain in an adolescent state even though they possess the talents and energies to assume adult responsibilities." They have little chance to contribute or earn their independence from adults. Because young persons have little chance to assume any serious responsibilities, "their need for independence is fulfilled by confrontation with adults and authority symbols."

This concern about schools failing to bring youth into adulthood because of their "narrow objectives" emerged from a Report of the Panel on Youth of the President's Science Advisory Committee. It stated:

At their best schools equip students with cognitive and noncognitive skills relevant to their occupational futures, with knowledge of some portion of civilization's cultural heritage, and with the taste for acquiring more skills and knowledge. They do not provide extensive opportunity for managing one's affairs, they seldom encourage intense concentration on a single activity, and they are inappropriate settings for nearly all objectives involving responsibilities that affect others. Insofar as these other objectives are important to the transition to adulthood, and we believe they are, schools act to retard youth in their transition, by monopolizing their time for the narrow objectives that schools have.[5]

WHAT ENCOURAGES STUDENTS TO LEARN?

Educators have spent decades sorting through learning theories in an effort to be more effective in promoting learning. Their search has been complicated by the diversity in intelligence and home backgrounds of young people to be motivated . . . by the spread in age from super-curious small children to (many) world-weary late adolescents . . . by the range in types of subjects to be learned, from memorizing the multiplication table to assessing evidence that the world is round.

Most modern educators seem to agree that the goal of education should not be just to promote learning per se. Rather, educators should seek to develop problem-solving, competent, self-confident future citizens able to cope in an increasingly complex society. Most agree too that encouraging an enthusiasm for learning should be a major goal. And most now also agree that learning should be an active rather than a passive process.

Traditionally, educators have mostly gone on the assumption that knowledge is best acquired if a teacher systematically transmits information to be memorized and repeated. Jean Piaget, the Swiss specialist on child learning, was a major figure in helping modify that assumption. He accepted passive methods for transmitting a set body of information but insisted that at best education is an active process of unleashing the youngster's intrinsic curiosity and pleasure in exploring and discovering. He or she rediscovers, reinvents. The task of the educator is to create conditions — and an environment — that enables the learner to extend these abilities.[6]

A few years ago I visited an elementary school in Columbia, Maryland, that was operating on the basis of a Ford Foundation study. The first thing I noticed was that the children seemed happy as they studied and worked on projects. There were spacious carpeted rooms and team teaching. Children sat in circles on the floor. Teachers were there to serve as resource persons rather than information feeders. Many mothers were helping out in the "media room," a broader concept than library. A ten-year-old girl who was working on a project explained to me: "You can go to any teacher for help if your teacher is busy. And you can choose the teachers you like to work with best."

I was impressed, but suspected some elements would have to be changed in an inner-city junior high school. However, two of the elements that would apply in any school were an enjoyable environment and parent involvement. Harold Shane of Indiana University has concluded after consulting many experts that "family involvement in the school program is a key factor affecting the social development and academic success of the individual child." Parents also play a critical role in conditioning their children to want to satisfy their curiosity, to achieve new levels of knowledge.

A few other generalizations seem possible. One is that encounters

with real-life experiences in the community stimulates interest in learning. Also it seems clear that youngsters in school settings need an environment that permits them to satisfy their sense of wonderment in an
enjoyable way. Given our present problems with giantism, pandemonium, and fear of violence, our most urgent priority in many hundreds of
schools is to achieve a more ordered environment where concentrated
student-teacher interaction can occur. Youngsters themselves want that
ordered, personalized environment. A survey of twelve thousand adolescents by *Read* magazine found that 87 percent of them would appreciate more discipline in their school. Students want to know what is
expected of them.

A number of researchers have approached the problems facing our
schools by searching for common elements in schools that do produce
high levels of learning. Ronald Edmond of the Harvard Graduate School
of Education, in his analysis of schools that have been effective in producing high levels of academic learning, came up with these five indis-
pensable characteristics: [7]

- teachers who have high expectations of all students;
- a principal who is an active leader;
- an emphasis on basic skills;
- standardized tests to measure those skills;
- an orderly climate.

TWO-TIER PUBLIC SCHOOLS?

Given our present disordered situation in many areas, perhaps it is time
we also think seriously about setting up in our big urban-suburban areas
a two-tier public school system starting right in fourth grade. Beginnings have been made within a few inner-city school systems. Under
this concept, "intensive" public school programs would be available to
any youngster of average learning potential who enjoys the challenge of
schoolwork. To qualify, the student and his or her parents would have
to sign a written commitment. This commitment would pledge the
youngster to maintain specific high standards of diligence and discipline.

This would be something quite different from the "fast tracks" some
schools reserve for very bright students.

For the type of intensive schooling proposed, new buildings need not be constructed if the school structures are large. One wing would serve.

Society can meet its egalitarian promise by doing the best it can to provide a sound education in a safe setting for those who are not yet ready to meet the high motivational demands of "intensive" school programs. Each year students at intensive schools who goof off by doing poor work or who are disruptive would return to the basic school system; and late-bloomers in the basic school system who are now willing to make the necessary commitment would replace them.

A glowing example of what can be achieved at an intensive-type public school is illustrated at the Beasley Academic Center in Chicago. A black school administrator, Alice C. Blair, was given a virtually free hand in creating it after she served as principal at a grade school in a tough area of Chicago that had chewed up a series of principals.

She is a firm believer in back to basics, not only in taught skills but in values. When she became principal only three out of eight hundred students were reading at grade level. Within three years she had that number up to four hundred.[8]

A Chicago student can get into Beasley only if he or she passes a test, behaves himself and applies himself. Both the student and his parents must sign a contract committing the student to abide by strict rules on discipline, garb, faithful attendance, and homework. The school is in a black neighborhood and 70 percent of the students, by design, come from that neighborhood. But as the school's repute has spread it has attracted students from more than a hundred other schools, public or parochial. About one hundred fifty of its students are white. Some commute long distances to attend.

A similar success has been achieved at the Edward H. Fitler Elementary School in a working-class area of Philadelphia.[9] Sixty-five percent of the students are blacks, Hispanics, or Asians. Four-fifths of its students surpass the national median on standardized tests. The school has a waiting list of two thousand from all over Philadelphia. It has a dress code. It has printed rules of behavior that are sent to parents. Parents must come in person to pick up report cards. Both parents and teachers must sign homework assignments. No pupil is promoted a grade without at least a C in reading and math. The principal explains the school's success: "We have expectations for these children." He believes there is a connection between an ordered environment and the probability that significant learning will occur.

Another important believer in homework is the famed black Chicago minister Jesse Jackson, who believes that progress for his people starts with diligence. His widely adopted Operation PUSH requires parents and their children to pledge that the student will spend at least two hours a night studying with TV and radio turned off.

Assaults on Children's
Minds and Bodies

"Many of us allow our children to watch junk, eat junk,
listen to junk, play with junk and then are surprised
when they come out to be social junkies."

— *The Reverend Jesse Jackson*

As an institution television should be viewed as nearly as powerful as
the public schools in terms of impact on the minds of our children. In
the average U.S. household the TV set is on about six or seven hours a
day. The voices that millions of children hear most often come not from
live humans around them but from boxes that emit TV or radio signals.

In one generation the circumstances of growing up in America have
been profoundly changed by television.

Depriving a child of access to television is becoming a more common
punishment for misconduct than spanking or sending the child to the
naughty chair. In the toilet training of children many parents reward
performance by putting the potty in front of the television set.[1]

It is difficult for some to grasp the sheer amount of time children
devote to TV viewing. The A. C. Nielsen Company, an audience-meas-
uring organization, found, as indicated earlier, that in 1980 preschool
children watched TV more than four hours a day. Grade school children, despite required school attendance, still managed to average about

twenty-six hours of TV viewing a week. Since school lets out for three summer months, this means that during the full year of 1980, they spent more time watching television than attending classes. Children as a group watch TV more than adults. And most of the programming the children watch is so-called adult programming. The specific programming aimed at children Saturday mornings accounts for only a small amount of their total viewing.

The Nielsen findings on *when* children are watching TV are astounding. Most of America's children, including preschoolers, are watching TV during the prime-time hour eight to nine at night, which probably accounts for the networks' catering to juvenile or childish tastes then. But now we come to the surprises:

- Nearly a quarter of all preschoolers and nearly 40 percent of grade-school children still are watching TV between nine and ten at night.

- Close to 10 percent of the preschool tots and nearly a quarter of grade school children are watching TV between ten and eleven o'clock at night.

- Nearly 5 percent of preschool children and 10 percent of grade-schoolers are watching between eleven and midnight.

- About a million children are watching the tube between midnight and one A.M. when the vast majority of U.S. adults have long been asleep. One explanation is that nearly half of the U.S. homes have two or more TV sets, one often being in a youngster's room. (Another may be the increase of parents coming home from work late at night.)

The majority of grade school children in the U.S. feel free to turn on the TV set in their home whenever they want, and many are not controlled in what they watch by any means. Nicholas Zill, an official of the Foundation for Child Development, told a conference on the family, perhaps with tongue in cheek:

"I think more and more children will be raised by neither parent but by interactive television sets, computer controlled, which will be prepared according to principles laid down by . . . child-development psychologists."

In West Germany children under eight — unlike those in the U.S. — do considerably less viewing than children over eight, which suggests German parents are much more active than American parents in controlling the TV viewing of young children. In West European countries advertising is banned from almost all programs geared to children.[2] And their networks have considerable weekday afternoon programming for children.

In contrast the U.S. major commercial networks' main offerings to children are manic cartoon programs, particularly on Saturday morning, heavily interladen with advertising aimed at children.

Much that is on U.S. television can be rewarding to children. Often there are early evening programs that are magnificent achievements in photography showing nature at work — from the activities of bats, beavers, bison to those of blowfish. Public television has stunning ballet, opera, and chamber music. TV is very good at covering important events, such as space launchings and inaugurations, and superbowls. Occasionally TV comes up with illuminating dramatic productions. Public television has fine children's shows such as *Mister Rogers' Neighborhood* and *Sesame Street*. Then there are the Muppets and Charlie Brown specials for everyone.

The disgusted or harassed parents who put their TV sets in the attic are probably overreacting, unless they have an out-of-control situation with their children.

The advent of television as an institution was a promising historic development, and perhaps the promise can be fulfilled as we move to cable TV with its potential for special-interest audience, to two-way cable TV with its great potential for interactive participation in shows, to videotapes which offer good shows of your own choice, to video games (which at least don't carry advertising). However, overdependence in the home on any kind of electronic diversion has its hazards.

As for television in its present form in the early 1980s, it clearly has its darker side, particularly as far as children are concerned.

For one thing it is addictive. Some children involved in experiments of abstaining from TV viewing for a week report desperation. One fourth-grader moaned, "I thought I would die."

THE IMPACT OF HEAVY TV-VIEWING ON THE MENTAL WORLD OF CHILDREN

The noted educator Harold Shane in his *Educating for A New Millennium* sought the views of more than a hundred scholars on their major concerns about the world of tomorrow. He found a number of them expressing concern about the impact on people growing up today of the assault that television makes on "reason and emotional stability." There was a feeling that TV "confuses our reason, our time sense and our feeling for 'real world' geography by jumbling so many impressions into too few minutes."

Others are concerned about the value distortion and cynicism created in children by the continuous barrage of commercials.

By the time the average U.S. youngster has finished high school he has been the target of more than fifteen hundred *hours* of TV commercials. If you divide that by the thirty-five hour work week, you come up with a figure that stuns: the average youngster has spent nearly a work year listening to advertising messages.

The barrage of more than ten thousand advertising messages heard by the average child each year does more than influence their brand preference. It influences their concept of what life is all about: seemingly high materialism. If the child is from a low-income family, the unrealizable desires instilled by constant repetition can be cruel.

The purpose of much of the advertising aimed at children is to make them very effective naggers. An ad man in *Advertising Age* was quoted as observing: "If you truly want big sales you will use the child as your assistant salesman. He sells, he nags, until he breaks down the sales resistance of his mother or father." If the parents can't really afford the product you have the seeds of parent-child conflict. That children do nag for products they have seen promoted on television was demonstrated at the University of Georgia, where researchers established a small store carrying 163 items. Mothers and children could go shopping after viewing a cartoon. Six ads for sweet or salty food products were also shown. The commercials obviously caused the children to nag for the six items advertised.

U.S. networks have lately been carrying messages telling small girls to experiment with kid cosmetics. One company in its trade advertising showed a seven-year-old girl applying eyeliner. It said, "She's your market. She is four to nine."

Jean Piaget found that children were uniquely vulnerable to the kinds of verbal curves commonly tossed out by TV's pitchmen. Those most avid TV listeners in our society, the preschoolers, are close to total believers in what the adults tell them. They typically receive the messages as directions.

It is only when children reach the nine- or ten-year-old level that they start becoming upset about misleading advertising statements. Many become tense and suffer from conflict as disillusionment sets in, according to a report in the *Harvard Business Review*.[3] It adds that "there is evidence the conflict is harmful.'' Perhaps the youngsters may start becoming wary of accepting the word of adults in general.

By age eleven or twelve, the report states, the youngsters have become cool cynics. But is that good? The report thinks not: ''TV advertising is stimulating *pre-adolescent* children to think about socially accepted hypocrisy. They may be too young to cope with such thoughts without permanently distorting their views of morality, society and business.''

The U.S. Federal Trade Commission came under heavy pressure from such parent groups as the very active and effective Action for Children's Television, headed by Peggy Charren. ACT consists of about eleven thousand mothers. This organization badgers government agencies and provides mothers with guidance on dial control. The FTC finally agreed to hold hearings when its own staff concluded that it was an ''unfair trade practice'' to beam television advertising at children too young to understand its selling purpose. Hearings were held on eliminating commercials aimed at young children. After considerable counterpressure was brought to bear on the FTC by commercial interests working through the congressional unit controlling FTC funds, the hearings ended in stalemate. The FTC administrative law judge ruled that a whole new set of hearings would be required if any action was to be taken. This ruling came at a time when the Louis Harris–ABC poll showed that three-quarters of all U.S. parents wanted a ban on all advertising directed at children under eight.

TV AS A PROMOTER OF PASSIVITY AND A TIME STEALER

This works several ways. For the older youngster the fact that he or she spends an average of three and a half hours viewing TV every day throughout the year decreases the chance that much homework or reading for pleasure will occur. In discussing seventeen-year-olds, the federally funded firm the National Assessment of Educational Progress stated in 1978: ''In general, the students who report . . . the least amount of television watching performed best on the assessment.''

The preschoolers watching TV four hours a day are losing out on a lot of valuable things in terms of personal development. The boy or girl doesn't look at books as much, or play as much. TV does not challenge the imagination, as reading and play do. It requires less mental activity than reading. Creation of fantasy worlds, which is so crucial to child development, occurs during solitary play, not in front of a television.

A heavy-TV-watching child is losing opportunity to develop verbal skills. The kind of learning important to a child's growing up does not occur during passive TV watching. Jean Piaget was pretty emphatic about the importance of a child having concrete experiences in order for learning to occur:

"It is absolutely necessary that learners have at their disposal concrete material experiences (and not merely pictures) and that they form their own hypotheses and verify them . . . themselves by their own active manipulations."

A child who spends hours every day in a trancelike state looking at the Tube apparently is not developing the part of his brain essential for good verbal interchange.

Children Today carried a report on "The Electronic Fix," which cited two similarities between drug-taking and heavy TV viewing on children: both blot out the real world and promote basically passive states.

TV, like swaddling, offers mothers a chance to get things done or to be by themselves. I know a mother of a two-year-old who lets her son watch *Sesame Street* three times a day. When she was reminded that it was the identical show she grinned and said, "He doesn't seem to mind."

Then there is the loss of richness in family life when everyone is staring at the Tube at night.

DOES TV TEND TO CREATE RESTLESS CHILDREN?

The flickering screen usually does not present a child with a view of a subject for more than a minute without a shift from camera A to camera B. The picture zooms up and jumps back. People on the screen seem to be under orders to be in motion. Even the esteemed children's show *Sesame Street* leaps every few minutes to a new, unrelated subject. On TV news programs, any interview lasting more than ninety seconds is a long interview. Commercials come of course in eight-, fifteen- or thirty-second bursts. All this has caused some behavioral scientists to wonder if television is contributing to short attention span and hyperactivity in growing children. Real life does not afford such a barrage of visual spurts.

DOES TV VIOLENCE PROMOTE SUSPICIOUSNESS AND AGGRESSIVENESS?

Something certainly is happening. Television began to go national in the early 1950s and had nearly saturated American homes by the 1970s.

By the late 1970s three-quarters of all network shows contained some violence. A youngster in his or her middle teens had seen quite a few thousand depictions of people being killed.[4] During the three decades that TV was growing to such importance in children's lives, the number of juveniles arrested for serious and violent crimes increased by 1600 percent.[5] There are numerous explanations for the increase in juvenile violence, but TV viewing is certainly one.

A three-year study by the U.S. Surgeon General's office concluded: "The more violence and aggression a child sees on TV, the more aggressive he is likely to be in his own attitudes and behavior. These effects were not limited to youngsters who are in some way abnormal, but rather were found in large numbers of perfectly normal children." In 1981 it was revealed that a follow-up study found the evidence of connection between TV violence and later aggressive behavior was "overwhelming."

And in 1982 the National Institute of Mental Health also checked in with a long report concluding that the evidence was "overwhelming" that violence seen on TV spills over into the child's daily activities and has a lasting impact on young minds.

Increases in aggressiveness among young heavy TV viewers have been reported from numerous laboratory-type studies. Perhaps more impressive is a six-year study in London correlating specific everyday acts of violence in the lives of 1,565 randomly sampled teenage boys with their TV viewing habits.[6] The investigator studied the viewing habits, for example, of a boy who explained, "I kicked a boy in the crotch as hard as I could." His overall findings, the investigator reported, were "very supportive" of the view that long-term exposure to violence increases the degree to which boys engage in violence or a serious crime. He added: "It looks as if television has reduced or broken down the inhibitions against being violent which had been built up in the child by parents and other socializing influences." TV may also desensitize youngsters to brutal behavior. Someone who is bashed in one episode shows up hale and hearty in an episode the next week.

TV violence apparently does more than beget violence. Kids who are heavy TV viewers are twice as likely to report they are "scared" about going outside their home, according to the Foundation for Child Development study of the lives of 2,300 youngsters aged seven to eleven.

The American Medical Association has reported that a study it helped sponsor, of children and adults alike, found that people who spend the most time watching police and crime programs are far more likely to buy locks, dogs, or guns to protect themselves. They are also more likely to be afraid to walk alone at night. The heavy viewers also tend to have low faith in people. Such viewers say people have to look out for themselves and that you can't be too careful in dealing with people.

SO WHAT CAN BE DONE?

All indicators are that television-viewing will be an even more time-consuming activity than it currently is in the Western World. The energy shortage that looms in the decade ahead will keep people at home more. And the telecommunications revolution promising four-foot screens, videorecorders and various cable innovations may make TV even harder to resist. However, it also promises parents more control if they want to use it. For example, with videotapes or discs the set can be turned on at the time of day that is most convenient to mother. Some of the discs being made promise child participation, even using special crayons on the screen. There is experimenting with read-along programs with book pages shown on the screen.

Parents can tackle the *content* of current TV programming — such as violence and commercials — by supporting the reform movements of such organizations as Action for Children's Television and the National PTA.

The TV cable network operators have tried to introduce children's channels such as *Nickelodeon* and *Calliope*. We may be seeing a considerable upgrading of what is available for children *if* parents search the cable and public TV offerings. The cable networks seem, at present at least, to be planning to ban or tightly control advertising on children's programming.

As for the sheer presence in the home of the TV set as a dominant force, control must begin with the parent. Presently only a third of U.S. parents seriously attempt such control.[7] T. Berry Brazelton, noted Harvard pediatrician, has written that children under five years of age show signs of exhaustion if exposed to more than one hour of television a day.

Action for Children's Television (46 Austin Street, Newtonville, Mass. 02160) supplies parents with program evaluations and guidelines for handling all aspects of television viewing by one's children. Here, I feel, are some particularly important points to bear in mind.

- Access to TV should not be used as reward or punishment. It should bc handled matter-of-factly.

- Modeling helps. If parents are not avid TV viewers their children are not likely to be either. If parents expect to control their children's TV watching, they should examine their own viewing habits and if need be modify them.

- Children under fifteen certainly should not have uncontrolled access to television in their own rooms.

- Children under six should have only occasional and supervised access to television.

- As for grade-school children there should be a daily time limit during school days of one hour (unless there is some really marvelous two-hour show, such as *Nutcracker*) and a total of five hours over weekends. That would add up to ten hours of TV a week, more than some child experts would recommend but at least less than half the viewing that now actually occurs in the typical home.

TV news personality Tom Brokaw has been tougher with his own three youngsters, now teenagers. For years each was permitted to choose and watch three shows a week. Often, Brokaw reports, they were so busy with their projects and reading that they did not use up their viewing time.

Two of the best strategies I have heard of are those of two young couples I know in New York. One of the couples has a son and daughter, ages seven and nine. The father and mother keep the TV set in their own bedroom. The children go in to see TV only when told that they may do so. As a result, the children organize their lives around reading, play, projects and study, not TV viewing. The other couple, with sons age twelve and fourteen, has a rule that there be no TV-watching on weeknights when the boys should be studying. However they all recognize that some of the best shows appear on weeknights. That is the main reason the family invested in a videorecorder. They tape weeknight shows of particular interest for weekend viewing.

In Germany I have talked with families who have locks on their TV sets. The key is available to the children at what the parents feel are appropriate periods of the day. Such sets should be widely available in America. In Austria many parents buy timers that automatically turn off a set to which children have access, after a specified time.

As for commercials. When a child is first introduced to commercials, his or her parent should explain — and explain repeatedly with examples — that the commercial is something separate from the regular programming. As the head of ACT pointed out, "Children can't deal with the television commercial because they don't know why it is there." Parents should explain that the purpose of the commercial is to make people want to buy the product, and that such buying makes profits for the sponsor. When the first good example of overstatement is made, they should explain that the makers of competing products often try to outpromise each other.

A good house rule for children under eight is to keep the TV set tuned to the public television station. The child should know that only a parent can turn the set on or dial to other channels.

THE OTHER BOXES WITH SOUND

For youngsters over ten a big fact of life is the amount of time they spend listening to radio, mostly rock music, and to the record player or tape deck. On an average day, nine out of ten U.S. teenagers spend a substantial amount of time with the radio on. An advertising journal has made the astonishing revelation that average teenagers listen to radio nearly three hours a day.[8] Since they also listen to TV three hours a day, it suggests they spend about six hours a day listening to some sort of box — unless, as some do, they listen to both simultaneously.

Radio listening or tape listening can of course accompany study or shooting the breeze with friends . . . or making out sexually. Some of the recordings featured on radio programs aimed at youths have been referred to as "fucking music." A poll of North Florida high schools indicated that almost all the unmarried girls who became pregnant did so while listening to pop music.

Up until the mid 1970s, music on the stations geared to young people was suggestive, not explicit. Then suddenly the airways became filled with sounds of coital panting, climactic yelps. "Love to Love You, Baby" consisted almost entirely of coital noises. The record had sales in the millions thanks to radio promotion.

I noted at a Pittsburgh radio station that the chart of top hits at that time included "Foreplay," "Into You," "Back in the Saddle." In lyrics, girls beg boys to do it to them again.

The impact of so much throbbing sensual noise, when at high volume, can also be physical. Damage to hearing ability often occurs. A study of seventy disc jockeys at discotheques found that a third of them suffer from significant loss of hearing. They were all in their twenties, so the loss was about thirty times normal expectancy. The study was done by the New York League for the Hard of Hearing. A New York psychiatrist, John Diamond, found in a three-year study of twenty thousand records that a beat common to about half of popular rock music — the "stopped anapestic" rhythm consisting of two short beats followed by a long beat — triggers a distress signal that upsets the balance between the brain hemispheres. The result is a temporary 60 percent loss of muscular strength.[9]

Most recently youngsters, particularly males, have become so obsessed with another box, the videogame in arcades or on home TV, that many adults, at least, have become disturbed.

The youngsters flocking to the arcades have often been using their lunch money or book fees — or in some cases quarters gotten from breaking into parking meters or their mom's purse to feed their pleasurable "addiction." The sum of the quarters they have been inserting in the arcade machines is stupendous: close to eight billion dollars a year.

Some towns have been passing ordinances forbidding youngsters under sixteen from using the arcade machines, or at least during school hours. The United States Surgeon General, E. Everett Koop, entered the controversy in late 1982 by announcing that videogames might be hazardous to the health of young people using them. He said they are becoming addicted to the machines "body and soul." However he offered no scientific evidence of harm. He simply predicted such evidence would soon emerge from health care studies underway.

Other scientific observers are less certain. MIT sociologist Sherry Turkle, after a study, suggested some positive effects of videogame playing. It is training youngsters in total concentration at a time when many seem to have low concentration. She said the machine becomes an extension of the young, which can be exhilarating. The integration of the youth's mind and body during this concentration, she said, gives the games something of "a sexually charged feeling."

Many of the videogames do promote hand-eye coordination and give many low-esteem youngsters a sense of mastery. They are also helping induct youngsters pleasantly into the new Computer Age, so that they are not as intimidated by computers as many adults.

On the negative side, it is suggested, a passion for videogames does promote compulsive, even addictive, behavior and steals a lot of time that should be spent on homework. A sociologist at the University of

California, Berkeley, suggested that the arcade machines promote an assembly-line mentality. You try to do what the machine tells you to do.

In this sense home videogames are less dictatorial than the arcade ones. Youngsters at home can feel free to reset the button anytime they want and to start again, improvise and develop their own style.

ASSAULTS FROM EDIBLE JUNK

Nutritionist Hugh Powers, in talking about the rise of obstreperous behavior in the schools, says, "We believe very strongly that a significant relationship would be revealed between the deteriorating American diet and the deteriorating behavior of its young." An interesting hypothesis, though, as we have noted, the obstreperous behavior seems to have a number of causes.

Children are insistently bombarded by selling messages to eat food high in sugar, fat, and salt. All three ingredients, in excess, spell trouble for young and old alike. In 1982, for example, a panel of experts of the National Academy of Sciences studying links of nutrition to cancer warned against the habitual heavy consumption of fatty or salty foods. And for those who think cancer is a hazard only to older folks, it cited "the long time frame" over which most cancers develop.

Take sugar   When the Lord created Man, He/She didn't have sugar in mind as a significant nutrient. Mother's milk has only a trace of sweetness in it. In 1815 Americans consumed, from all sources, about fifteen pounds of sugar a year. Today American youngsters consume close to one hundred fifty pounds of sugar a year, ten times as much.[10] It comes to about four-tenths of a pound per youngster every day of the year.

One of America's most respected nutritionists, Jean Mayer (recently president of Tufts University), has declared that habitual overeating of sugar is dangerous to health. There is powerful evidence that sugar rots teeth. The U.S. Surgeon General, in 1979, in talking about the promotion of sugary goods to children, said tooth decay has become the "No. 1 chronic disease of childhood." Heavy sugar consumption is linked to overweight not only because sugar's delicious taste promotes a "sweet tooth" addictiveness but because of its "empty calories." Sugar contains almost nothing in the way of essential nutrients for humans. There is some evidence linking heavy sugar consumption to the onset of diabetes.

Also many children developing a pattern of heavy sugar consumption may be increasing their chance of being among tomorrow's addicts of such substances as nicotine and drugs.

Janice Phelps, a medical specialist in addiction, now believes that all forms of addiction, from nicotine to drugs, is caused by the proneness of the pancreas of many people to overreact to sugar in the blood. Her remedy is for the person with this common malfunction to cut way back on simple carbohydrates, especially sugar.

Until it was recently forbidden, sugar was widely used as a filler by baby food manufacturers to cut costs. Many breakfast cereals promoted to children contain up to 50 percent sugar, more sugar than grain content. Count Chocula, a cereal promoted to children on TV and other advertising as a "complete breakfast," contained more than 43 percent sugar.

Most of the commercials aimed at children on Saturday morning TV shows have been for heavily sugared cereals, candy, or sweetened soda pop. A Federal Trade Commission study found sugar in some form was being promoted between eight and fourteen times an hour on each network's programming for children on Saturdays.

Other studies show that mothers overwhelmingly bow to their children's demands when it comes to purchasing breakfast cereal.

As with its proposed ban in ads aimed at small children, the U.S. Federal Trade Commission was stalled on a staff recommendation to ban the advertising of heavily sugared products to children. The sugar, cereal, candy, and broadcasting lobbies persuaded the House Appropriations Committee to refuse funding for enforcing such a ban. It said the FTC could continue studying the matter.

Or take fat   Americans in general have greatly increased their consumption of fat-laced foods in this century. When our consumption of fatty foods regularly exceeds a third of our caloric intake — according to a Harvard Community Health Plan newsletter — we get into a definitely unhealthy situation.

Many medical scientists have long been convinced that prolonged heavy fat consumption is frequently associated with reduced efficiency of blood vessels. French fries, a great favorite of youngsters, are about 50 percent fat. So are the whopper hamburgers dispensed by the leading burger chains. The McDonald chain carried a network ad at the beginning of the camping season in 1980 showing a boy at camp crying because he missed his french fries.

And there is salt   French fries can taste flat unless they contain salt. So can potato chips and soda pop and sugar-enriched baby food. A study at the Louisiana State University School of Medicine involved a test of monkeys who were, for just eight weeks, put on a diet containing the level of salt and sugar contained in the typical junk foods American children consume. The monkeys developed abnormally high blood pressure. Such high blood pressure if continued over a number of years contributes to hypertension in humans.

A series of studies at the Brookhaven National Laboratory not only suggest a relationship between hypertension and high salt consumption but that the disease is appearing at much earlier ages, even down into the teens. The chief of the laboratory said: "A child gets a salt appetite which then must be satisfied the rest of his life."

Hundreds of U.S. public schools have been involved in battles on how much junk-type food should be available in school lunch programs or in school vending machines. One pro-junk argument has been that kids now throw away a lot of food (be it from the school cafeteria or home-packed) that is supposed to be well-balanced in nutrients. A typical fast-food take-out meal consists of a hamburger, french fries, and a milk shake or soft drink. It is not only overloaded with fat, sugar and salt, but contains only a third of the recommended allowance for eight critical nutrients. Some schools have tried serving up junk food and lacing it with needed nutrients so that it meets federal standards. That, of course, doesn't eliminate the sugar, fat and salt.

The federally supported school lunch program has caved in recently on both quality and quantity. In 1978 the federal government proposed that the sale or serving of junk foods such as candy, frozen desserts, soda water, and chewing gum be banned in school lunchrooms. There was an incredible outcry from producers of such products, and virtually all restrictions were abandoned. Meanwhile under President Reagan's budget-cutting, the long-time rule that the school lunch program provide children with one-third of the essential vitamins and minerals needed for good nutrition was lifted. In the summer of 1981, the Department of Agriculture proposed that the government's lunch program need supply only 18 percent of a child's needed calories. Under the proposals, catsup and pickle relish could be counted as vegetables; cakes, cookies, and corn chips could be counted as bread. (When Democrats on congressional committees began demonstrating this lunch on national TV news shows, the administration said there had been a mistake and the proposal would be changed.)

Nutritionists assert that the fast-food chain pattern is becoming widely adopted in school food service operations. If so, what are the children getting — even when the fare is "fortified" with nutrients? *Consumer Reports* made an analysis (in September 1979) of the fare of ten fast-food chains offering burgers, fried chicken, pizzas, etc., with french fries a mainstay with milk shakes to wash the food down. It reported, "Fat content was high in most of the entrees. . . . Sodium (salt) was abundant in just about all the fast-food entrees. . . . Even the shakes. Americans would do well to do with less. . . . In general burgers were higher in calories, fats, sugars (from the sauces) and sodium than all the other fast food entrees." It added that "The Pizza Hut pizza turned out to be the most nutritious fast-food entree we tested."

Perhaps the answer, for those who can afford it, is to go back to the school lunchbox packed by Mom. But she may be too busy getting off to work.

2

Children Whose Parents Work

Life in Homes
Where Mothers Work

"The number of mothers of children age five or under who work outside their home . . . has more than tripled in twelve years."

— *Harold Shane, Indiana University professor of Education*

The recent flood of women into the job markets in the Western World is called "the single most outstanding phenomenon of this century" by Eli Ginzberg, an economist at Columbia University. He says it is having a greater impact than the rise of communism or the development of nuclear energy. And its consequences are still "really unchartable."

It is hard to realize that forty years ago three-quarters of all Americans disapproved of wives who worked if a husband could support them! Today in the U.S. about half of all youngsters under the age of fifteen have mothers who have jobs outside the home. And in 1980 about 40 percent of all children under age six had mothers holding outside jobs. *Monthly Labor Review* has projected that in the half-decade leading up to 1985 the number of children under six with mothers in the work force would grow by three million.

The situation is changing rapidly, but today more than a third of all children under age three have mothers with jobs, two-thirds of them full-time jobs.

Children under age three are of particular concern because they are relatively helpless and have attachment problems with parent figures; the way they are reared in those first years will significantly affect their social, intellectual, and verbal development.

The three- to six-year-olds are probably the next most critical group. When youngsters reach age six, the schools take over supervision during about three-quarters of the hours the typical working mother is away at work, for nine months of the year. That still leaves a need to arrange some sort of supervision, especially for the younger school-agers, for perhaps several hours a day. And in the summer months working parents are back to trying to arrange full-time supervision (or to training their children to take on responsibility for themselves at an early age).

The problem of parental oversight doesn't end even when the youngsters get into early adolescence. The youths can take care of themselves, but how? They are going through the rapid growth of puberty when many tend to be low in self-control and are experiencing sexual awakening. Whereas parents used to worry about what their children were up to when out at night, today, if both parents are working, they are more likely to worry about what the youngsters are up to in the late afternoon when so many houses are empty of adults.

The reasons mothers are working in such great and growing numbers go beyond material need. They include: the drop in the challenge of being "just" a homemaker because of smaller living units, smaller families, increased appliances and packaged foods . . . a felt need to get out of the home because of the increased loneliness of urban, high-mobile living. . . .

Harvard psychiatrist Alvin F. Poussaint has made the generalization that when both parents work outside the home "frankly it interferes with the nurturing of the children." Some would say he is too sweeping. I know many couples where both parents are working and they seem to be doing a fine job of raising children. Still, as a generalization, particularly if confined to infants and toddlers, Poussaint's statement has at least the merit of public support.

In 1981 General Mills released a survey on families in which the mother works. The well-known opinion-sampling firm of Louis Harris and Associates had interviewed a national cross-section of 1,503 adult family members. Also sampled were 235 teenagers, 104 corporate personnel executives, 56 labor leaders, 49 leaders of the "pro-family" movement, and 52 active feminists.[1] Results:

- All the groups except the feminists agreed that "the trend toward both parents working outside the home has a negative effect on families." Even the working wives concurred.

- The main strain cited by the adult family members when the mother worked was "lack of time with family/children, less time to see each other."

- The teenagers' views were particularly interesting. They felt on balance that for teenagers the effect of both parents working was primarily good for teenagers. But when questioned about children under age twelve, these 235 teenagers were emphatically negative in their responses. By a four-to-one margin they said the effects were generally bad.

  The same teenagers were asked, "Do you feel if parents have young children who aren't in school yet, they should both work outside the home if they want to, or should one parent stay home, or doesn't it matter?" A majority (55 percent) said, "One parent should stay home." If the children were older and already in school (age not defined), nearly half the teenagers thought it was okay for both parents to work, and a quarter said it didn't matter.

Some mothers of recently born children go back to work soon after the birth, even though economic pressure is not severe and there is no special concern about career status. They are influenced by the opinion of job associates, to whom the paycheck may represent personal worth and independence and proof their mind is not turning to mush. A bright young schoolteacher near Syracuse who went back to work six weeks after her infant was born told me:

"I now see my working as a copout that I was pressured into. I really would rather be home with my child, at least for the first couple of years."

Another young mother told me:

"After I left my job at the publishing house to have a baby it took me about eight months to admit to the people back at the office that I really enjoyed motherhood. Now, after four years at home the thing I miss most is not having my own checking account."

Or they may go back, even though their husband has a good job, because of anxiety. He's in an industry where a lot of people are losing jobs. Now that they have a baby at least one parent has to be working.

In 1982 young women planning to combine an outside job with child-rearing were given a new reason to ponder the wisdom of postponing motherhood until their thirties. *The New England Journal of Medicine* reported a French study involving 2,193 wives of sterile husbands who sought impregnation by artificial insemination. Fertility seemed to decline more sharply than expected after age thirty. Whereas 74 percent of the wives in their late twenties became pregnant within a year, the number dropped to 61 percent for the wives in their early thirties.

This led many young wives to wonder if they should launch their families first and turn to a career after thirty when they would have about thirty or more uninterrupted years for working. Some who are strongly career-oriented contend that that's a dumb idea because the late twenties are crucial years for launching a successful career, at least in the business world, especially if they have received educations specifically geared to their prospective career.

Some contend that women who feel fulfilled by going out to a job every day make better mothers because of their satisfied state of mind. A restless stay-at-home might take her frustrations out on her children. Actress Meryl Streep, talking on national television about the imminent birth of her child, said she still had not worked out a satisfactory care arrangement for the baby but that she hoped to be back acting within a few weeks after its birth. She explained: "I love my work. I wouldn't be a good mother if I didn't keep myself happy."

CHILDREN WHO HAVE THE HOUSE TO THEMSELVES

Many school-age children today carry keys on strings around their neck. Some just keep the key to their house in their pocket and may or may not go home. In any case the number of these "latchkey kids" has soared in the past decade. A *Newsweek* study reported there had been an "explosion in the number of children who spend at least part of every weekday without any adult supervision."[2]

Some children left on their own after school may spend their time hanging around the pinball or video arcades. Or they may go home and carefully lock themselves in their home and start on their homework. Kids of the well-to-do can go from school to tennis, flute, or ballet lessons. Poorer kids have fewer options. There are all sorts of patterns. Recently I was checking out the qualifications of a seventeen-year-old girl as a possible companion-sitter for my three-year-old granddaughter.

She laughed and said, "My Mom worked as a department store buyer so that when I was eight years old after school I was diapering, feeding and sitting for my baby sister. I did it until I was eleven." (She proved to be an impressive, highly responsible, and likable person.)

As indicated, one problem that arises if children are past puberty and both parents work is that in an empty house they may feel free to play sex games. The empty, accessible home is certainly a factor in the recent lowering of the age of first intercourse.

A girl named Rachel who had been having sex in the afternoons since the age of fifteen put it this way: "Both my parents work and . . . I have the whole house to myself when I come home from school. . . . So Bob and I just make ourselves comfortable. A lot of times we just study together. Sure, we have sex a lot. But I think that is only natural."[3]

Self-reliance can emerge. *Working Mother* carried a report about a nine-year-old girl whose mother has a job as a typist. The girl explained that she washed the dishes, made up not only her own bed but her mother's, and often cooked her own meals. Who taught her to do all that? She replied: "Me."

Some children who cope well still don't like it. The *Newsweek* investigators encountered an eleven-year-old girl who took care of her younger brother while her mother worked. She said her aspiration in the future was to make a lot of money quickly so she could be home with her children after school.

LIFE IN THE HOUSEHOLDS OF WORKING MOTHERS

Mornings in the two-job-holder family with children are likely to be a whirl unless there is live-in help. In millions of homes young children find that bowls are tossed out for their cold cereal. Dirty laundry is thrown in a pile. In their rooms covers may be thrown loosely up on the recently emptied beds. Their mother has been dubbed "super-woman" for her capacity to lead two lives.

Children often find their job-holding mother is bushed when she gets home at night. She usually has an array of homemaking functions to attend to but tries to get in some "quality" time with her youngsters between chores. Many do succeed in making evenings with their children into a rewarding time for all concerned by making it a point to dine together, by playing games, by going to school events, and reading to the young ones every night.

The sociologists who recently revisited Middletown, U.S.A. (Muncie, Indiana) after four decades found a lot more mothers with jobs and children living in a lot more untidy homes.

Working under pressure can be more stimulating for some mothers than having too little to do. Many homemakers with kids already in school fight off boredom in slack hours by looking at soap operas or looking for bridge partners. The more imaginative and thoughtful ones involve themselves in community activities, which can yield considerable satisfaction (and make their communities function better).

If the mother works, some problems and concerns of her children may get slighted. A junior high school official in Darien told me, "Many problems at school stem from the fact that both parents are away from the home working. I frequently have to contact parents about disciplinary problems and I can't find either of them." (Some schools now ask not only for home phone numbers but office phone numbers.)

And some things usually get slighted because of work overload, such as taking the children to see grandparents, cousins, aunts and uncles (according to a report in *Psychology of Women*). Most important, for society and the parents, is the drop in home activities that involve children and community activities that involve children. An investigator for *The Wall Street Journal,* Joann Lublin, took an intensive look at the impact of job-holding women on life in Morton Grove, Illinois, a prosperous suburb of Chicago.[4] Here are a few of her observations:

- The League of Women Voters felt something ought to be done to provide care for the growing number of latchkey children in town. But there was doubt the League could muster any significant resources for the project because its membership had dropped 50 percent in eight years. "Everyone has gone back to work," the League president explained.

- At the Parent-Teacher Association meeting for three schools, about fifty parents showed up. A school superintendent blamed the low turnout on working mothers. A decade ago, he said, they would have a full auditorium with 300 parents four times a year.

- Daytime burglaries were soaring. Most occurred in homes where both parents had jobs. And most of the burglars were teenagers.

- The busiest hour at a major local supermarket was from five to six in the evening. The manager said: "We sell a lot of frozen pizzas,

TV dinners and convenience foods like lunch meat — any quick meal, the kind where they don't have to spend much time at the stove.''

- At a local elementary school whose doors open at 8:30, mothers on their way to work began depositing children outside in the school yard around 7:45. By the time the door opened, quite a crowd of children were waiting.

- The elementary school nurse spent many of her hours every week caring for sick children while she tried to get word to working parents to come and take their children home. She didn't like spending so much of her time being a baby-sitter. A sixth-grade teacher said parents were delegating a lot more of their responsibilities to the school.

WHERE MOM'S JOB REQUIRES A SEPARATE HOUSEHOLD

With the large increase of professional women in high-paying or high-responsibility jobs, many today are receiving job offers that are hard to resist but that are in other geographical areas. Many are married and have children. The wife may be a professor who gets a better offer. Or a job opens up in Washington as the federal government seeks to meet its commitment to put more women in high positions. Or to cite a specific case, the mother may be a cosmetic executive transferred from Los Angeles to New York while her husband, a network correspondent, remains stationed in L.A.

The wife-mother living separately is producing a new family form — a form, it is predicted, that is going to grow.

In some cases the women's husbands have gotten themselves new jobs in order to continue living daily with their mobile wives. This happened when the housewife-mother Eleanor Smeal was elected as president of the National Organization of Women. The job required that she move to Washington. Her husband, a metallurgist, got himself a new job in the Washington area.

More commonly, where there are children, the pattern is for the wife-mother to take an apartment in the new location. She leaves the children with their father back in their home neighborhood and gets "home" weekends. Or if the distance is great, gets home every few weeks. These setups are being called "weekend marriages" or "commuter marriages'' or ''long-distance marriages.'' When the couple can afford it, they hire some sort of housekeeper to help Dad. Or if the young are teenagers they may be sent to boarding school.

Many allot a greater portion of their budget to telephone bills so that mother can call every night and talk to each of her children. Younger school-age children frequently can return to their former day-care center and do homework or play under supervision until Father can pick them up. At home young daughters get early experience in helping their father cook meals. Some have said they are pleased to be able to sleep in their mother's bed. Crunches come for father when a child comes down with such childhood diseases as chicken pox, but that is an experience all working mothers in one-parent households have to learn to agonize through and somehow handle.

These commuting setups, no matter how boldly launched, create strains, particularly where there are pre-teen children. Harriet Engel Gross, who studied twenty-eight long-distance marriages, observed:

''Husbands who take pride in their wives' accomplishments still resent the increased child care and household maintenance burden. Wives in their turn miss their children and worry about lessened input into their children's lives.''[5]

Another investigator, Ohio sociologist Betty Frankle Kirschner, studied 160 married couples living apart. She concluded such arrangements survive best if they are assumed to be temporary. Children, she said, became symbolic embodiments of the fact that there is a marriage.[6]

One wife who commutes from New York to Los Angeles every few weeks spoke proudly of the ''quality time'' she spends with her infant. She plunged into being a loving nurturing mother. But she confessed considerable distress on one visit when the infant didn't recognize her.

STRATEGIES FOR NORMALIZING CHILDREN'S LIVES WHEN PARENTS WORK

When mothers have outside jobs there are practices that help keep life for children reasonably normal. My doctor's nurse takes ten minutes off every afternoon at three o'clock to call home and chat with her thirteen-year-old daughter about the day's events and the daughter's plans.

Mothers who successfully combine parenthood with career strive to give the children a sense of their *presence,* even though they are busy and frequently away from home. They not only keep in touch from their job, but when busy with problems at home they promise a specific time they will have for a heart-to-heart talk with each youngster about any problems. Children in a well-run home know they always have their mother's ear. A very busy New York clothing designer, the mother of a seven-year-old daughter, was enormously gratified when she got a Valentine Day card on which the daughter wrote this message: "Why do I love my Mommy? Because she is always there for me."[7]

Parents with very young children can adjust the bedtime hours of both their children and themselves to get maximum awake time together. Parents can go to bed at nine o'clock instead of eleven and can be up with their children at five o'clock in the morning and have a couple of good relaxed hours in their presence. This may, of course, curtail socializing on weeknights.

Some parents can adjust their work schedules so that one of the parents will be in the house during most of the waking hours of the children (and as a result see less of each other). Many New York policemen ask for night shifts for this reason. In Akron, Ohio, where a number of companies still operate around the clock, many fathers take the midnight-to-dawn shift so that they can spend several morning hours with the children while their wives work. They usually go to bed sometime after noon and have evening hours with their children.

An architect in Chicago, the father of a two-year-old daughter, rearranged his job so that he could work at home mornings while his wife commutes to her job as an advertising copy writer. He sees much more of the daughter than the mother does. The arrangement works out quite well because he is a devoted, nurturant father. He did make this interesting comment to me about his daughter: "She loves her mother, but when there is trouble she's her Daddy's girl."

Mothers looking for jobs will find some types are more desirable than others from the standpoint of child care. Being a teacher at a nearby school is one of the better full-time jobs for mothers of young children. If the hours are eight to three, the mother can have a good hour with the child before she goes to work, and five hours after work.

Having one's own business, even if it is outside the home, gives a mother more flexibility of working hours. Three mothers in Springfield, Virginia, set up a business that cleans up newly built houses to get them ready for occupancy. The profits are good. They all start work after their children leave for school and are home before the kids return.

In the ancient town of Ochsenfurt, Germany, I talked with Barbara Remling, the lovely daughter of the Lord Mayor. She was studying economic research at the nearby University of Wurzburg in order to complete all the work necessary for a doctorate except the thesis. She wasn't interested in the doctorate title because her life, in her mind, was already mapped out. She said:

"I want to get married and have babies, so the usual economic career doesn't interest me. I am arranging to become a consultant on investing for business clients of one of our insurance companies. That way I can pretty much set my own hours."

Many thousands of mothers of young children can handle most or much of their paying jobs from their home. In the U.S., women, from their home, can write business pamphlets, engage in family counseling, handle design work, and serve as an Amway distributor of home products.

In the very near future the opportunities for doing most of one's job at home will explode, thanks to two-way communications technology.

If the job does not require materials handling, face-to-face conferring, or being at a specific location, probably it will soon be possible to do it more economically at home. The high energy costs of commuting and the soaring costs of downtown office space are causing many companies and management consulting firms to look at home work installations with new interest. Devices such as word processors, facsimile machines, computer terminals and teleconferencing equipment are starting to make it attractive to both companies and enterprising individuals to put work centers in the home.

Already it is feasible for parents to handle pool typing, computer programming, monitoring distant chemical plant operations or acting as a stock broker or investment counselor without leaving the house. This is something quite different from the textile piecework mothers who hour after hour have worked at home at wages well below the union scale.

Gradually the dilemma facing many bright young brides — motherhood or career? — may fade. But at the moment millions of young wives still do face the challenge of deciding whether to go back to an outside job after a child is born. And if so, when?

10

How Important Is Mother to a Child's Development?

"More and more prospective mothers in Muncie say that the right amount of maternity leave is three to six months. Three weeks, if I can help it, says one."

— *Edward E. Scharff in reporting on four decades of change in Muncie, Indiana, known to sociologists as Middletown, U.S.A.*

When can a mother return to a job or look for a job if she has small children?

We are in an area of controversy in seeking an answer. Even some child experts say we are in such turmoil in terms of role changes that they are confused.

The mother can find some support for anything she chooses to do after her child is a few months old. Or she will be told that the answer depends to a large extent on her personal circumstances. Hundreds of thousands of desperate mothers heading one-parent households have little choice as to the time of returning to a job.

Some respected investigators of child development such as Selma Fraiberg of the University of Michigan have cautioned that a child can readily tolerate separation from its mother without distress only after the third year of life.

Jerome Kagan, the highly influential investigator of infancy at Harvard's Department of Psychology, used to hold a roughly similar position, but now holds that if the circumstances are right, separation can begin a few months after birth. He has concluded that the first couple years of life are not clearly make-or-break times for young children. He found, for example, in his study of Guatemalan children that severe retardation produced by terrible living conditions during the first few years of life appeared to be reversible.

Others contend that certain enormously important things happen or don't happen at certain critical periods in the first two or three years and that the mother should be around at least part-time to help these changes occur in a positive way for the child.

So many millions of mothers of children are working today that the argument among experts is pretty much confined to whether she should be present full-time during the first three years of a child's life.

The gap in the views of the experts is due not only to differences they attach to the importance of mother being present when certain events are occurring in the young child's life but also due to their views about the optimum role for modern women.

Some investigators admit they are so admiring of the Women's Movement as a step forward in history that they are reluctant to make recommendations that might dump a load of guilt on a young mother seeking to lead her own life. They stress that it is not just the child that is involved but the mother-child relationship. If the mother feels aggrieved in a lonely, nuclear family situation, they contend, she may make a much better mother if she can get out and work at a job she relishes.

Also there are the practices of many employers that discourage any delay in return to work. The employers may give only a few weeks of maternity leave. They may make it clear a young woman's chances for advancement in her career will be in jeopardy if she drops out for a year or two to concentrate on being a mother.

For the mothers of young children who do have an option about when to take up working outside the home, I would offer two expert opinions that particularly impressed me. Both are those of highly respected child experts are in a position to be fairly objective about the controversy as to when mothers can work.

William Kessen, head of psychology at Yale, told me, "There can be no doubt about the importance of early caretaking of children. What is distressing to me is . . . that the issue is cast polemically and in an exaggerated form . . . and that we know so little about the particularities of early care, the subtler ways of exchange, after all these years of observation and speculation.''

The other opinion comes from T. Berry Brazelton, professor of pediatrics, Harvard. He says: "Each extra month of mothering is like money in the bank for both mother and child."

WHO CAN SUBSTITUTE FOR MOTHERS?

At this point we will consider as possible caretakers for a child only people who will be in the home or are well known to the family.

The answer to the question above is anyone age fourteen or over who has the time, who is fond of the child, who has an affectionate disposition, and who has a lot of patience. If the child is quite small it will benefit from a lot of cuddling and stimulation.

How about father, if he has the time? Sure, if he feels up to it and qualifies on the above traits. With the great increase of marriages where the spouses think of themselves as truly equal partners — and particularly where the wife brings home a paycheck — the younger husbands have been expressing a new willingness to share in home responsibilities.

A very small child will respond to either a male or female adult who is loving. The only question is whether the male adult will respond comfortably to the child.

A series of observational studies by developmental psychologists Douglas B. Sawin and Ross D. Parke of the Universities of Texas and Illinois were made of the nurturing behavior of both mothers and fathers while in charge of newborn babies.[1] Mothers were observed for ten-minute periods in their hospital room. Fathers had their ten-minute testings in a quiet hospital room nearby. The authors concluded that "fathers are as competent as mothers in providing affection, stimulation and the necessary care for newborn infants." There was, for example, little difference in the amount of milk left over in the feeding bottles used in all cases.

The fathers presumably were well motivated since they had just become proud parents and they were in a testing situation. For the long haul of parenting some observers still feel that hormones and the experience of being tuned in to a fetus for much of nine months gives most mothers some natural advantage at nurture. Remnants of instinct may also favor the mother. Sociologist Alice Rossi has pointed out that almost all mothers — whether right-handed or left-handed — cradle their infant in their left arm and against the left side of their chest where the infant can be soothed by the maternal heartbeat familiar from uterine life.

Still let's accept the fact that many fathers can be excellent caretakers of children. I have seen at first hand a number of examples of superb parenting by young fathers. As for older youngsters entering their teens, fathers probably have a natural superiority, at least with sons. They can better tolerate their youngster's drive for independence. They are often better authority figures for youngsters going through the confusions of puberty. And as New York psychologist Richard A. Gardner points out, fathers may excel in sharing in sports and other activities with youngsters.

But what about their natural inclination to pitch in and involve themselves in the day-to-day parenting and other home work under the new egalitarian mood? The advertising agency Benton and Bowles questioned 452 husbands on a family consumer panel about household activities they perform. The researchers found these four groups:

1. Progressives (who really do pitch in) 13%
2. All Talk But Little Action 33%
3. Ambivalents (help some but without conviction) 15%
4. Traditionalists 39%

Apparently a great deal more acculturation is necessary before males in large numbers will gladly take over all-day care of small children while their wife goes out to a job, unless he is unemployed. Today such a father is commonly a graduate student who is home a lot anyhow and his wife may be providing the main paycheck.

Competent people can be brought into the home to watch over children while mother works. But often there are problems.

If a mother of a small child has a full-time job and wants to hire a full-time, competent, in-house mother substitute (nannie) she will need lots of bucks, say $150 or $200 a week, and plenty of perseverance. Nannies are a disappearing breed. One New York agency specializing in such help says it gets a hundred calls from mothers for every job it can fill.

Nurses or nurses' aides are somewhat easier to locate. Also one may hire a full-time housekeeper who doubles at mothering.

One can often get student nurses from a local college which trains nurses. Their fees are relatively low, say $2.75 an hour plus cab fare. Unfortunately they have to attend classes and so are rarely available full time. Some mothers are able to get two such student nurses to take shifts, but that can take a lot of juggling and leave an infant confused as to who is its real caretaker. Also good prospects at moderate fees are students at local colleges who are majoring in early child development.

Older siblings, say those over eleven, can fill in after school in care of younger siblings, but unless they are fourteen years old it would be rather chancy to trust a typical sitter with infant or toddler care, in the view of the Child Care Resource Center, Cambridge, Massachusetts.

Adult sitters such as older women also are available in most urban areas. They will come into the home when the mother is off working. Care should be taken to check references. I know a mother who saw an ad placed by an available woman who said she had a lot of mothering experience. During the interview the applicant seemed pleasant and motherly. She was hired. The mother turned a three-month-old baby over to her care and cheerfully went back to work as personnel manager of a fairly large company. Within a few days she got a call from a neighbor that she better come home; her child had been crying for an hour. She rushed home. The baby was on the woman's lap. The woman, a lush, had passed out. The mother was distraught. She informed her employers that she would take her chances on getting a good job back after a year or so of full-time mothering.

More than a third of all children of mothers with jobs are cared for by informal arrangements with relatives, neighbors or friends. Yet astonishingly little is known by child experts on how these arrangements work out, how they are handled, and what the impact is on the children involved.

Relatives are believed to be the best choice because the child already knows them and there is a fair chance the child will get loving care from them. Grandparents, if they are not busy, may even come into the home.

These informal, makeshift arrangements may have to be at the convenience of the relatives, friends, or neighbors. If a neighbor becomes temporarily unavailable the mother is forced into a hectic search for alternative arrangements.

WHAT ABOUT THE PROBLEM OF FEEDING AN INFANT?

This question arises as an important issue only because the mother who takes a full-time job soon after birth may not be able to breast-feed the baby. At least she won't be able to do so during the nine or so hours when she probably will be away from the home, unless she takes the infant with her or unless she extracts her milk during rest periods on the job.

Oddly, breast-feeding has been increasing at a time when more and more mothers of young children have been leaving the home for jobs.

About one U.S. mother in five now is still breast-feeding her infant five months after its birth. Once out of vogue, breast-feeding has been staging a major comeback for some sound reasons.

The new naturalism coming out of the counterculture may have helped account for the new interest in breast-feeding. A bigger cause, however, was scientific findings, still emerging, on the superiority of breast-feeding to bottle-feeding, once considered both chic and scientific.

Statistically, at least, bottle-fed babies are off to a less favorable start in life than babies who are breast-fed for several months. *The Medical Bulletin* of the International Planned Parenthood describes the medical advantages of breast-feeding as "overwhelming." Human breast milk is ideal and fully satisfies the infant's nutritional requirements for the first six months. The American Academy of Pediatrics now agrees that human milk is superior.

Here are some medical reasons given why bottled milk is somewhat more risky than human milk: Bottle-feeding involves more chance of gastrointestinal infection, digestive upset, diarrhea; more probability of skin disorders; more proneness to obesity later in life.

There are also possible psychological losses for the bottle-fed infant. The baby needs the warmth and security of a caretaker's arms and body while feeding according to, among others, Grantly Dick-Read and Selma Fraiberg.[2] Food from a bottle can be administered in many nonintimate ways, especially by an inexperienced person struggling to hang onto the infant.

Then there are possible psychological losses to the mother which are rarely mentioned but are nonetheless intriguing. Some women profess that breast-feeding is a bother and a bore. Perhaps some with that view have had little experience at it themselves.

Sociologist Alice Rossi, in a footnote to her report on the biosocial aspects of parenting, had this comment: "Provide a woman with a rocking chair, and the far-away look of pleasure one often sees among nursing mothers is much closer to the sensual Eve than to the saintly Mary.''

One psychologist in reporting occasional incidents of orgasm by the mother during breast-feeding suggested that Nature meant breast-feeding to be pleasurable. It helps assure the survival of the species.

Some years ago two anatomists at the University of Minnesota found, in studying several lactating females, a correlation between the amount of milk the breasts ejected and the women's degree of sexual arousal.[3] The pro-breast-feeding organization La Leche League International simply calls such feeding ''one of the most restful and enjoyable times of the day.''

Some mothers with jobs manage to have their infants brought to their job site for breast-feeding during lunch hour or job breaks. A mother in Iowa City lost her job with the fire department for doing this. A kindergarten teacher in Orlando, Florida, sued her school board after she was forced to take a leave of absence because her principal barred her from breast-feeding her infant who was brought to her during her duty-free lunch period. This practice, it was alleged, violated a rule against bringing one's child to the school. She claimed her constitutional rights to liberty were violated. The federal district court judge dismissed her claim as frivolous. With the help of National Education Association affiliates she appealed. The appellate court sided with her to the extent that it agreed that the Constitution indeed ''protects from excessive state interference a woman's decision respecting breast-feeding her child.'' It directed that the case go back to the district court to determine if that particular school board's ruling served a legitimate ''state interest'' sufficient to override the teacher's ''liberty interests.'' The same federal judge held in March 1982 that the school's rule was ''reasonably related to the state interest in an efficient and effective public school system.'' The teacher and the N.E.A. groups may appeal. Meanwhile the state's N.E.A. officials are pleased that a constitutional right to breast-feed was established.

The noted English actress Lynn Redgrave left the popular U.S. television series *House Calls* because she claimed the producer would not allow her to breast-feed her baby Annabel during production hours. After that she worked as a star for all three major U.S. networks, breast-feeding every working day.

There are now quite a few reports of mothers breast-feeding on the job with no problem at all. For example, a receptionist and bookkeeper for a doctor in Aberdeen, Washington, keeps her infant son in a reclining baby's chair right on top of her desk. He sleeps most of the time and feeds from her in a private part of the office.

Two state senators in Madison, Wisconsin, permit their cherished secretaries to keep their babies near them so that they can breast-feed on demand. A number of laboratory workers in Australia now are permitted to bring their infants to work and breast-feed them there.

More common now are the working mothers who express milk from their breasts into plastic containers and keep it chilled in a refrigerator (and en route home in a chilled thermos jug). The milk is bottle-fed to their infants next day by the infant's attendant while the mothers go back to work.

An airline stewardess in Georgia has been taking a hand pump with her on her three night flights a week and pumps milk every three or four hours while away.

The expressing of milk can readily be done by hand. Or if desired the mother can obtain a suction pump that imitates the baby's sucking action. There are a number of hand pumps on the market. The La Leche League International, which operates out of Franklin Park, Illinois, and distributes a manual for working mothers, cites in particular as effective a cylindrical pump designed in Japan and distributed in the U.S. by Happy Family Products; the Lloyd B Pump which has a trigger action like a spray attachment on a household cleaning product; and the Ora Lac pump. With the latter, the mother creates suction pressure by sucking on a tube.

Electric pumps are more expensive and often can be rented from a druggist or medical supply house. The La Leche League mentions as effective Egnell and Medela, both based on Swedish designs. Any pumping equipment that comes in contact with the mother's milk must be sterilized before use.

If mothers of infants continue to be at jobs in increasing numbers, companies with large numbers of female employees should have small lounges where women can nurse infants brought to them — or can use breast pump equipment.

Thus far La Leche League has heard of no such special company facility. Most on-the-job mothers express their milk by going into the washroom several times a day or to some private room or office or an unused storeroom, or to a first aid station, which usually has a refrigerator. Some go to their car.

HOW SIGNIFICANT IS THE ALLEGED PARENT-CHILD ATTACHMENT?

A strong preponderance of investigators of child development seem to agree that attachment, or bonding, to one or more adults should occur for a child to get off to a good start in life. Some call attachment absolutely vital. A few are not sure what "attachment" is. Absence of attachment, many experts feel, can have a lasting ill impact.

A human infant is relatively immature at birth, considerably more immature than most mammal infants. It apparently does not start developing significant attachment to a specific adult until the sixth or seventh month of life. Before that, however, some other very important things should be happening.

For a baby to develop a sense of trust it needs a considerable amount of cuddling and molding, belly to belly, to the body of an adult. Home movies made during the infancies of children who later needed psychiatric attention show a pattern of the mother resisting the baby's instinctive attempt to mold to her body.[4] Typically the infant tries to mold to the holder's left side where the heart is beating. (On the other hand young children who develop psychiatric disorders are often remembered as having actively resisted molding to the mother's body early in life.)

The new baby, immature as it is, thrives on attention. It needs a familiar person or persons to nuzzle it and give it things to explore with its hands and mouth. Infants getting such attention receive an important head start in life that seems to persist.[5] Leon Yarrow, as a top official at the National Institute of Child Health and Human Development, made this strong statement:

"Perhaps the most striking finding is the extent to which mother's stimulation influences developmental progress during the first six months. Its amount and quality are highly related to her baby's IQ." (For "mother" you can probably substitute any adult who is very fond of the baby and capable of nurturing it.)

Ideally in these early months of life the mother has been developing a strong attachment to the infant. The child's attachment to the parent figure comes more slowly and becomes significant only after the first half year of life.

As the infant moves toward becoming a toddler it wants to be near the adult to whom it is most attached. It will show disturbance when separated from that person and show joy or excitement on the person's return. And typically it will show some anxiety when left with or even approached by strangers.

Its attachment intensifies and becomes more and more important until about the eighteenth month of life. This attachment reflects itself in the intensity of its anxiety when separated from its mother figure. The drop in anxiety seems to coincide with its increasing ability to communicate through language. T. G. R. Bower of the University of Edinburgh has charted the decline in separation anxiety from a peak at eighteen months to about the twenty-sixth month, when the anxiety at separation levels off to a moderate level until about the beginning of the fourth year of life when the anxiety again declines.[6]

A psychologist at Children's Hospital, Boston, suggested to me that a child's attachment to its caretaker doesn't necessarily decline along with separation anxiety after the eighteenth month but may take different forms. She explains: "The toddler and preschooler are less reliant on the caretaker for close physical contact, but are still critically dependent on him/her (witness the toddler's intense need for visual contact with his mother, or the preschooler's continuous verbal bids for attention)." And as we will see, four-year-olds are particularly vulnerable to sustained hurt by divorce. But that may reflect a high need for stability then as much as a need for attachment.

Many researchers investigating the impact of substitute care have set up tests, usually under laboratory conditions, to test any attachment behavior differences between children who have been receiving considerable substitute care and those who have not.

Two factors should be pointed out, as they confuse any such measuring of attachment:

1. The infant who has plenty of loving care from its mother or surrogate mother in the first year of life feels more secure and thus by the twelfth month is less likely than average to show distress when the mother figure leaves for a while. Insecure toddlers, whatever the reason for their insecurity, may *seem* more attached because they are more prone to clinging behavior than the secure child.

2. The infant who has a variety of caretakers before attachment normally begins may show fewer of the anxiety symptoms of attachment loss. Hence some believe that a child will be less bothered by substitute care if it is put right into it during the first six months of life. But such a child often will have its own special problems unless the substitutes are very few in number and skilled in giving the child plenty of devoted attention. When their normal period of

yearning for attachment arrives they may display upset behavior unless a substitute parent can serve as a good attachment figure.

One of the towering figures in human development, Erik Erikson, has cautioned about the hazard of not giving small children a good chance to develop attachment. Erikson stressed that consistent, continuing loving care plays a critical role in ego identity. He also cautioned that the very small child who has not known a trust relationship with adults may grow up with a sense of mistrust.

The most emphatic warning about nonattachment came from psychoanalyst Selma Fraiberg of the University of Michigan. She talks about the "diseases of nonattachment" that can develop during the first eighteen months of life.[7] The distinguishing characteristic of this disease, she says, is "the incapacity of the person to form human bonds. . . . In the absence of human ties a conscience cannot be formed, even the qualities of self-observation and self-criticism fail to develop." This, she contends, can be a permanent impairment. At its worst, the diseases of nonattachment create bondless people who "constitute one of the largest aberrant populations in the world today, contributing far beyond their numbers to social disease and disorder." They are handicapped in work relations, friendships, marriage, and child-rearing.

ARE THERE IMPORTANT DEVELOPMENTAL PHASES THAT A MOTHER CONSIDERING A JOB SHOULD BEAR IN MIND?

A great many modern mothers seem to assume that their nurturing role is of decreasing importance with every passing month starting with month one. Millions believe that by the time their child is six months old it is well launched. This is a serious misconception.

As indicated, the first six months *are* important in terms of needing lots of body contact, good health, stimulation, the encouragement of interest in the world the infant has entered, and promotion of a deep sense of trust. The last is reflected, Erik Erikson has pointed out, in the ease of feeding, the depth of the infant's slumber, and the relaxation of his bowels.

But even more important things are about to start happening. The infant is about to burst out as a self-aware, mobile human. Burton White and associates spent a decade making notes on the behavior of small children as part of Harvard's Preschool Project. White, who now heads the

Center for Parent Education in Newton, Massachusetts, has charted this emergence in step-by-step detail through three years.[8] Here, briefly, is his interpretation.

White says the first eight-month period of a child's life in terms of making choices "is probably the easiest of all times for parents. If they provide the baby with a normal amount of love, attention and physical care nature will pretty much take care of the rest." White adds that parents should stop worrying about spoiling a young infant by picking it up. It is virtually impossible to spoil a child under eight months of age by picking it up whenever it cries. But a child in its second year of life can become spoiled.

The eighth month, in White's view, is when the most exciting and chancy phase of child development begins. Parenthood suddenly becomes more demanding. More choices must be made. This period starts, he says, at about the time the child starts to crawl.

"The educational developments that take place in the year or so [after] a child is about eight months old," White states, "*are the most important and most in need of attention of any that occur in human life. . . . To begin to look at a child's educational development when he is two years of age is already much too late. . . .*"

White asserts that four key goals in early human life are language development, social development, nurturing the roots of intelligence, and the development of curiosity. All four, he contends, can be significantly affected by what occurs in the year or so starting with the eighth month of life. For example, he states:

"We have never come across an eight-month-old child who was not incredibly curious."

White cautions parents of crawlers and toddlers that it is not inevitable that this curious eight-month-old will have its curiosity deepened and broadened by events in the coming year. Nor is it "inevitable that a child will learn language . . . that his social development will take place in a solid and fruitful manner . . . [or] that a substructure for intelligence will be built." It is White's belief that the vast majority of children never achieve the level of ability of their potential in these four areas.

What environment is being provided to the child if this period is indeed the beginning of extraordinary receptivity? Are parents who are working (or estranged) short-changing their children in these apparently critical months? Or are they resourceful enough to arrange affairs so that their very small, curious children receive plenty of stimulation and enrichment?

White stated that he was impressed by the fact that during the first years of life "the child's own family seemed so obviously central to the outcome."

Some specialists in child development are less certain, as indicated, that there is any single make-or-break time phase in a child's development. Those who lean to Jerome Kagan's conception of early childhood as a period of considerable resiliency wonder if White may have stated the critical phase concept too strongly. Clearly the situation calls for more study.

As for preschoolers, those youngsters three or four years old, there is one developmental thesis that should be of interest to a mother not then working but considering taking a job. Some experts contend this is a period when many children are said to be in a don't-rock-the-boat period. Mothers accepting this view should be careful to prepare the child for a coming significant change of life pattern. If a job is planned, she should take the child to the place where she will work and show the child what she will do and the plans she is making for the child. The noted New Haven investigator of child development Louise Bates Ames stated that this is a period for many children when "everything has to be just the same" even within its house or room. If a move to a new neighborhood is planned, put the child in a room furnished as closely as possible to its present one.

Children who are of elementary school age and are in what psychologists call their latency phase don't mind the idea of their mother working. In fact they may take pride in her career. They just don't much like the idea of coming home to an empty house. So arrangements need to be made to see that this experience happens as infrequently as possible, and when it does happen the child should be left with the feeling that there is someone in charge.

With the onset of puberty and early adolescence, Erikson points out, "all samenesses and continuities relied upon earlier are more or less questioned again" as the youngsters undergo a physiological revolution and see themselves facing adult tasks. In their search for a new sense of continuity and sameness they have to refight many of the battles of earlier years and may set up perfectly well-meaning people such as parents as their adversaries.

Working parents may feel they somehow are failing their youngsters when in fact these young adolescents may be going through a normal period of turbulence.

We should look at care sharing from a child's view. A child is not just something nice to have around in free hours to play with and to have as a source of emotional warmth. It will need a lot of parenting for several years in order to thrive. Married couples should think twice about having a child if they plan to put the child fairly directly after birth into full-time substitute care, unless they can afford a warm-hearted nannie or housekeeper. Margaret Mead was a champion of working mothers but she startled some feminists by stating, shortly before her death, that thoughtful women shouldn't be having children with the idea of packing them off to day-care twelve hours a day.

The realities are that millions of mothers of small children have —or are considering — full-time jobs. So the question for many becomes: what arrangements offer the better chance of being agreeable, and not painful, for the child? The most thought should center on the under-threes, since they would seem to be most at risk because of the skills that are achieved or not achieved in those years. What are the main considerations to keep in mind if full-time substitute care is needed? Here are my own conclusions:

If there are no compelling reasons for the mother to go to work full time, she should wait until the infant is at least eighteen or twenty months old before making a move. By that time the child is fairly well on the way to being launched in life. If substitute care is needed before the eighteenth month on any large-scale basis, it should, if possible, involve only a single surrogate mother.

In the early years it is important that substitute care be as individualized as possible. This would suggest a preference of care in this descending order for those earliest years:

1. A grandparent or other relative your child knows and likes. Such a person often is most likely to have that extra devotion to your child that is so important.

2. A warm-hearted housekeeper or an affectionate and competent sitter over fourteen who does the sitting within the child's own home.

3. A competent neighbor who enjoys mothering, who is known to the child and has a couple of children of her own, who will care for the child in her own home.

4. A competent mother who has obviously done a good job raising her own children and is now running a small licensed "family day-care" home. A trend is developing to organize such family day-care services into systems. Parents may find that in their area an agency for such a system is available to help them find an appropriate home nearby.

5. A "group day-care" center. These may be largely federally funded centers for children of low-income families, or nonprofit services by a community organization, or a mothers' cooperative, or a center run for profit. The big growth appears to be in the last category.

I will examine the question of day-care in greater detail in the following chapters.

11

The Dilemmas of Day-Care

"Children are stashed away all over the city."

— *Erma Napoleon, Massachusetts Office for Children, speaking of Boston*

Federal officials report that child care has become an eleven-billion-dollar industry. For the typical working couple with children, the cost of child care has become the third largest item in the family budget. Still, the organized facilities available have the capacity to accommodate only a fraction of the preschool children whose mothers work. And then there are the millions of young school-age children who need some sort of supervision when school is not in session (and no adult is at home). We will get to the school-agers later.

What really is known about the impact, if any, of child care by others on a small child's development? When is a child ready for day-care?

Any reasonably precise answer to the question of the impact of day-care must depend on whether we are talking about top-quality, individualized day-care or typical day-care (or even worse, unlicensed day-care) . . . whether we are talking about part-time day-care or full-time day-care . . . whether we are talking about family day-care or group day-care . . . whether we are talking about middle-class children or slum children . . . whether we are talking about infants and toddlers or preschool youngsters.

The question of impact has been under considerable investigation. I have examined a couple dozen of the better-known studies and have had the benefit of fine published overviews of the whole body of credible research prepared separately by Urie Bronfenbrenner and Michael Rutter.[1]

Despite all the studies the body of certain knowledge is relatively small. There have been several problems with the research. Bronfenbrenner neatly summarized the most serious distorting factor:

To an overwhelming degree, research on day care has been conducted in . . . university-connected centers with high staff-child ratios and well-designed programs designed at fostering cognitive, emotional and social development. Yet most of the day care available to the nation's parents is not of this character.

Some of these high-quality test centers cost more than $10,000 per child a year to run, not counting free time contributed by graduate students. One report mentioned that each child had a single caretaker through the first year and that staff turnover was minimal.

Another distorting factor perhaps is that many of the children in experiments have been drawn from inner-city low-income homes, the kind of children most likely to benefit from high-quality day-care.

A third problem is that so much of the early research was focused on the effect of day-care on the child's attachment to its mother. Some of the researchers seemed primarily bent on reassuring mothers that despite their child's contacts with surrogates, the mothers were still number one with the child.

Still another problem is that very few of the studies have looked for any long-term effect. In 1977 a critic pointed out that there had, after more than a decade of research, been only one study of long-term effect. That had simply measured IQ, and the sample had included only eleven comparison pairs. They were at the fifth-grade level.

Highly qualified observers differ on what effect, if any, group care has on children's development. Consider the conclusions of two highly qualified observers, Jerome Kagan, developmental psychologist at Harvard, and Michael Rutter, child psychiatrist at London's Institute of Psychiatry.

Kagan, who used to worry about the impact of group care, changed his mind partly as a result of helping run, on a research basis, a group day-care center, the Tremont Infant Center in Boston. Children were taken in during early infancy. Kagan still believes in the importance of attachment but he also believes a good day-care center permits a child to attach to "both mother and auntie (caretaker)." In 1978 he and his research associates stated that recent studies

reveal that group care for young children does not seem to have much effect, either facilitating or debilitating, on the cognitive, social or affective development of most children. The one exception to that statement seems to hold for children from poorly educated and less privileged homes. If these children attend special, well-run centers, they tend to perform a little better on the standard tests of cognitive development. . . .[2]

Rutter's overview of the various findings was summarized in *The American Journal of Orthopsychiatry* in these words:

Although day care for very young children is not likely to result in serious emotional disturbance, it would be misleading to conclude that it is without risks or effects.

Here are my impressions regarding some of the areas of contention in terms of effect or noneffect on day-care. (Bear in mind that the quality of any substitute care and the age of the child are especially important variables.)

Impact on intellectual development   As yet there is no impressive evidence of any difference in rates of learning between home and center. Jay Belsky and Laurence Steinberg, human development specialists, reviewed forty investigations and concluded that the day-care experience "has neither salutary nor adverse effects on intellectual development . . . of most children. For economically disadvantaged children however, day care may have an enduring positive effect."[3] Bronfenbrenner in his overview of day-care's impact reached a similar conclusion. There is some suggestive evidence that for older preschool children, those cared for by sitters or family day-care do not thrive intellectually quite as well as those in good group day-care, where there may be more intellectual stimulation. Also there is some suggestion that these older preschoolers who spend a half a day in nursery or kindergarten do somewhat better in school.

Impact on emotional development   One study that showed a clear emotional impact of day-care was reported in *The Challenge of Daycare* by Sally Provence et al.[4] This study at "Children's House" was sponsored by a number of directors of the Yale Child Study Center. The investigators described the early reactions of children to experiencing day care at three *very well run* centers. The hardest hit initially were children entering day care between the ages of ten and twenty-four months (all high parent-attachment months). Some of these children showed clear signs of anxiety or anger. Some became apathetic. Some lost previously acquired skills. The investigators said that infants under ten months of age showed less vivid reaction than those who were older; and they adjusted more easily at first with few signs of distress than did the children who entered between ten and twenty-four months.

This was not to say, they emphasized, that it was better for infants to come into day-care before the tenth month of age. In infants placed in full day-care at an early age "there is some interference or delay in the formation of a close attachment to the parents."

A small infant adjusted to day-care may become surprisingly disagreeable when it reaches the attachment period. Videotapes have been made of children in day-care by the Infant-Toddler Research Project funded by Pittsburgh foundations (reported in *Children Today*, Nov.–Dec. 1981). Officials, as an example, tell of the strange behavior of Mike who entered day care at five months:

Mike's entry into care was rather uneventful. . . . Signs of stress were barely discernable. . . . Four months after placement however, to everyone's surprise, morning separations suddenly became a source of stress for Mike. . . . After finally settling down from these morning upheavals he fussed constantly, became increasingly demanding of the caretaker's time and refused to let her out of his sight.

The emotional impact of placing infants in day-care can also be on the parents. Bronfenbrenner has mentioned this as a concern in citing 1974–75 studies by W. Fowler and N. Khan (published by the Ontario Institute of Studies in Education). They investigated changes in the family home environment when children went into day-care during the first year of life. The results raised serious questions. The investigators indicated that mothers who enroll their children in day-care early in the first year may undergo a drop of interest in their children. That of course could have a detrimental effect on a child in the long run. It certainly is a subtle hazard which thoughtful parents should keep in mind.

Impact on social development   Here the evidence of the impact of day-care seems to be most emphatic and least questioned. I have before me reports of eight investigations involving the impact of day-care on social development, made in the U.S., England, and Sweden. Seven are consistent in finding that day-care children are lower in socialization. (Historically a vital role of the family has been the socialization of children.) For example, all seven found the day-care children less cooperative with adults.

A major center for studying social development of children in day-care has been at Syracuse University, with many investigators involved, some from other universities. One of the studies pertinent to our interest was conducted by a group headed by University of Connecticut psychologist J. Conrad Schwarz.[5] The occasion was the opening of a new day-care center at the university. Nineteen of the preschool youngsters were old hands at experiencing day-care. They had been in high-quality day-care since infancy. Children in a matched group were having their first brush with day-care. A few months after this new center opened, all the children were tested on nine behavior traits. The veterans of day-care were found to be significantly more aggressive, more physically active, and less cooperative with adults. They did a lot of running around. Their aggressiveness, verbal and physical, was vented toward both peers and adults.

In general, however, they got along all right with their same-age peers. Day-care, it was suggested, "may slow acquisition of some adult cultural values." Kagan, who has been skeptical about most findings of any difference in day-care kids, agreed that the Syracuse findings "suggested" that children who have been in day-care the longest "were less cooperative with adults, slightly more aggressive and more active."

The social effects of substitute care seem not only to persist but to become more striking with age. In T. Moore's study in London he checked back on two groups of youngsters when they were teenagers, about fifteen years old. One group of boys had been raised at home until they went to school. The other group had experienced "diffused mothering" such as day-care from about the age of three.

The mother-raised teenagers tended to be more sensitive in conforming to adult standards rather than to peer group standards, they were high in self control though somewhat reticent, and were high in academic interests. On the other hand, those teenagers who had experienced "diffused mothering" tended to be rather aggressively nonconforming in terms of adult values. They helped themselves to things they knew they shouldn't use and tended to hang out with friends the parents didn't approve of. These of course are simply tendencies, but parents should bear them in mind in shaping their parenting patterns if full-time substitute care is used on a long-term basis.

Because of all the questions and variables, the decision as to when a specific child can be considered "ready" for organized day-care can be better answered after we take a look at the varieties of day-care that have emerged in the U.S. and abroad.

THE CHILD-MINDING INDUSTRY

Many other modern societies have coherent policies toward assuring good care for young children whose mothers have jobs. The United States is still fumbling the issue. What day-care we have is seen primarily as an aid to parents, not something good per se in the way of enrichment for the child. That at least is true when full-time care for children under the age of four is involved.

In the U.S. the search for some organized provider of substitute care for children is a source of family distress in hundreds of thousands of homes. A three-year study of two hundred working mothers made by investigators at Columbia University School of Social Work concluded that finding adequate child care was "a source of constant stress" for all the women interviewed.[6]

Ms. Erma Napoleon, who heads group day-care licensing in Massachusetts, says many parents are so desperate for affordable day-care that they don't ask many questions. Like whether the place is licensed or not. They don't know what to expect from day-care except help for themselves. Very often, she stated, they never see the inside of the place their young children spend their long days. The parents assume, incorrectly, that a day-care center is sort of like a school. And they are gratified that the center has a van that picks up and returns their child or children, even if they haven't seen the place the van is going.

The U.S. has licensed day-care facilities for roughly one-fourth of the preschool children whose mothers work. The absence of facilities is far more acute for infants and toddlers. And it is the mothers of infants and toddlers who have shown the largest surge into the job market. One operator of a day-care chain told me there is a "terrific demand" for infant and toddler care. Since infants and toddlers inevitably need a lot more care, costs tend to run much higher — about $30 or $40 more per week — for reasonably good care for the under-threes. Many centers will not take children until they are toilet-trained. Others specify the child be two and three-quarters years old. In Massachusetts, for example, the great majority of licensed day-care centers won't take infants and toddlers. Hence the long, long waiting lists. Faced with this shortage of licensed spaces for preschoolers, many turn to illegal organized care facilities. Some hire illegal aliens.

Decent group day-care for one child at a private unsubsidized center can cost about as much as the family rent. Day-care for two children at a private center can often cost two-thirds as much as the working mother earns.

Surprisingly, some of the better group day-care centers in America are basically for children on welfare. They are supported primarily by public funding, such as the recently reduced federal Aid for Families with Dependent Children program.

Mary Keyserling, who made an extensive study of day-care several years ago, found that profit-making day-care centers were five times as likely to deserve a "poor" rating as licensed nonprofit centers.

One of the harsh facts about private group day-care centers is that employees tending our children are paid less than half as much as the average schoolteacher. Typically, the maximum that the average day-care worker can expect is very close to the prevailing minimum wage.

In the 1968–1972 period, many U.S. companies faced up to the brave new world of millions of job-holding mothers by setting up day-care centers on company premises for the small children of employees. During rest breaks and lunch mothers could go to check on, and even breast-feed, their children. The Russians already had become deeply involved in such on-site day-care centers.

With a few notable exceptions the U.S. movement collapsed. Among the reasons for its demise was the very deep recession in 1973–74. Also, day-care costs were soaring because the minimum wage kept rising. It was assumed, erroneously, by the companies that the federal government was about to move in and fund day-care centers on a massive scale. The company centers did not seem to be reducing absenteeism. Perhaps most important, the centers were not used as much as expected, especially those in cities where mothers might be caught up in rush hour bus or car traffic and didn't like lugging small children with them. Finally, many unions took a dim view of day-care as a benefit. Some worried that day-care centers would lock employees into too much dependency on employers.

Recently, starting in 1982, with the big change in tax laws, companies have been given a new incentive to help employees with their childcare problems. Companies can get favorable tax treatment (1) on money spent to set up a program to run an on-site nursery, or (2) subsidize an outside child-care center, or (3) reimburse employees for some of their within-the-home child-care expenses. Whether this will significantly change the long-prevailing wariness of employers remains to be tested.

For more than a decade the Women's Movement and some family organizations have been pressing the federal government for free or low-cost day-care for all job-holding mothers of young children. The National Women's Conference in 1977 also specified that the centers be nonsexist (meaning that men as well as women be hired). This is an excellent specification because so many children in day-care centers come from mother-headed households. In 1970 the White House Conference on Children voted that the number-one need of American children and families was quality day-care. In the Congress, then Senator Walter Mondale was in the forefront in trying to awaken the nation and the government to the new needs of children.

But public resistance to any large-scale program to provide low-cost child care has also been massive, except where welfare clients are involved. One reason day-care is favored for people on welfare is that it helps get the mother herself off the welfare roles by enabling her to work. Recently, because of cutbacks, the working mother often can't afford the "sliding scale" tuition and is forced back on welfare.

Some particularly conservative politicians have labeled public support of day-care as a plot to Sovietize America. In 1971 the U.S. Congress passed a Comprehensive Child Development Act which would have deeply involved the federal government in general support of day-care for working families. President Nixon vetoed it. His explanation centered not so much on cost as philosophy. He thought the act "would commit the vast moral authority of the National government on the side of communal approaches to child-rearing over against the family-centered approach."

Nothing approaching the comprehensiveness of that act cleared Congress for the following decade.

The federal role in helping families not on welfare with child-care costs consists mainly of permitting a tax credit for a part of the cost of child-care services. Until 1982 it was a maximum of $400 per child (or about 15 percent of the cost for moderately decent day-care for pre-schoolers; and less than 10 percent of the cost for decent care for infants and toddlers). Starting in 1982 the maximum allowable credit for people with family income under $10,000 was raised to $720 per child, but for the family with a total income over $30,000 the allowable credit per child was raised by only $80 a year. If a low-income family owes less in taxes than the amount of the tax credit it can receive, it does not receive a refund.

There seems to be looming in the U.S. a massive pressure to put day-care — at least from the age of three on — into the public schools. Some proponents such as Michigan psychologist Roger Ulrich have suggested that public school education start at age two.

Joseph Coates of the Congressional Office of Technological Assessment has even forecast that soon schools will be under pressure to "compensate for reduced parental care" by teaching young children such skills as how to dress, eat, and drink along with deportment and self-control. That's probably some way off.

The American Federation of Teachers has been particularly interested in getting the money federally funded for aid to dependent children into the school coffers. There is some logic to this because of the relatively small number of children born in the 1970s. Many elementary schools have schoolrooms that are empty much of the time, and tens of thousands of teachers are out of work.

Organizations, such as the Children's Defense Fund, which are trying to improve day-care for low-income families, are wary of the politics that would become involved if federal funding for small children (already being slashed) went to school budgets. Many day-care professionals in the National Association of Education for Young Children are wary too. They view the care of small children as a separate and distinct profession requiring talents that often can't be assumed by schoolteachers. The biggest complication that would arise from any move to put day-care into the schools is that teachers would balk at accepting the low pay scales common in the day-care field. Teachers usually work only nine months a year for their salary whereas day-care professionals work year-round for a much smaller annual income.

At any rate, let's review the facilities for child care presently available in the U.S. (and, later, abroad) for parents who cannot be with the children. Children in need of care include not only those under school age but also the elementary school children whose schools let out a few hours before either parent will be home.

CHILDREN IN FAMILY DAY-CARE

This is the most widely used form of organized day-care. A woman (or occasionally a man) will take children into her home each weekday for pay. It's a cottage industry. Sometimes the proprietor has children of her own. Such proprietors take into their homes more than one or two million children whose mothers work. The exact number is unknown because in many states small operators don't bother — or are not required — to get a license. Many operate illegally.

Some operators are dreadful, like the little old lady in the shoe. But many are an excellent alternative when substitute mothering is required. For example, a well-educated warmhearted young mother I know only as "Barbara" has often taken care of my three-year-old granddaughter, Kendra. At this writing Barbara has two fine children of her own in kindergarten and elementary school so that for much of the day she has only two or three children. In late afternoons her own kids may be home along with a couple other "aftercare" schoolchildren whose mothers work. In the backyard there is a wading pool, sand box, and climbing rig. She handles the client children just as if they were her own. She takes them along when she goes shopping or to the doctor, to a gym where she works out, to a senior citizen center where she does volunteer work. Once a week she takes them on Girl Scout or Brownie field trips.

A friend close to the day-care situation in Massachusetts told me of being at one family care home where there were six babies in one play-pen without a single toy in the pen. The babies were left there all day long. She added that this was not extraordinary.

Some states specify that an operator can have no more than six children under her wing, including her own. In Massachusetts an operator must have six months' experience with small children, but motherhood for six months is accepted as experience.

Family day-care homes as opposed to the more structured, bigger group day-care centers are better in some ways, and worse in others. For example, the family day-care setting assures that your child has just one substitute mother, rather than a crew of caretakers, which is common in group centers. A good family care operator is more likely to provide a homelike atmosphere. This is particularly important if infants or toddlers are involved. Family day-care normally costs less — typically at least a fourth less — especially for infants and toddlers since there is no overhead, and since the "center" is already in place and serves also as a home.

Some ways they can be worse Typically there is relatively little educational component in family day-care, which is important for those children over two and a half years old. And there is probably a higher chance the operator may have had relatively little education. In one study of twelve infants in family care homes who were followed for two years, one-third showed losses of mental development quotients and half scored lower on social quotients.[7] (That of course was a small sample.)

There is less inspection of family day-care operations and thus theoretically a greater chance of getting a really bad situation, unless the parent doing the choosing has personally inspected the proprietor and facilities. In the survey by the National Council of Jewish Women a few years ago, one interviewer came upon a "family day care" home in a mid-Atlantic state where she found eight children strapped to high chairs in the kitchen, twenty children huddled before a flickering TV set in the basement, and a fenced-in backyard full of children. There were altogether forty-seven children at the "home" which was licensed for a maximum of six.

A family day-care licensing official in Massachusetts told me she had come across licensed homes with twenty children. One adult was in charge. The children in the seven-room house ranged from infants to five-year-olds. The operator kept her license by cutting the number back to six. She claimed she just couldn't say no to desperate working mothers.

In family day-care there is a greater probability that the operation will place heavy reliance on television to keep the children occupied. One study made in New York City found that a third of the "family" centers had virtually no play materials.

Some states required only that a family day-care operator obtain a license if she takes in four or more children. A dozen states simply "register" home day-care facilities without bothering to inspect them.

COOPERATIVE CARE CENTERS

These come primarily in three forms:

Pure cooperative   These are usually small. They are formed by parents and staffed by parents. They may operate a few hours a day in a church basement, an unused schoolroom, or a private home from two to five times a week. Nationwide there are apparently several hundred. The precise number is unknown since they do not require a license. One hears about them by word of mouth, checking at the children's room of the local library, talking to a minister or school counselor. They are not for the working mother with a full-time job but may appeal to a mother with a part-time job. Mostly they appeal to full-time mothers who want their child to have more contact with other children, and to be in an early education program.

Parent cooperatives that have a hired staff   These still require that parents contribute a few hours a month as teacher aides, and be otherwise involved in seeing that the center thrives. These seem to be particularly popular in academic centers such as Cambridge, Massachusetts, and Ann Arbor, Michigan, and often emerge from pure cooperatives that can no longer be managed because most of the parents are working. They appeal to faculty members and married graduate students partly because such people have open hours during the week when they can work at the coop. Also they appeal philosophically to all thoughtful parents who believe, correctly, that top-quality day-care is associated with a high level of parental involvement.

In Cambridge, at least, this type of cooperative is not necessarily for bargain hunters. The average cost of group day-care in this high-cost area in 1982 was $75 a week for preschoolers, $100 a week for infants and toddlers.

Parents who take the trouble to form cooperatives are usually concerned first of all with obtaining high-quality care for their children. They pay more to get good teachers and aides, and have more of them than the average care-for-profit center.

Cooperatives that are administered by parents but staffed by professionals   Parents may, or may not, help out in emergencies, help build climb structures, etc. The Aldrich Nursery School in Co-op City, New York City, is such a school. Also the Family Center at the Bank Street College of Education in upper Manhattan is run by a steering committee of parents. The parents at the Bank Street center all work within a couple of blocks of the center and typically lunch with their children and take them on walks. The center was organized like a typical New York apartment home, with living room, bedroom, kitchen, bath.

To avoid the common pitfall of cooperatives of losing momentum when the children of the founding parents leave, the Bank Street center tries to take only children at a young enough age that they will be able to spend three years at the center.[8]

The large organized coops that have hired staffs really come under the broad heading of "group" day-care centers, which we will look at now in some depth.

The Big "Group" Day-Care Centers

Most of the activist organizations that are calling for more free or low-cost day-care for mothers with jobs have group centers in mind, not so-called family day-care run by one person.

There are now many thousand group day-care centers. Most are run for profit, legally or illegally. Some of the legal ones are nonprofit. A few of the very best centers are university research facilities. Poor parents entitled to federal aid can usually enter their children in most such centers.

In the Boston area some group day-care centers have factual names such as Hawthorne Day Care Center, but many others — mostly run for profit — have names on the cute side, such as Wee Care, Wee Toddlers, Busy Bee Day Care, Kiddie Kollege, Our Place to Grow, Kiddie Country Club, Tiny Tots, and Goose Gander Nursery.

Two of the group care centers I visited in Boston were within the same block. At one, motherly types were busy picking up and rocking toddlers in rocking chairs, and male aides were playing games with the children. At the other center nearby four young female attendants stood chatting with each other for at least fifteen minutes while toddlers wandered around aimlessly or gnawed on their playpens.

SOME REALLY BAD CENTERS

In Boston, which ranks above most cities in day-care quality, there are still, as indicated, horrendous situations. Most, but not all, are illegal.

Occasionally the state's Office for Children shuts down a fast operator who has managed to get a license. The legal process of revoking a license, however, can take up to a year.

Some of the unlicensed group day-care centers operate something close to straight warehousing of children. They pick the children up in vans, store them away in places with few play materials, deliver them back home at night. Parents are so desperate they typically complain to authorities only when their child comes home hurt.

A state licensing official said: "We see a van packed with say sixteen small children, early in the morning or late in the afternoon, and try to follow it at least long enough to get the van's license number and run it through the registry. The illegal operators store the kids in houses all over the city. We get after them. They disappear and later we discover them somewhere else.''

I talked with eight licensing officials in Massachusetts. Here is some of what I learned.

They often get a complaint that a program is overenrolled, with twenty children per attendant, but if they go to see it they may not be allowed to enter without a court order.

One said, ''If we fine them, all they do is move. There is one operator we have been chasing for a good many years. One of the times we found her she had forty children in a five-room apartment.'' The children ranged from infancy to age six. She uses a van, picks up and delivers, mostly in the Dorchester and Mattapan area of Boston. The officials said it is very hard to get complaints against her because she has a reputation for threatening parents who file complaints against her.

Some centers using vans will not even allow a parent to walk into the center without an appointment. They want the parents to call a day in advance before coming. They know parents might be disturbed by a place that is dirty or not serving adequate food. In some centers, cans of food are just dumped together to make a meal. The children may simply be left to wander around. One official added, ''When transportation is provided, parents are less inclined to go check the site.''

I asked how would parents subscribe to a service like that. An official explained: ''They get the phone number from an ad and make the arrangements over the phone. Sometimes they are stalled if they ask to visit. Or they are shown a site, but it is not where their child actually goes. The operator may take the child to a low-rent place outside the city. The use of vans makes it very easy for the provider to isolate the center from the parents.''

Another higher-level licensing official in Boston told me this startling story:

''A mother left her toddler off at the licensed center. An hour or so later she remembered she had not left medicine which the toddler was supposed to take and she hurried back. She found that her child was not at the center she had seen, and demanded to see him. She was taken to a three-family house several blocks away. Her child was on the second floor, which was entirely covered with dirty mattresses. The mattresses were fully occupied by infants and toddlers. Her child was one of them.

There were more than twenty children attended by a woman and a helper. Now this was a legitimate day-care operation, but it had not been licensed for infants and toddlers.''

One of the investigators of the National Council of Jewish Women's survey found one eastern day-care center where babies were stacked in cages.

In many states a license to run a group day-care center does not mean it is necessarily even of average quality. Most states focus on such things as safety, food quality, amount of space, and fire hazards.

Cleanliness in both facilities and practices can be an important factor, it turns out, in all kinds of child care facilities. In early 1983 the *Journal of the American Medical Association* carried a report that day-care facilities had become "networks" for spreading diarrhea, dysentery and other intestinal diseases. An official of the National Association for Child Care, in commenting on the report, put the focus of the problem on children up to the age of two, because their immune systems were not as developed as those of older children.

A day-care center may look fine physically, but after you have visited it for a while you notice that the handling of children may be mechanical: there may never be any eye contact, never any smiling or cooing to infants. Some centers have plenty of toys to display to parents but keep them in storage most of the time. It is simpler to let the kids sit in front of a television set than to bring out equipment, supervise its use, then put it all back at the end of the day.

These of course are just the bad examples of what you can get into in putting a child at a center without properly investigating it.

PROBLEMS IN FINDING QUALITY GROUP DAY-CARE

Millions of parents want *quality* group day-care for their children, and some achieve it. The major reason why most of the group care presently available ranks from mediocre to poor is money. That is one of the major current dilemmas of day-care.

In the Boston area a really good infant and toddler center needs close to $500 per month per child to function well unless there are volunteers or a special deal on rent. Most of the cost of running a day-care center is payroll. When the center is run for profit — without volunteers —the expense for teachers is only about $450 to $550 a month and for aides about $365 to $400 per month. This poor pay produces very high staff turnover, which of course is bad for the children.

For general day-care, if you increase the staff load from say five children per caretaker to eight children per caretaker, the staff costs drop about 40 percent. Some states specify the maximum number of children per staff member. It may or may not be enforced.

From the child's standpoint an even more frequent and more acute source of feeling ill at ease is the sheer numbers of children at a center, regardless of staffing. Even if there are a total of fifteen caretakers, a child who finds itself amid a hundred other tots running around often feels stress, if there are not solid, soundproof walls dividing up the children into small groups. The adults in centers get free periods but the children almost always are together, even when they are asleep.

Another common trouble with group day-care is that staffs may work on a team basis. Teams are tolerable for preschoolers. They are bewildering, however, to an infant or toddler under two years of age, for whom attachment to one adult figure is still very important. It is like having four substitute mothers at the same time. Some centers assign a primary caretaker (or caregiver) to each infant and toddler. In practice, however, several caretakers are apt to be in touch with the tot each day. A special person, for example, may run the nap room. Attendants tend to operate a kind of zone defense, to use the football phrase. The probability of multiple caretakers is also enhanced at many centers because they have a shift of staffs around midday. Most centers stay open ten to twelve hours a day because parents may have a long commute, need to shop, etc. Most caretakers consider ten hours too exhausting to tolerate. The caretakers are relieved by another crew in early afternoons. The fact that a ten-hour day at the center may also be seriously exhausting to a child is given less thought. When the new crew comes on this may mean two or three more substitute mothers for the child. In the course of a ten-hour day the infant or toddler may find itself being supervised by a half-dozen attendants.

At the parent-managed day-care center I visited at Co-op City, New York — a nursery which was restricted to children more than two and three-quarters years old — many of the children were picked up by parents or relatives at noon. But at least ten children were staying on for the full ten-hour day. The director thoughtfully puts those who will stay on in a separate room at 11:30 so that they won't be depressed by all the mothers or relatives coming to pick up their playmates. The separate room has cots and an adult supervisor. Some children nap. When I peeked in some were asleep, some were still bouncing on their cots. At one o'clock they were brought out to begin the afternoon session with a new set of playmates. Since these were older children, they probably could handle all the change. But hundreds of thousands of infants and toddlers are left at day-care centers for the full ten-hour day with shifts in both children and caretakers. For many of them the experience must be like enduring a nine-hour cocktail party.

EMPLOYERS' EFFORTS TO PROVIDE CARE

One of the more impressive group day-care centers I visited was created by a corporation, primarily for its employees with children. It is on the premises of the Stride Rite Corporation, a major maker of children's shoes. The center is one of the few established by corporate employers that has survived. The location: in the blighted South End of Boston.

The day I visited, there were about fifty children present, all over two and three-quarters years old. About half were children of employees, two of them in management. The other half were from the community. Stride Rite founded its center as a tax-deductible community contribution. The operating costs in 1979 came to about $3,000 a year per child. The cost is shared among the company, the Massachusetts Department of Public Welfare, and the parent-employees. A parent who is a Stride Rite employee pays 10 percent of his or her gross weekly salary for the weekly fee of each child enrolled.

Since Boston has a host of colleges and unemployment is currently high among certain types of college graduates, the Stride Rite center is staffed largely by people with at least some college education. The pay was minimum wage. Some attendants were male. As you approach the center you pass a playground built entirely by parents with materials supplied by the company and community. It is sort of an adventure-type playground with lots of tires, chunks of telephone poles, blocks of wood.

Inside there are two main areas: (1) green floored, where children can run and yell, and (2) blue floored, located behind the kitchen area, where a child is supposed to do quiet things. During my visit they were getting ready for lunch. Children were setting the tables. A three-year-old hollered: "I need two more forks." Shortly after noon, nearly a dozen working parents at the company ambled in to join their children for lunch. I asked Mariam Kertzman, the director, if the center had a TV set. She said:

"Never."

Every month or so the center has a supper, picnic, or outing for the school's children and their parents.

A few other New England companies, such as Polaroid and Connect-icut General Insurance, have been getting into day-care for employees' children indirectly. They make payments per child to independent day-care centers which the employees' children attend.

In Freeport, Texas, a maker of heart pacemakers, Intermedics, set up a day-care center as a business subsidiary for quite practical business reasons. Officials concluded that much of their problem with absentee-ism and tardiness was caused by the problems female employees had in arranging child care for their children. Also they concluded that a day-care center would give them a big edge in attracting new female em-ployees with young children. Within a year it had a center with 250 children. Employees pay only about $10 of the $55 a week per child it costs to run the center. The company picks up most of the rest, but at relatively little real cost after it makes deductions from company taxes for operating losses of its day care subsidiary. It viewed as business gains a sizable drop in turnover of personnel and a drop of about six hundred hours a week in absenteeism.

THE KID-CARE CHAINS — AND THEIR COLONEL SANDERS

The yawning gap between the number of mothers of young children with jobs and the number of facilities to handle the children has struck some entrepreneurs as spelling business opportunity, if cost factors can be overcome. Demand awesomely exceeds supply.

Into this gap have come the day-care chains. They grow on the basis of brand-name familiarity, savings through economies of scale by stand-ardization and mass production, colorful facilities, promises of enrich-ment programs, and most important, fees that many desperate parents of moderate means can bear. Most of the chains began looking into this child market around 1970. Some seem sincerely interested in the chal-lenge of making quality day-care more widely available; some seem primarily fascinated in empire-building with parents' dollars.

Quality varies from quite good to not so good. You don't get horror stories regarding day-care chains. Like Burger King or motel chains, they couldn't survive really bad publicity. Some people in day-care as-sert that children and profits don't mix. The final answer on that is still not in.

The chains listed below are among those that have attracted the close interest of Wall Street investors quick to recognize a potential hot growth situation. A couple years ago *The OTC Review* for investors had an article on "the burgeoning child care center industry" and advised investors of five stocks they could buy to get a handle on this growth industry. They were then all over-the-counter stocks. All had attractive earnings per share.

The five listed in order of size of dollar revenue were:

1. Kinder-Care Learning Centers, headquartered in Montgomery, Alabama.

2. La Petite Academy, headquartered in Kansas City as the then most profitable division of the conglomerate Cencor, Inc.

3. Children's World, headquartered in Evergreen, Colorado.

4. Living and Learning Centers, headquartered in Waltham, Massachusetts.

5. Mary Moppet's Day Care Schools, Inc., headquartered in Tempe, Arizona. It is primarily a franchiser.

Since that listing was compiled the number one, Kinder-Care, has absorbed Living and Learning Centers, then fourth. Meanwhile a big newcomer has emerged, National Child Care Centers, Inc., headquartered in Houston, Texas. At this writing it is still privately held. It features, "Laughter, Learning and a Lot of Love." National Centers are mostly for children over two years old but some units take infants. Its average center accommodates 150 children. The company advises me that TV is "not emphasized."

As for parent involvement, it advises: "Working parents are too busy to be involved in policy formulation and are satisfied to let NCCC's professional staff develop each program." A Living and Learning official, before it was absorbed, said that parent-participation really didn't work there. "The majority of our children are coming out of recent divorces. The mothers have lots of adjustment problems."

Of the major chains, Children's World, with around a hundred centers, seems by far to be the most idealistic and serious about trying to serve the needs of young children. It has not tried to get a standardized Kentucky Fried Chicken type of image. Some of its centers are highly innovative in design. Its president, Robert Benson, once worked with the National Urban Coalition and has been active with the Public Agenda Foundation, which has been studying "childcare" as one of America's major problems in the coming years. He also seems to be highly regarded by officials of the National Association of Elementary School Principals.

At Children's World centers, parent suggestions and participation are actively sought. Head teachers have college degrees. Although the pay to staff is modest, only 30 percent of its staff get minimum wage whereas at some of its rivals the proportion of minimum wage runs up to 70 percent. Children's World offers and encourages employee ownership of stock. It scrimps on overhead and tries to avoid anything gimmicky. Its centers are mostly in Colorado, California, Texas, and the Midwest.

It averages about 100 children per center. At first it tried an "open" format with "classrooms" divided by low lockers. But now it is moving to "more contained" classrooms with permanent walls.

Children's World will not take children under eighteen months of age (infants) except at one hospital-based center. Ten of its centers are in housing developments.

And now we come to the giant Kinder-Care Learning Centers, renowned for its money-making prowess. A New York financial writer spoke of Kinder-Care's zeal for profits and was critical of the fact that the company was using its tens of thousands of children as a "captive market" to sell life insurance.[9] And that's not all it sells.

Kinder-Care, with close to fifty thousand children, has expanded in about a decade from three centers in Montgomery to at least 750 centers in thirty-six U.S. states and two Canadian provinces. Many centers take infants and toddlers, but mostly the day-care children are two and a half to six years old.

In five years its earning per common share leaped more than 700 percent. In March 1981 the big investment counseling service Value Line Special Situations Service singled out Kinder-Care as its top new recommendation. Nine months later, although a national recession had cut into profits, the service forecast that the price of the stock might well triple in four years.

Kinder-Care mostly stays out of inner cities, catering to middle-class and lower-middle-class suburban-urban clientele. Its centers are open eleven hours a day on weekdays. They also often operate in the evenings and on weekends for "drop-off care," where parents can leave a child while going to a party. It employed Joyce Brothers, the famous columnist, to promote Kinder-Care in television commercials.

The founder of Kinder-Care, Perry Mendel, has been called "The Colonel Sanders of Child Care." He foresees doubling the number of centers, and has said that he owes much of his success to a careful study of the merchandising techniques of the fast-food chains. "There's always been a hamburger, but it took McDonald's to bring it along," he said in 1978. Some of his centers are near fast-food outlets since both have the same respect for high-traffic areas, except that Kinder-Care prefers to be one street back from the heavy traffic because such sites are lower in cost and somewhat quieter.

When all the excitement about the need for group day-care began in the 1968–1970 period, one of the first day-care chains was developed by the same company that owned Minnie Pearl Chicken franchises. It didn't thrive.

At about this time, Mendel, a Montgomery businessman, got interested. He is a sharply dressed, polite but hard-driving man who has driven around Montgomery in a white Cadillac. His business background was in auto parts and later in real estate. When he got wind of the opportunity presented by so many job-holding mothers with young children he persuaded eight businessmen to put up about $200,000 to help him launch Kinder-Care. His first idea was to sell franchises, where local owners of centers would buy use of Kinder-Care's name, know-how and equipment, to raise the "front dollars." He did indeed use a Miami promotional firm that had helped launch Lums restaurant chain. But his ads for franchisers drew too many "ex-teachers and ex-ministers" who would love to get into day-care but didn't know the first thing about getting buildings up and operating. So he chose to keep ownership and turned to selling stock.

Mendel's director of operations responsible for setting up the educational aspects of Kinder-Care was a sharply dressed man somewhat in his own image, Col. Arthur E. Boudreau, who was former registrar of the Air Force Academy. Colonel Boudreau retired in 1981. The official who now handles the chain's operations division, Gene Montgomery, had fast-food and other food management experience.

The business journal *Forbes,* in an article entitled "Perry Mendel's Golden Diapers," quoted Mendel as explaining: "Truly I think the one secret of Kinder-Care's success has been the development of a sophisticated real estate department . . . that can work with developers." A contract with a developer to build a dozen centers permits economies of scale. One developer in the Southwest has built more than twenty-five Kinder-Care centers. Also Kinder-Care now makes deals with developers of apartment complexes to put centers in or near the complexes. The developer can then advertise the center as an amenity to attract families with job-holding mothers. This I consider an excellent trend, if the centers are good.

Mendel shrewdly locates his centers "on the morning side of the street'' for a parent driving from her or his home. Thus harried parents dropping off children aren't bothered by left turns and having to cross a median line on their way to work.

Kinder-Care is seeking to make its image as familiar to Americans as the McDonald's golden arch or Howard Johnson's orange tile roof. Its basic image now is an orange tile steeple at the entrance. The steeple is topped by a black, plastic nonringing bell. Inside, the typical center is pretty much open space with four or more ''classrooms'' vaguely divided by low closets where the children hang their clothes. There is a walled-in area in the center of some buildings for infants and toddlers. Outside typically there is a playground. Mendel says his company ''makes no provision for television.''

The standard center with few inside walls is built to accommodate 100 children. Some can accommodate up to 280 children. The ratio of children to staff runs around ten to one, or considerably less staffing than is mandated in a licensed facility in Massachusetts. Still, the staffing is not far from the present national average. Mendel told me he complies with state regulations, which tend to be minimal.

Staff people start work at or very near the U.S. minimum wage, which as indicated is not unusual. Directors of centers in 1977 were paid about $35 a day. A Kinder-Care executive told security analysts in that year that maybe a third of his people had a ''degree'' and the rest ''some education.'' This ratio with degrees may be improved now. One benefit offered is that staff people with children get a reduced rate for their own children.

Tuition fees are moderate by the standards of the privately operated end of the industry. In 1982 the weekly charge varied from $35 to $75 depending on geographics and age category. This moderate rate is helped on the low end by the fact that a large majority of the centers are in the Sun Belt where living costs, including heating costs, are low.

One secret of Kinder-Care's success that some consider questionable is that it uses its child populace of about fifty thousand (and still growing) as an outlet for all sorts of selling strategies. In 1979 Kinder Life Insurance Company added $147,000 to the parent company's profits. Kinder-Care has a competitive edge in selling insurance on children since its sales costs are minimal. Kinder-Care's merchandising branch promotes to the parents of its children T-shirts, totebags, and wooden toys. At least thirty thousand parents also have bought a package of photographs of their child. Now Mendel has decided he has enough children to sell a host of children's items to parents by the catalogue showroom concept. Mendel is even thinking now of working with manufacturers of products to let them try out products and services aimed at children on his children.

Kinder-Care promises to develop children. It has in its effort developed an $85,000,000 empire. Perhaps it might reasonably be said that Kinder-Care is profitably meeting a very large demand by applying the very best techniques available to private enterprise.

KINDER-CARE CENTER NO. 578

From its now vast experience in competitive profit-making day-care, Kinder-Care has learned some lessons on how to makes its services agreeable to parents and children alike. I should add that there appear to be noteworthy differences in the quality of care among its more than 750 centers. Many of its centers, for example, are acquisitions.

Though there were numerous Kinder-Cares near my Connecticut home in New England and upper New Jersey, almost all were acquisitions. I wanted to see at first hand one of the newer now standard bell-tower centers. The nearest was in Mt. Laurel, New Jersey, so I journeyed there.

The center, eighteen months old, had a standard bell-tower design and a capacity for ninety children. Yes, it was located on the "morning side" of Route 537 going west toward Philadelphia, Camden, and the big RCA plant. It was not only on the morning side but was located by a bus stop. And it was located on the edge of a large new housing development of $100,000 homes. The center was growing but was still operating at only about two-thirds capacity because of its recent start between sessions, because of the recession that hit while it was trying to open, and because of the fact that many of the nearby development houses were still sitting empty.

This Kinder-Care center number 578, an integrated facility, is open from seven A.M. to six P.M. The inside design was standard: a big U-shaped open space divided only by children's coat-hanging space into four "classrooms." Everything seemed clean. Walls were covered with colorful numbers and flowers.

About forty-five children were in the main open area when I arrived. They had been resting or napping all over the place on lightweight plastic "cots," really oversized trays that stood about six inches off the floor and were slightly sloped so that the child's head is higher than its feet. Most children had their own blankets.

As the children were told that the nap period was over, some went to drink water from built-for-small-children spigots. In a couple minutes the teachers and aides — average age about twenty-one — had tossed all the tray-cots onto stacks along the wall. The staff members were cheerful and seemed to have pretty good rapport with the children. One called out, "All right, you guys, it is time for the good resters to have snacks."

Apparently that day all had been reasonably good resters. They gathered ten to a low table for the snack. Some looked droopy or forlorn, but most seemed refreshed and were noisily chatty.

The enclosed central area of the building contained a nursery. The Mt. Laurel center was then accepting only toddlers for nursery between one and two years old — no babies. And most extraordinary — it was then charging only a dollar a day extra for nursery care and that was said to be a diaper-changing fee. There were then ten toddlers with two staff persons attending.

The center's director, Nancy Pete, a slim, cheerful, candid young woman, had her small office right in the entrance of the center. There she says she can watch what is going on inside and added, "I get used to the noise." She has a degree in early childhood education from the University of Delaware. The overall staff ratio was about nine children per staff person; in the nursery five to one. Child-care experts would call both ratios on the skimpy side, but not really bad.

Those two staff persons in the toddler room acted as a "team," which might well cause most experts to frown. A child apparently was not assigned to a particular teacher as a surrogate mother. One of the nursery staff women explained to me: "I take five of them and the other takes five. They are never the same five. We play at peg boards, block boards, string beads and after that free play. Any toddlers still around after 4:30 are put in the open area with two-year-olds."

While the center is open eleven hours a day for children, no staff person works more than eight hours. The fee for full-time day-care five days a week was only $48, more attractive I gathered from parents than most other day-care centers in the area.

The pay of the staff is astonishingly low considering the caliber of the staff. Aides start at the minimum wage (then $3.35 an hour in New Jersey). And teachers earn just ten or fifteen cents an hour above minimum. Teachers get ten- or fifteen-cent-an-hour raises depending on performance. Yet three of the five teachers had some advanced schooling in early education. One possible explanation for the seemingly good caliber of the aides — given the very low pay — is that a nearby community college supplies students taking early childhood education courses for child-care experience at the center.

Regarding the use of Kinder-Care children as a market for commercializing products and services, Ms. Pete said that the insurance option is on every child's application form. The most subscribed sales venture with Mt. Laurel's parents is the portrait-taking. Parents are notified as to when a picture-taking team will be at the school in the fall or spring. Parents can, if they want the picture, dress up their children. The teams, I gathered, photograph every child interested in posing and parents pay if they accept the pictures. The main office of Kinder-Care arranges by contract the portrait-taking of its tens of thousands of children by an international portrait-taking corporation. Corporations in the business of taking children's portraits on a mass scale in the U.S. have grown to more than a billion-dollar-a-year industry.

By late afternoon the center's day was starting to wind down slowly. Parents dropped by in a fairly steady stream to pick up their children. By five o'clock day care had boiled down pretty much to baby-sitting with children mostly milling around or playing outside.

Some of the mothers walked in and without a word wrote out their $48 weekly checks. Others chatted with Ms. Pete about medical problems or brought in a new bottle of medicine. One mother called to explain she would be late because of extra work. Ms. Pete told her, "I'll be here until six." It is not unusual, she said, for parents not to show up by closing time. The center charges $5 for every fifteen minutes the parent is late. If a parent is frequently late the center imposes a flat $20 charge for lateness.

A few fathers came. One looked startled when I asked if I could get his thoughts on child care. He said, "Oh, you want to talk to the boss." He led me out to the car where his wife was sitting. Some fathers have never even seen the center.

Altogether I chatted with more than ten parents. One said, "I tried a dozen places before I found this and I'm not going to change." The following day I got in touch with four of the parents for more extended talks.

The four seemed generally satisfied with Kinder-Care center number 578, though I heard a few mild reservations about play equipment or food. The staff, as one put it, "is good with kids." Two of the four mothers said, however, that they had had quite negative experiences with other Kinder-Care centers in the lower New Jersey–eastern Pennsylvania area. One mother complained that a previous Kinder-Care center which she had tried was overcrowded, with a poor ratio of staff to children. The staff members acted as if they didn't really want her to get past the reception office. And she asserted it used television at times to keep the children occupied. The Mt. Laurel school, she said, does not.

Two of the four mothers, Sandy Opfer and Barbara Birkett, cited isolation of their children as the main reason they had put their children into group day-care instead of using other available caretakers in or near their home.

None of the four parents had bought insurance through Kinder-Care. One said she didn't receive a photograph because her child screamed when the team tried to take her picture. None of the four seemed to resent — or even be aware of — the fact that Kinder-Care was using their children as a captive audience for its merchandising projects.

Kinder-Care center number 578 had no parent's organization nor did it encourage parent participation as far as I could find. Ms. Pete said, "Most parents are so busy with their children and outside interests that they don't have too much time to be involved with the center. The center does have Parent Nights a couple times a year to explain and discuss its programs."

One of the parents, Mrs. Denise Hardy, an RCA technician and the wife of a bricklayer, confirmed that there was no parent organization. She said that she goes to Kinder-Care every day during her lunch hour break to be with her fourteen-month-old daughter Lisa. She helps feed Lisa her lunch and plays with her for half an hour. But she is exceptional. She said her women friends at the plant who had children in day-care thought her odd to make the trip to be with her daughter at lunch. She said they tell her: "That's what I'm paying them for."

SOME UPSET PARENTS

At about the time I visited Mt. Laurel in 1982 there was an uproar among parents at a Kinder-Care center only thirty miles from my home, in Brookfield, Connecticut. The Brookfield center had been acquired by Kinder-Care as part of a package deal when Kinder-Care bought out the Living and Learning chain of thirty-five centers in New England, which had a reputation for above-average care. I had in fact checked out one of its centers in Waltham, Massachusetts.

The uproar in Brookfield occurred when Kinder-Care gave one week notice to parents that it was closing down the Brookfield center. It had also closed down two other acquired centers in Torrington, Connecticut, and Pittsfield, Massachusetts. Apparently only the Brookfield parents fought back.

Their center, which they liked, was in a two-story converted barn on the wrong side of the highway for morning traffic into the city of Danbury, where many parents work. The management cited rising costs and declining enrollments. The parents charged that if the center was in trouble it was because Kinder-Care had done almost nothing to advertise the center after acquiring it and did not even list it in the phone book.

A management spokesman meeting with the parents seemed eager to pacify them, presumably because of all the bad publicity being generated by the parents. He promised to keep the center open for at least a few more months.

Another reason the management was upset perhaps was that it was just then building in nearby Danbury its first standard design bell-tower center in all of New England. It was to become Kinder-Care center number 755.

In a chat with me a national official of Kinder-Care mentioned casually that the chain was getting rid of some of its acquisitions that were "not on the morning side of the street." This official added:

"Parents just don't take to them. Convenience is the biggest consideration."

Kinder-Care has apparently reached the business decision, probably soundly based, that most parents are primarily thinking of themselves, not their children, when they select a day-care center for their children.

HOW OTHER SOCIETIES COPE WITH CHILD CARE

Most modern societies outside the English-speaking world and Japan have been quicker than English-speaking countries to face up to the problems — and the institutional gap — created by the job-holding mother. They have introduced institutional adjustments. That does not mean they have always come up with neat solutions from the child's standpoint.

Outside the U.S. the societies that seem to have gone the farthest in trying to fill the child-care gap are:

- those countries seriously concerned about maintaining population growth, such as France and Israel;

- those concerned about recruiting more women into the work force, such as China and Russia;
- those countries which have traditionally been alert to social trends and been quick to make social innovations, such as Sweden and Denmark.

Here are some specifics on coping activities outside the U.S.A.:

England and Canada   They have tended to resist the idea of group day-care centers for children under age three. For very small children they seem to prefer some kind of home setting, handled by someone well known to the child. They have preferred to stick to informal arrangements.

England has a relatively small proportion of job-holding mothers of small children. Only about a million children under age five have mothers who work. England has registered child-minding facilities for about eighty thousand children. One guess is that there may be three hundred thousand children in unregistered facilities. About a fifth of the preschool children go to nurseries for a couple hours a day. The country has a pretty well-organized hierarchy of child-minders: two grades of live-in nannies, live-in teenage girls from mainland Europe seeking to learn the English language, and baby-minders (usually mothers) who come in by the day.

Japan   This society has been slow to relinquish its once-strong conviction that the place of the mother of young children is in the home. Facilities for the care of children under the age of two are very hard to find. Some companies do guarantee to a woman having a baby that she can have her job back after a couple of years. Still, there has been, quite recently, a rapid rise in career women who want to get back on the job within a matter of months after the child is born. An array of informal, often unregistered, facilities have sprung up to meet this demand for help. Alice H. Cook, who studied the problems of working mothers in nine countries, described one such facility outside Tokyo that probably was an extreme:

"I found twenty children under eighteen months cared for in two tiny rooms on the ground floor of what had once been a shop. Babies were swaddled and laid on shelves, toddlers were confined to a large playpen. . . ."[10]

France   This nation cherishes its children and has introduced a host of official policies to encourage parenthood, a movement begun long before the emergence of job-holding mothers of small children. For more than a century starting with the Napoleonic wars, the nation's population was repeatedly drained to the point that population growth became a national concern.

Out of this concern has come a far-reaching policy for assisting families with children. There are financial allowances for families with children, allowances for mothers who remain in the home with their children, maternity leaves for both mothers and fathers who have jobs, and two very extensive programs for the care and development of small children:

- Creches. Working parents can deposit their children during work hours from infancy until they are two or three years old. Parents pay a fee geared to their income. Some are primarily rooms full of cribs with attendants, others are more stimulating.

- Écoles maternelles. These are in effect free public nurseries and kindergartens run by the nation's educational system and are available for children from age two to six, where there is space. They can take children full day or part day. A relatively small proportion of two-year-olds of the nation have been going to these centers, but by age three a majority of the nation's children are enrolled at least part of the day. The national government pays 80 percent of the cost, the local municipality the remainder.

Scandinavia   Most of the Scandinavian countries have comprehensive government-aided child-care programs with parents paying fees geared to their family income. These programs include both family day-care and group care centers. In Sweden this care is available as soon as a child is six months old. Since there is a shortage of facilities, some kinds of families receive priority treatment. These include single-parent families (which are unusually prevalent in Sweden), low-income families, families in which both parents have jobs or are studying. Staff ratios tend to be excellent, commonly one adult to four or five children.

Perhaps more notable, Sweden passed a law allowing sick leave to parents with jobs if a child is ill.

Denmark also has some remarkable innovations. The national and local governments pay about 70 percent of all costs of day-care. Their programs stress parent involvement, and at least a fifth of the staff of a town's day-care facilities must be male. Copenhagen has bought more than twenty farms near the city and has established child-care facilities on them. Children are bused out to these centers.

One of Finland's more novel concepts is to pay a "mother's wage." The mother of young children who does *not* hold a job and who does not use the forms of day-care made available by Finnish society is paid a modest salary. This is considered fair, and gives mothers somewhat more options.

Also common in Scandinavia are "park mothers" who watch over and supervise the play of children left at the parks by their mothers. In some cases where mothers work the children spend the mornings in nurseries and the afternoons in the parks. Or the mothers simply use the parks when they have to shop or want their child to get some outdoor play without having to sit and watch.

All these Scandinavian innovations have been adopted after spirited debate and free democratic vote. They represent a willingness of people to pay more taxes in order to see that their children are well taken care of in these changing times. (Few Scandinavian countries have heavy defense budgets as a tax burden.)

The Soviet Bloc   Moscow is relatively rich in child-care facilities, according to Alice Cook, who made the nine-country survey. Still, many parents prefer to leave children with grandmothers (who still often live in the same dwelling as the family) or relatives or neighbors. Less than half of the Soviet Union's young children ever see the inside of a day-care center. Soviet ideology promotes day-care for a number of reasons. Communist doctrine going back to Lenin stresses the importance of the liberation of women from the drudgery of home work. Further, in Soviet Bloc countries women seem to be urgently needed in the work force and often are made to feel they are being less than good citizens if they don't have jobs. And finally the Soviet leaders have a clear interest in getting children early into situations where they can be indoctrinated with group values.

A quarter-century ago Soviet leaders proclaimed that by 1980 all Soviet children would be group-reared. Many parents tend to dote over their children, and think of group day-care as a last resort. Commonly the Soviet centers hold 150 to 250 small children, which makes for an upsetting environment except where there is strict division by rooms. Many of the Soviet state nurseries are attached to the place where the mother holds her job.

Other nations in the Soviet Bloc are far from monolithic in regard to child care, though all have a substantial involvement in day care. In most of the East European countries the movement is away from use of group day-care for children under the age of three.

China   In terms of sheer numbers the Chinese have vastly more children in day-care than any other society. And the children often enter earlier, when the mother's two-month maternity leave is up. Perhaps 40 percent of China's young children are in nurseries that are either free or charge a small fee, or that are cooperatively run.

Chinese children strike many foreign experts as remarkably sunny, well-behaved and perhaps docile. Day-care as it functions there does not seem to be producing any notable increase in emotional problems in children.

Since China is in transition from an intensely family-oriented society to a collective society, it is probably early to assess the long-term impact of the large-scale shift of mothers into jobs. However, some things should be noted as peculiar to China. Places of work are still normally very near to the child day-care center. The mother leaves her job to breast-feed her child twice a day and is permitted an extended lunch period with the child. Grandparents often are attendants of nurseries. It is still the Chinese custom that children under age three sleep with their parents or grandparents.

SOME GUIDELINES FOR SIZING UP CARE POSSIBILITIES

Let's assume at this point that you are a parent in a bind. Perhaps you head a one-parent household. You have no option but to seek — and immediately — some form of full-time child care for a small child. You have no relatives, friends, or neighbors who could reasonably be expected to help out more than on a temporary basis. A full-time nannie, let us assume, is too expensive. A sitter if she works more than twenty hours a week must be paid minimum wage, which would run costs up at least to $130 a week, counting free lunch. If you split the job up among lower paid sitters, the price comes down but the anxieties about failures to show go up. And so in the U.S. many are basically left with the facilities and services available under the U.S. day-care system.

The choice you make can be enormously important to your child. Yet an Arkansas-based day-care chain concluded from a survey of middle-income parents that the number-one consideration in choosing a center is convenience to the parents. The second-ranking consideration was cost. Quality came third.

It is barely possible that your area has a child-care information center that will save you a lot of legwork, and provide you with important information on available services and their costs. An excellent, and rare, example is the nonprofit Cambridge Child Care Resources Center in Massachusetts. It has comprehensive lists of group and family day-care facilities and sitters in each general neighborhood and their costs. This helps take a lot of the panic out of emergency needs for help. In any case, here are some factors and possibilities to keep in mind in approaching the search.

Join forces   If you have a child under three, the first possibility in terms of attractiveness is to join up with two or three other mothers in a similar fix and hire a nurse or a mother known to be skilled to come into one of your homes. An alternative is to hire two student pediatric nurses or student teachers specializing in early childhood who can take morning and afternoon shifts while continuing their studies. The advantage of this joint approach is that you have a better chance of getting expert help, the ratio of adults to children will be good, the cost should be affordable, your child will be in his own home or a friend's home, and you will have considerable parental oversight.

Family day-care   This should certainly be seriously considered next if you have an infant or toddler since you will have a home setting and only one substitute mother. While interviewing possible family day-care proprietors, keep these questions in mind:

- Does she (or he) have children herself? How do they look as samples of her mothering ability?
- Does she seem to have a cheerful or affectionate disposition, or is she putting on an act? How do she and your child interact?
- How many children will she be tending, including her own? If you have an infant or toddler a total of three would be a good number. Walk out if there would be more than four infants and toddlers. If there is an assortment of infants, toddlers, and preschoolers, be wary if the total is more than five.
- What kind of a report docs she get from a mother who already is using or has recently used her services?

- Does she seem to maintain a nice clean home?
- How busy is she going to be with housework, television or with neighbors coming in for coffee?
- Does she have play facilities at least as good as your own and have access to a safe outdoor area?
- If the operator has a husband who is going to be in the home part of the day, check his disposition and attitude. He may be annoyed that she is cluttering up his house with kids or be an upsetting presence.
- Are there books or serious magazines in the home? In short, does she seem to be a reasonably literate, articulate person?
- Since she will presumably have a TV set on the premises, what is her policy about using it as a child pacifier? How much time will she sit in front of it herself?

Group day-care   If group day care is considered, there are more variables to weigh. Here are some pertinent questions to keep in mind, with the first six being of particular importance.

How many caretakers (or substitute mothers) will be having regular contact with your child?   In general, the fewer the better. A small child has an urgent need for continuity of relationship, especially if it is under three. The Princeton Center for Infancy has concluded that "nothing is worse than a series of caretakers."[11]

A really well run center will assign one staff person to be in charge of providing motherlike care to each child under three years old, one person who will be responsible for comfort, help, and learning for the child. Observe the center to note how much the staff works as a team, rather than individually with children. If there are two shifts, see both staff persons who will be primary caretakers.

If you select a center, insist that the staff person assigned to your child comes to your home, at your expense, to get acquainted with your child on its own home grounds. And the mother should spend at least an hour of the first day the child is at the center helping it to get acquainted with its new environment. Check also the napping situation. Who will be in charge of that?

England's Michael Rutter cites studies showing that if you have five caregivers and twenty very small children in one room, then no matter how much assurance you are given of individual attention for your child — say four children are assigned to each staff person — the probabilities are that the child will get relatively little individual attention. How well defined is each staff person's area?

What is the total size of the group of children who will be mingling with, or circulating in sight of, your child?   Again, the fewer the better. This, investigators are finding, is a top-priority question. The trend is toward larger and larger groups either to achieve economies of scale or higher profits. According to a federally sponsored study by the Abt Associates of Cambridge, "group size" is the most significant factor in determining the quality of care provided by day-care centers.[12] For example, you get better results by having two caregivers per twelve to fourteen children than by having four caregivers for twenty-four to twenty-eight children.

The younger your child is, the smaller its group should be. There is less chance the child will suffer from apathy or stress. Even for three- and four-year-olds, the child's specific group should not number more than fifteen to eighteen. For the under-two child, its group should not exceed six or seven at most.

How many children are there per staff member?   This is usually referred to as "the ratio." Once again, the fewer children per staff member, the greater the likelihood of achieving quality day-care. If a staff person has so many small children assigned to him or her that the adult can give only sporadic attention to each child, the child may suffer confusion, loneliness, and also has little chance to develop any significant attachment (very important for the under-twos).

Investigators at the Yale Child Study Center have recommended that for infants and toddlers there should usually be one attendant for every two children.[13] Otherwise both adults and tots become overtaxed. We are talking now about high-quality care. Edward Zigler, also of Yale and formerly chief of the U.S. Office for Children, thinks that as a maximum there should be a ratio of one adult for three infants or toddlers. He explains: "One only has to think of the burdens of the mother of twins or triplets to wonder how our caregivers could regularly care for four hungry babies or curious toddlers."

For the over-three-year-old group, many experts recommend as a maximum one adult for eight or nine children. Yet many U.S. day-care centers, even some that include a number of infants and toddlers, have one adult per dozen kids.

A federally funded national day-care study found that three-quarters of the proprietary centers examined had more than ten children per caretaker. They also tended to have the highest staff turnover rates.

In the mid 1970s the U.S. Department of Health, Education and Welfare sponsored a study directed by Henry Ricciuti, human development specialist, which came up with a more precise scaling for infants and toddlers. The proposed ratio of attendants to children:

	Ratio
Under two months	1:2
Two to twelve months	1:3
Thirteen to twenty-four months	1:4
Twenty-five to thirty-six months	1:5

What are the qualifications of the staff person who will have direct contact with your child?   I am not suggesting that caregivers, to use their phrase, have advanced degrees or even bachelor degrees, although that would certainly be a plus. There are many talented college graduates attracted to the early childhood field as a career, or are attracted because they have small children and can bring them to the center at a discount. But don't settle for anything less than a high school graduate with some formal training, perhaps at a community college, in child care and the psychological needs of children at each age level as the primary caregiver of your child — or someone with ample experience in child care. As aides, seventeen-year-old high school students are acceptable. In many areas of the U.S. there are literally no educational or training requirements for day-care personnel. Some of the critical skills of a good caregiver can be taught, some come from disposition and experience, so you need to make your own judgment. One skill relates to "affectivity." In our context it means being good with children. People high in it are not easy to find. Helen Maley, founder of the early childhood program on Martha's Vineyard, advises:

"Don't get sidetracked by equipment, though equipment is important. Watch the children's faces. How much eye contact is there with the teacher? Is the contact warm and friendly?"

Does the caregiver seem to rely heavily on do's and don'ts? (That's unfortunate.)

Does the caregiver seem relaxed when lifting or talking with children? Does she speak conversationally, or in baby talk (unfortunate)?

Does she really listen to what the children say? And does she seem good-natured? That can be vital for people putting in a long day at a child care center.

What is the center's real attitude toward parent involvement?   One of the problems of many day-care centers, particularly the proprietary chains, is that they see themselves as running a business just like auto servicing and don't want or need any help from the customers. Their manuals of procedures come from national headquarters. The parents as bill-payers are jollied with cheery newsletters. Real parent involvement often is viewed as a nuisance.

Two early childhood specialists at the University of Minnesota call parent involvement "a key ingredient in any pre-school program and one notoriously hard to come by."

Here are some reasons why high involvement by parents is important:

1. Parent involvement helps assure that the center will be well run by parent standards.
2. It helps the child think of the center as an extension of home.
3. It helps integrate the center into community life.
4. It makes the parents better parents and helps relieve any guilt they feel about being away from the child all day.
5. Parent involvement can significantly lower emotional costs and may lower dollar costs per child.

But if parents work all day at jobs, can they be involved? Yes, in many ways. They can have regular consultations with the child's primary caretaker, which help both understand the child's interests and problems. Each family has its own style and that should be known by any substitute parent. Parents can work weekends to improve the play area, build shelves, and make materials for the children to use. They can attend weekend picnics and outings to help create an all-one-family feeling. They can visit the center at lunchtime. And they can help raise funds.

One of the better-known day-care centers, The Children's Pumphouse in New York City, is truly parent-controlled. The parents set policy. Each parent is a member of the board. Meetings are held every month and attendance is mandatory. If parents miss two consecutive meetings, they are fined. If they continue missing meetings, their child is dropped.

At the Montessori school which my five-year-old granddaughter attended, all parents were pledged to put in twenty hours of volunteer work during the term. This eased school expenses. But the main aim was to promote parental involvement. At that it was highly successful. I saw the high involvement one night at a fund-raising auction the parents organized.

Will the center help your child's overall development?   This of course is a hard one to answer but should be considered. Do the center's staff, facilities, and programs combine to provide a congenial, cheerful, stimulating place for your child to grow? Or is it oriented to being simply custodial? Is the daily program apropriate for each age level? Is the atmosphere homelike or institutional? Will your child have a variety of materials to work with? And are they reachable?

For older children, does the center have learning excursions and have interesting people such as local firemen to come in to talk about their work? Do the children have a very good chance to develop language skills? Are they given responsibilities such as picking up, setting up the lunch table, and spending time helping a young two-year-old with play materials?

Those are the main questions. Here are, briefly, two more to bear in mind.

Will your child have a chance for plenty of interchange after age eighteen months with children of other ages, or is he lock-stepped with one age group? Some highly regarded centers such as The Learning Center of Philadelphia are arranging an age mix with each unit of ten children.[14]

Does the center have males on its staff as well as females? This is a particularly important consideration for mothers heading one-parent households. A center in Sherman Oaks, California, where there is a very high proportion of single-parent families, is run primarily by males.

We began this chapter by noting that in the U.S. we have a severe institutional imbalance: plenty of jobs for mothers but relatively few good arrangements for substitute parenting while mothers work. Our society must face up to this imbalance. One approach is to make available more abundant high-quality substitute care. Another approach is to make social arrangements that encourage mothers of infants and toddlers to postpone their return to full-time jobs, and provide the parents more flexible working arrangements when the mothers do return.

12

Who Watches School-Agers When School Is Out?

"The needs of young school-aged children requiring some support or supervision before and after school hours have been largely unmet."

— *Louise Guerney, human development specialist, Penn State University*

When mother has a job the problem of child care may be eased but does not go away when her youngsters reach school age. Typically, the school day doesn't start until an hour or so after she has to leave for work. And schools lets out usually two or three hours before she can get home from work. Also there are the three-month summer vacations from schools, and the long winter and spring holiday periods to contend with.

A leading expert on child care during all these hours, days and months when school is out is Michelle Seltzer, director of Wellesley College's School-Age Child Care Project. She says these periods when neither parent nor school is in charge "leave much room for anxiety. Arranging care for children when school is out has become an urgent national problem." Quite suddenly in the last three years there has been a greatly increased groping for ways to handle the problem. Let's look at the main approaches, starting with the simplest:

GIVING CHILDREN KEYS TO THEIR HOME

This, as indicated, is being done by millions of parents. No one really knows just how many. The *Newsweek* study concluded that the phenomenon was "astonishingly widespread." It cited a ten-year-old daughter living in a Columbia, South Carolina trailer park (and instructed to stay inside when alone) as saying wistfully: "Sometimes I would like to go outside and play but there is nothing I can do but stand at the door and watch."

When are children old enough to be left on their own? There is no clear consensus. For example, a lot of parents are concerned enough to be organizing programs after school for their junior high school children. Michelle Seltzer feels that the ages where it is *imperative* for school-agers to have some sort of after-school supervision is up to eleven or twelve, depending on the youngster's self-sufficiency and neighborhood.

Many children age six to eleven who are left on their own by working parents develop skills in shopping, doing laundry, cooking, and disciplining themselves to do homework at a set period every afternoon. James Garbarino, professor of human development at Penn State, cites as more typical however some latchkey children who are left pretty much "on their own." Mary, age ten, theoretically was in charge of her little brother and sister after school, but mostly she just sat and watched television all afternoon. John, age nine, was supposed to fix supper for himself and his younger brother because his mother, a dental assistant, didn't get home until seven o'clock. Actually they played on the streets with other kids until all the other kids had gone home, then they would go in and watch television until their Mom came.

Some children respond well to responsibility thrust upon them. For others it can be thrust too early with ill effects, particularly if the child feels neglected and unsure of parental love. Some parents, too, rationalize promoting self-reliance as positive because it saves them quite a bit of money. (Other parents don't like to but see no other choice.) A few children, at least, develop generalized fearfulness and are panicked by thunder, persist in keeping the TV turned up loud, or crawl under their blankets.

Specific families manage to handle the latchkey approach with positive results. The evidence overall, however, is not favorable. Urie Bronfenbrenner has reported that in general latchkey children "contribute far out of proportion to the ranks of young people who have reading problems, or are dropouts, drug users and juvenile delinquents.'' *The Journal of Social Issues* carried a report that school officials were finding more absenteeism and homework problems among children who came from homes empty during the day.[1]

Penn State's James Garbarino finds there are four types of risks to weigh in considering latchkeying: that the children may feel bad (rejected, alienated, nervous, or lonely); that they may act badly (delinquency, vandalism); that they may develop badly (academic slump); or that they may be treated badly (accidents, possible sexual victimization, etc.). He says, "All four are quite real." The nature of the community and the child's bond with the family determine how minimal or serious the risks are in specific situations.

If the latchkey approach is adopted, here are some things parents can do to help children cope well with the situation. Child development specialist Hyman Rodman of the University of North Carolina, Greensboro, proposes these strict parental rules: no visitors without permission, check in daily by phone with a parent, regulations about snacking, cooking, studying, and TV watching. Latchkeying works best too, he finds, if parents set aside a time when they will be interacting with the youngster after they return home.[2] It helps if friendly neighbors or relatives look in on a latchkey kid regularly, even for the eleven- and twelve-year-olds. Also it helps if the youngster comes home to a be loved pet her or she can fondle, nurture, and talk to.

Meanwhile, some outside organizations are trying to help the latchkey kid cope. An official of the American Home Economics Association is promoting courses in elementary grades that teach both boys and girls "survival skills" such as handling laundry, shopping wisely, cooking. The Boy Scouts of America has launched a new program to help children, age six to twelve, cope with being home alone. Instruction includes handling emergencies, helping take care of younger brothers and sisters, preparing snacks, home safety rules, and developing self-esteem.

RENT-A-MOTHER

Hiring a sitter for a school-ager is not as burdensome economically as hiring a sitter full-time for a toddler or preschooler. If a sitter is required full time, you are not only dealing with someone working a lot of hours, say forty a week, but someone who must be paid at least minimum wage (which is required for people working over twenty hours a week).

In such a situation the pricetag may be in the $125-a-week range. But for someone who drops in, say, three hours a day to be with a school-ager, the pricetag may come down to around $30 a week.

A sitter may be particularly appropriate if a family has two or more children under twelve, including a preschooler. The per-child cost comes down and the day-care pick-up hassle is eliminated.

Whether selecting a sitter for school-agers or preschoolers, a good deal of thought should go into the process, especially if you are dealing with strangers.

A first screening can be done by telephone. The best prospects should be interviewed in person. Anyone seriously considered should supply at least two references from former or present employers. The person referenced should be questioned particularly about the applicant's honesty, disposition under stress, drinking habits, if any, dependability, and skill in dealing with children.

An adult with mothering experience should be preferred; but a sensible fourteen-year-old who has had to take care of younger siblings may be acceptable. A discussion of the activities teenage prospects participate in and what they read will offer clues to how responsible and levelheaded they would be. If you expect the sitter — whatever the age — also to handle household chores, be prepared to pay at least fifty percent more and make sure the chores will not interfere with good child care.

Parents getting seriously involved in use of child care of any kind — preschool or after-school — would benefit by obtaining the federal government's brochure "A Parent's Guide to Day Care."[3] It details, for example, the agreement one should make with an in-home caregiver. One point: "Agreement about visitors, phone calls, television and radio while the caregiver is working."

LETTING ENTREPRENEURS TAKE CHARGE

In upper Manhattan the Billdave Sports Club has vans that pick up youngsters after school. The driver-counselors take the youngsters to Central Park for supervised play activities such as soccer, hare and hounds, treasure hunts. In bad weather they go to a gym. Then they deliver the children to their home when they know the parents will be home from work. The charge is about $48 a week. Also, on Saturday mornings, the driver-counselors will pick up and drop off at the home. Sometimes, a spokesman said, a kid may be picked up at one home, dropped off at another. Quite a few of the parents are divorced.

Most of the day-care chains have begun setting up special programs to provide care and interesting activities for school-agers whose parents work. Children's World centers all have vans that deliver and pick up children at school. It tries to confine this service to the six-to-ten-year-old group. It doesn't stop at ten because the need for oversight ends there but because the over-tens tend to have different interests. Also, President Benson explained to me, "such older children tend to turn their noses up at the idea of attending a 'baby school.' "

Others report that even the younger six-to-tens may get some static from their age peers at school about having to play with "babies" unless day-care centers take pains to put them in special programs.

The giant day-care chain Kinder-Care, which has recently pushed aggressively into the care of school-agers, has invented a special snob-appeal "club" which its school-agers from age six clear up to twelve can join. It is the "exclusive," patented Klubmates, a "School Age Club of Distinction." Klubmates seems to be inspired by Cub Scouts and Brownies but is coed and age-broadened.

Each Klubmate is given a "membership card" upon entering Kinder-Care that can be used as an "entrance pass" to Klubmate activities. He or she is given a Klubmate T-shirt. Each Klubmate can work toward winning achievement badges in such areas as music appreciation, food fun, physical fitness, and ecology.

School-agers upon arriving at a Kinder-Care day-care center after school go to their own area of the center, and have their own teacher. They are given a snack and are permitted during the first hour to hack around, letting off steam after being "regimented" at school. Or they can do homework. Klubmate activities usually run for one hour starting at four o'clock. Those who are not picked up after that hour by their parents may be mixed in with the pre-schoolers and other tots for what often amounts to simple custodial care.

GETTING HELP FROM ONE'S EMPLOYER

A good many corporate employers now are at least staffed with counselors who are qualified to give an anxious employee sound advice on care facilities for school-age children that are available in their area. Honeywell, Inc. and Polaroid are examples.

Those few day-care centers supported by corporations on company sites or near where many of their employees live are starting to add programs for school-agers. Michelle Seltzer advises that the Northside

Child Development Center in Minneapolis, funded by local industries, has a couple dozen school-age children. Public school buses pick up and drop off the youngsters at the center.

A number of employers in the major computer-producing city of Sunnyvale, California, pay for school-ager "slots" at the Sunnyvale Child Care Service Center.

BRINGING IN A COMMUNITY AGENCY

The YMCA, which regards itself as a primary nurturing and developmental influence in children's lives, has belatedly plunged on a large-scale basis into programs for young school-agers who otherwise will be on the streets or going to empty homes. It made a survey of the hundred largest YMCAs in North America as to any new programs needed by local YMCAs and got back a plea from most of the hundred that the YMCAs move more vigorously into school-age child care. At this writing the YMCA is getting up a manual on school-age care for its local YMCAs and has started nine pilot programs for young school-age children. It is advising members:

"There is a tremendous difference between the involvement of a child in a sports program twice a week for ten weeks and the involvement of a child every day after school and during the summer for up to six years. The responsibility is awesome."

One area where the YMCA already is deeply involved in school-age care is in Alameda County, Oakland, California. It is operated by Fred Stickney who has seventeen different "Latch Key Child Development Centers" functioning within the county. Youngsters with only an empty home to go to have opportunities to involve themselves in crafts, drama, music, field trips, sports, photography, etc. He recommends at least one staff person for fifteen children if they are under eleven. If they are older the ratio can go to twenty-to-one.

Community colleges and hospitals in a number of U.S. cities — such as Modesto, California — are also moving into school-age care.

ENCOURAGING SCHOOLS TO EXTEND THEIR DAY

Perhaps one hundred out of the several thousand U.S. school systems now are running their own "extended day programs" for the benefit of children of working parents. These include systems in Minneapolis,

Jacksonville, and Arlington, Virginia.[4] The school doors stay open from soon after dawn until late afternoon.

Austin, Texas, got into a school-run program largely for practical reasons. It was trying to find uses for half-empty school buildings because of declining enrollments. Such uses of once-unused facilities also seemed to help cut vandalism.

Arlington, Virginia, probably has the largest "extended day" program operated by the school system itself.[5] Every one of the county's twenty-two elementary schools has a school-age child care program operating out of its schools. Parents pay about two-thirds of the extra cost to the school; the county pays the rest. And community facilities are drawn upon.

The hundred-odd teachers and aides are not a part of the regular school staff. Many are college students. The teachers are paid about half as much as classroom teachers. However the school principal supervises each center. There are long waiting lists at most of the schools and people say they are moving to Arlington because of "extended day." Still, the programs remain controversial. There are legal and other grounds for questioning whether schools should be getting so directly into child care, especially with school budgets often being cut.

Private schools are under even more pressure than public schools to move into providing child care when school is not in session. Many of the new-style parents (dual career or divorced) who are shopping for a private school for their children now ask each school being considered whether it offers the option of a full-day of child supervision. In New York City about a third of all private schools now are prepared to answer yes.

BENEFITING FROM JOINT SCHOOL-COMMUNITY PROGRAMS

This seems to be the most popular of the routes now being taken on a nonprofit basis. In this "partnership model," the school may provide an unused class area or it may also include access to gym, library, and the homemaking room. It may ask to be reimbursed for custodial and electrical costs, and even rent, or it may not. The main thing is that someone else manages and raises most of the money for the service. For example:

Park district sponsorship   One strong advocate of school-community cooperation is John Ourth, a school principal in Highwood, Illinois, and retired president of the National Association of Elementary School Principals. He told me he had worked out a "sweetheart deal" with the local park district. The school furnishes already existing facilities, the park district furnishes the school-age care program. He explained that his school has the facilities and even trained personnel but no "money." The park district does have "money" and by its charter is responsible for working with children of the community. And the parents of the children make a nominal contribution by paying a fee ranging from 50 cents to $1.25 an hour depending upon the activity. The activities range from gymnastics and model building and playground activity to "clown classes" which he says are a lot of fun.

The Wilton, Connecticut school system near my home has a similar situation of a sweetheart deal. Its afterschool child care program, which runs until six o'clock, is sponsored by the Park and Recreation Department. The cost to parents is about $4 a day.

A nonprofit child care agency acts as sponsor   In Denver, which has about three hundred empty classrooms in its elementary school buildings, rooms are rented out on a per-square-foot basis to the nonprofit Mile High Child Care Association.

A government bureau acts as sponsor   In Fairfax County, Virginia, it is the county's Office for Children that runs the programs in twenty-eight county elementary schools, according to a report in *Education Times*. Parent fees cover about two-thirds the cost.

A parent group administers the school-agers care program   In Brookline, Massachusetts, a group of working parents (mostly mothers) formed a nonprofit organization which made a deal with school officials to run an "extended day" program in all eight Brookline elementary schools.[6] About five hundred children are involved. Tuitions average around $25 to $30 a week per child. School officials feel that a couple of additional pluses of the program (beyond child care) are that (1) it tends to bring closer involvement of parents in school affairs, and (2) it is serving to attract new younger families to a community with a growing elderly population.

Schools arrange with neighbors of children to provide family-type care   Some educators think that, no matter how you slice it, keeping kids involved on the school premises for eight to ten hours a day can be hard on kids, even with field trips. Schools in Orlando, Florida, and Lincoln, Nebraska, are arranging for a network of neighborhood families to take in young school-agers whose parents work.[7] Costs to the parent in Lincoln run around $1.75 an hour. These programs encourage children to engage in quiet activities of their own choosing such as doing puzzles.

THE LONG, HOT SUMMER

Many of the programs described above shift onto a full-time basis during the three months of summer when school is adjourned.

In Highwood, for example, the school and the park district cooperate on a program that runs for six weeks immediately after the summer vacation begins, at a cost to parents of about $20 a week. The school district runs the morning program. This is staffed by certified teachers who are not paid their regular salary but are paid at about $10 or $11 an hour, still a lot more than day-care teachers receive. The park district takes over at noon. Its personnel are paid less.

The Kinder-Care's Klubmates go onto full-time care basis for the six-to-twelve crowd two weeks after school adjourns. At the Mount Laurel, New Jersey, center I visited the fee is $53 a week. Much of the activity takes place at the day-care center but there are outside events.

Eight Kinder-Care centers in the eastern greater Philadelphia area, including Mount Laurel's, combine to run a camp on a private lake near Clemington, New Jersey. As a group the centers also arrange field trips to pick blueberries and to visit local radio stations.

As for corporate involvement in summer care, an example is Fel-Pro Industries in Skokie, Illinois, which makes gaskets and industrial chemicals. Children of employees can go to a two-hundred-acre summer camp which the company purchased. Parents pay a nominal fee of about $10 a week. The company's president said his company felt it had a "commitment" to the children of employees.

Every community, I believe, should be moving to provide after-school programs, which the working parents will help pay for. A case can be made that employers, schools, and the local and federal government should all be involved. The morale and work performance of the working mothers would be improved. And conditions promoting delinquency and emotional upset of present latchkey children would be greatly reduced.

The schools should even question the wisdom of their nine-month school years (with vast facilities empty during the summer). The nine-month school year made sense when most youngsters were urgently needed to help bring in the hay. The availability of year-round programs for children of working parents (and others who want them, or would rather take their three months off in some other season) deserves to be tried on a pilot basis. Year-round programs might well make teaching more attractive by offering the possibility of increased pay.

And even where educational programs are not in progress during the summer, the school facilities should be made available at low rental to community groups that wish — perhaps with their own staffs — to provide supervised child activities.

We have seen that a number of approaches are possible. With experimentation, the best would gradually emerge.

3

Children Whose Parents Split

13

How Divorce Affects Children

"Children are becoming less and less of a deterrent to
divorce."

— *Lucile Duberman, family life investigator*

A thirteen-year-old girl was talking on television to Phil Donahue about
divorce. She said, "Mom shows me old pictures that include Dad. They
seem happy. I wonder why they broke up."

A schoolteacher was telling investigators about an eight-year-old girl
who one day seemed disturbingly withdrawn. After class the teacher,
suspecting something serious was wrong, asked the girl to remain a few
moments after class. At first the girl denied any problem, then blurted
out that the night before her parents announced they were about to be
divorced. The teacher went into her regular counseling routine and
pointed out that a number of children in the girl's own homeroom had
divorced parents. The girl responded: "But you don't understand. They
were smiling. They just sat there and smiled."[1]

We have noted the increased fragility of marriage contracts caused by
a swirl of social changes and changing individual attitudes. It is often
overlooked that marriage and family are not coterminous. Marriage is a
legal unit, the family in its fundamental meaning is a biological unit

which assures the perpetuation of both the species and personal heritages. If there was a better understanding that despite divorce the family goes on — even into legal remarriages — there would be less rancor, confusion, and irresponsibility. There would also be less pain for the children involved in such transitions.

As it is, marital disruption when children are involved has been rising faster than the divorce rate itself. Since 1960 the divorce rate has doubled, but the number of children involved in divorce has tripled. The challenge of coping with young children under today's conditions can add to the strain on a weak marriage. About two-thirds of all U.S. divorces now involve children. At this writing the latest annual report on the number of children involved in divorce is at an all-time high of 1,181,000. Altogether now about a third of all American youngsters under the age of eighteen are no longer living with both their natural parents. For younger children, the proportion is still higher. America is not alone in this divorce surge. In Czechoslovakia 40 percent of all marriages end within a few years.

There are many reasons for the great increase of divorce in America, but perhaps foremost are new life-styles (particularly the exalting of do-your-own-thing), family and community fragmentation created by mobility and rapid urban growth, and a decline in religious belief as a force in daily living.

Studies in California indicate that *actual* divorces peak in the fourth year of marriage and then decline steadily.

Persistent thoughts about divorce lead to low-level tension, avoidance, perhaps chilly silences around the children, and often increased arguing frequently in front of the children.

If parents are good at communicating with each other, they talk about their grievances or regrets. After a series of talks they either go back to living in reasonable amity or agree on a course of action for ending their marriage that will least upset their children. Unfortunately, most aggrieved people are poor at communicating when their emotions are involved.

Soon they find themselves quarreling more and more often, more and more stridently, and more and more openly. Some let their rage move from verbal assaults to slaps, fistpounding and flinging things.

Social welfare professor Doris Jacobson of U.C.L.A. interviewed thirty persons in Los Angeles who had undergone a marital separation within the past year and she sought to assess the conflict leading up to the separation.[2] More than half of these persons reported some type of physical violence, half in front of the children. One-third of these parents reported efforts by one parent to turn the children against the other parent.

Caught in such conflict, small children often regress in behavior. Some go back to crawling after starting to walk. School-age children at these times often get into fights at school, or develop psychosomatic symptoms. Young teenagers are substantially more likely than average to turn to drugs. Michael Rutter, the London child psychiatrist, listed six factors strongly related to psychiatric disorder in ten-year-old children. Number one was "severe marital discord."

Sometimes the appalled children try to referee the conflicts. A college student whose parents divorced when he was eight years old told an investigator of such an attempt in these words: [3]

"Once at the dinner table they were screaming as usual. I started to write on a piece of paper, 'Please stop fighting,' but I couldn't remember how to spell 'fight.' My mother saw me and asked what I was writing. I started to cry and couldn't stop."

A family counselor in California told me of a girl there who crawled under the living room table whenever her folks started fighting.

In the tapes I have of teenage girls in Lexington, Massachusetts, talking about the parting of their parents, the comments of one girl are particularly interesting.

This girl, on receiving the news (when she was age twelve) that her parents were parting: "I feel so guilty because when my Mom first told me about it we were in Florida. She said we were moving up to Maryland and getting a divorce. All I could think of to say was that I would finally see snow . . . which was really rotten of me. But all I could think of was snow. I was just thinking, well, it's just another move in my life because up to that point I was in seventh grade and I had been in seven schools. Now I am in my twelfth."

The lucky youngsters are those who can find someone to talk to — preferably within the extended family — about their own feelings.

As marital disenchantment intensifies, one of the partners may simply desert the household with no talk of divorce. Historically the husband-father has left. The margin was about three hundred deserting husbands to one deserting wife. Today increasingly it is the wife-mother who departs, and without the children. An executive of Tracers Company of America, the largest company specializing in searching for missing persons, confirmed to me an enormous upsurge in runaway wife-mothers. In some years his company now searches for more wives than husbands.

During the 1970s its business in tracing missing husbands declined while its caseload of runaway wives nearly tripled. Other search specialists around the country report a similar picture. As one put it, a "tremendous switch" has occurred. The runaway wives tend to be persons who married young and have school-age children. They feel trapped, want to "do their own thing," as one West Coast searcher of missing spouses put it.

A study of thirty-eight runaway wives in the Toronto area revealed they had abandoned a total of 103 children.[4] They cited lack of communication or lack of common interests as major reasons for taking off. Most claimed it was best for the children to leave them at home with the father, who was more secure financially. A majority professed that they missed their children.

Most of the wife-mothers in the study had indicated to their spouses that they were thinking of taking off, but quite a few of these failed to mention they were going to leave the children behind. Only one-half of the mothers discussed with their children their plan to leave.

Some offered the explanation that their children were too young to understand. Those who reported they did try to explain their planned departure to their children reported that about half said they understood. Others were upset. One mother who had left confessed wondering if her children would hate her when they were older. About half of the 103 children were actually in the household at the time the mothers went out the door.

More commonly, disaffected spouses try separation before divorce. Here the children typically stay with the mother. Divorce may not even be contemplated because of religious restraints or because one spouse wants to prevent the partner from remarrying. Sometimes the couple has a trial separation either to see if absence will have a healing effect, or to ease the blow of marital dissolution to the children. When the father prepares to leave, whatever the explanations, the children may scream and clasp him and implore him not to leave.

For parents who really want to leave each other, the legal act of divorce has been made to seem easy. In San Diego a judge divorces couples by the roomful. And in widely available literature, divorce has been made to seem courageous and life-enhancing. Books have such titles as: *The Courage to Divorce; Divorce: Chance for a New Lifetime; Divorce, the Gateway to Self Realization; Divorce: the New Freedom;* and *Creative Divorce.*

The author of the last, Mel Krantzler, suggests that the "real" family is no longer necessarily "the best structure for raising children."

A marital breakup frequently comes as a complete surprise to the children even though the partners may have quarreled before the children. Doris Jacobson, in her study of thirty separated families, cited earlier, found that a third of the children had not been prepared in any way by their parents for the separation. The best-adjusted children were those who had been given the most preparation.

The wear-and-tear on children who live in a household where the parents are in a state of silent or noisy warfare has caused some observers to argue that divorce can be good for children. Divorce may come to the children as a relief from tension. They'll be better off, it is said, living in a one-parent household where they can at least have a good relationship with one parent.

There may be something to that argument if there is an absence of any real desire on the part of the parents to work toward an accommodation. But, as we shall see, a petition for divorce does not bring instant tranquillity for the children. There are some "civilized" divorces where the transition is eased for the children. But civilized divorces are the exception. Some involve "empty shell" marriages in which for years the relations between the spouses are increasingly perfunctory as they lose interest in each other although they may be doing an adequate job in their role as parents. For such cases the parents may find relief by separating, but the children involved may lose more than they gain by the parting.

In the great majority of cases of divorce involving children, relief is not the first reaction of children. They bleed awhile.

CHILDREN'S REACTION TO THE FACT OF DIVORCE

Some children can, with seeming coolness, handle the news that their parents have parted. They may exhibit bravado and deny that anything important has happened. Most parents are so preoccupied by their own fury or grief at the time of parting that they simply do not notice what is happening inside their children's heads.

The fact is that the act of parental divorce is a devastating blow to most youngsters.

Their first reaction, if they are under ten, is panic. The shock to the child's own self-esteem is likely to be particularly severe if he or she had a loving relationship with the departing parent.

Younger children commonly believe the departing parent is abandoning them (which he or she sometimes is), and some fear that in all the turmoil both parents will disappear.

Morton and Bernice Hunt, investigators of divorce, tell of an eight-year-old boy named Mark, whose father had left a full year earlier and was a thousand miles away in Florida. Mark had resumed bedwetting, and suffered from recurring nightmares. The Hunts report:

"He would awaken, crying wildly and clinging to his mother . . . would ask again and again, 'If you go, who will take care of me?' "[5]

Another common source of panic in younger children is guilt. Because the young child's thinking tends to revolve around himself, he is likely to feel that the divorce somehow is all his fault. He has not been a good child.

E. Mavis Hetherington, a leading authority on children of divorce, found that children from the age of three to eight were particularly prone to have these guilt feelings.

Most children of divorce sink for a while into a state of grief, particularly those under twelve years of age. However, they cannot accept the idea that the cause of their grief is more than temporary. They keep expecting the departed parent to return. Albert J. Solnit, Yale pediatrician, said: "For the rest of their lives, children whose parents divorce when they are young will long to and make partial efforts to reunite their parents."

The longing for the parent to return takes subtle forms. A nine-year-old girl refused to wear a coat in the winter in an effort to get sick enough that both her parents would unite in helping her get well.

Lora Heims Tessman, clinical psychologist at the Massachusetts Institute of Technology, tells of a girl named Linda. Her father left home when she was eleven. For a full year Linda insisted on sleeping in her father's bed. Even in adolescence she wrote a poem that ended:

"From the depth of my spirit I call to you; come with the rising sun."

In her memoir actress Lauren Bacall recalls that when she and her second husband, actor Jason Robards, divorced after an erratic marriage their son Sam kept hoping that "we would get back together again." Even after six years he still had fantasies of their reuniting. His fantasies by then were so unrealistic that arrangements were made for him to undergo counseling.

As noted, children are remarkably resilient. Given certain conditions, they can take a lot of turmoil. Still, for some the emotional disturbance created by divorce can be a serious matter. John McDermott, chairman of the Department of Psychiatry at the University of Hawaii, says:

"Divorce is now the single largest cause of childhood depression."

A review was made of the family backgrounds of several hundred children who had been seen consecutively for psychiatric evaluation at the Department of Psychiatry of the University of Michigan.[6] It revealed that children of divorce showed up at the clinic at nearly twice the rate of their occurrence in the general population.

We now have two particularly well-done studies on what happens inside a household where there are children living with their mother after the onset of divorce. (One parent has departed and divorce has occurred or is in the works.)

First I will describe the comparative study focused primarily on one age group. The principal investigator here is E. Mavis Hetherington, long affiliated with the University of Virginia. Her associates were psychologists Martha Cox and Roger Cox.

Their study involved ninety-six families who had children of nursery school age. Half of the families had recently gone through a divorce; the other half had intact marriages. The two sets of children were matched by sex, age and birth order, and came from the same nursery school. Behavior of the two groups of children was compared, after one group had gone through divorce. Extensive assessing was made of both the divorced parents and their children two months after the divorce had occurred; then again one year after divorce; and finally two years after divorce. In all cases the children were living with their mother.

The stresses of adjusting to the divorce peaked at about one year after the event. By the second anniversary of the divorce most of the stresses had receded and parenting had improved, but some of the boys had taken on some distinctive behavior patterns as we'll see. Little boys much more than little girls seemed disoriented by parental divorce.

During the entire first year after divorce life in the divorced households was far more disorganized than in the intact households. Meals were more likely to be pick-up events eaten at irregular times. Newly divorced mothers and their children were less likely to eat together. Bedtimes were more erratic. The children were read to less before bedtime than were the intact families' children, and the children of divorce were more likely to arrive at school late.[7] Even the absent fathers were living what one father called "a chaotic lifestyle."

Two months after the divorce, relations between the divorced parents in all but four of the forty-eight divorced couples were characterized by acrimony, anger, feelings of desertion, and resentment. Oddly there was a good deal of ambivalence. Attachments persisted and in some cases improved now that the couple was not obligated to face each other every day. A half-dozen ex-couples even had sexual intercourse in those first two post-divorce months. And four fathers baby-sat while their ex-wives went out on dates.

At the two-month mark, about a fourth of the divorced men and women were experiencing "an ebullient sense of freedom" tinged with apprehension. By the end of the first year the elation was largely replaced by depression, anxiety, or apathy. Those feelings gradually eased in the second year. Parental self-esteem was low at the end of year one, particularly for mothers of boys. If the mothers had jobs, there was less of a collapse of self-esteem. They were steadied by social relationships with fellow employees — but they experienced considerable harassment in arranging child care so that they could work. The investigators observe:

"It is hard to nurture if you want nurture yourself." This feeling contributed to the typically poor relations the divorced mother had with her children. Another factor contributing to her poor job at mothering was the loss of support and authority she had received in parenting from the now-absent father. If the children still had frequent contact with the father, they were less apt to behave obnoxiously.

The divorced mothers tended to become more restrictive with the children and to issue commands that were commonly ignored or resisted. These divorced mothers, beset by their own troubles, were typically given a bad time by their children, particularly by boys. The children tended to nag, whine, and make dependency demands. Boys tended to become belligerent. One mother reported that the first post-divorce year with the children was "like getting bitten to death by ducks."

The more that conflict continued between the divorced parents, the worse the children behaved, and the more troubled they seemed.[8]

At the end of a month following divorce the children showed more constricted play patterns. Play is particularly important at this time in reducing tensions. These children were less imaginative and more repetitive than their counterparts from intact families. Often they just watched others play. Girls soon were back to playing like the girls from intact families. But even after two years, boys were more solitary, less cooperative, more constricted, and less imaginative in their play than their counterparts from intact homes.[9] Additionally, boys from divorced families generally were unpopular with their male peers, had difficulty gaining access to play groups, and were spending more time with females and younger peers.

As for the parents, one of the surprising findings was this: *at the end of two years of divorce the majority of former marriage partners thought the divorce might have been a mistake and that they should have tried harder to resolve their conflicts.* (Sixty percent of the men and 72 percent of the women were of this regretful opinion.)

Psychiatrist John McDermott did a smaller study of sixteen children at a nursery school in Ann Arbor, Michigan, that helps illuminate the impact of divorce on children at this nursery school age. He followed their development for several months after a parent had filed for divorce and divided the children's overall reactions into three categories:[10]

- Essentially unchanged. There were only three of the sixteen in this group. They still had good relations with both parents. The parents had apparently cooperated in preparing the children for the break.

- Severely disorganized. Here there were only two youngsters. McDermott called them "lost, detached children." Possibly they were already in ego trouble when the divorce struck. They seemed in a daze. The boy forgot where his locker was. The girl chewed on her hair and on her stuffed animal, messed her pants, and kept asking the teacher to retie her shoe laces.

- The sad, angry children. These accounted for more than two-thirds of all the children in McDermott's sample. In school they displayed anger, depression, grief. Typically they became possessive, noisy, restless. They pushed, kicked and occasionally bit peers in contrast to their pre-divorce behavior. One four-year-old boy cited as typical of this group had been well socialized. Now he began knocking down blocks and throwing other children's toys, dishes, and puzzles. Then he would sit for hours in a swing looking tired and sad.

McDermott got the impression from his small sample that boys showed more dramatic reactions to the news of divorce than girls.

THE DIFFERING IMPACTS BY AGE

Does the hazard of pain to the child vary by age? Yes, in some interesting ways. Experts seem to agree that the two least threatening times to divorce are when the child is under fifteen months old or more than fifteen years old. In all the years between there is a strong likelihood of pain, but there are wide varieties by age in its form and intensity. At different age levels children seem to cope with their disrupted family in different ways.

Infants feel the impact of a marital disruption only indirectly. The anger and distress generated by divorce may disrupt the mother's capacity to nurture, or her ability to build in the infant a sense of trust. For the younger toddler — when attachment is so important — the main attachment typically is the mother. Thus the disappearance of a father probably will not cause any long-term distress. If the father has been a major caretaker, however, his disappearance will cause the child to be distraught.

Lora Tessman tells of a seventeen-month-old boy who kept searching every crevice of his mother's apartment for his father and crying. This went on week after week, even though the father picked the boy up for weekly visits. During the boy's first year of life, the father had been the primary caretaker.

Several systematic studies of the immediate impact of family disruption on children at different age levels have been made. The most comprehensive look at the impact of divorce across the age spectrum of children occurred in the high-divorce, well-to-do Marin County north of San Francisco. A total of 131 children from sixty divorcing families were studied and followed. All were drawn from the general population. A series of studies by age groupings of the children were made. The children of divorce ranged from two and a half years to adolescents. For most of the work the principal investigator was Judith S. Wallerstein, who is on the faculty at The School of Social Welfare, University of California, Berkeley. She is also executive director of the Center for the Family in Transition. Joan B. Kelly, formerly of the University of Michigan, was the co-principal investigator. There were four others on the staff.

They saw the youngsters and their families soon after divorce; did a follow-up study one year later; then still another after five years. They issued reports on several age categories. A report on the overall California Children of Divorce Project has more recently become available in a book by Wallerstein and Kelly, *Surviving the Breakup*. Here are some of the reported findings by age of the Wallerstein and Kelly group.

Reactions of the preschool child   The youngsters in this group ranged in age from two and a half years to six.[11]

In the Wallerstein and Kelly study a majority of the preschool children seemed to be getting back into developmental stride by the end of year one. This may have been influenced at least partly by the fact that the divorced families had access to counseling during the post-divorce crisis at the Divorce Counseling Service of the Community Mental Health Center with which Wallerstein and Kelly were affiliates. Even so, 44 percent of the preschool children in the Wallerstein and Kelly study "were found to be in significantly deteriorated psychological condition at the follow-up a year later." None of these children had any prior history of psychological difficulty. Many of the children felt that somehow they had been responsible for the divorce. To use Piaget's term, they engage in "magical thinking." They develop prelogical, magical explanations of cause and effect.

Unlike Hetherington and associates in their study of nursery level children, Wallerstein and Kelly found among their preschoolers that girls seem to be more vulnerable to the stresses of divorce at this age. However, the significant problem found in boys by Hetherington's group — developing relationships with peers — was primarily noted two years after divorce. The time-frame was different.

Wallerstein and Kelly divided their preschoolers into three groups.

Youngest preschool group (two and a half to three and a quarter). All of the youngsters in this group showed acute regression in toilet training following divorce. They had few mechanisms for relieving their suffering. The most enduring symptom was a "pervasive neediness" for relationships. This showed itself in a too-quick reaching out to strange adults. They wanted to sit on strange laps or hold any adult's hand.

A boy named Alex who had been very close to his departed father spent hours a day listening to his father's phonograph records or trying to call him on his toy telephone. The three children who were worst off at the end of a year all came from households where the parents were still feuding.

Middle preschool youngsters (three and a half to four and three-quarters years). These were closest in age to the nursery school children Hetherington studied. These middle preschoolers are of particular interest because virtually no feuding was reported among the parents. Thus any behavioral change was likely due to the parental separation per se. After divorce these children as a group became more whiny, irritable, and aggressive. They still were unable to master their hurt through play, even though one child played house by placing both doll-parents in bed together.

The most notable finding, however, was that even though there was little open parental discord, most of the children in this group were worse off psychologically at the end of one year than those in either of the other two preschool groups. This would indicate perhaps that four-year-olds are the most vulnerable to sustained hurt by divorce of all small children.

The oldest preschool group (five to six years old). For the first time we have children who seem to have a reasonable understanding of what had happened to their family. They could articulate their sadness and their longing for their father. Many of these children were disturbed before the divorce by the growing tension between their parents, so the fact of the father moving out was not so stunning as it was to the younger children. When the news of divorce came, there was a general increase in anxious and obnoxious behavior. In a matter of months some of these children had regained their liveliness and self-confidence and showed no basic setback in development. About a third were worse off psychologically at the end of a year.

The early elementary school youngsters   There were twenty-six children, aged five and a half through seven, in this group. Kelly and Wallerstein termed these children in "early latency."[12] In psychological terms, latency means the post-oedipal years when sexual urges lie dormant.

With these youngsters there was no longer any guilt about having been responsible for the separation of their parents (presumably due to more sophisticated cognition — they have become more logical, less self-centered). A year after divorce they did not cling unreasonably to fantasies that the absent father would return, though most — especially boys — still held a strong loyalty to the father.

After the initial shock, the primary response of this age group was a pervasive sadness. Roger, age seven, said he was very, very sad about the split. . . . He said he had to hold it in or he would be crying all the time. It would be embarrassing to cry at school.

In the first interview Dan denied the divorce had presented any particular problems for him. He was glad the divorce was over. Several months later he asked for an interview to talk about the "awful bad problems I am having at night."

Most of these youngsters found their world shaken by the divorce and began showing fear about how it would affect their own future.

Another new kind of problem began afflicting these first- and second-grade youngsters. There was a clear tendency for them to worry about antagonizing their mother. They were now old enough so that one or both parents often sought to enlist them in an ongoing battle with the other spouse. Kelly and Wallerstein found that among most of the parents of children in this age group there was still considerable bitterness and self-righteous accusations. The children were not shielded from the accusations.

Some of the children became notably overweight. One girl had eaten her lunch by ten in the morning. About half of the children at some point suffered a noticeable decline in school performance. And about a fourth of the children in this group were judged to be significantly worse off psychologically at the end of a year following the divorce.

(An elementary school counselor in Lexington, Massachsetts, advised me that children of divorce seem to him at this age to "get extremely frightened because they don't know who is in charge of their lives anymore.")

The later elementary school youngsters Wallerstein and Kelly termed the thirty-one children, aged nine and ten, in this group as being in the late latency sample.

At first these children, they reported, seemed to fare better. Many went into their first interview with "presence, poise and courage."[13] Their soberness, clarity, and occasional bravado at first startled the investigators. There was little of the disorganization and immobilization that characterized the early latency youngsters. Some seemed eager to talk. A girl Mary said that if she didn't talk about it soon she would fall apart.

Instead of being immobilized they tended to be galvanized by the divorce. One girl embarked on a frenzied campaign to reunite the parents by scolding and yelling and often made it impossible for her mother to have dates. She almost succeeded in reversing her mother's decision to proceed with the divorce petition.

The single most conspicuous reaction of these youngsters was intense anger. The anger — often close to fury — was directed at one or both of the parents.

They still thought their parents were dumb for getting a divorce. In one family both children strongly opposed their mother's decision to proceed with the divorce even though they had seen the father hold her down on the floor and stick bobby pins in her nose.

These youngsters had trouble thinking through what the divorce did to their identity. They exhibited a strong impression of loneliness.

Another thing new with this age group was that these children — now fully capable of logic — voluntarily began taking sides in the feuding between the father and mother.

Again in half the cases schoolwork dropped notably at some point during the months following divorce but most recovered by the end of the first year.

While these youngsters seemed more poised in the face of divorce, they were still showing more problems at the end of year one than the younger early latency children. Fully half, at the end of a year, were showing more distress in interviews than they had in their initial visits.

The adolescents   While the overall sample of the Wallerstein and Kelly study was large (one hundred thirty-one) it happened that only twenty-one were teenagers. Still, the impressions gained are interesting. The investigators expressed surprise at the degree of initial distress shown by them to the news their parents were parting. However, most recovered relatively rapidly and several showed marked increase in maturity at the end of a year.[14]

They displayed sharp anger and a substantial amount of shame that their parents had broken up. Often they did not tell their closest friends. Perhaps this was because they wouldn't feel comfortable making explanations.

Some of their distress was practical. The divorce threw a great big question mark over who was going to finance their plans for college and career preparation. Another source of discomfort was the sudden heightened awareness of their parents' sexuality at a time when sexuality was becoming so important in their own lives. The father's dating and the mother's overnight male guests caused uneasiness. Several of the subjects themselves began showing a high level of sexual promiscuity. Some reacted by expressing aversion to the idea of ever marrying.

Like the preteenagers they got caught up in the loyalty conflicts put to them by the parents. However, they were better able to handle this than the preteenagers. They handled it mainly by withdrawal, by putting distance between themselves and their bickering parents.

By the end of the first year those teenagers who had been reasonably stable before the divorce had almost all bounced back. Those who had most clearly gone into withdrawal now were realistic about the situation and even showed compassion for their parents. For example one girl who had withdrawn into a cool, self-centered stance had now willingly taken over much of the care of younger siblings and seemed genuinely concerned about her mother's welfare.

The sharpness of the initial pain and the defensive act of withdrawal have since been noted by others assessing reaction of teenagers to divorce. For example:

- Pediatrician Murray Kappelman of Johns Hopkins University notes: "Many parents wait until their children reach adolescence to divorce, believing that this is the best time, since the children are now grown up. This is . . . false, for teenagers react extremely badly to divorce. An adolescent who is rebelling anyway finds it very difficult to deal with the disintegration of the home." (Wallerstein and Kelly would probably agree, but note that adolescents seem better able to bounce back over time.)

- Bonnie Robson, a Toronto child psychiatrist who did one-time interviews with twenty-eight adolescents, said that as a group they went through shock, anger, and some relief before finally accepting the situation. Their main concern was to "know where they stand."

- Lora Tessman, in her study of teenage reactions, found some vigorously taking sides and expressing their disapproval. They lapsed into depression and withdrawal. She described the withdrawal this way: "Many adolescents temporarily turned against a previously much loved parent figure during the aftermath of divorce. Their own need to disengage themselves to some extent from their past affection at this time in their lives played into the volatility of their reactions."[15]

For a while in the 1970s, when the divorce rate was soaring, there was a tendency to look on the bright side and stress the resiliency of children. Divorce was becoming a part of the new life-style. Child psychologist Michael Lamb, of the University of Wisconsin, said, "The effect of divorce on children is not necessarily harmful." The large survey by the Foundation for Child Development of 2,300 youngsters aged seven to eleven concluded from responses that "many children got through divorce without being upset or disturbed by it and apparently without developing emotional or behavior problems, at least not by the time they are 7–11." (It probably should be noted that this was a survey of opinion.)

More recently a number of experts have been taking a dimmer view.

The focus of their concern is not so much that youngsters of divorce may suffer developmental setbacks and long-term emotional disturbance. (Some do and many do not.) Rather, their concern is with the attitudes these youngsters may take into adulthood. The editor of the professional newsletter *Marriage and Divorce Today* interviewed a large number of therapists at a recent conference of the American Association of Marriage and Family Therapists. Some may unwittingly reflect a vested interest in seeing people involved in divorce as having problems. At any rate the editor found that many "expressed increased pessimism about the future of children of divorce. They see massive troubles ahead unless something is done to counteract the trauma, depression, etc. that these children are now facing." This did not mean they would be traumatized ten or twenty years from now. The editor paraphrased one respected therapist in these words:

But there are bound to be patterns which develop from these experiences — patterns which many already see developing. One such pattern is the refusal of the child of divorce to make a serious commitment to any relationship. To this group serious commitment such as marriage means the beginning of the end of any relationship. Another pattern: taking marriage lightly — the minute you encounter problems follow in your parents' footsteps — get a divorce. All married couples face problems, but too many of this group refuse to make any commitment to working them out.

In short does the divorce surge today beget a far bigger surge of divorces and singlehood tomorrow?

Child psychiatrist Richard A. Gardner of New York, who has testified in many divorce proceedings involving children, put much the same apprehension in these even stronger words:[16]

Because of their exposure to these extra traumas and stresses it is not surprising that children of divorce do not fare as well as those who grow up in intact, relatively stable and happy homes. Children of divorce are likely to be less trusting of human relationships and to look upon them as unstable and unreliable. When older, they may avoid and shun marriage altogether in order to protect themselves from what they consider . . . a relationship doomed to failure. If married they may feel insecure in the relationship with the spouse — expecting rejection and abandonment.

He was speaking, I assume, of broad tendencies, not inevitabilities.

One of television's more prescient dramas of 1981 showed a bride bolting from the wedding scene before the ceremony occurred. She was a child of divorce. When she was finally located, she sobbed: "I'm afraid of what happens when the loving stops."

The reduction of our spectacularly high rate of divorce where children are involved should be considered as a national challenge. Meanwhile, we need to work to minimize the short-term and long-term effect on children already involved in the divorce process, through smarter parenting and more widely and readily available counseling services before and after children arrive.

While the averages suggest trouble ahead for children of divorce, many youngsters come through in fine shape. Who are they? This deserves more long-term studies.

To a very great extent the prospect of an agreeable outcome for any particular youngster depends upon the custody and visitation arrangements that are made by the parents and the nature of the youngster's future relationships with both the divorced parents. Let's look into the poorer and better arrangements and relationships specifically regarding custody and visitation.

14

Children as Prizes
or Pawns in Court

"You simply cannot divide a child fifty-fifty."
— *Sally Provence, Yale Child Study Center*

Some months ago a divorced mother of two children was thrown in jail by a Maryland judge for falling behind in her child-support payments. Her husband had won custody of the children, aged six and eight. He earned $300 a week, which may have been a factor in his winning custody. She made $165 a week and was supposed to pay $30 a week for child support.

Yes, things are changing swiftly regarding the dissolution of marriages where children are involved. And the court battles are getting uglier.

More and more tens of thousands of children each year find themselves anxiously waiting as their estranged parents, or the parents' lawyers, parry over who will get custody and what chances the children will have to see their noncustodial parent.

A decade ago it was assumed that the no-fault divorce laws would end the acrimony long associated with divorce cases. Much of the nastiness *has* disappeared for childless couples. If children are involved, however, the acrimony can be prolonged and intensified. Charges of marital misconduct, parental incompetence, a lack of moral behavior or mental stability are valid points of contention in settling arrangements for child custody, support, and visitation if parents get into court contests.

Legal contests over custody have greatly increased not only because of the great upsurge of divorce but because old assumptions about handling custody have been overturned.

Nearly half of all divorces involving children end up one way or another as court cases, and about a third require a number of court actions, according to a study cited in a 1979 issue of *Journal of Divorce*.[1] In many states the courts are so swamped with battles over children that there can be a two-year wait, with the children living in a kind of limbo.

A spouse who loses a decision can come back at the winner with a series of court challenges on the grounds of changed circumstances. One custody case in San Francisco was in the courts more than twenty times in four years.

Father may demand custody now because under the new sexual equality they have often been sharing or partly sharing child care with a job-holding mother. The sharing of care may have deepened their love for their children. As divorce approaches, some parents actively compete for the affection and loyalty of their children.

But some fathers have other reasons for getting into a custody contest. They may be trying to embarrass the now-loathed wife. Some husbands fight for custody when they really want the house, not the children. Or they seek custody as a bluff to force the wife to accept less of a contribution from them in child support. *Money* magazine carried the assertion that "more and more fathers take one look at the child support schedules and immediately ask for custody." A law review article stated that one often hears counsel cynically remark, "It is amazing how custodial claims can be shifted by relinquishment of an appropriate number of dollars."[2]

A recent development has been the fighting between the parting spouses on who is going to be able to claim the children for tax deduction purposes. These deductions include not only about $1,000 per dependent but medical bills which can be high if a child is getting psychiatric counseling (perhaps because of the stress of family turmoil) or orthodontia.[3]

The general rule is that the parent who has custody the most months of a year gets the deductions, but there are a couple of exceptions if the noncustodial parent is contributing significant support.

Or a custody claim may spring from a desire for revenge because of infidelity. Nancy Weston, who works to try to unscramble continuing custody battles in the Los Angeles area, told me that sometimes it is very hard to find out what it is they are really fighting about.

Weston explained that a parent who feels abandoned — such as a mother who has been left for a younger woman — may have a deep psychological need to hold on to the children out of a sense of isolation. There is so much pain and loneliness associated with divorcing that both parents may cling to their children out of their own need for comfort and connectedness instead of putting the needs of the children first. They may not be aware of their motives.

You can even have husbands suing for custody because they feel a need for a male heir and want to control the last name of the child. Ordinarily the parent receiving custody decides what last name the children will have. Older children may insist on deciding the matter themselves. Occasionally they start using a hyphenated name incorporating the last names of both parents.

Children often are misused in the court contests. Attorney Marion Robinson of New York, an expert on family law, has been involved in many dozens of custody cases. She told me that emotions run so high in these disputes that whether consciously or unconsciously "the child becomes a pawn more often than not." This is the case, she said, even though the child may be loved.

Family law authorities have deplored the "revolving door litigation" over custody and visitation. The realities, however, are that run-of-the-mill matrimonial attorneys may encourage an adversarial mood in their clients. The bigger and longer the conflict, the higher the fees. Lawyers are often the only winners. Their fees in custody cases typically run between $6,000 and $14,000, at least in urban areas. A leading New York judge, Charles D. Breitel, complained in 1977 that protracted custody cases are often handled on the basis of how much the lawyers can make out of them.

I sat in on a number of cases. One in New York City stands out as an example of a child thrown into a traumatic situation and the competing parents thrown into turmoil by a hard-pressed judge trying to cope with a mass of custody contests.

The courtroom was packed with present and former husbands and wives, stepparents, and a thirteen-year-old girl. A lot of lawyers impatiently paced about, looking at their watches while waiting their turn.

The judge was middle-aged, softspoken, and a bit bald. As the morning went on it became clear that he was trying to run a tight ship. He bawled out his aides if anything was out of order. In making decisions he spoke slowly, but when questioning witnesses he rattled out the standard questions so rapidly the witnesses seemed stunned.

Then the Walker case was called. (The name is changed.) The father and his new wife were seeking to gain custody of his thirteen-year-old daughter from the mother and her new husband. The father, a small businessman, was testifying. He was attended by a plump, weary-looking lawyer whom I will call Ms. Leopold. The judge was trying to refresh his memory. To the father:

"You say you are seeking custody of a thirteen-year-old daughter?"

"Yes, she is right there." He pointed to a chubby, nicely dressed girl with glasses seated in the audience.

The judge stared at the child and, addressing the lawyer in a thundering voice, ordered her to get that child out of the courtroom immediately. The lawyer tried to explain, but the judge would not listen.

Addressing the room the judge announced sternly: "I don't want a child in this courtroom. And I will deal very peremptorily with any attorney or litigant who brings a child into my courtroom."

The child was led out by her father, who immediately returned because he, like the other principals, didn't know what was going to happen next. The judge, apparently to punish the attorney, said he would come back to the case in a little while. He began rapidly processing some other routine cases with his aides.

I went out into the corridor. The girl sat alone in a chair by the door. She looked distraught but was not crying. I tried to cheer her up by observing that courtrooms were not very nice places for kids. She simply said she wanted to live with her daddy.

I went back into the room and sought out Ms. Leopold. She looked disgusted. She whispered that the judge had specified that the child be on hand to give testimony. He had simply forgotten. I asked if children really were forbidden. She said that children quite often were in that courtroom. "He just doesn't like to have small children around because they are apt to cry and created a disturbance," she said.

After about fifteen minutes the judge returned to the Walker case and called up the two attorneys for a conference. Then he announced that he had concluded that the child's testimony was relevant and would talk to her in chambers. Ms. Leopold went to fetch the girl. The other lawyer, a pug-nosed young man, went into chambers with the judge.

In about twelve minutes the judge returned and resumed hearing cases. The two lawyers called both the families out into the corridor. In a few minutes I strolled out. The two families were seated in two clusters about fifty feet apart in the hallway. The girl was seated between her father and stepmother and had her arm on her stepmother's lap. I gathered that the judge had ruled for the father but had ordered that the lawyers work out details about visitation before he announced his decision.

Each lawyer would confer with his or her client for a few minutes and then return to a midpoint in the corridor. There the lawyers would whisper a while and return to their respective clients. This went on for about twenty minutes. The natural mother, a plump woman in bulging slacks, was apparently being stubborn about something.

Finally they all went back into the courtroom, except the child who was told to remain outside. The lawyers signaled the chief clerk that everything was in order. After the judge had disposed of the pending case he called the two attorneys for a whispered conference, then called for the litigants of the case to come up before him. The father and stepmother went and stood before the judge. Ms. Leopold, the lawyer, stood nearby. The judge swore them in. Then belatedly the natural mother and her lawyer joined the group. The judge looked bewildered. He addressed the mother:

"Who are you?"

"I am the girl's mother."

The judge looked at the other woman and said, "And who are you?"

"I am the girl's stepmother."

The judge clasped his forehead, shook it a few times, and directed the stepmother to go back to her seat and reprimanded the woman lawyer for her carelessness. The stepmother, he said, was not a litigant.

The judge had his decision along with all the agreed provisions read into the record. He kept amending details. The father was to have custody of his daughter but the mother was to have the right to see her daughter for a twenty-four-hour period every weekend if she wished, but not on the father's premises. The father was not to leave New Jersey with the daughter for any reason without giving the natural mother written notice thirty days in advance.

PROBLEMS IN HANDLING CHILDREN IN COURT

In a legal contest over custody it is generally agreed that the principal party of interest is the child facing possible loss of an important affiliation in its life. The competing desires of the parents to possess the child are secondary. Yet the child is usually on the sidelines.

How are the child's interests protected?

Courts traditionally have held that children lack the competence to judge what is good for them.[4] Older children may have firm, emphatic preferences. Yet traditionally a fourteen-year-old's view was considered as incompetent as a four-year-old's. Young children may not even be competent to give a coherent indication of their preference. Take the poignant case of a six-year-old boy who had been handed over to his mother for custody. When the boy was asked in court what he thought about it, he said he wanted to live with his father. His feelings were probed on this. Where should his mother then fit into the picture? He said: "I already have her." What he wanted was both his parents.

Boys have been thrown in jail for leaving the parent who won custody of them and going to the parent who lost custody. One fourte-year-old boy's intensity of preference regarding custody in the late 1960s helped bring awareness among judges that a youngster's preference deserved attention. The boy was in the custody of his grandmother on his father's side. His mother petitioned the court for custody and the right to send him to military school (*Marcus v. Marcus*).[5] In a wild court hearing the boy flatly refused to accept the judge's approval of his mother's petition. The judge sternly told the boy that if he didn't obey that he, the judge, would have the sheriff enforce his decision.

On appeal, the appellate court decided the judge had gone too far in refusing to take into account the intensity of preference of a "young man of fourteen years of age."

HOW DO YOU LEARN CHILDREN'S PREFERENCES?

Some judges still do not attach much significance to the preferences of youngsters as to custody. But in about half of the U.S. states the judges are now required by law to give "due weight" or otherwise take into "consideration" the preferences of youngsters involved in custody disputes.[6]

However, you also have a strong feeling on the part of the child experts that in a custody dispute a younger child should not have to make a choice as to the parent he or she wants to live with. One finding in a three-year study of the Child Custody Research Project, Cambridge, Massachusetts, was that children have frightening fantasies of being ordered by a judge to choose one parent over the other.

Although youngsters occasionally are still put on the stand in some states, most judges in recent years have been balking at the idea. In Utah a father demanded that his two children, both under ten, be permitted to testify as to their preference between parents in open court. The judge was vehement: "I don't think you people ought to have even the remotest desire in God's world to prostitute your own children in that way."

A general trend in the U.S. has developed to take the testimony of children, when it is sought, in chambers. A New York Court of Appeals approved this since "the welfare of the child is paramount." But this procedure has not been without hazard.

In North Carolina at one point judges who used this procedure were overruled for committing reversible error. Normally, due process requires that testimony be given in open court and that witnesses can be subject to cross-examination.

The courts in most U.S. states now accept that custody cases are special and that judges can handle the matter in chambers. However, the regulations to permit this vary. Commonly they state that a judge *may* talk privately to a child but he may need the consent of both parents. Further, counsel may be required to be present, and there may be a requirement that a recording of the judge's talk with the child be made. Later either parent can inspect the transcript.

It is clearly inequitous that the interests of children in court custody battles are not better protected in most U.S. states. They are the prize being sought and the acknowledged principal parties of interest. Their needs may well conflict with those of adults who are so angry with each other that they are acting like children. Yet in most states nobody speaks for the child.

Several states now specify that a judge "may" or "shall" appoint separate counsel to represent children in custody cases. Where it is a "may" power it rarely is used, perhaps because it would lengthen cases in the already crowded dockets. Connecticut is one of the states where it is mandatory. Michigan has a "Friend of the Court" that provides some representation. In New Hampshire and Wisconsin it is now mandatory that a guardian *ad litem* be appointed for the youngster in any contested custody case. Wisconsin also has provided judges with a ten-point list of the rights of children in custody cases.

The Conciliation Courts Review carried a proposal that a trained representative for children serve on the court staff. It was felt this would be preferable to appointing a counsel, since a counsel would simply lengthen the adversary process.

Philadelphia has been experimenting with a Child Advocate Unit, with the help of federal funding. It represents children and monitors court orders. An official of the unit points to a paradox in America: the rights of delinquents are far more fully safeguarded than "innocent" youngsters who are in the courts with their futures being arranged by a harassed judge trying to appraise the disrupted family situation at hand.

JUDGES START CALLING FOR HELP

In the face of the upsurge of custody cases, their inherent ugliness and the changing ground rules, many judges have been looking for ways to shift the burden of assessing these disputes. Why, they say, should they be stuck with all these hundreds of thousands of battles over children, especially since the old presumption that mothers know best is gone? What are the guidelines that these modern Solomons untrained in children's needs should follow? The embittered parents have often hired experts such as child psychiatrists to reinforce their claims on what custody arrangement is best. The conflicting pictures painted in esoteric psychological language on the two sides can further bewilder a hard-pressed judge.

Increasingly the judges have been trying to turn the squabbles over to various types of experts for recommendations. In some states they have ordered probation officers to sort things out. In northwestern Pennsylvania judges assign a local lawyer to serve as a "custody master" and almost always accept the custody master's recommendations. But the main new trend is to call upon family experts, psychiatrists and child psychologists, to make professional evaluations for the court.

These experts try to see the principal parties involved, including the children. They watch how everybody interacts. Younger children may not be asked about their preference as to which parent they want to live with directly, but may be asked to draw a picture or play with a doll house in which the dolls can readily be seen to represent various family members. Another strategy is to ask a parent and child to do some task together, such as building a skyscraper from blocks, while the evaluator watches and listens behind a one-way window.

In the northeastern United States a child psychiatrist who has been frequently called upon by judges for an evaluation is Alan M. Levy. When I saw him he was working on three cases. I passed one young father seeking custody when I entered his ground-floor office in an old upper West Side apartment building in Manhattan. Levy explained that he first likes to see the parents separately and the children separately. Then he sees each child with each parent. Still later, he sees each child with both parents. Finally, when possible, he chats with the whole family.

Some people handling custody think it is a waste of time to ask a youngster below the teenage level for his thoughts about custody. One judge said, "I'll be damned if I will let an eight-year-old tell me what to do." Levy disagrees. For all ages the preferences of children capable of expressing their thoughts are important. Levy added:

"I advise asking kids their preference right in front of their parents." That struck me as putting a heavy load on the kid. This was his explanation:

"By the time I see children they have already certainly been asked about their custodial preference, in one way or another, by their parents. . . . In almost all instances of divorce and separation the children feel themselves caught between two parents, and even if no one else is asking them their preference, they themselves are struggling with the idea. So often, however, parents openly state to their children, 'Wouldn't you like to live with me rather than your mother/father?' Or, 'Don't worry, the judge will say you can live with me.' "

Levy feels that asking the children to indicate any preference is "an effort to help them deal realistically with what is a fact of their life, and to minimize the unfettered fantasies that can accumulate in this area."

When alone with Levy a youngster may state his preference in a way that is extremely negative to one parent. He said, "When the same issue is discussed with the child and each of the parents separately, the stated preference may remain the same or be modified considerably. As a final step when the child is together with both parents and myself, the stated preference may either remain the same or still shift to a more middle ground. Stated preferences that remain constant in these various situations tend, in my view, to reflect a more valid statement of position by the child than a preference which vacillates or starts out strongly and then comes down the middle. Such a vascillating custodial preference reflects the persistence of divided loyalties and equal regard for both parents.'' He added that this stating of preference is always to some extent painful, ''but at times may be something a child has been desirous of doing for some time.''

One is left wondering how much quizzing of the child is needed to protect his best interests.

VISIT TO A CENTER EVALUATING PARENTS REGARDING CUSTODY

Organizations too are springing up to provide judges with recommendations on disposition of children in custody disputes. The most fascinating I encountered is the Center for Legal Psychiatry, a nonprofit group, in a building on Wilshire Boulevard in Santa Monica near the Los Angeles city line. It is headed by John M. Suarez. He is on the clinical faculty of the Department of Psychiatry at the University of California, Los Angeles. The group is assigned tough cases that can't be resolved by the conciliation court in the limited time available. The center also gets cases when couples come willingly to try to avoid a long and costly court battle, and cases where opposing lawyers get together and recommend the center in the hope of keeping the case out of the courtroom.

The waiting room of the center has a lot of interesting things for children to play with. The staff of about fifty experts — psychiatrists, child psychologists, marriage counselors — mostly work part-time for nominal fees. The center makes custody evaluations for numerous courts in the Los Angeles area. It also has a Divorcing Family Clinic headed by Nancy L. Weston that does counseling work, including group therapy, for parents who are fighting, often in the courts. It offers therapy for children caught in the middle of such in-fighting. The clinic also conducts a course for divorced parents.

The focus of the Center for Legal Psychiatry is entirely on the welfare of children, not the property aspects of a custody dispute. It seeks *the least detrimental* arrangement for a child of divorce. This means it seeks to get the whole picture. In each case assigned to it by a court, it assigns a professional evaluator to talk with every party that has a significant bearing on where and how the child should be settled. This can include not only the separating spouses and their children but any of their ex-spouses, new live-in parents, grandparents, even housekeepers and teachers.

Younger children are given projective tests. ''If you are on a deserted island whom would you like to have there with you?'' Or, as described earlier, they are asked to draw a picture of a family. One evaluator told me:

"I had a little girl who in drawing a family left out her mother. She had in the picture her father, her brother, and a female adult she identified as her stepmother. This was all unconscious on her part, but she was telling me something."

In playing with dolls, another girl had her father falling out of an airplane. Changes in a child's voice as it talks about family members also often are revealing.

Once the evaluator is ready to make a recommendation he (or she) presents an analysis for review to a staff conference. About ten professionals including the director were at the three reviews of cases I attended. The reviews took place in a large temporary trailer behind the center because the center was short on space.

A young psychiatrist offered the first presentation. (To protect identities I have modified some details.) Before the talking began she swiftly designed the Hispanic family's tangled setup with chalk on a blackboard, like a football coach setting up a play. Sex, ages, and relationships were indicated by squares (male), circles (female), numbers and lines reaching down (children), out (new spouses or bedmates), and up (grandparents). Altogether, fourteen figures were indicated.

Cheerfully the psychiatrist then opened the case conference by presenting the issue at hand. The children were presently living with the mother's parents. The father wanted custody. She said it had been hard to get a straight story out of any of the adults. The husband claimed that the wife he was leaving was unfit to be custodian. She was a marijuana user and had been caught stealing money from the cash register of the store where she worked. Furthermore, the husband had shown the psychiatrist a knife cut on his arm which he said his wife had inflicted.

On the other hand, the husband wasn't such a shining character. The maternal grandmother with whom the daughters lived had told the psychiatrist that when he had had his daughters to his new apartment for visits there would often be an overnight girlfriend there. The older daughter confirmed that she had twice witnessed intercourse between her father and another woman.

The psychiatrist said the one person in the whole layout with whom the children seemed to have a close relationship was their stepsister Maria, age twelve. She lived nearby. Maria spent a lot of time watching over her stepsisters and helping them with their schoolwork. The psychiatrist joked that they might advise the judge that the twelve-year-old girl was the most competent and loving "adult" on the scene and should be awarded custody. More seriously, she recommended that the prevailing setup was the "least detrimental" one available to the children and that the judge be advised to reject the father's claim for custody, but to assure him reasonable visiting privileges (with a provision that he not have sleep-over girlfriends when his daughters were visiting).

The conferees asked a lot of questions. In the end they concurred with her evaluation.

The next case was to be a "live" one. This meant that after the briefing the parents themselves would be brought in for inspection and questioning.

A male evaluator chalked a diagram of the situation. The father, we'll call Tom, was forty-one years old. The mother, Cynthia, was thirty-three. They had two children, Peter, age nine, and Jane, age seven.

Father Tom was helping support two daughters and a son by a previous marriage. He was a prosperous wheeler-dealer in boat and auto dealerships. The investigator said some of his accounts were inconsistent and that sometimes he had not shown up at agreed times to pick up the children for visits because he was busy. The mother, Cynthia, had had a bout of heavy drinking, but the separation had sobered her. She was working full-time as a dental assistant and going to school three nights a week to qualify as a dental technician. This meant the hiring of a lot of sitters. In the psychological testing, the daughter Jane had seemed to have a closer feeling toward her mother. Peter, a bright boy, was careful not to indicate any preference. The evaluator had surmised that he did not want to come down on the losing side. Whom would he like to have with him if he was marooned on a desert island? Everybody. Both his parents. He wanted the marriage to continue.

Tom, while asking for full custody, had hinted a willingness for some sort of "joint" custody. He claimed that Cynthia once had a lesbian affair and professed concern she would lapse back into serious drinking.

After the briefing the conferees talked about handling the "live" assessment. The parents were waiting outside in separate cars.

They came in a few seconds apart. Tom was a lean, smooth-looking redhead in sports shirt and polished boots. Cynthia looked like a well-organized person but she had a face suggesting severe strain. She looked sharply at the diagram on the blackboard, then sat down in a chair beside her husband but with her body turned away from him.

At this point I slipped out, as agreed. A staff person briefed me afterward.

Director John Suarez had led off the discussion by asking each in turn to talk about the two children. The mother talked first and had seemed quite analytical. Tom, on the other hand, spent most of his time talking about what a bright, wonderful boy Peter was. He discussed his daughter more briefly and matter-of-factly. Each was asked to present his or her case for being awarded custody. She insisted that despite her heavy work and study schedule she was being a good, loving mother. He repeated his contention that her schedule was hard on the kids and might push her back into heavy drinking.

Tom was reminded that he had hinted that joint custody might be acceptable. He was asked to spell out what he had in mind. (Joint custody actually comes in several forms.) It turned out that he really had in mind "split" custody. He wanted his bright son Peter and the wife could keep the daughter Jane. He claimed he had gotten higher grades in college than his wife and he wanted his son exposed to the more intellectually stimulating environment he was capable of providing.

After the two parents left the conferees discussed their impressions. It was agreed without any notable dissent that the evaluator had been correct in recommending that the mother have custody. The father should be given considerable opportunity to have the children, especially his son, with him.

I asked if the children were ever brought in during these case conferences. The answer: occasionally. It occurs only if the evaluator wants an impression confirmed about a particular child.

"If it is a boy," I was told, "we ask him about school and sports and what he most enjoys doing. We don't ask particular questions about the divorce. We don't ask youngsters whom they want to live with; we try to interpret what they say based on our training and experience. A fifteen-year-old youngster knows whom he wants to live with. But it is not fair to ask a preteen child where he wants to live."

Only the more enlightened judges in America awarding custody of children have the benefit of such carefully considered opinion of qualified professionals. Much more of it is needed if divorcing couples continue taking their custody arguments to court.

The court route to deciding custody is expensive and very slow, and because of the slowness it is hard on the kids. A court route is also hard on kids because the rival lawyers often freeze the parents into adversary roles over the long period of time that the legal contest lasts, as noted.

The first decision a divorcing couple with children should make is to stay on civil terms, as far as the children are concerned. This will help ease the anguish of the children. The second decision they should make is to keep their argument regarding custody out of the court.

A Canadian study found that agreements made out of court were much more likely to be permanent than court-ordered arrangements and to be more generous to the noncustodial parent regarding visiting rights and unlimited telephone rights.[7]

Be wary of lawyers who even suggest litigation. Their motives can be selfish. Try to agree on a single neutral lawyer who will act as a go-between and help thrash out custody as a part of an overall divorce agreement. Or if necessary use two lawyers and order them to seek accommodations.

If that doesn't seem feasible turn the argument over to a professional mediator. Mediation is faster, far less painful for all concerned including children, and puts a premium on rationality rather than contest. Mediators are readily available in many Western countries. For guidance look in the phone book or ask your lawyer, or a local marriage counselor, or a professor of family life or family law, or a minister, or an officer of the local court. In many U.S. cities there are now mediators who specialize in family problems.[8] The Family Mediation Service now has a thousand members. It is headquartered in Washington, D.C. In 1982 *Marriage and Divorce Today* carried a report that in Fridley, Minnesota, the local mediation and counseling center was harassed by local lawyers claiming that this center dedicated to peaceful settlement of family disputes was "bordering on the unauthorized practice of law."

Michigan has taken a major step to keep bitter custody or visitation disputes out of the courts. A portion of marriage license fees goes to family counseling services. In Grand Rapids, for example, more than 130 custody or visitation disputes have been referred by the courts to a Family Services Association. It seeks to arrange mediation of the disputes between parents. If the parents cannot agree, the association makes its own recommendations to the judges.

Some states such as California have conciliation courts which offer essentially the same sort of resolution. All contested cases involving custody or visitation must, by law, go to the conciliation court for mediation; and about half of the contested cases are resolved at this level. Jeanne Ames of San Francisco's Superior Court told me, "Mediation is the new kid on the block." That court's load of *full* court hearings of custody battles had shrunk from 280 in 1976 to five in 1981. If certain issues seem too difficult for mediation, the cases may be turned over to an arbitrator, who is also readily available. The arbitrator differs from the mediator in that both sides agree to abide by the arbitrator's decision.

In short, we should get the overburdened courts clear out of the business of dictating relationships between children and their divorcing parents except where novel claims are made. We should keep children of divorce out of the court process; and liberate harried judges from the role of playing Solomon.

15

Who Really Should Get the Children?

"Fathers don't make good mothers."
— *A California judge, during a custody argument, 1972*

We have seen how children are treated as prizes or pawns when battling parents turn the question of custody over to the legal system. But we did not deal with the heart of the matter: in these modern times what *is* the best way to take care of the children when parents have split? Some ways can be a lot less painful for the child than others.

Until well into the nineteenth century, the child usually went to the father (if he wanted it) as a part of his rightful chattel. During the first six decades of this century the situation was reversed. The assumption was that a young human in his "tender years" should be assigned automatically to the mother if she was of sound mind. It was taken for granted that mothers knew best how to nurture the young.

A few states still cling to the tender years doctrine for young children. But now basic assumptions have shifted again, largely because of new emphasis on the sexual equality of roles and the fact that husbands have been getting much experience at nurture during hours when the mother is off working at a job. As a result, a host of novel concepts for custody and visitation have emerged.

THE DIMINISHING PRESUMPTION THAT MOTHER KNOWS BEST

The assumption that husbands should be allowed to have custody of children after divorce only if the wife-mother was gravely unfit was undone several years ago largely by the noted child psychologist Lee Salk, associated with the Cornell Medical College. When he and his wife parted both felt they would be the better parent for their two children, Pia, age eight, and Eric, age fourteen.

The case got into the newspapers with quite a splash partly because of some colorful aspects of their battling. He refused to leave ''home'' even though divorced because his children were there. But the crucial aspect of the case was that he never suggested in any way that the mother was unfit or neglectful. Nor did he dispute that the children loved their mother. He rested his case purely on the fact that the children liked being with him more. He met them more often after school and was reported to have more talks with school officials about their development. The judge talked with the children in chambers and got assessments of a psychologist and a child psychiatrist who interviewed the children.

The court report in *The New York Law Journal* (October 29, 1975) indicates that both youngsters were bright and articulate. Both expressed love for their mother. Eric, the older youngster, was apparently quite emphatic in wanting to live with his father. He thought it would be more exciting and intellectually stimulating. He considered his father the more understanding and felt the father did things better. The situation with his eight-year-old sister Pia was apparently a bit more complicated. The child psychiatrist found that she desperately wanted to keep the family together but since her parents were divorcing she was clinging to her older brother Eric as her ''family.'' Eric had been very protective with her. Perhaps partly because of this, she reportedly opted to live with her father even though she knew it would make her mother sad.

Ultimately the judge concluded that this particular father could best ''nurture the complex needs and social development of the children.'' The children were awarded to the father with a provision for liberal visiting arrangements for the mother.

He added the view that it was beneficial for the children to be reared together and that courts are reluctant to separate siblings for split custody unless necessary. Split custody is rarely granted for younger children. But it often happens that a youngster — particularly a boy — will upon reaching adolescence simply move in with his father without a revision of the custody decree.

Today more than a dozen states have statutes specifying that sex does not give one parent an advantage over the other if both are seeking custody.

The presumption in many state laws that the father must provide support if the wife gets the child also is being eliminated in a number of states. Courts now frequently specify that the husband pay child support only if it seems to be needed. The situation is influenced by whether the wife has a job or has access to child support under the federal government's now shrinking Aid to Families with Dependent Children program (for the poor). Some judges have been sympathetic to a husband's plea that he contemplates remarriage and will have children in a new marriage to support, according to Morton and Bernice Hunt, authors of *The Divorce Experience,* in citing a report of the U.S. Senate Committee on Finance.

If the wife insists on custody the husband may retort, ''Okay, but you've got a job so don't expect any support from me.'' That of course is an unfair premise. Child-raising is sufficiently expensive today that both should contribute no matter what the arrangement for physical custody is, if she has a good income.

At any rate, many tens of thousands of husbands are now getting outright custody of the children. Other tens of thousands are getting ''joint custody.'' In practical terms this can be two-thirds custody, half-custody, one-quarter custody, or simply joint custody on all important decisions affecting the children, such as health and education. We'll examine some of these father-involved arrangements shortly.

WHERE NEITHER PARENT REALLY WANTS CUSTODY

Children commonly have nightmares involving fear of abandonment, as we have seen, even if the fears are unjustified. Georgia Dullea, writing about custody in *The New York Times,* told of a six-year-old girl so panicked by her parents' separation that when she went from one parent's house to the other's she would leave a trail of marbles to mark the way back.

Children's nightmares of such an outcome — of abandonment — are not always fantasies. Increasing numbers of cases are coming to light where neither divorcing parent actually wants the children in the sense of having responsibility for physical custody. If the mother has a job and is thinking about the possibility of attracting a new mate, children — whether loved or not — may be seen as encumbrances. And the husband may see custody as a whole new complicated way of life he would have to learn.

Jesse Rothman, whose New York law firm specializes in matrimonial cases, mentioned to me he had handled cases where neither parent really wanted custody. ''The whole thing is changing rapidly,'' he said.

At the center in Los Angeles county which makes recommendations regarding custody for courts, an official put it this way:

''Once in a while we'll have a case presented in a case conference where the evaluator will say, 'It's really sad — these are two adorable children and I don't think either parent really wants them.' But one parent or the other has got to take them. The foster home situation is very limited . . . and typically creates a lot of moving around for the child.''

A young architect told me of parting from his wife who, he said, tended to run away from responsibility. While they were talking about dividing up the property he said he would take Leigh, their five-year-old daughter. His wife, with obvious relief, said, ''Oh, would you!''

Two investigators of custody arrangements tell of the real damage inflicted in a thirteen-year-old girl named Valerie when her two parents were going through the motions of conventional custody contest but with both parents thinking of her primarily as a burden.[1] In addition, a new stepfather resented her. Valerie was an ''unusually bright, alert girl'' but she was having severe problems at school. The father reluctantly went to talk to school officials because the girl's mother ''didn't want to be bothered.'' Valerie's schoolwork had become deplorable. She couldn't get along with others. She was disruptive. And she was starting to disappear without explanation. The father agreed to pay for increased psychiatric counseling, but admitted he was becoming afraid to think about Valerie's future.

For some children custody arrangements can be bewildering in their complexity. Investigators for the Foundation for Child Development came upon a young girl who at the time of the first interview was living with her father and stepmother. At a follow-up check six months later she was living with her grandparents during the week and going to alternate mother-stepfather and father-stepmother households on weekends. An official of the Foundation suggested the situation called for psychiatric attention.

PUZZLES OVER A CHILD'S "BEST INTERESTS"

For parents who are parting, the goal should be to determine which of the available settings will make the child feel most comfortable and least apprehensive, and will be best for the child's long-term welfare.

A youngster's preference between parents, while important, is of course only one factor that must be considered. This is particularly true for preteenagers.

There are practical considerations. The children will need sustenance and acceptable caretaking. They will need a good home environment. They will need continuity, especially the younger children.

Which parent can best offer such conditions?

Child experts have recently been badly split about how much importance to attach to continuity. Which alternative is more important: that everything possible be done after divorce to assure the child a solid, undisturbed connection with one parent, or that everything be done to assure the child's regular access to both parents even though this may involve some awkward passing of the child back and forth?

The storm over which course is least undesirable was triggered several years ago when three distinguished experts on children wrote a book called *Beyond the Best Interests of the Child*. These authors were Joseph Goldstein of the Yale Law School, Anna Freud of the Hampstead Child-Therapy Clinic, and Albert J. Solnit of Yale's Child Study Center.

They came down quite firmly on the side of providing the child with stability. This, they concluded, meant assuring the child a solid relationship with its custodial parent, even if it meant substantially cutting out the departed "visiting" parent. They contended that where there is a contest the parent receiving custody, not the courts, should have *full say* in deciding the conditions under which he or she will raise the child. The authors wanted to abolish complicated visitation formulas worked out by the courts for the parent losing custody. That parent who lost the argument would see his or her children on terms agreeable to the custodial parent.

The authors felt that the child of a bitter divorce was already "greatly at risk." That risk should not be heightened by further parental squabbling over the loser's access to the child. Judges often have to allow for the possibility of changed circumstances, and the losers may be quick to make such claims.

These authors also contended that children have difficulty profiting from contact with two "psychological" parents when those parents are not on good terms with each other. They started from the premise that every child has a need for "unbroken continuity of affectionate and stimulating relationships with an adult."

Occasional visitations with an adult (parent) not on friendly terms with the custodial adult might "themselves be a source of discontinuity."

The full power these authors would give the custodial parent to control the noncustodial parent's access to his own children started an argument among experts that still persists. E. Mavis Hetherington, who headed a major study of children of divorce, was impressed by the widespread longing to see departed parents. She has called the authors' thesis "destructive, appalling." Wallenstein and Kelly, who likewise did a major follow-up study on children of divorce, said in 1980 that "we offer a view diametrically opposed to that of our esteemed colleagues Goldstein, Freud and Solnit. . . ."

I have the impression that if the proposal of the three authors was put to a vote among children of divorce capable of a reasoned response, the vote would be overwhelmingly against the authors' proposal. Most children seem desperately to want to see their departed parent. On the other hand, if the setup the authors proposed was generally accepted by custody courts, I can see at least one good result beyond stability. The divorcing parents, faced with an all-or-nothing verdict from the courts, might lower the level of their feuding, become more "civilized." They might even decide divorce wasn't such a good idea after all. And if they went ahead with divorce, they might see the wisdom of working out an accommodation themselves, out of court, rather than leave the matter to a judge's verdict.

WHAT ABOUT JOINT CUSTODY?

Among the more severe critics of the thesis of *Beyond the Best Interests of the Child* are the increasing number of proponents of joint custody.

Is joint custody a better way to handle "best interests" in our brave new world of family arrangements?

Nancy Weston, head of the Divorcing Family Clinic and a resident of California, offered me this analysis:

"Families that are not fighting can handle joint custody very nicely. It solves many problems. For example it relieves the mother of the entire burden of feeling she has to raise the children alone. Father then becomes an active participant in the children's lives. If mother can't go to the children's school because she has to work, he can go. Or they can go together. Or she can go away for a weekend once in a while and know Dad will take the kids, and vice versa. They talk to each other about their children's lives."

More recently Pennsylvania, for one, has enacted a joint custody law. It not only calls upon the courts to consider joint custody, but requires that certain of the child's health and educational records be available to both parents in any case.

Couples who have divorced don't have to like each other to make joint custody work, but they must be on speaking terms. Constance R. Ahrons, who studied several dozen couples with court-awarded joint custody, found that the great majority liked their arrangement.[2]

The details of the "joint" arrangement can vary greatly. The jointness of custody may be just philosophical: although the child or children may live primarily with one parent, both parents agree they still have a joint responsibility for the upbringing of the youngsters they created. The father and mother in such a situation typically confer in making decisions about their child's health problems, schooling, church upbringing, summer camps, etc.

If there is a "joint" physical sharing of custody, it can be on an equal basis. Or perhaps the husband has the children on weekends, summer vacations, and has unlimited telephone privilege with his children. Children and grandparents get liberal rights to see each other.

If the physical custody is truly joint, the usual pattern is for Mom to have the kids one week and Dad the next. Or they rotate the kids every few days. Both homes have separate rooms for the kids. Both are equipped with their children's clothes and recreational materials. Usually such shared custody is feasible for school-age children only if both parents live in the same school district and within easy biking distance of each other. Ideally the children are free to drop in on one parent without getting the other parent's permission (unless it becomes so excessive that it threatens to violate the spirit of the joint agreement.) Ideally also the parents get together with the children for birthdays, Christmas, important school events.

I have reports of joint physical custody arrangements that seem to be working well after eight or nine years. Youngsters in joint custody say they sometimes are unsure what address they are supposed to use when they register for school, or which house their basketball is at. But many seem to do well. They usually say their friends know where to find them.

Preschool children typically have difficulty comprehending custody arrangements based on split weeks or alternating weeks or months (because of their low time sense) and may spend a lot of time wondering or worrying about when they are due to be moved again.

Mel Roman, a New York professor of psychiatry, studied forty families that had entered into joint custody. While most encountered occasional troubles, his conclusion was that joint custody did work in the great majority of cases. Most of the children were thriving, not just adjusting.

He offers as a typical case a father in lower Manhattan who is a social scientist and a mother who is a writer, and must travel quite a bit. Their daughter Morgan was only three when they divorced. They had gone into joint custody warily, because their breakup had created so much anger. Morgan split each week between her parents, with a bedroom of her own in each house. She has been doing fine in school and has many friends.

While the parents have not become chummy, they did establish a basis of trust and an easy habit of cooperating where Morgan was concerned. If she became ill in her Mom's house she stayed there until she was well enough to go back to school. And when her Mom had to go on trips, Dad would keep her a few extra days.

Susan Steinman, who studied thirty-two children in joint custody arrangements in the San Francisco Bay area, found that joint custody was no simple solution.[3] The youngsters (age four and a half to fifteen) overwhelmingly wished their parents would get back together, but greatly appreciated the trouble the parents had gone to in order for them to maintain contact with both parents. About a third felt "overburdened by the demands and requirements of maintaining a strong presence in both homes." This was particularly true of the younger children.

Some of the youngsters were so grateful to have access to both parents that they were almost obsessive about being even-handed. Steven, age ten, who had lived alternate weeks with each parent for six years, was "religious" about making up time with one parent if because of sickness or vacations he had "short-changed" the other. Patty, age nine, said, "I am always really equal about things" in order not to appear to be taking sides. "If I am nice to my Mom and he [Dad] isn't there I'll go and be nice to him at his house."

The older children maintain a "clarity about their schedules and the location of their homes that was impressive."

Some of the children handled the traveling to homes two miles apart with ease; others were frightened about getting lost or going to the wrong house. During the gasoline shortage an eight-year-old boy worried that the shortage might cause him to lose contact with his mother. An eleven-year-old boy, Jim, on the other hand, who had parents living on opposite sides of the Bay, found the shuttle between homes a real inconvenience involving several changes of buses. And he didn't know many kids in San Francisco where his father lived. In responding to a question about what he would want if given three wishes, his first response was "wings." Then, he said, he would be able to drop in on his dad every afternoon.

A few really thoughtful, loving parents accept that the burden of the marital disruption should be on them, not their children, and they do the shuttling. The children remain in the original home and the parents take turns living with them. This of course is the best arrangement for the children. It can be expensive for the parents if they each have to establish separate part-time places to stay.

A divorced couple in New York City with two children handled this rather neatly. Both parents are architects with separate offices. Both have rigged up living space in their studios for the week when they are not in their brownstone house with their children.[4] Both the children expressed great satisfaction with the arrangement. The eleven-year-old son said, "When most parents break up it is usually the kids that have to travel. But we're lucky because we get to stay where we have lived all our lives." The parents said the arrangement would become a complication if either became seriously involved with someone of the opposite sex. Their agreement provides that if that happens the children will do the shuttling, as in conventional joint custody.

Some parents with joint custody live in different communities, perhaps 120 miles apart, and rotate the physical custody on an annual basis. The children have permission to visit the parent they are not living with. In the Steinman study a ten-year-old boy made such an annual trek with some sadness and anxiety. It meant going into the "country" where his mother had moved. This was saddening because it meant giving up for a year his main base of friends and favorite hangouts.

Here are two innovative court-ordered arrangements that I hope will influence legal thinking.

In northern Michigan the Grand Traverse County Circuit Court Judge Charles M. Forster startled an older couple seeking joint custody of their three sons, ages eleven to fifteen, by decreeing that the sons continue to live in the family home while the parents take turns living with them on a monthly basis. He said it seemed logical because the parents put the welfare of their sons above their own convenience. Both parents professed to be pleased. During the first month of adjustment the father moved in with his own parents. The boys expressed enthusiasm for the arrangement. One explained that now "we get to see our parents." The divorce had started out on a tense basis but the parents handled it so sensibly the oldest boys remained on the honor roll at their Traverse City Junior High School.

New York State Supreme Court Judge Richard Donovan ordered joint custody in a case involving two sons in grade school but made this interesting provision: every six months they, the sons, would each decide which house they wanted to live in for the next six months. Also they were awarded unlimited visiting privileges.

There are cases where joint custody has survived even into remarriage of both parents. That, however, seems hazardous. Couples making a joint custody agreement should have a provision making it possible for either to call for a new arrangement if one of them remarries.

Joint custody agreements can become disastrous if the divorcing couple lapses back into wrangling over such questions as what hospital a sick child should be taken to for an operation. Divorcing couples considering joint custody should test their capacity to be civilized on a trial basis during a separation before the arrangement becomes official.

In general, joint custody seems to deserve consideration. A study at the Philadelphia Child Guidance Clinic of ninety-one children of divorce indicated that those in joint custody were just as well adjusted as those in single-parent custody. One interesting advantage for the mother turned up. Fathers in joint custody arrangements were twice as likely to keep up support payments as were those where the wife had full custody. That certainly is an advantage for the children also.

In January 1982 *The American Journal of Psychiatry* carried a report on what happened over a two-year period to parties involved in 414 consecutive custody cases in a Los Angeles court. A comparison was made of the aftermath of sole custody awards versus joint custody awards. It turned out that in the cases where one parent was given custody there was twice the likelihood of renewed litigation. Joint custody awards, it seems, would at least ease the congestion of the courts.

One big question that arises when joint physical custody is considered is whether the father has the capacity to nurture the youngsters and run the household. The same question comes up when husbands seek full custody.

FATHERS AS CHIEF CUSTODIANS

How well, really, can fathers handle the whole gamut of roles that go with obtaining custody? We have an argument. As indicated, women as bearers of babies were assumed to have a big edge at nurture. The modern mothers holding down jobs usually have been pleased to praise their husbands for any evidences of competence in handling the infants. Psychiatrist Robert Coleman of the University of Nebraska recently observed to colleagues: "The most forceful motivator of active fatherhood has been the voice of feminism." Men who take on full custody or joint physical custody are often regarded by acquaintances as heroic figures.

The age of the child unquestionably is one factor to consider in assessing the relative competence of men to take charge of their youngsters. For most fathers, ability to take over complete charge without difficulty probably improves with the age of the offspring.

I have before me three different reports of youngsters approaching adolescence who left the mother to live with the father. A fourteen-year-old girl was quite analytical. Her dad, a scientist, gave her more freedom, had somewhat more money, and seemed more understanding. A twelve-year-old boy took the initiative of telephoning the court repeatedly to demand the right to live with his father, whom he felt sorry for. The boy claimed his mother abused him, but his real motive was to try to cheer up his depressed father. A fifteen-year-old boy, after summering with his father, defied the court order that he return to his mother in another state. He said he and his father both liked to fish and work with tools. And his father was willing to treat him as more of a grown-up than his mother was.

In contrast it would be very risky for a father to take custody of a one-year-old child if that child has become attached to its mother.

Researchers on parenting behavior with infants have been using a variety of instruments to make a microanalysis of the motion pictures taken of fathers and mothers as they handle their infants. Hormonal studies also have been made. And parents handling infants have been viewed from behind one-way mirrors.

Some of the researchers conclude that either a father or a mother can cope with an infant equally well when they put their mind to it. We have mentioned (under the discussion of who can substitute for mothers) the Sawin-Parke study finding fathers competent in handling babies only a few days old.

Others have found differences, perhaps not critical differences but still differences. The Harvard Medical School's Infant Follow-Up Center has been studying the parenting habits of men and women. Its director, James Herzog, told the American Psychoanalytic Association that men and women have distinctly different patterns of nurture. Man's ability to be a good nurturer may come out of the depth of his feelings for his wife, and Herzog had reservations about the man estranged from his wife. He explained: "A woman can care for a child well without also being involved in a relationship with a man. But we're not sure the opposite is true. In other words, a woman can be a good single parent, but maybe a man can't."

Sociologist Alice Rossi has become impressed by biosocial factors in parenting, at least as far as infants are concerned. Her research has led her to believe that a mother has an innate predisposition to relate intensely to the infant. In her view physiological factors such as hormonal cyclicity, pregnancy, and giving birth are at work to promote intensity of feeling in mothers.

Infants can become as attached to a father as to a mother. That is not the point. Rather, she suggested, it is that the "predisposition to respond to the child may be much greater on the part of the mother than the father, a reflection . . . of a heritage that links mating and parenting more closely for females than males."[5] She suggests the difference can be overcome only by compensatory training or experience of males in child care.

An interesting difference in the way mothers act with infants has been charted by researchers at Children's Hospital Medical Center in Boston. The mothers' interaction was more enveloping, secure, modulated, and controlled. The father's was more playful, exciting, and physical. Mothers do more cooing and playing verbal games; fathers play more physical games.[6]

The Educational Testing Service found that older children tend to talk less to fathers, more to mothers.

Whether such differences have a biological base or are due simply to the way males are socialized in our society still is undetermined. A parenting study conducted in the Boston area with forty-nine custodial fathers found they were reasonably comfortable handling homemaking roles and entertaining children but were less at ease in handling nurturance.[7] They tended to be unsure of themselves when the children were upset and often turned to others for help. One father said, "I was afraid. I didn't know how to listen or respond to them." Presumably repeated experience would enhance confidence. Fathers often were uneasy in such roles as going to PTA meetings, calling baby-sitters, buying clothes for the children, or taking children to birthday parties. But the fathers who willingly undertook the role of primary parent and had been able to handle it felt good about their performances.

16

Persisting Problems
with Split Parents

"We've had fathers kick down doors, break in windows when they don't get to see their children."

— Nancy Weston, Director, The Divorcing Family Clinic, Greater Los Angeles

In Toronto a father misses seeing his child so much between allowable visits that he frequently parks his car in front of the school and, from a distance, watches his child in the playground during recess.

And in Denver a four-year-old boy who had managed to comprehend the calendar recited his visitation pattern to a psychologist in these words: "Mondays, Wednesdays and Fridays at Mommy's house, Tuesdays and Thursdays at Daddy's house. Weekends they take turns." The psychologist noted: "He never mentioned 'my' house!" Except for the recitation, the psychologist said, he was "a pretty confused" kid.

After a divorce involving children the mother still ends up with physical custody of the children in about 90 percent of the cases. Thus despite sweeping changes in family functioning and the beginnings of custody arrangements that involve the father, the "noncustodial" parent or "visiting" parent is still highly likely to be the father.

The kind of arrangements made for this absent parent to maintain contact with his children, and how well he handles his available contacts, will importantly affect how well the children survive the disruption of the home.

Consider for example those 131 youngsters in Marin County, California, whose lives were followed by Judith Wallerstein and Joan Kelly. Recently the researchers checked back on the youngsters five years after divorce. One finding was that no matter how much they saw their divorced father, they didn't think it was enough. Wallerstein reports that the youngsters who saw their divorced father only infrequently or on an erratic basis tended still — after five years — to be afflicted with periods of depression and low self-esteem. These represented one-fourth of the whole group. On the other hand, those youngsters who after five years had a good relationship with their natural father tended significantly to be high in self-esteem and ego functioning.

Even after five years children were keeping careful count of their sessions with father. Wallerstein tells of chatting with an eight-year-old boy named Bobby who had seen his father, a policeman, only occasionally during the five years despite the fact the father lived only a few blocks away. The subject of the father came up. Abruptly Bobby became vague and somewhat incoherent. At this point they both happened to hear a police car siren. Bobby's look went blank. After a moment of silence Wallerstein softly suggested that the siren may have reminded Bobby of his father. The boy started to cry and sobbed for more than half an hour.

Doris Jacobson of U.C.L.A., in her study of fifty-one youngsters of divorces, found that those youngsters who had experienced a sharp drop in personal contact with their fathers were most likely to have high maladjustment scores.

Many youngsters of divorce also badly miss their former contact with their often adoring grandparents on the side of the absent parent. Some angry mothers with custody return any presents the paternal grandparents send. Frequently the children only see such grandparents when the father arranges it during his allowed visiting period. Such strains in maintaining relations with grandparents can make Christmas and birthdays more painful than pleasant when the custodial mother takes such attitudes.

Some custodial mothers have contended that contacts with paternal grandparents are just a painful reminder of the louse of an ex-husband they are trying to forget.

Grandparents seeking visitation rights have been getting considerable legislative or case law support. Officials of the Family Law Section of the American Bar Association report that in the last few years there has been a movement in at least eighteen U.S. states to uphold grandparent visitation rights. These include such big states as California, Florida, Michigan, Minnesota, Missouri, New Jersey, New York, Ohio, Pennsylvania, Texas, and Wisconsin.

DECLINING CONTACT WITH NONCUSTODIAL PARENTS

What are the odds that significant contact between children of noncustodial parents will persist? Not high. For example:

- E. Mavis Hetherington and her associates found that two years after divorce only about a third of their children were seeing the divorced fathers at least once a week.
- Wallerstein and Kelly found that at the five-year mark after divorce only about a third of the fathers still played a "significant parenting role" in the children's lives.
- The Foundation for Child Development in its survey of youngsters ages seven to eleven found that roughly a third of those whose parents were separated or divorced saw their fathers on a "regular" basis.

Some fathers fight the trend toward disengagement. A father in New Jersey went to court seventy-six times in two years in an effort to get more reasonable visiting rights and to have them enforced.

Often fathers gradually stop seeing the youngsters even though they love them and have a legal right, because of the pain involved for themselves. The visit may give them a sense of guilt. As Hetherington put it, some felt they "had failed as fathers." These fathers commonly protest that the idea of visiting their own children is awkward and phony, with no counterpart in an intact marriage. The whole business often depresses them.

Men complain that they become discouraged by the nastiness they encounter from their ex-spouses when they come to pick up the children.

Wallerstein and Kelly found that the large majority of mothers with custody were conscientious, even if annoyed, in honoring the father's visiting time. But one out of five tried to sabotage each meeting, sometimes in bizarre ways. One mother, when her ex-husband appeared at the door, reached forward and smeared his face with dog feces.

Dread of painful encounter causes some fathers simply to sit outside in the car and blow the horn. Wise parents have an agreement that any talk about their personal differences is taboo in the awkward moments when children are picked up or returned.

If the parent with visiting rights lives nearby, the older youngsters simply drop over. It also helps if there is no restriction on the right of the children to phone the absent parent. Some angry mothers switch their phone to an unlisted number so that the absent father cannot call. Tens of thousands of children have to sneak calls to their fathers.

PRACTICAL PROBLEMS OF VISITATION

One factor that discourages the father from keeping up regular visitation is the awkwardness of being a visitor to his children for a specified number of hours. It makes a normal home atmosphere difficult. The father unwittingly often finds himself in the sugar-daddy role. He takes the kids to the zoo, the museum, ball games, skating, the movies then out to dinner. The bills run up, but Daddy wants to see the children again. He tends to be far less restrictive than he was as the in-house father. If they get back to his apartment with a couple of hours to kill, the youngsters may act bored unless there is something they want to see on TV. At home before the divorce there was never any awkwardness. The kids buried themselves in their own projects or went out to shoot baskets and occasionally chatted with Dad. Wise weekend fathers get their children involved in helping them prepare stews, meatballs, lasagnas, or homemade ice cream.

Often the logistics of arranging regular visits become a major deterrent. A divorced mother in New Jersey told me she usually sent her eleven-year-old daughter Molly by bus to visit her father. He had an apartment near his job in New York City. The arrangement was that he would be waiting for her at the Port Authority Building at the bus's arrival gate. Okay. What could be simpler?

One Friday night when the mother and Molly arrived at the New Jersey bus depot they found the scheduled bus had been canceled and the next one would not leave for two hours. The mother drove to a nearby railroad station where she knew a train would soon be departing. She found in fact that the train, the last of the day, was just leaving. She put Molly on the train and went to a phone to advise the ex-husband to go to Penn Station instead of the Port Authority building. No answer. He was visiting a friend. She called Port Authority to have him paged at bus arrival time and tell him to call "home." She returned to her home. In about half an hour he called. She told him to get over to Penn Station and gave him the train number. Shortly after the train arrived the ex-husband called in angry panic. Molly was not on the train.

After a while Molly herself called her mother to say she was at Penn Station and had waited and waited for Daddy and then had gone to the station police. She left the telephone number. Mother had Daddy paged in Penn Station. He called. She gave him the new information. The police knew of no such girl. And the phone number was wrong. It was, they thought, a New Jersey number. After another twenty minutes mother got another call from Molly, asking why Daddy hadn't come. Mother asked to speak to the policeman. After a few minutes of bewildered talk the puzzle became clear. Molly had gotten off at the Newark, New Jersey, station. The conductor had hollered "New Ark," which Molly mistook for New York. By 1 A.M. Mother received word from Daddy that Molly was with him in New York City.

The really big discouragement for a noncustodial father, however, is that the custodial mother often badmouths him to the kids or uses them to carry ultimatums about money. Nancy Weston of the Divorcing Family Clinic, located in Santa Monica, explains:

"A child wants to be able to look up to both its parents. I have heard kids say to their parents at our sessions 'I refuse to tell you what's happening at the other house. I will not carry stories back and forth.' "

A study of 295 children of divorce by Judson T. Landis indicated that almost half of them felt they had been "used" by one or both parents.

When mother and father are not speaking to each other, some of the brighter children start manipulating their parents. Nancy Weston told of children living with a mother who was weak and still adrift from the divorce experience. Every time she attempted discipline they would both run to a phone, call Daddy, and cry, "Help. Help. Come get us. Mother is beating us." The father would storm over and take them away. He began suing for custody to protect them. When the therapists at the clinic explained to the father that his children were manipulating him, his behavior changed. After that, whenever the children would call for help he would say, "Well, that's between you and your mother. She is in charge." Weston added: "That, of course, stopped the craziness. The mother became less angry with the father and they began to talk and negotiate, and in the process he stopped his lawsuit for custody."

A major goal of the Divorcing Family Clinic simply is to persuade the father and mother to talk with each other rationally about the children. This often involves getting them together and letting them argue while someone on the clinic staff moderates. Often a parent is angry simply because she or he feels nobody has listened to her or him and there are things that must be said. Some of the hurt must be expressed before the ex-spouse can be free of it. Weston said: "It's amazing what talking something out does."

The parents are first seen separately at the clinic and then together. Weston went on:

"When the father and mother can participate in parenting together, even though living separately, the child is then freed of the terrible burden of the conflict and can go back and forth and be with either parent. He or she can live with either parent in a comfortable way. One of the things we see with fathers is that if they have access to their children they become more reasonable." Until then the situation can be ugly for the children.

SUPERVISED VISITS IN DENVER

Custodial parents may be so fearful of the rage or influence of the other parent, or the hazard of kidnapping by the other parent, that they try to get the judge to impose various kinds of controls on visiting.

In Denver this kind of apprehension led to the creation of a novel facility on an upper floor of the Children's Hospital. It is a kind of high-security visiting center used when there is a "significant risk of unmanageable stress."

The noncustodial parent must visit his (or her) children under the observation of a behavorial specialist seated behind a one-way mirror. The observer can also listen to all parent-child conversation via a microphone.

This center is a part of the Department of Behavioral Sciences at the hospital and has been under the direction of Meredith Ringler-White, a pediatric psychologist. She has done most of the monitoring from her office next door. If it has seemed necessary she has intervened by imposing limits on the way the talk was going or offered support when things were going badly. And she has commended the parents when things are going well.

The center also provides "supervised" visiting exchange. If the mother and father are so embittered that abusive language by a parent is possible when a child is picked up at its home, the center becomes a safe, neutral "pick-up" and "drop-off" place. The two parents are requested to arrive fifteen minutes apart so that there is no possibility of encountering one another. The fifteen minutes also sometimes allows a child being returned by a loved parent to get some crying out of its system, or talk about feelings of conflict, before the custodial parent arrives. Experts at the department are often concurrently counseling the problem parents so that the center's services will eventually not be needed. The center also makes evaluations regarding custody and visitation for the courts. In about 40 percent of the cases the recommendation favors the father.

At the time of my visit the center was unique in the U.S. Ringler-White's office has Mickey Mouse posters on the wall, a blackboard and table where children can play with toys while waiting to be picked up or to be observed. By her desk is the window (one-way mirror) where monitoring occurs. The window is shown to parents and to children old enough to comprehend it.

The larger visiting room next door has a table and comfortable chairs. There is a closet full of games, building blocks, dollhouses. Visiting parents often bring along their own games and refreshments.

The visitation supervisor takes notes on how the parent and children are behaving during a visit in case a judge asks how things are going. Are they relaxed, or is the parent trying to pry or pressure the kids? If the parent and children want to go down to the hospital cafeteria for a snack, the monitor will accompany them. Says Ringler-White: "It is not the greatest place for visiting. To be with your own kids and have someone watching is not a pleasant situation."

Some children have been conditioned by their custodial parent (usually the mother) to view the absent parent as a terrible person. Then the visits can be pretty stressful, particularly because of the initial strangeness of the center. The children don't know that this parent they are seeing for the first time in months or years has been fighting in court for the privilege of seeing them. Two little girls stepped on their father's feet, kicked his shin, and refused even to wish him a happy Father's Day. One shouted, "I don't ever want to see you again." Another child kept her head buried in a pillow throughout the "visit."

Other reunions go more pleasantly. The children have longed for the return of the absent parent or perhaps they were infants when the parent left. Now they are intensely curious about the parent who is a part of their roots.

During the week when I visited the center ten cases were on the week's schedule. Samples:

Case P. The mother was the monitored visitor and was still considered to be dangerously angry. There had been a switch in custody of her five children, and Ringler-White thought for good reason. The mother was a clinger who kept trying to treat her children as toddlers, though they were not. She was not on speaking terms with the children's father, who had remarried. Said Ringler-White:

"It's amazing how much the children have improved since they have gone to live with their father and stepmother."

Case J. A nine-year-old boy was to have a supervised visit with his natural father. The boy was living with his stepfather and his stepmother. His natural mother had died after the remarriage to the stepfather. The stepfather managed to keep custody after remarrying; he fought off the natural father's claim to custody by charging that he was dangerously unfit. The natural father had an ailment that caused him sometimes to act aggressively and unpredictably. Ringler-White recalls his first visit with the boy: "It was a really touching reunion. The father was able to explain to his son, 'You know I love you very much and I have been trying to see you because I do care for you.' " The child seemed greatly gratified.

Case R. A father was to have a monitored visit with his three-year-old daughter and five-year-old son born of his second marriage. His wife in the second marriage had a teenage daughter from a previous marriage. When he and this second wife split up, the teenager allegedly confessed to her mother that her stepfather had made sexual advances to her and she once had finally succumbed. Ringler-White said this father always needed close monitoring with his young natural daughter. He often asked her to sit on his lap, a natural thing for a normal daddy to do. And he would softly ask — until Ringler-White intervened — such questions as, "Is your mother still sleeping with that man?" Ringler-White turned the sound up high during his visits and counsels him on responding more appropriately with his daughter.

Case F involved an alcoholic father who wanted very badly to continue visiting rights with his six-year-old son. He tried to sober up for the visits. Ringler-White checked him out in her office before permitting the visit. If she decided he was not in shape for the visit she let him look at his son for a moment, through the one-way mirror, and later told the boy that the father called to explain he couldn't make the visit because of a pressing business matter.

In *Case G* Ringler-White would simply accept a seven-year-old boy from the mother for a "supervised exchange." The adoring father would arrive fifteen minutes later to pick the child up for an overnight visit. There were still very bad feelings between the father and mother. Two months earlier Ringler-White had tried to mediate their differences about custody, but feelings still were quite high. The father, ordinarily a calm bank official, became "volatile" at the last meeting in her office. I asked what she meant by "volatile."

"Well, he started yelling and shaking and made wild accusations against his ex-wife and then lunged to strangle her. I had to pull them apart."

Case H was the most fascinating visit scheduled for that week. It was to be between a father and his twelve-year-old son, Paul, who clearly was having torn feelings about his father. The father would be accompanied by his new wife and perhaps her two young boys.

It would have been improper for me to watch this or any of the visits through the one-way mirror, but I was fortunate in being able to arrange something better. I went to the homes of all the principals for talks and also conferred with the lawyer of Paul's mother, who had custody.

Paul's mother, Mrs. Helen Mittern (the names and identifying characteristics in this account have been altered), had fought to prevent her former husband, Josh Wilsin, from ever seeing his son. The boy Paul had been a baby when the father disappeared into prison for hijacking a trailer truck. While he was in prison, Helen got a divorce.

After five years in prison Josh was paroled from a twelve-year sentence for good behavior. One stipulation of the parole officer was that he not try to visit his son, at least for a few years.

Josh observed that stipulation for five years. In the meantime he drew upon old flying experience to become a charter pilot. In the late 1970s he resumed legal efforts to obtain visitation rights with his son, and finally the judge said he could do so on a trial basis under the watchful eye of Meredith Ringler-White.

First I went to visit Mrs. Mittern and, I hoped, her son Paul. I was told she supported herself and Paul by working in a typing pool. The cab pulled up to a two-story apartment complex near the airport with the Rockies in the background. A dark-haired, slim twelve-year-old boy standing by his small bike greeted me cheerfully and asked: "Are you the person who is coming to see us?"

I asked if he was Paul. He nodded and led me down a corridor and, picking up his bike, led me up a flight of stairs to his mother's neat, snug apartment. His mother greeted me courteously. A male friend who was going to escort her somewhere later lounged off to one side. Here are excerpts from the conversation after some preliminary conversation in which Paul revealed he liked skiing, biking, and baseball and that his grades "need improvement."

MRS. M: We were married for about a year and divorced shortly after that.

VP: (*to Paul*) So you didn't know your father?

PAUL: Yeah, I didn't know him.

VP: What developed to cause the marriage to dissolve?

MRS. M: Well, there were personal problems and the fact that he was sent to prison with a long sentence.

VP: Did you correspond?

MRS. M: I wrote him when he first went to prison but after that, no.

VP: (*to Paul*) Did you know he had been in prison?

PAUL: Well, my mom told me that, yeah.

MRS. M: The first time I saw him was in court. He wanted visitation rights. We went to court four times and it was postponed all four times and we finally went and the ruling was that he was to be supervised at all visitations and it has been like that ever since. It has been seven or eight months.

VP: (*to Paul*) So when was the first time that you met him? At the visitation center?

PAUL: Well, when we went to court I was sitting in a room when he went by into the courtroom. I figured that was him.

Mrs. Mittern said all the talk about visitation had been through lawyers. Now they are waiting mainly for Meredith's report on what she feels is best. "We'll just go by what Meredith says. Because I trust her judgment," said Mrs. Mittern. Paul was now going once a month for the monitored talks with his father.

VP: (*to Paul*) Has he remarried?

PAUL: Yeah, he married a lady named Maria.

VP: What is your attitude toward the visiting?

PAUL: I don't know yet.

VP: Do you mind the visiting?

PAUL: No, I don't mind.

VP: Do you find it interesting or not?

PAUL: Well, it seems like he straightened out better since what my mom told me.

VP: What do you mostly talk about with him?

PAUL: What we've been doing since the last time we've seen each other and stuff like that. And about his trips. I enjoy that. It seems like he's been in a lot of wrecks or close calls. He broke his shoulder once.

VP: Do you want the visits to continue or do they bother you?

PAUL: Really, I don't know very much about him so when I see him I can find out more. . . . I don't care whether we have them or not really. I kind of like seeing my dad though.

VP: Do you ever leave the hospital with him?

PAUL: No, we stay in one room with a two-way mirror with the lights on.

VP: Does that bother you or not?

PAUL: Kind of, you talk about something and then you remember that you're being listened to.

VP: (to Paul) Does the two hours visiting you have seem quite a long time to you or does it go pretty fast?

PAUL: It goes pretty fast.

VP: Is there anything he can bring in and show you like home movies?

PAUL: Just pictures. Photographs.

VP: I am going to be seeing him in a little while.

PAUL: Josh?

VP: Yes. I am not going to tell him what you say. I might not even tell him I talked to you. Did you meet his new wife Maria?

PAUL: Yes, she comes. She has two boys. One is named John and the other Jimmy.

We are now strolling out to the cab that Mrs. Mittern has called.

VP: Do you get along all right with Maria?

PAUL: Yeah. I like her all right. She sells tickets at the airport.

VP: You're having sort of a complicated life aren't you?

PAUL: Yeah, it sometimes bothers me.

vp: In what way would you say it bothers you?

PAUL: I guess I'm still mixed up.

I thanked him very much for talking with me and stepped into the cab for a trip down the East side of Denver to the home of Mr. and Mrs. Josh Wilsin and their two boys in a southeastern suburb. They live on a street with lawns and nice middle-class-type houses. Two handsome cars were parked in front of a two-car garage.

Josh, the ex-con, was quite a surprise. Pug-nosed, articulate, very relaxed and cheerful, rather tall. As our talk proceeded he seemed to be speaking frankly. His wife was a pleasant, light-haired woman, also good-natured. And her two boys were exuberant. They came up, pumped my hand and then returned to their play in the kitchen.

I began by saying, "My main interest I guess is why you have pursued the visitation right and I am just trying to get your philosophy about it."

Josh reviewed the case. He contended his ex-wife, as a part of the divorce, had agreed to let him have visitation rights with his son upon release. He was to pay child support. After release she refused to accept his support checks and got the parole officer to ban visits. After five years he appealed to the court for visitation rights. "This time," he said, "the judge, a lady, got a psychologist to make a report. It was detrimental to me because it said that at that particular time Paul was having psychological problems."

vp: Paul seemed like a nice lad; I saw him briefly.

JOSH: Oh he's — he can be funny, he can be ornery too. But anyway the judge said it would be a detriment and let it go again until I brought it up again about a year ago, and we went through the whole thing again. The judge and I had a long discussion. He said, "Well, what if Paul doesn't want to see you?" I told the judge I would go by the boy's decision after he had seen me. He asked me if I would be willing to pay child support even though he didn't want to see me and I said, "Yes, I would." Anyway, we finally got this visitation going on a trial basis with supervising from either Meredith or another psychologist through a one-way mirror. The only bad thing about this visitation is that Paul knows he is being watched. He doesn't really let go. He doesn't like the setting at all. I know that. He is very restrictive in his conversation. Basically he is hyperactive and sitting there and talking is not one of his fondest things in the world. We start joking occasionally and then things get better. From what I understand and can gather Paul didn't even know I existed until June of last year.

VP: I'm told Paul knows the past record now.

JOSH: Oh, yes sure. But it doesn't seem to bother him. As a matter of fact, from his discussions with us, he's not come out and directly said it but he has hinted a desire to stay with us. Why, I don't know.

VP: You mean on the visits?

JOSH: No, to live with us. . . . We haven't stated anything one way or the other . . . and it would cause problems . . . it would put him in the middle because he doesn't want to hurt his mom and he doesn't want to hurt me and he doesn't know what in the world to do. I can understand his position.

VP: That would make it a custody case.

JOSH: Yes, and she definitely would fight that. If I pursued custody then the judge would probably base his decision on whatever Paul told him. He'll soon be a teenager.

VP: This is interesting. You have not conveyed any interest in some kind of custody to anyone officially. It is just an impression you have gotten from talking with Paul?

JOSH: Yes. He has just subtly mentioned how nice it would be to fight with a couple of brothers.

I remembered Paul's last words to me, that he was "mixed up."

Meredith Ringler-White recently advised me that the requirement of supervision was withdrawn. Paul now regularly sees his father. In fact, with Mrs. Mittern's permission Paul spent most of a recent summer at his father's home!

KIDNAPPING ONE'S OWN CHILDREN

Some of the visitations Meredith Ringler-White supervises, as indicated, involved children who are believed to be in jeopardy of being kidnapped by the noncustodial parent.

Child-snatching is undoubtedly the messiest part of the great upsurge in contests over possession of children. The parental kidnappers may explain to their children that the other parent has died suddenly, and take off with the children.

Somewhere between 100,000 and 150,000 American children now are being kidnapped each year by angry parents. The lower figure was the 1980 estimate of Children's Rights, Inc. It has a network of people who cooperate in locating abducted children. Its members all have had their children kidnapped. Other organizations that have sprung up are Stop Parental Kidnapping (Rochester, New York), Stolen Children Information Exchange (Anaheim, California), and Citizens League on Custody and Kidnapping (Long Island).

Mexican police have become so weary of coping with parental kidnappers from the U.S. that at some border points its guards have been turning back single adults accompanied by children under sixteen unless they have documentation to account for the missing parent.

Children are snatched at school on the pretext of a dental appointment, or during visitation, or right from the home of the custodial parent. (Occasionally children, unhappy with the custodial arrangement, are willing abductees; many, however, are simply bewildered.)

In one case where the noncustodial mother was the snatcher of her two daughters she used nine different names and lived in fourteen different motels or hotels to elude searchers hired by her ex-husband. Two hired agents posing as FBI agents finally resnatched the children and returned them to the father.

In another case the husband was awarded custody of the children by an Alabama judge. The father had declared his wife unfit. While the children were visiting her, the mother got them awarded to her by a Massachusetts court. Thereupon the husband, who had dyed his hair and hired two agents armed with tear gas and handcuffs, physically snatched the children and fled with them to his Alabama haven.

In Oklahoma a mother, while her son was in her care, happened to see her ex-husband and some other men making off with her four-year-old son. She gave chase. During the chase the kidnappers' car overturned and both the son and the father were killed.

A number of psychiatrists examining children who have been kidnapped have testified to the probability of severe emotional reactions, such as intense clinging to the favored parent. A boy who was taken to another state by his father with the explanation that his mother had died was recovered by her two years later. He had lost the power of coherent speech for nearly a year after hearing his mother was dead.

Until recently U.S. parents felt little apprehension while snatching their children because such acts were exempt from the kidnap laws. They were family matters. At most, the acts were misdemeanors. With the great surge of custody battles and ensuing kidnap attempts, many states began passing laws specifiying that in custody matters their courts would respect the court decision in the state where the grant of custody originated. But there were always "safe" states, a dozen or so, including Illinois and Washington. Also, many states have declared kidnapping a felony but law enforcement officials often do not seem aware of changes in state laws.

As the family kidnapping continued to mount, Congress finally took action in the closing days of the Ninety-fifth Congress. The Parental Kidnapping Prevention Act, which went into effect in 1981, requires all U.S. states to respect custody and visitation decrees imposed by courts in other states. Also it makes available in child-snatching cases the services of the Federal Parent Locator Service, previously used only to locate husbands delinquent in child support payments. It often can track a parent by way of Social Security numbers, bank deposits, etc. A parent cannot apply directly for this help. It must be authorized by a court or a state official. The new act also makes it possible to bring the FBI into the search for child snatchers (a role the FBI has not been eager to assume).

Outside the U.S., at least twenty-seven countries now have signed a Hague Convention provision agreeing that they will return a child abducted by a parent to the child's country of origin.

THE NEED TO NORMALIZE VISITS

We've seen that the right to have access to one's own child after divorce has taken some painful turns from the youngsters' standpoint. The monitored visits and the snatching of children back and forth are just extremes. But court-ordered, tightly scheduled visiting is common. Frequently it is painful or tedious to the children because of the constraints of time and because of the artificial setting. These constraints thrust the parent being visited into the role of host rather than a real live parent.

For the youngster, casual, frequent short contacts with the noncustodial parent are more enjoyable and reassuring than long but occasional visits.

What the youngster really wants is not hosted entertainment but rather the assurance that he can follow his or her own interests — woodworking, softball, class projects in the proximity of his other parent. He or she wants to go shopping with that parent and help in cooking a meal. The child also wants freedom to telephone the other parent without getting a court order. And he doesn't want to have to feel guilty if he drops in on that other parent to say Hi on the way to school.

The parents acting together brought these children into the world. Hence they have a moral responsibility to continue functioning as a family unit and promote their children's best interests even though their own marriage contract has ended. Only cruel or thoughtless parents compete for a child's time, affection, or loyalty.

Nancy Weston of the Divorcing Family Clinic in Santa Monica summed up her convictions about the importance of relaxed visiting arrangements in these strong words:

"A child's life becomes lopsided if he has access to only one parent. . . . It is the children who are seeing both parents regularly and frequently who are doing the best, who have the higher self-esteem, who are suffering less depression and who are doing better in school."

17

Better Ways to Handle
Family Disruption

"The nature of the post-divorce relationship between
the parents profoundly affects the life of their
children."

— *Richard Chasin, Harvard psychiatrist and co-director
of the Family Institute of Cambridge*

As our Western societies are presently functioning, it is likely that the
divorce rates will increase rather than decrease in the coming decade.
We have seen some of the painful impacts of typical divorces on children; and we've also seen that divorce is causing substantial torment
and disruption in our society at large.

For children of divorce there is a strong likelihood, at the least, of a
lengthy drop in inner security, sense of self-worth, and willingness to
trust adults.

If you add up all the stressful things likely to happen to a typical
child going through a typical divorce and subsequent readjustments, you
get a stress score of 217 on the Social Readjustment Rating Scale
(Holmes & Rohe). That is the estimate of Penn State University researchers in human development.[1] They point out that a score of 300
puts a youngster at "high risk" of clinical symptoms.

Divorce itself rates a score of seventy-three, second only to death of a spouse (100). Some of the other relevant stresses that went into the 217 total:

> Change in financial state — 38
>
> Mother beginning to work — 26
>
> Change in living conditions — 25
>
> Change in residence — 20
>
> Change in schools — 20
>
> Change in number of family get-togethers — 15

One reason for the 217 score is that marital disruption is typically handled so badly in our society. Wallerstein and Kelly found that 80 percent of the divorcing parents of preschool children in their sample had given their children no explanation why they were splitting.

It seems reasonable to suggest that national efforts be made to ease the impacts of the divorce epidemic on children and on society.

A first step would be to reduce the chance of divorce by taking steps to enhance the likelihood that people who marry are well-matched. We should discourage impulsive marriages. A young man and woman can test their ability to live together only by a sustained acquaintance that involves handling emotional and practical trials of daily life. If this suggests that society tolerate cohabitation of people seriously interested in each other, so be it (though cohabitation certainly isn't essential to the testing of relationships). Some early north European societies experimented with a requirement of bedsharing before the couple was eligible to marry. States should require a six-week waiting period between the application for marriage license and the issuing of it. Such a requirement might make young people more prudent about embarking on marriage on the basis of binges or quickie romances.

Divorce laws should remain liberal for married couples without children. The laws should become more strict, however, for couples with preschool children. This is when marital disruption is hardest on the mother, and the children are least able to comprehend and manage what is going on.

In our new era of having the option of creating only wanted children it should be considered a serious offense against society and children for a married couple to bring a new person into the world and then not have the will to keep their marriage intact for the still helpless toddler. The fact that the young husband and wife decide they no longer are "happy" should not be enough. Perhaps they just haven't bothered to make a real effort. We have seen that a year or so after divorce a majority of divorced people have conceded regrets that they didn't try harder to make a go of their marriage.

Married couples with children under age six should be given more chance to reconcile their differences and explore the possibility of keeping their marriage intact. Community opinion used to inspire such second thoughts.

Two months before a divorce can be granted, if preschool children are involved, both partners should be required to meet, preferably together, with a court-appointed family counselor. The counselor would help them explore the roots of their grievances and the possibilities of modifications in behavior patterns that would make their union more viable. Such a meeting would be mandatory for the partner petitioning for divorce.

After a month, if one or both still wish to proceed with divorce, they would both be requested to meet again with the same counselor, together or singly. This time the aim would be to resolve how best to handle the marital breakup as far as the children are concerned. This second meeting would be mandatory for the partner filing the divorce petition.

If a divorce is definitely planned here are thoughts (beyond those already mentioned) on proceeding through the various stages to possible remarriage:

BREAKING THE NEWS

Divorce comes as a stunning surprise to most youngsters, even when (as in perhaps a fourth of the cases) there has been frequent, open quarreling. Their family is the basic fact of their life. How could they lose it, or survive without it?

No matter how well the explanation of the decision for divorce is handled, the youngsters probably are going to be angry, frightened, and grief-stricken. Probably they will plead for reconsideration. Older ones may receive the news with stony silence or try to play it cool. But they all deserve an honest explanation, one that will make sense to them if they are over one and a half years old. This will substantially reduce the hazard of prolonged trauma.

It is a cop-out by parents when they tiptoe out of a marriage quietly, as so often happens, "because the children wouldn't understand." Even if the parents are furious with each other, they owe it to their children to make the parting as cordial and understandable as possible.

If the ages and levels of comprehension of the children are fairly close, child psychologist Lee Salk recommends that the father and mother should break the news at a family meeting. Children can benefit from the sense of closeness in being in a crisis together. If age differences are large, the children can be told separately.

An explanation which parents prepare and present jointly greatly reduces the chances the parents individually will give hostile, conflicting, self-serving explanations. It also symbolizes the fact that the family is continuing despite a change in housing arrangements and a legal dissolution of the marriage.

If the decision to divorce is mutual, either parent can start the explanation. A united front is by far the best approach. If only one parent wants the divorce, the one not wanting it should open the discussion by saying, for example, "Your mother/father has decided she/he does not wish to continue living with me as man and wife." The parent opening the discussion should recall the couple's earlier happiness in marrying and having children. Lee Salk has suggested the parent then say something like this:

"As time went on, some things began to change and did not work out the way we thought they would, or the way we both wanted them to. Now we find that we are not happy living together. We have tried to work things out, but there does not seem to be any way that we can. Because of this, we have decided that is best to stop being unhappy and live more happily apart." I would put it more strongly. It should be stated that the degree of the unhappiness in marriage is so great that they fear it is affecting their ability to be good parents to the children.

Children should not be burdened with details of infidelity, if such has occurred. It can be stated that the departing parent has "taken up with friends I object to" or "I don't approve his long pattern of gambling" or "he doesn't approve of my desire to take a job" or "unfortunately we now seem to argue most of the time we are together."

Still it should be made clear that the person seeking the divorce is a good person and a good parent. The parents deeply regret and apologize for the fact that they are not going to continue living together as man and wife. But they both still love the children very much and will both try to continue being good parents.

The parent who will be leaving the household should assure the children that he or she will continue to love them and the changes will not affect the fact that they are still an ongoing family. Then to the details of the ongoing arrangements, as many as can be given. A few points should be made and repeated:

- The child is is no way to blame for the split, only the parents.
- Details about arrangements should make it definitely clear to the child he is not being abandoned.
- Both parents are still going to be acting as parents to the child, the family will continue, the father and mother are just going to be living in different places.
- Questions and comments from the youngsters should be encouraged, even if the children are in tears or furiously protesting.

If the treatment of the children during this crisis period in their life is handled well, it will increase the chances that the youngsters will handle the situation with only moderate and short-term distress.

HANDLING THE BREAKUP OF THE HOME

If possible the departure of the parent who is moving out should be in phases, including the moving of possessions, over a week or two. The dramatic exit for parts unknown, suitcases in hand, may suit the mood of the angry parents but is a terrible experience for kids. If possible, the departing parent should take his (or her) children to the residence where he will be staying for an inspection even before he moves out of his present house.

During this transitional period both the parents — despite their probable preoccupation with their anger — should be having private chats with each child. They can talk of many things, but the focus should be on reassuring the child of their love and continued devotion. The parents should consider the week before parting as an armistice in their grievances between themselves.

Neither now nor ever should the parents test the loyalty of the children. Harvard developmental psychologist Jerome Kagan states: "Above all, in the whole struggle, don't force the children to take sides. This is very stressful to them."

A business friend of mine in Connecticut who went through divorce has some excellent ideas on handling the separation. He is the father of two teenage boys and has remarried a woman with one eleven-year-old daughter. His first wife divorced him because of a continuing disagreement about life-styles. He and his former wife live near each other. Each parent maintains a twin-bedded boys' room. The boys consider both places "home" and see both parents almost every day. Each month they work out their own schedule on where they will be officially staying and post it on bulletin boards in each house.

Some of the ways my friend and his now ex-wife handled their breakup may be of interest. For example:

"Rule number one is don't let a lawyer get into the scene except to type up the final papers in document form.

"My wife and I had long discussions and both tried to be fair. We played draw poker for the pieces of furniture we both wanted.

"I and my former wife still have dinner every week, with my new wife's permission. Sometimes she and the kids join us.

"I still mow her lawn. If I'm busy one of the boys does it.

"Friends know it doesn't bother us to be invited to the same party.

"We both still get along great with the boys; and I believe my stepdaughter is fond of me."

THE FIRST MONTHS AFTER DIVORCE

These months, as we have seen, are typically periods of high disorganization and turmoil. The custodial parent should understand the difficulties most preteen children have in absorbing what is usually a staggering loss. Their typical first reaction, to protect themselves, is one of denial. They may become withdrawn. A visit to a friendly peer already living in a one-parent home may help the youngster accept reality. After denial there will be anger, then depression because of inability to modify their fate, before acceptance of the reality of the change finally sets in.[2]

The worst course for a custodial parent is to urge the children to be brave, get busy and not think about the problem. Rather the youngster should be encouraged to feel free to let it all out — the grief, the anger, the despair. Only after a healthy mourning has occurred will the youngsters really be ready to cope with the new life pattern.

Let's assume the custodial parent is the mother. During the first month she is having her own problems with high stress and is prone to become erratic and overpermissive at mothering. If she understands this she will devote more than usual thought to introducing regularity into the children's lives, to setting standards and limits, and to being decisive.

She will be fortunate if she lives in a supportive community and the children are old enough to have outside interests. A sense of stability for the children can come from contact with grandparents, admired uncles, admired teachers, girl scout leaders, and a gang of cronies.

FAMILY RELATIONS AFTER THE SPLIT

Unless married people divorce simply because they have become bored with each other it is totally natural that their divorce is accompanied by considerable anger. One party may feel rejection. Both may be disgruntled with the financial settlement. Recent divorcés frequently refer to their mates as "real bastards" and "real bitches."

Natural as those feelings are, it is imperative that couples with children agree to keep in separate mental compartments their feelings as ex-spouses and their feelings as ongoing parents. Constance Ahrons at the University of Wisconsin, Madison, in studying fifty-four divorced couples, found that the most successful divorced parents were those who had such relationship rules which required them always to separate their parental and spousal roles. Harry Keshet, who was involved in a large study of divorced fathers, has concluded: "Kids do a lot better if both parents are cooperative and involved."

Evidence that "kids do a lot better" when parents are actively cooperating in watching over their progress is demonstrated in a 1976 study. It found that when fathers joined with mothers in discussing the child's school progress with the teacher, the children scored up to seven months higher in reading and math than children whose fathers were not involved.[3]

Here are some things that children of divorce are entitled to from their separated parents. These might in fact be considered as major points in a Bill of Rights for Children of Divorce. Thoughtful parents would take care to observe them.

1. The children of divorce are entitled to parents who set aside at least twenty minutes every month to discuss, in person or on the phone, the progress and problems of the children — and only the children. There should be no recriminations about any other topic, such as money. The children's schoolwork, health, mental state, activities, and apparent reaction to the divorce should be the focus of such talks.

2. The children of divorce are entitled to parents who go out to dinner together with them, if desired by the child, on their birthdays or on important holidays. The parents should also both go to school events important to the children.

3. The children are entitled to have separated parents who do not belittle the other parent in front of the children.

4. The children of divorce are entitled to have parents who refrain from any action that would seem to force the children to take sides.

5. The children of divorce are entitled to be free from any sense of pressure from either parent to serve as informants about the ex-partner's spending, dating, or other activities. If children freely choose to chat about the other parent that is another matter.

6. Children of divorce are entitled to have complete freedom to phone either parent. If distances are involved, the calls will be collect. The children's parents will also agree that it is agreeable for the noncustodial parent to call his or her children at least once a week.

7. Children of divorce are entitled to have parents who agree to notify each other in all emergencies or important events involving the children.

8. Children of divorce are entitled to have parents who by agreement are civil and avoid recriminations when they are in the presence of the child.

HANDLING CUSTODY AND VISITATION

Whatever the details agreed upon, custody and "visiting" should also be handled on a co-parenting basis. Such an approach has several real advantages. It reminds the children that their family is still functioning. It greatly reduces conflict over support and visits. Since the modern divorced mother is probably going to be having a job, she will — when she stops feeling bitter — be grateful for breaks in her child-care responsibility.

Some form of legal joint custody has clear advantages for those parents who can separate in their mind their parental responsibilities from their spousal anger. This does not require that the child live an equal amount of time at each house, just equality of responsibility for major decisions affecting the children's lives. If there is also equality of physical custody the main consideration is that it not disrupt the child's routine of school, activities, friends, and contacts with important kinfolk. For those parents who just can't handle custody alone, a social worker or family counselor or an admired friend might be consulted.

It is vital that the parents — not lawyers and judges — work out the custody arrangement.

State laws should require that when children are involved any application for divorce must be accompanied by a written agreement by the divorcing persons on how custody and visitation will be handled. A lawyer can draft the document and offer technical information on what needs to be covered. But the agreement will be more acceptable to both sides and be more enduring if the principals thrash out the details themselves. If they can't agree among themselves they should turn to a mediator. Fortunately we are starting to see the emergence of attorneys specializing in family law who are committed to the conciliatory rather than the adversarial approach. They are qualified mediators. John Fiske of Cambridge, Massachusetts, is an example. If mediation fails, the contesting parents should refer their case to a family life specialist for a recommendation to the court.

As for visitation, the more rigidly structured the permissible visiting the more unsatisfactory it will be to the youngsters. Judges often spell out visitation in detail because it gives them a ready-reference guide if the parents bring their quarrels back into court.

"Visitation" is a poor word. It probably should be discarded to describe what both the child and the noncustodial parent want. They really want "access time" with each other. Visitation puts their get-togethers on an artificial basis, makes the parent feel responsible for entertaining the child.

A child should be guaranteed access time with the noncustodial parent that is both regular and frequent. He needs the assurance of regularity. If the noncustodial parent lives in the vicinity, and he should, a youngster capable of biking should also have the right to drop by and chat with the noncustodial parent whenever he wishes.

Ideally the noncustodial parent's place should be seen by the youngster as his (or her) second home. It should have a room, at least a reserved space, he can call his own. He should be able to bring friends to the second home, and have a place for doing homework. When he stays overnight the youngster will be expected to make his bed, help out with meals, do his homework or read. Trips out to movies, restaurants or ball games should be thought of simply as occasional treats.

If there are two or more children, they should do some of their visiting as a group, to give the custodial parent time-off from parenting. But the noncustodial parent should also have some exclusive time with each child.

OPTIMIZING THE ONE-PARENT WAY OF LIFE

Probably the first thing to remember is that the well-being of the children depends very greatly on the morale of the mother. If she permits herself to remain in a funk, or to be ground down by role-overload, the children will feel defeated too.

The mothering role in a one-parent family is so challenging that it often seems to bring forward a blithe spirit and a lot of ego strength. Such a feeling is contagious. It will bring out the best in children; they take on unusual responsibilities, become intensely loyal to Mom, and feel like junior partners.

The mothering role will be greatly simplified if she manages to get a job with some flexibility and if she has an understanding boss. If boys have little chance to have contact with the father because he is in another county or state, the wise mother will see that they have frequent exposure to admirable adult males, whether uncles, neighbors, or male acquaintances. She will get the boys into Cub Scouts, Boy Scouts, and camping.

And for her own morale the mother will seek an active and community and social life for herself.

Most mothers will find it greatly supportive to join a local chapter of Parents Without Partners at least as a start. The local chapters have monthly programs on problems relating to single parenthood. They have discussion groups and they have recreational social activities for *both* single parents and their children. Parents Without Partners has community projects for both adults and children, and it has outings such as visits to museums or parks for family units. Teenagers in PWP have their own clubs.

Many PWP chapters have a dad's committee of males who head one-parent families because of death, divorce, or separation. Its members take the children on outings or volunteer to baby-sit and in general serve as role models.

Parents Without Partners will accept into membership only certified single parents. References are required. The aim is to keep out prowling husbands (or wives) looking for a date. Here are a few notable comments from the two-hour-long talk I had with eight PWP mothers in Connecticut:

"It is easier for me to meet interesting people, including men, through my children than to meet them by myself."

"If you meet an interesting man at PWP, you know at least that he is interested in children. A lot of men aren't."

"Having a place to talk is most important."

"We're kind of an extended family."

"There is a lot of remarriage within PWP."

"PWP helps people become a lot more relaxed as parents."

If parents can be relaxed in their roles, be compassionate, and do things together with their offspring, the youngster appreciates it enormously, whether living in one-parent or two-parent homes.

4

Major New Patterns of Family Life

Growing Up in a
One-Parent Household

"I don't miss my father so much as I miss the
Daddy-Mommy business. It's a curious thing to have,
instead of family dinners, just me and mother. And on
Christmas when you get downstairs there is just you and
Mother."

*— A fifteen year old girl cited by sociologist Robert
Weiss of the University of Massachusetts, Lecturer,
Department of Psychiatry, Harvard Medical School*

During the flick of time between 1970 and 1980 there has been an absolutely astonishing change occurring in the proportion of children in the Western World living with only one parent. In the United States, for example, there was a two-thirds increase of such children, according to U.S. Census Bureau figures. Today, more than a fifth of all the nation's children live in a one-parent household. That adds up to more than twelve million youngsters. The vast majority are children of divorce, separation or desertion. One-parent living is up throughout the Western World, but America has twice as high a proportion of one-parent households as, say, Great Britain.

Is it a hazardous trend for society? We'll get to that later, but first I want to describe my talk with Katie Powell, who heads one such family. Her three daughters have all impressed me as delightful. Mindy is eight. Maggie is ten. Loddy is fifteen. They live in a suburb of Baltimore. I had been struck by the sight of the mother Katie and her three daughters spending more than a half hour in animated conversation at the table after they had finished breakfast. I had been struck by the sight of young Maggie spending more than an hour by herself figuring out backgammon moves; and the fact that Mindy is already quite a good figure skater. I was impressed last summer when Loddy went all by herself to Idaho for two months to work on a ranch.

How did all this relate to the contention made by some respected professionals that children raised in one-parent households are at risk? Was there something somber in the situation I didn't see? The story of the Powells doesn't exactly contradict the professionals, but it is illuminating. Below are excerpts from my taped talk with the mother Katie, an attractive, articulate woman in her thirties. Since her account is highly personal, I have changed her name, but she didn't request it. The words are right off the tape.

Katie now works for a firm that helps companies select sites for new plants. Her ex-husband Joe has remarried a divorcée with three children of her own. Joe is a coach for a high school a half hour from Katie's home. Two issues causing the divorce were that she, with a master's degree, wanted to work, which he strongly disapproved; and the fact that his work kept him away from home a lot. Her first job was helping to reconstruct an early-nineteenth-century iron factory. After their separation that job ended and she worked at several jobs — secretary, nursery school teacher, etc. — until she got her present job, which involves some travel.

VP: Was it nasty all the way through or have you maintained an amiable relationship with Joe?

KATIE: I don't think it has been amiable. There were certain basic things we agree on that have to do with the children. But we don't get along very well when it comes to finances and a lot of other issues.

VP: How often do the children see their father?

KATIE: Ideally they see him every other weekend. It doesn't work out quite that way, but close to it. In the summer they generally spend anywhere from the whole summer to six weeks with him. It's a very ideal situation because he has free access to things like swimming pools and tennis.

VP: Does he ever come to visit you, or not?

KATIE: No.

VP: Does he do the honking thing?

KATIE: Oh, he comes in when he picks up the children.

VP: Was the divorce difficult?

KATIE: We didn't fight openly. It really wasn't too grim around the house for the girls.

VP: They were not in a tension-ridden home.

KATIE: No. So I think it was quite a surprise to the girls. The one thing they still can't get over is that they want us to be together. They are reconciled to seeing us separately but in their hearts they want to see us together under the same roof. Yes, even though he has re-married and we have been apart five years.

VP: Which of the girls seemed to be most bothered by the breakup?

KATIE: They all were, I think, in different ways. In some ways Mindy might have been least affected because she was so little. Maggie developed skin diseases. And Loddy just sort of verbalized a lot that she was upset.

VP: Some studies show that one-parent households tend to be disorganized for a while after divorce. Did that happen to you?

KATIE: Well, yes, in fact it still often is very confusing. Sometimes there is not enough in the house to eat and the dishes don't get done and you have to remember which child you are supposed to pick up where and hold down a job at the same time. These things are somewhat threatening to the children, also. *I know that Mindy still worries that I am going to leave her somewhere and forget to pick her up* [italics mine].

VP: Do you think you try to compensate because you are the only parent in the house and have a job?

KATIE: Yeah, I think that's right. When you're working and come home to your children I find that I am really glad to see them. I like to have dinner with them and we talk about the day and sometimes if there's time we play a game. I try not to overdo it.

VP: You seem to talk to them like adults.

KATIE: I do. I think I do it more now because I think of us as a team, as sort of good friends. We are all sort of in this together. I didn't do that so much when they were little, but I think I've always tried to treat them with respect, if possible.

VP: Mindy was three when you were divorced. Did that create a problem for you in getting jobs?

KATIE: She was in nursery school. I was very very lucky because I had a good friend that took care of her every day for two hours after school. She did it for free. She was a mother and had two children of her own.

VP: What have been the most difficult problems in terms of raising three children on your own?

KATIE: The sheer organizing can become pretty exhausting. Trying to keep everybody's schedules straight while holding down a job. The older two get out of school at funny hours and they take lessons in the afternoons and there are lots of advantages I would like to give them but can't because I can't be there to drive them. They just have to skip it.

VP: Like what?

KATIE: Like ice skating. Mindy is a good figure skater but there is no way she can get down to the rink to get lessons. A lot of nights I have to work late so I can't guarantee that every night I can come back at five and pick them up. There are constant dentist and doctor appointments and things like that which are really hard to handle. Then financially it is hard. I guess I understand how men used to feel when they had the complete responsibility for their family's future.

VP: Has Joe been a good father?

KATIE: Yes, an excellent father. Very involved with them personally.

VP: He still is even though remarried?

KATIE: Yes, and we've always had an agreement between us that we would never contradict each other. In other words, we wouldn't have the girls coming to one parent and that parent saying no so she goes to the other who says yes. We have backed each other up.

VP: Is that still true since your divorce?

KATIE: Yes, we do the best we can to be consistent.

VP: Has his remarriage changed things much?

KATIE: The girls get along fairly well with their stepmother, although there are tensions at times.

VP: The eldest and youngest of your girls are seven years apart in age. Does that create problems in talking with them together?

KATIE: Every year it has become more fun to talk and share ideas. It's hard to describe.

VP: They don't think of you as an adult figure at all or a mother figure?

KATIE: I think they do in some respects. If I am angry at them, they know it. They're miffed and sometimes they react to me. They sulk. But mostly when we are together I feel the spirit is one that we're having a good time together. I like to take them on trips I have to make.

VP: What kind of trips?

KATIE: Last fall, I took the two little ones out to Seattle. We traveled all around the Olympic Peninsula and we just went from one motel to another. I was on a work project. They were incredible. They carried in the suitcases and every morning they packed and put them in the car. Sometimes they had to sit in the rain in the car for a couple of hours while I had an interview or something. But it was all just a big adventure and we did it together. Half the time I am as scared as they are. They support me an awful lot. I've had tremendous comfort from them.

VP: Are they concerned about your overworking?

KATIE: I think so, a little bit. They want me to be happy. They want me to have friends.

VP: Do they still like their father very much?

KATIE: Yes they do.

VP: Is it awkward for them to go to his place?

KATIE: I think they like to go. They love the kids there and all. They do get sick of packing and unpacking for the trips.

VP: Do the girls have to take on responsibilities beyond what one might expect for their age?

KATIE: They have to cook. We take turns. I'll cook two nights. Maggie (age ten) will cook two nights. Mindy helps with the cooking another night. They all do their laundry.

VP: Mindy does that? She's eight now.

KATIE: Yes. I still help her some but the other two do theirs completely on their own. Mindy was able to take her own penicillin three times a day when she was ill. The girls all take care of their own rooms; change their own beds and vacuum their room. Sometimes it looks like a disaster area, but generally they get organized and fix it up about once a month.

VP: Have you ever had any really bad times in terms of the visits to Joe's place?

KATIE: There have been a few. For example, as I said, I insist the children do their own packing. I think this is great but Joe and his wife don't seem to think it is so hot when the girls get to their house and don't have the proper clothes. I get yelled at because I don't supervise them enough.

VP: He yells at you in front of the children?

KATIE: No, on the telephone.

VP: Is this house you live in the one you had before the separation?

KATIE: Yes. That I am sure has helped. Joe felt strongly about that. He wanted them to stay in the same house to have some continuity. They love the house. . . . We still jointly own it.

VP: What has been the worst period from your standpoint?

KATIE: The first year probably, though in some ways it is worse now because I am more realistic. After you have been at it for five years you realize it may never end. The first year you're in such a shock you don't know what will happen next. You think maybe you'll get married again and your problems will go away. The way it looks now I think I might be single for quite a while, and have a long period of responsibility. . . .

VP: The girls have never gotten after you to remarry?

KATIE: No, in fact every time it comes up . . .

VP: They want you to go back to Joe?

KATIE: No, they're realistic. They say they like it the way it is. I think what they don't want is to have to divide my attention with some man. I say, "Someday you will grow up and move away" and they start to cry.

The Powells prove that one-parent living can work out very well for all concerned and be a kind of adventure. But it should be noted that they had a lot of things going for them that millions of one-parent families don't have (in addition to the fact the girls have an excellent mother). For example:

• The parents have remained sensible and responsible despite the disruption of their marriage. They confer about the children.

- The girls still have a loving father, and their mother cooperates in their visits to him, even though he has remarried.
- The parents still back each other up regarding decisions about the children.
- There was comparatively little nastiness between the parents at the time of the divorce, or afterward, regarding custody or visitation.
- The girls are still living in the same house and among the friends they always had.
- The mother has an understanding boss who permits her to leave the office when she has to transport the children, etc., as long as she gets her work done.
- There isn't any serious financial privation.
- The Powell family does not include boys. There is some evidence that boys have a harder time in a Mom-only household than girls.

There is no full consensus among experts but several investigators have found evidence that boys seem more vulnerable. Texas psychologist J. W. Santrock reported in *Child Development* that school grades of boys in father-absent households are more likely to suffer than those of girls.[1] The studies of Hetherington and of Michael Rutter in England found boys were more disrupted by separation and loss caused by divorce than girls. And Michael Lamb, psychologist at the University of Wisconsin, said that boys are more likely than girls to be damaged at all ages. However, there may be a sleeper effect for girls when they reach adolescence, which we will note shortly.

Regardless of how well or how poorly a one-parent family handles its arrangements, there are some common problems that must be dealt with by most one-parent families, particularly after divorce.

Role overload   Katie Powell's harassment with "sheer organization" was no more exhausting than that of most divorced mothers with more than one child. She had an understanding boss and no infants or toddlers under three years of age. A staff report of the National Association of Elementary School Principals states:

"For the working single parent, the very mechanics of child care can be a logistical nightmare."

One such divorced mother summed up the overload vividly to divorce counselor Mel Krantzler in these words:

"My life is a series of spinning plates. One false move and they all shatter. If the baby-sitter calls up sick at the last minute, I can't go to work and the whole routine is thrown off. I never knew that just getting through twenty-four hours took so much planning. I have to decide three days in advance when to wash my hair."[2]

Most divorced mothers probably would find jobs for themselves even if they didn't need one to survive. A Wilton, Connecticut, divorcée with children told me: "Work is therapeutic for a divorced person. Better than sitting at home — oh my god!"

A curtailed outside life   This is not inevitable but it does seem a common pattern. Partly it may be due to the mother's busyness and preoccupation with her own new way of life. Divorce often leads to moving into new, strange neighborhoods. Friendship and socializing patterns tend to be almost split in half for a while by a marital disruption.

Partly too, there is curtailment because the mother feels engulfed in problems. A study of nearly a thousand single parents caused Ohio psychologist Michael J. Smith to conclude they participate less in community affairs than the heads of two-parent families. He found they socialize less and are more apt to be affected by feelings of loneliness, alienation, and powerlessness. And this is not just a temporary situation.[3] He considered the drop in community participation particularly important because single parents "may need *more* participation and a *greater* sense of control over their lives than the heads of two-parent families."

The mood of a mother in such a state inevitably influences the frame of mind of her children. A mother told me that one of the few times she gets out among male adults is when she takes her son to his Little League ball games; and that seems embarrassing to her son.

Many enterprising mothers shake off such an understandable proneness to isolation and set out to lead a full life. A first step as mentioned earlier is to join a local chapter of Parents Without Partners.

Severe financial problems   Some investigators have reported that any alleged bad effects on children of life in a single-parent home tend to become small when the investigators provide adequate controls for the amount of income of intact families versus one-parent households.[4] There is some evidence to the contrary, but perhaps the argument is made moot by the fact that lowered economic status is one of the most pervading characteristics of mother-headed households created by divorce.

About three million children in mother-headed households live below poverty level in the U.S.

The first inevitable discovery that even the most cooperative divorcing couples learn is that two households are more expensive to maintain than one. Mother still typically "gets the children" even though the national odds are that she has only 60 per cent of the bread-winning capacity of the father, if she works. This inequity is presumably corrected by alimony and child support.

Alimony is fast fading as a corrective because of court decisions and modern women's desire to be independent. Only about one father in fifteen pays alimony beyond a few months.

As for child support payment, that has eroded sharply too. Only about a fourth of the mother-headed households in the U.S. receive child support payments from the father six months after the divorce. A year after the divorce the proportion drops still lower. And only rarely are the payments sufficient to support the children fully. The mother who gets $1,500 a year per child is lucky. That is not much in these inflationary times.

The upshot is that about half of all mother-headed households are living below the poverty line, at least for the first couple of years after divorce. Some of course were near the poverty line to start with. But millions of mother-headed households undergo a sharp decline in their material level of living.

Robert Weiss, an authority on one-parent households, told me of an analysis he and Mary Jo Bane of Harvard made of an income dynamics study at the University of Michigan. When couples with incomes in the upper third of U.S. families divorce, it would appear, the mother with children found their available income slashed almost in half. The cut was considerably less for mothers whose families were in the lower third. But there was less to cut.

Psychologist Dorothy Burlage of the Harvard Medical School reported a couple of years ago that in most cases the payments from ex-husbands are late or less than stipulated, which can be very upsetting to the mother trying to make ends meet. According to the U.S. Census Bureau, only about one-half of mothers who are supposed to receive child support actually receive it. Burlage quoted one mother as saying: "My greatest fear since the separation has been money. It keeps me running scared and depressed all the time." Burlage added the obvious: "Of course, the mother's emotional state has repercussions for the children."

Weiss in his study got a sample of such "repercussions" on the youngsters from an adolescent girl who told him, "You don't have the freedom of not worrying about things, of not worrying about money."

Single mothers often find themselves moving to cheaper neighborhoods, which for the children means changing schools and neighborhood friends.

Some mothers become ingenious in finding ways to cut living costs without moving. A neighbor of mine who has been active in Parents Without Partners, Judy Gans Nathanson, despaired of her high costs for home and auto repair. She is a mother of two. After her divorce she got herself a job driving a bus and became a bus fleet coordinator. She took an auto repair course and began studying manuals on home repair and carpentry. She now rewires blown-out mixers, ailing vacuum cleaners, replaces worn out electrical cords, handles all toilet repairs, panels rooms, replaces auto fan belts, flushes out her furnace, installs towel bars and hanging lamps. She cut her cost of living by at least a fourth. More important, she is a very self-assured, buoyant young woman.

But most mothers heading households are forced to cut back from their former way of life. It is hard to get courts to prosecute fathers for nonsupport, at least outside a few states such as Michigan. In Michigan many hundreds of divorced fathers were jailed in 1977 for nonsupport. One reason husbands and courts have been lax about abiding by or enforcing support agreements has been the knowledge that the mothers often are able to go on welfare. About a third of all mothers who are separated from their husbands do go on welfare. Mothers with children have been able to get help under the federally sponsored Aid to Families with Dependent Children program. But since 1981 federal budget cuts have substantially eroded this safety net. Proof of poverty has also become more stringent.

In the late 1970s the federal government, weary of paying out billions of dollars in child support to one-parent families when the father was contributing nothing, began prodding the fathers. It set up the Federal Parent Locator Service to find the fathers who were flagrantly violating pacts committing them to provide some sort of support. The Internal Revenue Service has been authorized to hold up tax refunds of such scofflaws if notified by a local government.

One route that younger single-parent mothers in their teens or twenties take under the duress of making ends meet is to move back with their parents. That not only saves on rent but often on child-care costs. One price to the mother is that she may feel she has lost some of her independence. Another price, of course, is the extra burden of children on the grandparents, which they may or may not resent.

European countries generally have been quicker to realize that mothers heading single-parent families have a special problem that needs humane treatment. A housing association in Cologne, Germany, built a special block of apartments for one-parent families and provides child-care facilities so that the parent can work. Sweden gives one-parent families a number of advantages such as top priority for openings in nurseries.[5]

HOW IMPORTANT IS THE FATHER'S ABSENCE?

Hundreds of investigators have pondered this question. A dozen years ago researchers Elizabeth Herzog and Cecelia F. Sudia at the U.S. Office of Child Development reviewed about sixty of the studies least flawed methodologically and concluded that there seemed to be a near standoff. Almost as many investigators found no linkage between father absence (for whatever reason) and undesirable traits in children as those who did find linkages.

Herzog and Sudia's main focus was on the possible effect of father absence on juvenile delinquency, school achievement, and masculine identity. One conclusion was that "The number of parents in the home is likely to be less crucial to the child's development than the family functioning of the present members — which is far harder to assess." To illustrate they cited two well-known studies. One study was of the sons of Norwegian sailors who were away at sea a year or two at a stretch. It found the sons showed immaturity and dependency, with insecure masculine identification compared with the control group. When the study was replicated by Italian investigators on sons of Genoa sailors, unusual problems with masculine identification and peer adjustment did not seem to emerge. Herzog and Sudia suggested as an explanation that by tradition wives of sailors in Genoa were expected to demonstrate responsibility, independence, and self-sufficiency, whereas wives of Norwegian sailors were still expected to play conventional wifely roles.

Several years after the Herzog-Sudia study Michael and Jamie Lamb at the University of Wisconsin concluded that, by then, "The vast father-absence literature . . . indicates that such children are handicapped."[6] They conceded that there were a "number of confounding" issues that made it unclear whether the handicap was due to father absence per se or to the lack of his financial support. They also reported as a "consistent finding'' that the younger the child at the time of the father's departure, the more seriously the child appears to be affected. Harold Feldman of Cornell University suggested in 1979 that the father's absence has a significant impact only in those cases where the father has been interactive with his children, and that most fathers aren't really very interactive.[7]

Another complicating question: Why is the father absent? Has he separated from the family because of divorce, is he off to sea or fighting a war, or has he died? Apparently the absence of a parent due to death is less apt to have a long-term upsetting impact on the children than absence due to a splitting up of parents. Death is a clearcut blow. Once the grief has eased, the surviving family usually rallies and often feels it is responding to a challenge. Divorce, on the other hand, often brings the children dilemmas of loyalty, embarrassment at not having a father at home, and lingering fantasies of reconciliation.

Others suggest that the absence of father is most likely to have a significant effect if it occurs between the ages of two and six.

Those holding that the absence of the father (for whatever reason) is significant for children point to the following father roles — in addition to being a provider — as being notable losses:

Role model. Fathers show both boys and girls what it's like to be a man, and so add to their perception of human relationships.

Authority. In a typical family fathers have more control over children than mothers. Mothers give more commands but they are not as likely to be obeyed. As Hetherington has put it, "Mother doesn't have the aura of power." Perhaps this is just social conditioning. In any case, sociologist John Clausen of the University of California, Berkeley, finds that fathers play an important role in setting the "standards and values that provide the moral climate of a family."

Sex-role typing. For better or worse, a father is usually more concerned than the mother that his boys behave like boys and his girls behave like girls.

Helping mother to be a good mother. An investigator at the National Institute of Child Health and Human Development found that a father's emotional support helps a mother in her role of being a good mother.

SOME APPARENT PLUSES

Some of the impacts of one-parent living seem favorable. Robert S. Weiss, author of *Going It Alone,* interviewed more than two hundred single parents and about fifty children of such parents.[8] He was much impressed by a teenager who had been in a single-parent household since the age of ten, who said:

"In the long run — I feel sort of like I shouldn't say it — but a lot of kids are better off if their parents do get divorced, because you grow up a lot quicker."

If mother is working, the young tend rather quickly to have new responsibilities, as we saw with the Powell girls. Thirteen-year-old boys may be treated as man of the house and do most of the things a father would do. A teenage girl told Weiss of being angry with a friend at school from a two-parent home who had lamented that her mother hollered at her that morning for not making the bed properly. The girl said she had felt like responding: "You little twerp! I have to make my bed, my mother's bed. I have to clean the whole house. I have to cook the dinner. I have to take the trash out."

Some children regress when responsibilities are thrust on them so early, but many seem to thrive. Children want to be needed.

I mentioned a few pages ago about my divorced neighbor Judy Gans Nathanson who took the course in auto repair. I had a chat with her daughter Lisa when she was sixteen. She had been without a father in the house for six years. Lisa is a lithe, blond, handsome, cheerful girl. Her high school friends have often come to her house and watched in amazement as she bakes a chicken, cooks a casserole, or makes a chef's salad. When she was fifteen she went to visit her boyfriend, an eighteen-year-old freshman at the University of Connecticut one hundred miles away. She bawled him out because he had put a wet towel in the laundry hamper. To me, she slapped her forehead and said, "He'd know about mildew if he had to be on the other end of the laundering process."

She got after her high school acquaintances who were on pot and "walk around stoned all day in school." She told them it was an absolutely stupid habit. On out-of-town trips in the winter to high school basketball games she noticed the girls who had forgotten their mittens and reminded them to go back and get them. "They call me Mother," she said.

Another thing that commonly happens in the mother-children household is that the children come to feel they are partners, or at least junior partners, with their mother. There often is more intimate, confidential conversation, more consulting, and shared decision-making.

A divorced mother in Westport, Connecticut, who is a physical therapist told me that six years after divorce her teenage daughter confided: "You know, Mom, if I had graded you one to ten in that first year I would have graded you a one. Now as a person I would grade you as a nine."

This daughter knew her mother's great wish was somehow, sometime, to save enough money to go to the Galapagos Islands off South America, which had long fascinated her. This really extraordinary daughter worked on a production line of a bread factory until she was able to surprise her mother with a fully paid cruise to the Galapagos. The mother explained to me proudly, "She felt I needed it."

For a less-than-skilled mother, the thrusting of responsibilities and the increased confidentiality can create problems. She may be puzzled how to discipline a junior partner who does something really dumb or wild. Her need to confide in someone when she is at wits end over financial problems may dump more anxiety on children than they should be expected to absorb. A mother asked Weiss: "You're hit with these bills and who can you talk to about them but the kids?"

And when the kids visit their fathers, they may be hit by more talk about their mother's unreasonable financial demands on him.

Growing up faster in terms of responsibilities gives the youngsters strengths but perhaps also some problems, particularly for the youngster who spends several years being short-changed on nurture. Their precocity can turn them into loners or grave miniature adults.

SOME POSSIBLE HAZARDS TO KEEP IN MIND

Children who grow up in single-parent homes seem to show tendencies that some feel may not promote their well-being in life. I stress that this is just an inclination which can readily be offset by perceptive parenting. Here are some apparent problem areas:

Personality, particularly sex-role development   Large-scale studies of adults indicate that an above-average portion of those who were raised in one-parent homes were somewhat inclined to be apprehensive, lonely, and relatively low in self-esteem.[9]

Boys from such homes may be low in persistence. Hetherington mentions that such young men have been less likely to complete their tour of duty in the Peace Corps. Boys may have less drive to achievement and leadership, if they haven't somehow spent a good deal of stimulating time with their father or an admired father figure.[10]

In a typical two-parent household the father influences the sexual development by serving as a role model. Hence his absence for whatever reason presumably should cause untypical sex-role development, which is one aspect of personality. Apparently it does.

E. Mavis Hetherington conducted a comprehensive and fascinating study of the behavior of adolescent, lower-middle-class girls. Some came from two-parent homes; some had only one parent because of death of the father; others had not been in regular contact with their father for years because of divorce. Girls from all three groups regularly went to a community recreation center where they were systematically observed and interviewed.

Hetherington's principal conclusion was that the girls from homes where father was absent for whatever reason were somewhat uncertain and apprehensive in relating with males — both peers and adults. She attributes this to their lack of opportunity for constructive interaction with a loving, attentive father.[11] The father-absent girls scored high on the Manifest Anxiety Scale and many showed an unusual amount of pulling hair, lip, and fingers while being interviewed by male adults.

Most intriguing were the ways the two different types of father-absent girls differed in coping with their uncertainty. The daughters raised by widows tended to be quiet, shy, even timid when talking with male boys their age. In their interviews with a male adult they sat stiffly as far away as possible from the interviewer, with their knees close together. They looked everywhere but at the adult.

The daughters of divorcées, on the other hand, acted with startling if inept boldness with boys. They were flirtatious. They resolutely tried to be near, and to have physical contact with, the teenage boys. Despite their efforts they were no more popular with boys than the other girls. And with the male adult during the interview they sat as close to him as they could get, smiled a lot, tended to sprawl in the chair with their legs wide apart.

A study of one thousand teenagers by the Youth Values Project in New York City indicated that girls from single-parent households were startlingly more active sexually (33 percent more) than girls from two-parent homes.[12] Boys from single-parent homes were somewhat more sexually active than boys from two-parent homes. When controls for such factors as low socioeconomic or minority status were introduced, the differences in sexual activity held. One speculation was that teenagers with single parents felt a strong emotional need to be "popular." Another speculation offered for the higher level of sexual activity was that the single parent typically worked, which left the home empty for long stretches. The offspring had easy access to bedrooms or couches.

I should mention that a survey at Brooklyn College of twenty-four older college-age women who had been fatherless because of death or divorce found some differences in sexual attitudes but no differences in actual sexual activity. But that was a small sample.

The Gilmartin Report on sexuality found "swingers" were three times more likely than "non-swingers" to come from homes broken by divorce. And there are reports that females who had no meaningful affectionate contact with their fathers had more problems as adults in achieving orgasm. (This has been commented on by E. Mavis Hetherington and by Rhode Island University psychologist Henry B. Biller, who has been prominent in studying the role of fathers.)

As for boys from father-absent households, the preponderance of a considerable body of research seems to indicate that if father's absence occurs before the boys reach the age of five, there is a stronger than average chance that their sex role will be less firmly established. Biller has stated: "There is a wealth of evidence pointing to the importance of the father-son relationship in masculine development."[13] Emotionally distant or ineffectual fathers have about the same effect on their child's sex-role development as the physically absent father. Many divorced fathers who still maintain good contact with their young sons eliminate this tendency. Older brothers also often have an impact on little boys' sex-role development. So do divorced mothers who, if concerned, see to it that their preschool boys get plenty of exposure to adult male models. As Biller put it, "The child may also have a father surrogate in the form of a relative, friend or teacher, and such a person can be influential in his development." On the other hand, the child who has a father living at home may not have a very meaningful relationship with him.

Michael Lamb, who has researched the father role extensively, states: "One of the best established findings is that the masculinity of sons and the femininity of daughters are greatest when fathers are nurturant and participate extensively in the child-rearing."[14] In short, he adds, fathers are most influential when they are involved in what "are often portrayed as female activities." Paternal warmth is crucial.

Boys under the age of five in father-absent households may develop behavior patterns closer-than-normal to those of girls. In play patterns it may happen simply because male peers have shut them out. Hetherington noted in her group's study of children of divorce that small boys under five often showed play patterns more characteristic of preschool girls. For example they showed more verbal aggression and less physical aggression than did boys from intact homes.

But this does not necessarily mean that as they grow up they will take on effeminate characteristics. Peer consciousness may cause them to take on strongly masculine characteristics. D. J. West, from his extensive research on sexuality, pointed out that "pressures which drive one boy toward femininity . . . may turn another boy into a tough, defensive hyper-masculine personality."

If we have a mother-headed household, how the mother *and* father handle the situation has an influence on the sex-typing of the growing youngsters, boys or girls. As for boys Hetherington says:

"Fathers who are seeing their kids regularly have more masculine sons. We also found masculine sons in one-parent families where we found mothers reinforcing the boy's masculine behavior, mothers having a positive attitude toward males and the father, and mother permitting boys to explore and encouraging boys in rough-and-tumble activity."

Emotional stability   Judith Wallerstein and Joan Kelly in the five-year follow-up of 131 children of divorce stated that some boys and girls in all age groups who had been able to cope during a conflict-ridden marriage deteriorated notably in the five-year separation period. Thirty-four percent of the children after five years were "happy and thriving." Twenty-nine percent were doing "reasonably well." And thirty-seven percent were "depressed." The investigators considered the incidence of depression "dismayingly high." More than a fourth of the children were intensely lonely.

Most of these children of divorce did not, after five years, think their family situation had been improved by the dissolution of the marriage. About a third of the children were aware that an intense bitterness still existed between their father and mother. Wallerstein and Kelly in their report concluded that one major cause of the poor outcome for such children "was the failure of the divorce to result in a reasonable adjustment to it by the parents." The parents had flunked at human relations.

There was no way to distinguish what proportion of the depression was a lingering effect of the marital convulsion and how much of it derived from living in a single-parent household or other factors. The authors did suggest, however, that life in the single-parent household contributed. For example: "The fact remains that the divorced family in which the burden falls entirely or mostly on one parent is more vul-

nerable to stress, has more limited economic and psychological re-
serves."[15] Another problem they found was that such a family is handicapped by a lack of "the supporting or buffering presence of another
adult for the expected and unexpected crises of life." They called for a
network of supportive community services — including vocational, financial, and educational counseling for the single mother and enriched
child-care and after-school programs to ease this growing source of stress
in our midst.

The depression reported in a third of the youngsters after five years
of living in a single-parent home seems to some extent to persist to
adulthood. Richard Gardner, New York child psychiatrist, states that
the deprivation and strife in a post-divorce home "appears to be a most
important contributing factor to the development of adult depression. . . ."

Bed-wetting, an indication of emotional stress, also tends to be more
persistent in a single-parent home. In England the National Survey of
Health and Development followed the lives of 4,701 infants born in a
single week in 1946 for *twenty-three* years. One factor charted was the
rate of bed-wetting up to the fifteenth year. A report states: "At each
age, children from broken homes are apparently twice as likely to wet
their bed as children from unbroken homes." At age twelve, a tenth of
the "broken home" youngsters were still occasionally wetting. It is
noteworthy that the death of a father was not associated with increased
bed-wetting at any age.

These indicators of persisting stress presumably are accounted for primarily by those households where the process of marital disengagement
was ineptly handled, with long-lingering turmoil and bitterness.

Self-control and social maturity   We have seen that many youngsters in one-parent homes readily take on responsibilities that are surprising for their age. But many others in one-parent households have difficulty handling any kind of continuing responsibility or other mature
behavior. Again, it appears, it is the emotional environment of the home
and the relationship with the parents that makes much of the difference.

Hetherington states that "there is a lot of evidence on kids from single-
parent families not functioning as well in the area of social control."
She cites studies of the ability to delay gratification, cheating studies,
studies that measure impulsivity.

Then there is the matter of aggressiveness as an aspect of out-of-
control behavior. Kay Tooley of the University of Michigan suggested

in *The American Journal of Orthopsychiatry* that a substantial amount of the antisocial behavior and social alienation may be spawned by the growing matriarchal subculture. Her conclusion is summarized thus:

"Women raising children alone after divorce often find their new socio-psychological world frightening and unmanageable. Perceiving this, their young sons may undertake a counterphobic defense of themselves and their mothers, manifested as antisocial behavior."

She was referring to such behavior as "physically aggressive," "bossy and bullying," "unmanageable," and "hyperactive." Her impressions were based on "emphatic little boys" between age four and seven brought to the university clinic by "uncertain-looking young mothers." She added that it doesn't take long to penetrate a lad's facade of bravado to find a "very frightened, beleaguered little boy."

These lads of course are the extremes who seem to need either clinical attention or special attention from parents and teachers because of such offenses as clobbering another child over the head with a metal lunchbox.

It is noteworthy, however, that studies which find children of divorce more out-of-control than average do not find the same tendency of low self-control in children from widowed homes.

The causes of juvenile delinquency are both numerous and still controversial. Three of the clearest causes are poor reading ability, poverty, and discrimination. In street gangs, delinquency is more likely to have social than emotional causes. The gang leader may be surprisingly well-organized emotionally.

There is an abundance of evidence that an abnormally high proportion of delinquents come from one-parent homes created by divorce.[16] The proportion is even higher for girls than for boys. Perhaps this is because girls are more likely than boys to be branded delinquent for sexual reasons. But much of the differences in terms of the one-parent home probably could be accounted for by its overrepresentation among those with low economic or class status or minority status.

The long-term National Survey of 4701 English people mentioned above found delinquency was particularly associated with father absence due to divorce if the father left before the youngster was six years old. The survey also found the disproportionate rate of delinquency held more emphatically for middle-class boys from "broken homes" than for working-class boys from such homes.[17]

However a number of investigators insist that the simple absence of the father is not a major direct cause of delinquency. It is not a matter of a particular family structure but the family "climate," the intense interactions between family members, the lack of family cohesiveness that triggers delinquent behavior. In short, delinquency is high when you have a "bad home" situation. The bad home can be intact and still bad if the parents are fighting or the father is hostile or aloof toward the youngsters. But you also have many "bad home" situations where the father is absent. Two researchers at the U.S. Children's Bureau made a careful review of all the relevant research literature.[18] They concluded that the research findings "give clear support to the proposition that father absence in itself is less meaningful than are the climate and tone of the home and the kinds of supervision given the child."

WHAT ABOUT MOTHER ABSENCE?

Primarily thus far we have been talking about the father-absent home. Are conditions substantially different if father is in charge and mother is absent? An increasing number of fathers have been seeking not just joint custody but full custody. Divorce figures indicate that about 60,000 child custody awards go to fathers each year. Many thousands of fathers, I should add, have custody thrust upon them by circumstances such as their ex-mate's disappearance, low maternal competence or death. In one decade Census data indicate, sole male custodians of children tripled, to 600,000.

This situation is just starting to attract the attention of systematic investigators, but some things seem clear. In general, the older the children, the better things are likely to go where there is father custody. And the more the father has been involved before assuming sole child care and home care, the easier things will go. Many single fathers, after a few months of child care, report a new intimacy and camaraderie with their children they never had before.

But typically things don't go easily for the custodial father, at least not in the first year. Ira Victor and Win Ann Winkler, authors of *Fathers and Custody*, found:

"For every custodial father we have spoken to who described himself as managing smoothly, we have spoken to at least three who admitted that they didn't know what they were getting into."

One investigator, Helen Mendes, found that male "seekers" of custody — fathers who actively sought to gain custody — seemed better adjusted to their child-rearing role than those "assenters" who had child-rearing thrust upon them by such factors as death of a spouse.[19] The latter often confessed they had severe problems. Another study came up with a similar finding that divorced fathers obtaining custody were more likely to say they were well-adjusted than widowers.

Still another interesting finding, by John Santrock and Richard Warshak, in a study at the University of Texas, Dallas, was that fathers were much better at raising boys than at raising girls.[20] "Girls under the father custody arrangement . . . were observed to be less warm, show less self-esteem, be more demanding, show less maturity, act less sociably and be less conforming . . . than girls from intact families did with their fathers."

We talked earlier of three conditions common to women who find themselves with full custody. Let's review the same conditions with men in mind.

Severe financial problems   At first glance custodial men seem to have the big advantage. In general they have superior earning power. On average, a male-headed household has a $7,000 edge over a female-headed household. And they don't wrestle with the dilemma of the custodial mother: Shall I work or not work? They assume they will keep on working. They will just get in a housekeeper, or something. Soon they find housekeepers scarce and expensive. And the "something" is that in desperation they call upon female relatives to help out with the house and children. Or they turn to organized home and child care services, which can be expensive. If money starts running out, they have less chance than a mother of getting welfare assistance.

Robert Weiss tells of a wifeless construction worker who went through several hectic months trying to obtain care for his two small children. His parents could take them, but only at night, so he quit his job, got a night job as a nightclub bouncer, and stayed with his children during the day.

Role overload   Here custodial husbands usually have an even more stressful challenge than custodial wives. They start from a higher level of job ignorance. They are baffled by diaper rash or colic and convey to children their panic when the child runs a 103-degree temperature. How do they soothe the child with nightmares? For daughters entering adolescence, how do they explain the cramps of menstruation and how to cope with the blood flow?

Then there is the problem of seeing that the kids are not wearing dirty shirts to school. As for running the house, they have to learn how to cook nutritious foods the kids will accept. They have to learn to freeze batches of food at one cooking to save time. At the beginning they won't know how to wax floors properly, run the washing machine, and may not even know how to make a neat bed.

A curtailed outside life   This also probably hits custodial fathers harder than custodial mothers. Weiss quotes a father of three school-age children as saying: "The hardest thing for me when I first got divorced was getting over the resentment of being stuck with the kids. There are a lot of things I can't do because I have the children. I can't go off for a weekend even if I have the money. . . ."

Weiss points out that custodial men may have more difficulty than women in developing a helpful circle of friends. The men's social contacts have usually been with other males sharing such masculine interests as work, sports, and barroom drinking. Such male acquaintances can usually offer little help on the new problems foremost in the custodial father's mind. And the father might be embarrassed to ask.

A radio announcer in Eureka, California, Ralph McCarthy, one day was reading an announcement of a meeting of Displaced Homemakers. It was a group of northern California single mothers who hold meetings to pool ideas for entering the job market. Impulsively he blurted to listeners: "I'm a displaced homemaker too, and there should be something for single dads as well."[21] Many male listeners agreed and soon twenty to thirty single dads were meeting at his house every week to discuss their problems. And on problems that stumped them they called in a knowledgeable young woman for feminine input.

A better solution for such men would be to turn to an organization such as Parents Without Partners, whose members are mostly mothers of children. They usually know a lot more about child-raising problems than a group of single dads.

Both Weiss and Victor-Winkler note as a common pattern that single fathers who cannot afford housekeepers soon start thinking of remarrying or obtaining a wife-substitute to whom they can delegate some of the problems of child care.

Pupils from Homes
with One Parent

"We avoid many words such as 'mother' and 'father' when addressing groups of youngsters. We say 'parents.' "

— *Audrey Gillmore, principal of an elementary school in San Bruno, California, in which 41 percent of the pupils come from one-parent homes.*

America's school officials have suddenly become very much aware of the increased number of children in their schoolrooms coming from one-parent homes. In the average school today about a fifth of the student body comes from one-parent homes. In many schools, particularly in some areas of California, nearly half of the student body comes from such homes.

School officials have become acutely aware that students from homes where there has been a marital upheaval in the past year are likely to be troubled children. They also know that all the fighting over custody or visitation creates awkward problems for themselves. To whom do they report? And who can pick up the kids? Who has access the child's school records?

Schools can in fact play an important role in easing children of divorce over a crisis, if their personnel are sensitive to the problems. When a child's world at home is falling apart, the school can offer an island of stability and possible comfort for the child.

At the Lomita Park elementary school in San Bruno, California, the proportion of students from one-parent homes has recently been, as indicated, about 40 percent. The principal there, Audrey Gillmore, told me of ways the school has started adjusting to the situation. She explained:

"We have eliminated two functions, that Father-Son Banquet and the Mother-Daughter Tea. Instead we have an awards banquet for both sexes. We also hold all of our parent meetings at night so [working] parents can attend; and many parent conferences are scheduled in the evening.

"Often there is much tension between the single parent and the child. . . . The child usually wants more attention from the parent and may go to great lengths to get it. The parent is often resentful about not having time to pursue her/his own life and interests and has guilty feelings along with the resentment."

Then there is the matter of visitation as a school problem. She said: "We notice that Mondays are sometimes 'bad days' rather than the traditional Fridays. I believe it may occur when children have visited the other parent, or were supposed to and plans were changed. Either way, the child ends up disappointed or upset. Such children bring those feelings to school and explode over ordinarily insignificant incidents."

Lomita Park now has, along with its regular quite small P.T.A., a Single Parent Group where matters specific to children from single-parent homes are discussed.

An elementary school counselor in Lexington, Massachusetts, advised me that very often parents don't inform the school that they have split and have separate addresses. Teachers may start wondering if something is wrong at home when a child's school performance drops off rather abruptly or if the child seems very depressed, very edgy, and distracted.

Here are some of the traits that many U.S. elementary school teachers are being trained to watch for as possible signs of parental trouble: sudden gains or losses in weight, moodiness, inability to concentrate, fatigue, attention-seeking through negative behavior.

The National Association of Elementary School Principals suggests teachers pay more attention to such children. It advised: "A pat on the arm or a quick hug can go a long way toward reassuring a small child that there is another adult who cares." When the upset persists, the association recommends that a trained counselor talk with the youngster without seeming in any way to single out or stigmatize the child. Conferences with one or both parents also are suggested.

The association recommends that schools ease the parent's burdens of child care by providing before- and after-school activities.

An obvious need at schools with a high proportion of children coming from mother-headed households is a high representation of male teachers in the elementary schools. Traditionally that has been an area of education left almost entirely to females.

The problem U.S. schools have in maintaining contact with millions of divorced parents has become a major source of confusion for school officials. They are still working on mechanics for keeping abreast with the marital status of a child's parents and to cope with what one educator called "the unknown politics of the divorced parents' relationships." If the parents are divorced, are they cooperating or feuding?

Since a lot of parents think their marital status is a private matter, some schools are being advised to send a standard form home each semester. It asks for the names and addresses of the student, the mother, and the father. If the card shows separate addresses for the parents, the matter is noted. The school then tries to obtain both the home and work telephone numbers of both the custodial and noncustodial parent in case of emergency. Only about a third of the nation's schools yet have forms that permit such a doubling of information about parents. Some schools now have modified the student card so that there is a choice of listing "parents" or "parent."

School systems still tend to be baffled as to how to cope with a noncustodial parent who wants to see his child's school records or to receive a duplicate of the student's report card. Some traditional-minded judges specify in court orders that the noncustodial parent can see a child's school records or report card only after receiving permission from the custodial parent. The national law since 1974 has been that the noncustodial parent is entitled to inspect the school records of his children.

A young, divorced mother in Fairfield County, Connecticut, told me that at her school system she had to bring in a copy of her divorce decree to prove she had custody of each of her children. Then she had to put on record whether the father could see the child in school or pick up the child after school. She added:

"I let him see but not pick up."

School systems are also coming under pressure from organizations of divorced parents to end their "one-home" bias. Some organizations are calling for an abandonment of children's schoolbooks that feature the "Mommy, Daddy, Dick and Jane setting." It is contended that the books should include other family styles. One national organization claimed that children seeing only two-parent families in textbooks can be detrimentally influenced in their self-image if they come from one-parent homes. In counties north and east of New York City, a considerable amount of new-style literature is showing up in children's libraries. Parents Without Partners has been encouraging such change.

Dozens of U.S. schools now are offering short programs to help children of divorce adjust to and feel less uneasy about their new situation. School counselors in Newport News, Virginia, State College, Pennsylvania, and South Orange, New Jersey, for example, have been conducting regular programs for pupils concerned about changes in their family. Schools in Port Washington, Long Island, now have available film therapy for children of divorce. The film, which was written and produced largely by children of divorce themselves, is about one family's divorce and its impact on two children in the family. Themes such as grief, anger, and guilt are dramatized.

Two counselors in Minneapolis have been introducing into schools where more than a third of the students are from single-parent households a program on the *inevitability* of family changes. They cover not only marital breakups but change due to death, birth of another sibling, friends moving away. It involves readings, puppetry, role playing, etc.

In Lexington, Massachusetts, a program called the Divorced Kids Group has reached from high school down into elementary school. It is run pretty much by adolescents, mostly girls, with a counselor often present. They visit divorce courts. They arrange for sessions with such experts as sociologist Robert Weiss, authority on single-parent households. Or they just sit in a circle and compare notes about how they are handling their problems of living in a single-parent home. The older students also talk about their legal rights or how to relate to Mom's new boy friends.

One of the girls who has been active explained to me: "It makes you feel like you are not the only one."

IS SCHOOL WORK AFFECTED BY SINGLE-PARENT STATUS?

Many schools also are becoming aware that children from one-parent homes seem to have an above-average chance of being affected in their school performance. Schools are seeking ways to compensate for, or provide extra attention to, children from such homes who seem to be having academic problems. (And many concerned heads of one-parent homes are doing so too. Such increased interest can make a great difference.)

Some observers strongly deny there is any tendency for children from one-parent homes to have more than average academic problems. Certainly many such children thrive in classes and are outstanding on intellectual tests. But let's look at the evidence that, overall, a problem deserving attention does exist.

Dozens of investigations have been made to search out any possible effect that seems to be coming from a one-parent household that may affect a youngster's school work.

Findings differ because so many variables are involved. I examined about fifteen of the reports. Many did not pinpoint the reasons for the father absence (death, divorce, illegitimacy, or father simply being away on a job). They often didn't control for such things as socioeconomic status. And if divorce is the cause of father absence, how long has the parent been absent? Is the impact of the divorce action being measured, or the impact of father absence?

Judith Wallerstein and Joan Kelly found that in their particular sample of 131 youngsters of divorce these youngsters were hurt initially in schoolwork but after five years (mostly in a one-parent home) they had their schoolwork back up roughly to the level it had been at the time of divorce.

More research of careful design obviously is needed. A fairly recent review of all the research was made by New York University psychologist Marybeth Shinn. Her report appeared in *The Psychological Bulletin* of the American Psychological Association.[1]

She started with fifty-eight research reports and then narrowed them down to thirty that she felt provided "adequate methodological controls." What did she conclude from the thirty she judged to be adequate? Here are the highlights:

- Being reared in father-absent homes, *or* homes where the father provides little supportive interaction with the children, is often associated with poor performance on IQ and achievement tests.

- A rancorous home life before a divorce can have more detrimental effects on a child's cognitive performance than the simple impact of father absence.

- Four studies compared test results based on the various reasons why a father might be absent from the home (death, divorce, job-related duties such as being a seaman). In all four studies divorce emerged as most likely to have a negative effect on the children's mental functioning.

- There is suggestive evidence that if the father is absent before the child reaches school age, the absence is more detrimental than later absence.

Shinn was most impressed by these three explanations for the patterns she found:

1. If one parent is absent, there is a drop in the amount of mentally stimulating interaction a child has with parents. For one thing Shinn is impressed by the thesis advanced at the University of Michigan by Robert Zajonc that the ratio of adults to children in a family influences intellectual development. One child in a two-parent home is normally getting a lot more parental interaction than two children in a one-parent home. Zajonc has summed the one-parent situation up on the basis of his thesis in these words:

   "A one-parent home constitutes an inferior environment and should result in deficits, and . . . early loss of a parent should produce greater deficits than the loss occurring at a later date."[2]

   To support his thesis Zajonc reported that he found children in father-absent homes scoring ten percentiles lower in the American College Entrance Examination Test.

   It is not inevitable that a child gets less parental interaction when there is only one parent in the house. A mother heading a household who is not beset by problems and is well-organized may in fact interact more with her children than the average mother in a two-parent home. (Remember Katie Powell?) Children may get the attention that formerly went to the husband. In general, however, working mothers in one-parent homes have a lot of problems on their minds. The amount of interest a parent shows in a youngster's school work is also a critical factor.

2. Many children of divorce continue for years to be plagued in their mental performance by "anxiety interference," Shinn suggests. Children fatherless because of death do not seriously experience such interference. Children of divorce typically continue to do well in tests of verbal skills. Verbal skills are less likely to be disrupted by stress. In contrast, the children of divorce do less well in tests of

reasoning ability (such as math), where mental stress is often disruptive.

3. Financial hardship which often is present in father-absent homes also was accepted by Shinn as a substantial disruptive factor. The problems of adjusting to a drop in financial security, and worrying about it, can affect a youngster's ability to engage in sustained mental activity.

Hetherington comments from her own research: "In families in which the mother has good control over the children, in families where household routines were structured and carried through in some systematic way, you didn't get these cognitive drops in the children."

There have been reports that schoolchildren from one-parent homes tend to have more behavior problems in school than those from two-parent homes. These could affect school performance. The National Association of Elementary School Principals, for example, reported that a study of eighteen thousand youngsters in fourteen states disclosed that children from single-parent homes have greater discipline problems, more behavior problems, greater truancy and poorer grades than their classmates who are from two-parent homes.[3]

The report created quite a bit of controversy. It was argued for example that family income or sex of the children might account for the variations in achievement. So the sponsors commissioned an expert in educational policy, Wayne A. Barton of Penn State, to make a closer analysis of the status of 14,493 junior and senior high school students involved. A youngster's eligibility for free or discounted school lunches was used to determine, roughly, family income. (See *The Principal,* September 1982.)

Interesting variations did appear that were not related to the number of parents in the home. Girls in general were clearly higher achievers than boys, about 9 per cent higher. In fact, high-income girls from one-parent homes rated about the same as high-income boys from two-parent homes.

As for income as a factor, both boys and girls from higher-income families rated higher in achievement than boys and girls from low-income families. And the analysis showed that one-parent homes tended strongly to be low-income homes.

Still, the generalization of the original study held. For both boys and girls, those from two-parent households scored higher in achievement than those from one-parent homes. And for both high-income and low-income families kids from two-parent homes scored higher than those from one-parent homes.

As another part of the rechecking, school principals talked with 241 parents. One of the findings from these talks was that the number of parents in the home is relatively more important in the elementary grades than in high school.

Another study that attempted to control for differences in social class and for minority status was made in a suburban school district of Houston.[4] There were 3,644 children, all white, involved in the study. About 650 came from single-parent homes or homes where there had been a remarriage. Household heads were assigned to one of four social classes.

Teachers checked those children who exhibited any of five behavior problems (Conduct Problems; Personality Problems, such as anxiety; Inadequacy-Immaturity; Socialized Delinquency, such as organized stealing; Psychotic Signs). It turned out that children from mother-headed households had "significantly more difficulties" with all five problem areas. However, when those problems were analyzed for social class, it turned out that in two of the five problem areas (Personality Problems and Socialized Delinquency), the children from the lower social classes had more difficulties than those from the upper social classes. The investigators suggested that perhaps financial strain at home helped account for a lot of the problems that kids from mother-headed households have.

The report, interestingly, noted that children from homes where the mother had remarried seemed to have fewer problems. Remarriage, it said, "seemed to have a positive influence on children's adjustment."

Let's now look at how children experience remarriage — and the process leading to it.

20

The Shift to a Melded Family

"The start of a stepmarriage has to be approached the same way that porcupines make love — carefully."

— A stepfather cited by the head of the Stepfamily Foundation, Inc., New York

At a church in San Bernardino, California, about 70 percent of the congregation consists of single parents. The minister, a single parent himself, remarked:

"Most of the mothers are occupied with boy friends and changing men in the home. This is traumatic for parents and children." [1]

The typical single fathers are even more preoccupied with girlfriends. Both male and female single parents feel a new need for intimacy as a bulwark against the loneliness and uneasiness thrust upon them following divorce. The men are more likely to be seeking excitement, the women a renewed romantic feeling. Men can be extraordinarily active for a while because sex was increasingly unsatisfactory as marital strain developed.

Within a year the men usually start feeling morose and often a bit silly about acting like an adolescent. Even a divorcing man who has a committed lover waiting for him will often relive an adolescent-like fling before feeling ready to settle down in a committed way with another woman, according to Kristine M. Rosenthal of Brandeis University and Harry F. Keshet of the Divorce Resource and Mediation Center in Cambridge, Massachusetts. They made a study of 127 divorced or separated fathers who had been divorced at least a year.[2]

Mothers by necessity must proceed more cautiously and tactfully because they typically have physical custody of the children who can be a problem.

One divorced father in the Rosenthal-Keshet study explained the problem in this way: "I dated a woman with children and it was fairly complicated. She had a time commitment to her own children. Her kids entered into our relationship. So did mine. We each had to relate to and like each other's kids as well as liking and relating to each other."

I arranged, as noted, to tape record a session of teenagers in Lexington, Massachusetts, as they talked about their experiences as children of divorce. One of the more memorable comments was that of a girl who said:

"It is just weird seeing some guy put his arm around your mother and hearing your mother call him dear and 'can I get you this or can I get you that?' Dad and Mom didn't act like that around us."

Younger children may be quite scared about what is going on. They may see a setback in their aspiration for a return of the absent father. One woman recalled her childhood anxieties. "Every time men took mother out, I thought they were taking her away from me too."

Kids, if uncertain where they stand, may be quick to create a scene if they feel the least put upon. Investigators offer such accounts as these:

- A fourteen-year-old boy refused to go to a movie with his mother and her boy friend, who had brought along his own two children, age seven and nine. The boy's angry explanation: "They were just kids."

- A thirteen-year-old girl went into a rage because her father asked her to baby-sit with the preschool children of a woman friend so that he could take her on a date.

It is wise to start any dating with someone known to the child as a family friend or acquaintance. Fathers have to be careful too on weekends when their youngsters visit. Rosenthal and Keshet report that several of the 127 divorced fathers said that the children treat any date they brought in as an intruder. One father explained:

"It's hard to be romantic with a four-year-old around. Every time

Kathy and I would touch or just sit close Susan would hurt herself or in some way demand my attention.''

Every time one father took a girlfriend and his daughter for a ride, the daughter would insist on her usual place in the front seat beside him, as proof she was still first in his affection.

SEX AND THE SINGLE PARENT

The sexual needs of both men and women vary considerably from individual to individual. Women accustomed in marriage to obtaining frequent sexual release may well, after divorce, feel as sexually frustrated as their ex-husbands. In *Going It Alone* Robert Weiss quote one single mother he interviewed as saying, ''I can feel me getting frustrated. I can feel my stomach getting tight. . . . I get short-tempered with my kids. I say to myself, 'You just need a good screw.' ''

Some ex-wives said they turned to masturbation. And that was fine, one said, but didn't solve the problem of loneliness. Weiss cited one mother as saying, ''It's an awful, lonely thing to bring up children yourself.'' Some divorced couples, he said, miss sex so much that although they have no interest in reunion they do occasionally get together just for intercourse, months or years after the marriage ended. Melvyn Burke, a Dallas clinical psychologist who conducts ''after divorce'' workshops, puts the proportion of ex-spouses who get together for sex at a very surprising 30 percent.

From interviews with more than a hundred single parents, Weiss concluded that most of them followed one of two sexual policies after they start dating:

1. Sex is all right if there is affection. Women usually also want ''emotional commitment'' with the affection; men tend simply to want the other woman to be ''emotionally important'' to them.
2. Sex is okay if you know what you are doing, are considerate and not exploitive. That of course is a much more liberal attitude.

Rosenthal and Keshet found that after a year of separate living, three-quarters of the divorced fathers were having sleep-in dates. Typically they had been away from their children's home from four to six months before they let their date stay overnight on a weekend when the children were visiting. And most still felt uneasy about exposing their children to their sexuality. What kind of an example were they setting? One father told the researchers that he had cut back his dating to one girl-friend after his young daughter walked into his bedroom on a Saturday morning, looked down at the woman sleeping at his side, and asked: "Which one is this?"

Judith Wallerstein, in talking of the dating habits she and Joan Kelly found in their study of children of divorce, said that one reason fathers are uneasy about dating while children are around is that they have mostly been reduced to rather cramped bachelor-type quarters. One father who had a waterbed permitted his young daughter to sleep in the squishy pad with him while visiting. When he had a date he informed his daughter that she should sleep in the next room. He was taken aback by his daughter's tears of outrage.[3]

Mothers with live-in children tend to send the man home by two A.M. or they lock the bedroom door and set the alarm for five A.M. so that the man will be gone when the children awake. Problems persist, however, as they never know when a child, on awakening at night, will want to crawl in bed with them.

If a child feels secure in his or her mother's love, and has come to see she has a genuine admiration for the man who finally starts staying overnight, the child is much less likely to be disturbed by the arrangement. But casual sex by a parent — a parade of individuals through the parent's bedroom — is a heavy load to lay on a youngster, in the view of child psychiatrist Richard A. Gardner. He in fact does not feel parents should expose a child to each new date, only to persons with whom the parent has developed an ongoing and meaningful relationship. (The noncustodial father has an even more difficult problem in accustoming his children to a possible future stepmother. She either may pop into their life with little preparation — or is kept out of sight by the father until he is sure he wants to marry her.)

Dr. Lee Salk has cautioned that mother should consider the strength of her children's ties to the absent father before starting a pattern of heavy sleep-over dates. Will it threaten a child who feels intense loyalty to a biological parent who is absent? Teenagers can be quite sophisticated about parental dating after the shock of divorce has eased, perhaps because they are into it themselves. A teenage girl in Lexington, Massachusetts, said in the taping session:

"Mom's young. She is really pretty. She has a big career. Our relationship is changing. She has her boy friends stay over and that's okay with me. In that way, she has to come to me and almost ask permission. Some parents can't really handle that."

Lora Tessman, from her studies, notes that the parent preoccupied with dating preparations may stimulate sexual fantasies in adolescents exposed to it. A daughter, for example, may start going braless around the house.

Weiss says that parents can feel a lot less guilty about dating if they don't make their children suffer through uncomfortable introductions to someone with whom their emotional relationship is still tentative. The parent should make it clear to the children that at this point at least they (the children) are only incidentally involved. He quoted a mother who had had one post-marriage romance that had not worked out as saying that when she dates she rarely has the man come to the house to meet her or pick her up. "I don't get the men involved in any family stuff." Another mother with a similar experience quoted one of her teenage daughters as saying she didn't want to get to know anyone until the mother was pretty sure. Perceptive parents, he said, usually reassure the children that they come first.

Once a relationship gives promise of being permanent, the single parent, Weiss said, should be greatly pleased if the new person reaches out to the children.

GETTING SERIOUS

Robert Weiss, after interviewing dozens of children living in single-parent households, suggests that parents may be unnecessarily concerned about the impact of the sexual aspect of their lives on their children. (This assumes acts of intimacy are not performed in their presence.) The youngsters are typically not busy wondering what the parent is doing while entertaining a date. "Interviews with children of single parents suggest that the children are not nearly as moralistic as their mothers believe," he said. (They also may not be as moralistic as neighbors.)

The children's concerns, when they exist, are much more likely to center on what the meaning is to *themselves* of the appearance of this new person on the home scene. Will yet another parent be taken from their lives? Are their ties to the absent biological parent threatened? Will their live-in parent now start having less time for them or start considering them an obstacle? And if this new person starts becoming a live-in, will it impinge on the living space available to the child?

Such questions, he suggested, "can be a lot for children to absorb." One divorced mother with three kids had mentioned to the children that she was going "out" but hadn't bothered to minimize the importance of this first date. Her male date came into the family room. The three kids were sitting on the couch. Later he commented to the mother: "I never saw three such scared kids in my life."

It is the younger school-agers, vocal but not yet familiar with dating, who are most likely to react in an unsettled way to the appearance of a male escort.

Some divorced people fall in love again and start thinking of remarriage. The romance makes some women uneasy because they have come to cherish their independence. But most divorced people who are thinking of remarriage want it to happen because of a need for intimacy or "for the sake of the children." Many mothers are also motivated by their damnable economic crunch. About half the people who remarry do so within three years. Divorced fathers are much more likely to remarry within three years than divorced mothers. The fact that the mothers usually have custody of the children — an inhibition and a complication in dating — helps account for the difference.

Divorced parents who remarry usually do so with less testing for compatibility made by long acquaintance or around-the-clock living together. Cohabitation is now widely practiced among the never-married. Young mothers (and many fathers), however, sense (usually correctly) that cohabitation might seriously embarrass the children. Also a recent decision by the Supreme Court of Illinois (*Jarrett v. Jarrett*) may cause custodial parents to think twice about cohabiting. The divorced mother lost custody of her three minor children to the father-plaintiff solely because she had invited her male friend to move into her household on an open and continuing basis. The man began functioning as an affectionate and conscientious father. The court agreed that no tangible evidence of "contemporaneous adverse effect" on the children was presented, but held that the live-in situation was bad *per se* for the children's future moral well-being and development.

Teenagers may welcome evidence that Mom is thinking finally of remarrying if they see no prospect of their father's return. A teenage girl in Lexington said: "I've heard a lot of kids of divorce say they were against remarriage, but I've always thought it would be very nice for my mother if at some point she remarried. It would have to be the right person."

Younger children, and boys particularly, tend to be more wary of taking on a new, third parent figure. At first they reject him or her. Rosenthal and Keshet said virtually all of the 127 divorced or separated fathers reported experiences of having a prospective new partner rejected by their children. Fathers of male children reported this more frequently than fathers of female children.

As courtship continues and a wedding approaches, some but not all kids will accept emotional closeness with their parent's new prospective partner. If one parent plans to remarry, the children may get some heavy static from their other biological parent.

Rosenthal and Keshet found that fathers too are often wary about letting a prospective new wife have much to do with their children, except to be a helper. Partly the fathers are nervous about stirring up the wrath of the biological mother. In her anger she might jeopardize access to his children. She might get tougher about any financial arrangement (or nonarrangement) he has with her. In general, mothers are less likely to approve a remarriage of an ex-mate than fathers (who may sce an easing of a financial burden if their ex-wife remarries). But another reason fathers are wary is that they still haven't figured out how a third parent figure — the new wife — is going to fit into the picture.

If the Other Person also has children there will be attempts before marriage to get both sets of children acquainted. How well do they blend? Sometimes there is curiosity on the part of the children and the initial meetings go off well.

A recent trend has been to include one or both sets of children in the wedding ceremony. Many youngsters are invited to participate in the ceremony. A ten-year-old daughter may be a bridesmaid.

I recently attended a wedding of divorcés in a home at which their six children stood beside them. The minister called upon all sixty-five friends of the couple present to vow to lend their efforts to seeing that this union of parents thrived. In some ceremonies both the bride and groom take the vow while holding the hand of a son or daughter to convey to the children that the marriage is something they are all going into together. It can often promote acceptance. But some children don't want to indicate any acceptance. One adolescent girl was so angry with her father that she threw away the gown purchased for her and showed up in blue jeans and scraggly hair.[4]

The Institute for Juvenile Research in Children made a study of stepchildren brought in for therapy. In half the cases the symptoms showed up immediately after one of their parents had remarried. The upsets seemed to spring from a fear of loss.[5] They had not been sufficiently prepared for the new parent figure.

For younger kids a first reaction may be puzzlement about arrangements. A New York family therapist reported that when she and her second husband returned home from a two-day honeymoon and started taking the new husband's bags into their bedroom, her small son gave her quite a surprise. The boy asked his new stepfather: "Where are you going? Aren't you going to sleep in my room in the bottom bunk like you did before?"[6]

LIFE WITH STEPPARENTS

Each year about half a million children are involved in a remarriage in the U.S., to add to the seven million stepchildren under eighteen already on hand.

In published and televised reports of "melded" or "blended" or "reconstituted" families we have usually seen one grand mingling of affectionate people. Such grand minglings occur, but usually not within the first year of a remarriage. With patience and reasonableness such warm feelings usually develop. But they take time. *Stepfamily Bulletin* summed up this business of launching a stepfamily in these quite accurate words:

"Compare it to a chess game — challenging and complex. To a spider's web — delicate and intricate. Or to a toddler's birthday party — chaotic and confusing."

For a while it can also be bruising, especially for the younger participants.

In the long run, remarriages offer most kids a better deal than they had in the single-parent home. As a twelve-year-old named Neal told the Wallerstein-Kelly investigators, "It is nice to have two adults around." They promptly are back to having a day-to-day input from two adults as models and mentors. Thus their prospects of being well socialized as they are inducted into adult society are, on average, improved. Also many youngsters have the prospect of being relieved of the anxieties that go with the economic hardship of the typical one-parent household.

But the first year of remarriage where children are involved can be pretty disconcerting for all involved, even for Neal who had a real hollering match with his new stepfather before they settled down to being friends. The adults assume that the joy and love they feel after the wedding will be shared by the children. That is not likely to be the case. The kids are nervous. Some complain of feeling left out. Wallerstein-Kelly tell of an eight-year-old boy named Peter who complained: "They tickle and giggle a lot in the bedroom and they don't eat with us." If both of a youngster's biological parents remarry he or she may see himself coping with:

- two real parents;
- two acquired parents;
- some stepsiblings;
- two new sets of grandparents;
- possible new half-sibs.

Stepfamilies simply cannot operate like traditional families — at least not for quite a while. It takes more ingenuity, flexibility, and dedication to make a second marriage work, if children are involved, than is required in a first marriage. Evidence of this perhaps is that the divorce rate of second marriages (about 50 percent) is higher than for first marriages. (Or perhaps the higher rate may represent the fact that people who remarry may constitute a more restless cohort.)

The remarriage is in reality a merging of minifamilies, still a quite ambiguous institution in our society. A stepmother, for example, does not routinely become a real mother of her new husband's children even though they all now live under the same roof or spend the summer months and weekends together. If the youngsters still have warm ties to their biological mother, the best the stepmother can hope for is a role of "friend" or "other mother" for quite a while.

A stepparent has virtually no legal status in the U.S. as a parent, only as a marriage partner. If a boy falls out of a tree and the stepmother rushes him to a hospital, she may have no authority to sign a medical release authorizing treatment. Because of such complications it is prudent to obtain a power of attorney from a husband, or if he doesn't have custody, a written authorization from the custodial mother. If the custodial mother feels sour about her husband's remarriage, getting the authorization may take a heavy application of logic.

Stepmothers have a harder time getting along with stepchildren than stepfathers do. Stepmothers typically have less contact with the children because the children probably still are spending most of the time with the biological mother. A larger reason is that a new woman in a household has less chance of being accepted as an authority figure than a new man in the house. Confused or resentful children are less likely to sass a man who tells them to take out the garbage, or make their bed, or get down to their homework. Stepmothers may get a defiant response when giving the same kind of instructions that would be routine coming from a natural mother.

Helpful husband-fathers clarify the authority situation by having a chat with their kids, regardless of who has official custody, in the presence of their stepmother. We'll call her Jean. In essence he should say:

"Nothing has happened in my marriage to Jean that in any way affects your relations with your Mom. We know you love her and will continue to do so. As my wife, however, Jean deserves your respect. And as my wife she becomes the female head of this house. It is her responsibility to see that we all cooperate to make it a well-run, pleasant place to live. I promise to cooperate and expect you, when you are here, will do the same." The Stepfamily Foundation encourages such an explanation.

Alas, few fathers who remarry make such statements. Good habits fail to get started. Strains and a testing of limits typically soon develop.

Mothers too should give a similar talk soon after they bring home a new stepfather. She should make it clear that he is, by reason of marriage, the man of the house, that he and she after consultation will set the house rules and either can enforce these rules. Most children really want rules.

This "man of the house" news may be a bit hard on the egos of the older boys. They were told repeatedly by their mother during her singlehood that they had become man of the house. Stepfathers who assume they deserve respect as an authority figure may be in for a surprise. A prosperous male attorney married a divorced secretary who was having a desperate time financially in trying to raise her two children. They all moved into a nice house after the marriage. About a month later the stepfather instructed his ten-year-old stepson to straighten up his room. Tom replied. "Only my real daddy can talk to me like that," and ignored the instructions.

It is best in the long pull that a new stepfather be more than a new boarder, that he in time come to serve as both model and informal mentor for the youngsters. Serious disciplining of a wife's child should be left to her until the child has learned to like the stepfather and wants his approval.

For a youngster, the adjustment to a third parent figure is likely to be disconcerting for a while. Steve Gaskin, leader of the Tennessee commune, The Farm, has seen a lot of experimental innovative family arrangements. From his observations he comes back to this basic fact:

"Kids have a hard time copping to somebody who ain't their biological parent."

Writer John Leonard wrote an amusing and insightful column in *The New York Times* about authority problems of "stepping" (as well as the surprising pleasures). He didn't deny the difficulties. Both he and his wife are stepparents. His wife's daughter lives in. His children "visit" but check with him almost every day. Regarding authority he asks: "Can I explain to my stepdaughter that unless she turns down the volume on Styx or Queen I will feed her record player to the cats?" He said she was inclined to listen to him if he could otherwise be relied on to explicate a difficult poem, to listen to her opening argument in the next school debate, to correct her grammar and to admire her bizarre attire. Among other things, he said, a stepfamily is a series of trade-offs.

In Toronto, researchers at the Remarriage Research Project of the Clarke Institute of Psychiatry interviewed seventy remarried couples. Did they notice any differences in the kinds of problems they had in their first marriage and in their present remarriage? Yes. In recalling their first marriages those interviewed listed as first among difficulties their partner's immaturity, sexual adjustment, in-law interference. Problems involving child-rearing ranked low. But in remarriage there was no question about the number-one headache: difficulties with children. The researchers reported:

"They very often expressed surprise at their underestimation of the emotional upheaval involved for the children."

Wallerstein and Kelly found that even after remarriage of a mother, the large majority of the children still spent substantial periods of time with their natural father. The Toronto study of seventy remarried couples produced a similar finding of visits to natural parents. These visits indeed should continue but if they annoy a parent in the remarriage household the youngster feels stress and role ambiguity. Stepparents tend not to be cheered by evidence that the absent natural parent still has a strong hold on the children.

Emily and John Visher, authorities on stepfamily living, tell of a stepfather named Floyd who gave up trying to discipline his stepson. He had found the boy's natural father would make trouble, through the wife. The son soon began exploiting this by racing to the phone whenever the stepfather warned of any kind of discipline. He poured out an exaggerated lament to his dad. Once the boy was so dramatic that the father had the police come to force the stepfather to stop ''abusing'' his son.

A stepmother's personal strong qualities and efforts to be agreeable do not necessarily protect her from abrupt rejection in the early months of remarriage. The children may seem friendly with a stepmother one minute and then suddenly become rejecting. To a lesser degree a stepfather too may find himself getting this cool treatment. One couple in the Toronto study told of a small girl who asked her fairly new stepfather to tie her shoe laces. He did and she rewarded him by saying, ''My daddy could have done that much faster.''[7]

The age at which a youngster acquires a stepparent has a major bearing on how easy the transition will be. In general, the younger the child, the easier it goes; the older the youngster, the more likely sparks will fly. Age eight seems to be about the dividing time. Infants and toddlers seem only mildly aware they have a new parent. If the youngster has moved into puberty and is having problems of personal identity and sexuality anyway, rebellion comes naturally.

The NBC network carried a documentary about a melded family and the overall tone was that of new and old parents and a mix of siblings getting along in happy harmony. However, when some of the individuals were interviewed separately there were changes in tone. A lad of about ten said:

''You can miss your mom . . . like, I miss my mom a lot.'' His voice seemed to break.

Another youngster on the program said that favoritism was the worst problem. The husband-father said: ''I feel she favors her kids and I suppose I favor mine.''

Such favoritism probably springs from the tendency of the anxious children to be possessive about their natural parents. Those parents seek to reassure them that nothing has changed. If the recently married couple are not careful to present a united front, the children may be quick to pit parent against parent.

AND LIFE WITH STEPSIBS

If both partners of the new marriage already have children the stepsibling rivalry is likely to be more intense than any sibling rivalry the partners had to live with in their first marriage. That at least is true for the first year of remarriage.

Jane Ranson and associates reported in a psychiatric journal a case where the divorced father and mother were brought together in romance by the friendship between their children. Nothing could be nicer. Yet when the families were blended by marriage the husband's daughter became a hellion. She tangled repeatedly with all three of her old friends who were now stepsibs.[8]

Jeannette Lofas, the head of the Stepfamily Foundations in New York City, reports that one of the main problems raised at its sessions is: "We love each other, but the kids and our reaction to each other's children is breaking up our love."

First of all as problems there is the matter of turf. If the wife brings her two children into a home where the husband and his two youngsters have been living, both sets of youngsters keep a wary eye on sleeping arrangements. This wariness is deepened by the fact that in the new household there is likely to be more crowding.

The Vishers tell of a mother with two teenage girls who had been married for a year to a man with two younger children. His children visited every weekend. Since there were only two bedrooms in the apartment, the father's seven-year-old daughter slept on a cot in the room of the wife's teenage daughters. The husband's eight-year-old boy slept on the couch in the living room. They reported: "The tension in the stepfamily on these weekends is extreme." Beyond the bed situation there was the problem that the teenage girls, who had their own friends, had to take turns baby-sitting father's children while the parents went out to social engagements.

The Vishers feel that weekend visiting by one of the parent's children is more upsetting than if both sets of children are in residence. They all get accustomed to reasonable arrangements.

How chores are divided is also watched warily. Then there is TV. Each set of children usually has developed differing patterns of viewing. They are also likely to have differing views on what constitutes yucky food. When sparks fly and parents are caught in the fray, children are apt to lapse into the accusing talk about "your mother" and "my daddy."

Family specialist Lucile Duberman located forty-five reconstituted families with two groups of children and probed the parents regarding stepsib relations.[9] Thirty-eight percent of the parents rated the relationship of their stepchildren "poor" while a smaller number, 24 percent, rated the relationships "excellent". More than a third of the parents rated the relations "good," but some seemed really to mean "better" or as good as could be expected. One woman who had rated the relationships among the two sets of children as "good" explained:

"At the beginning you would find my husband's four children off playing in one corner and my two playing in another corner. But now they don't do that. There is no open hostility, and we handle it by trying very hard to be fair. Time and adjustment have brought an improvement."

Things go better, Duberman too believes, if both sets of children live in the same house rather than in separate houses. Duberman added that when a new half sib is born to the remarried couple, relations between the two sets of stepsibs seem to improve. Perhaps it was just the time taken to produce a half sib that did the healing. Or perhaps the half sib is seen as a symbol that the family has finally become a real family. (Or conceivably the new half sib is seen by the sets of stepsibs as a common threat and unites them.)

Once the fencing is over, if the parents have been fair-handed, the two sets of sibs may become really fond of each other. In the Wallerstein and Kelly sample, children of the divorced parents who remarried usually ended up on a friendly basis. Wallerstein and Kelly report they "usually settled down to friendship patterns which they enjoyed after an initial settling-in period of perhaps a year in most families. Overall, most of the children liked the availability of a larger group of peers. . . ."

Jeannette Lofas, head of the Stepfamily Foundation (33 West End Avenue, New York City) offered me this list of ten "Steps for Steps" to bear in mind during the often difficult first year of living in a stepfamily.

1. Recognize that the stepfamily will not and cannot function as does a natural family. It has its own special state of dynamics and behaviours.

2. Recognize the hard fact that the children are not yours and they never will be. We are stepparents, a step removed, but still in this position can play a significant role in the development of the child.

3. Super stepparenting doesn't work. Go slow. Don't come on too strong.

4. Discipline styles must be sorted out by the couple. The couple needs to work out what the children's duties and responsibilities are. What

is acceptable behavior, and what are the consequences when children misbehave? The couple together works out jobs and family etiquette.

5. Establish clear job descriptions between the parent and stepparent and the respective children. What specifically is the job of each one of us in this household?

6. It is vital to the survival of the parent to understand expectations for each member, especially the primary issues that produce upset, e.g., money, discipline, the prior spouse, visitation, authority, emotional support, and territory and custody.

7. There are no ex-parents . . . only ex-spouses. Learn how to best handle the prior spouse.

8. Be prepared for the conflicting pulls of sexual and biological energies within the step relationship. In the intact family, the couple comes together to have a child. The child is part of both parents, and generally pulls the parents' energy together for the well-being of the child. In stepfamilies, blood and sexual ties can polarize the family in opposite energies and directions.

9. The conflict of loyalties must be recognized as normal right from the beginning and be dealt with. Often, just as the child begins to have warm feelings toward the new stepparent, he will pull away and negatively act out. He feels something like this: If I love you, that means that I do not love my real parent.

10. Guard your sense of humor and use it. The step situation is filled with the unexpected. Sometimes we won't know whether to laugh or cry. Try humor.

PUZZLES ABOUT NAMES

The puzzle about what to call each other in the new stepfamily often causes uneasiness. If children called their parent's new partner "step-daddy" or "stepmommy" it would sound like they were deliberately being cool. "Step" has a negative ring. We have not developed the tact of the French who call stepmothers "belle-mère" (beautiful mother).

A common pattern among older youngsters is to call their stepparents by their first name — "Tom," "Ellen," etc. Yet the Toronto investigators found that when the same youngsters were introducing their new stepparents to friends they would call them "my father" or "my mother." Was this just politeness, or was it a case of not feeling comfortable indicating that the person being introduced was not a real parent?

One trouble with encouraging the use of first names is that it makes even harder the establishment of an authority relationship between youngsters and the new parent figure. Another problem: If a stepmother encourages the acquired daughter to call her "Mom," there may soon be an angry note from the "Real Mom" ordering that the practice cease. It is safer to develop a compromise such as Mommy Ann or Mommy Two, or a light word that lacks emotional connotation such as mumsy or popsy. A boy may be willing to call his new parent "father" but not "dad."

Then there may be the problem of deciding what the youngsters' last name will be. Older youngsters often cling to the surname they were born with if Mom remarries. They don't want to show up in school with a new last name. Also they may be loyal to their fathers. Some mothers who remarry keep the name of the ex-husband so that they and their children will have the same last name. If a youngster develops a fondness for his stepfather he may like the idea of taking the stepfather's name or hyphenating his last name to incorporate both his natural father's and his acquired father's names. The situation may be further complicated for children if their custodial mother after divorce reverted to her maiden name and then remarries. For a youngster it can get pretty bewildering if in three years he finds himself with three different names. The main thing is that the child be comfortable with his or her name. A toddler probably will not notice any change in his last name. If the family moves to a new town a youngster of ten may be happy to take his stepfather's name, assuming a warm relationship has developed. An advantage is that he will not have to explain to new friends why his name is not the same as the name on the mailbox. The great increase within the past decade of different names in the same marital household, however, has undoubtedly reduced such self-consciousness in the children involved.

PROBLEMS OF INTIMACY

The most troublesome relationship of all seems to be that of older girls with either a stepmother of stepfather. Often the girls are in turmoil and act in self-destructive ways.[10] Many are predisposed to try to give the stepmother a hard time; and some try to be aloof toward stepfathers. If there are male stepsibs their own age in the household, they may again be aloof, particularly if they see any signs of a stepsib eyeing them in an unbrotherly way.

I have more than a dozen articles from the professional literature which discuss the fact that incest is more likely to be a problem in stepfamilies than in natural families. The incest taboos which function quite firmly in the mores of first-marriage families may not be so firmly perceived by people without blood ties living in a family-like grouping under the same roof. Stepfamilies are so new as a major family form that rules regarding intimate behavior have not gained common acceptance. This development coincides with the emergence of reliable contraceptives and a softening of the incest taboo.

In many U.S. states marriage between stepfather and daughter is not prohibited. Stepfamily incest was described at the International Symposium of Family Sexuality in 1980 as "a recently emerging problem." In a study of stepfamilies Irene Fast and Albert Cain reported:

In some cases mothers "saw" potential incest in every intimacy between stepfather and daughter. In other cases highly sexualized fondling, hugging and kissing between stepfather and daughter alternated with horrified and embarrassed avoidance of any intimacy. And in a few, overt sexual relationships occurred.[11]

The comfortable relationship a stepfather may have with a daughter of nine may become uncomfortable, even stormy, as she moves into puberty. Pseudohostility may be exhibited by either one to stifle any sexual impulses. As for teenage sons and their stepmothers, Emily and John Visher tell of a stepson in his early teens who made these revelations about his inner feelings:

"I was always thinking about girls and I was always thinking about sex. And one of my fantasy objects was my stepsister. . . . There she was in various states of undress. . . . I was attracted to her. . . . Another one of my objects was my stepmother. And that was even worse! It was even more threatening to me because I was attracted to her sexually, and I went out to her emotionally too. . . . Really, my fear about my sexual feelings about my stepmother kept me from expressing some of my positive emotions toward her."[12]

One approach to removing the incest temptation between stepfather and daughter is for him officially to adopt her. That puts her morally out of bounds. It can be done if her real father does not have any custody rights regarding her. It should be considered however only in situations where the natural father no longer looms as an important figure in the girl's life.

Another way of handling incest is for the girl's mother — if she is concerned — to face up to the inherent hazards. She might advise her new husband to be careful to avoid situations that might generate inappropriate feelings.

AND FINALLY, REWARDS

One of the most enchanting eleven-year-old girls I know is a stepdaughter. Her father works with the Muppets. The first time his family came to my home to dinner I did not know until afterwards that he had remarried a few years earlier. The daughter Terri was a marvelous guest for three hours. She sat beside the person whom I thought was her mother. I asked her who made the fine design of a sunset on her denim jacket. She said: "My mom did it," indicating the woman beside her. When they left Terri had her arm around her "mom."

Paul Bohannan, the California anthropologist, has studied many stepfamilies. He tells of a chance encounter between a man's first wife and his second wife. The two had given birth to four of his children. They happened to find themselves talking together at the home of a mutual acquaintance. At first they were wary and annoyed by the encounter. As they made chitchat they found they had mutual interests and found each other nonthreatening. Soon they were planning events together and later began planning outings for the entire lot of children and parents. The husband at first was uneasy about the friendship, but finally concluded it was indeed a real plus for his two sets of children.

If handled right stepfamily living can be a plus for any parent. John Leonard in his column put it this way:

Having become a stepfather, I think I am a better father to my own children than I was when, as an amateur, I didn't have time to listen to them and I thought they owed me something. We owe them something: their dignity. Then maybe they will love us.[13]

Experiments in Family Forms

"A common feature of most of these new marital styles is that they seek to take some of the strain off the nuclear family by de-intensifying the husband-wife relationship."

— *Amitai Etzioni, Columbia University sociologist*

Millions of adults in our post-counterculture era have been exploring ways to improvise on, or test the boundaries of, the family form (in situations other than the conventional one-parent or remarriage household). Some of the explorations have been picturesque. Typically they have involved people with children. The two general thrusts of their experimenting have been with testing communal or sex-sharing family styles.

Parents who participate have a diversity of goals. Usually they are seeking more sense of community to escape loneliness . . . or more personal freedom . . . or additional intimacy from an extended family . . . or more novelty. Others have just been trying to lower living costs or ease the harassment of looking for baby-sitters.

Perhaps the simplest, most logical approach to the communal or group living is that of hard-pressed divorced mothers in Marin County, California. That county has one of the nation's highest divorce rates. Groups of mothers who find they are congenial and share similar standards on housekeeping and child-rearing rent or buy large houses. Rules are laid down on standards of discipline. In a typical instance each mother is in charge of three shifts a week for housekeeping and supervision of the school-age children. (A shift is a morning, afternoon, or evening.) Living costs, loneliness, and the stresses of combining job with motherhood are all reduced for the mothers.

One such home was established in Mill Valley by a divorced mother who underwent frequent periods of anguish because of the strains of finding care for her four-year-old son. She worked at night at a restaurant so that a day-care center for her son made no sense. Baby-sitters were expensive and sometimes gave ten minutes' notice that they could not show up. Several nights she was terrified because she had had to leave her small son alone. She advertised for single mothers in her situation interested in sharing a large house she had located. From the many who responded she was able to select a half-dozen single mothers who seemed to share her ideas about discipline, privacy, and a clean, orderly environment. Each mother was made responsible for cleaning her room and one other. Managers were designated for shopping and bill-paying. The mothers estimate they cut living costs by more than half. The children were reported to be doing very well in school.

A photograph of this group of handsome, smiling mothers and their exuberant children grouped together on the front steps of their house, which appeared in *The New York Times,* seemed to offer convincing evidence they were on to a good idea. Perhaps significantly there were no infants or toddlers among the children.

In several eastern cities similar groups of *intact* families have been sharing a large house or other common facility. They live together as a group of families to benefit from economies of sharing and from being able to be near people with common interests.

Experiments in communal or shared-facility living by people with children vary enormously. Two pediatricians who studied ten communes in the Northwest found considerable variation on how well the children fared. Some fared badly. In their particular sample they found that in one-half of the groups there was a conviction that children's views and thinking were "as important to the functioning of the commune as those of adults." The children were given adult responsibilities as early as possible and seemed to perform well. The investigators found that when an authentic extended family environment prevailed there were very few clingers or whiners or attention-seekers among the children.

In a great many communal situations, however, the children receive marginal attention from self-preoccupied parents. Most academic reports on variant marriage styles and family forms tend to focus on the adult life-styles and pay only passing attention to how the children fare. Alice Rossi made an analysis of fifteen reports, found only 5 percent of the total pages were devoted to children.

One of the best reports on the various ways children fare in communal living is *The Children of the Counterculture* by John Rothchild and Susan Berns Wolf.[1] Coming from the counterculture themselves, Rothchild and Berns packed her two children in their car and proceeded to crisscross America. The four of them shared the life of each commune they visited for a week or so. They covered a range of urban and rural communes and cults. Usually they and their children were well received. One reason, they suggested, was "We looked funky."

They spent quite a while with an urban commune they called The Cosmic Circle, founded by two psychologists. At the Cosmic Circle "freedom" for children was stressed. The children decided when to go to bed, what to wear, whom to sleep with, and whether or not they would go to school. One commune rule was that when a child had a problem "the nearest adult is the parent." This was observed. Still, for the most part, they reported, the children were just bumbling around. And what were the grownups doing? "They were talking. In fact the main purpose of the Cosmic Circle seemed to be analyzing every nuance of every relationship."

The Cosmic Circle had about twenty inhabitants. Partitions and doors were taken off to promote spontaneous community. The visitors were left with the impression that the children "were being raised in a bus station." Despite the founders' hopes and the children's household chores, the days at the Circle "were imbued with listlessness for the children, a state of affairs which resembled that in many other urban communes."

Rothchild and Wolf gave high grades to some of the rural communes. They encountered some admirable children. At a place called The Ranch they found the children "beautiful, disorganized and friendly. They lacked an urban aggressive edge." The youngsters remained in a perpetual state of savage innocence, and — for better or worse — they tended to run in packs.

On the other hand they found at the cultist nonrural commune of Hare Krishna the children were supervised and indoctrinated sternly.

The Hare Krishna people of course are the people with shaved heads and saffron pajamas that we see chanting and praying in public places in many U.S. cities. At their dwelling places small children sleep on floor mattresses right beside their parents. Rothchild and Wolf were assured by a mother that that posed no problem because the Hare Krishna believe that intercourse is a waste of important energy except for conception.

At age five children were separated from their parents and sent off for at least seven years to a special facility in Texas called Guracula; and in those years saw their parents only occasionally. They were in training in Sanscrit and for priesthood. Rothchild and Wolf were permitted to visit the facility but not to talk with the young priests-to-be. They found a prisonlike setting with play discouraged. Youngsters ate with their fingers. Each night at 2:30 they were aroused for a sway-and-chant worship service.

In another study made by three family-life specialists of more than thirty communes in urban and suburban New England, the investigators concluded that sharing authority over children among adults creates situations full of "inconsistency, ambiguity and contradictions."[2] Decision-making by the adults regarding a child's behavior was not handled as simply as two parents might handle it but rather led to a lot of "complications and uncertainties."

Married couples seem to lead more individual lives in communes. As parents they undergo a decline in standard-setting for their children and tend to become self-conscious about their role as parents.

In communes where group care is practiced, parental standards of discipline often come into conflict with the group's. At a commune of three families one set of parents was highly laissez-faire, another believed in strict enforcement of rules, the third strongly believed you handled problems by reasoning with the children.[3] In such group settings children soon figured out how far they could go with each set of adults.

A young mother, Virginia Rankin, has related her experiences in spending a year at a commune with eight other adults and six children.[4]

They had spent a half a year planning how best to eliminate family units and "knock down the walls of dependency, jealous competitiveness" by achieving freedom, trust, and community. Every kid was to trust every adult equally. They would all become parents of the youngsters.

Right from the outset, she relates, "The kids quite simply freaked out. Most of them became very dependent. Each child wanted *everything* done for it by its own mommy. They fought loudly, constantly and brutally." She added, "Not only were we disappointed in terms of our visionary goals but on a practical level the child care was harder rather than easier." Ms. Rankin's own three-and-a-half-year old son was not satisfied to have anyone but his own mommy put him to bed.

The commune concluded that "when responsibility is divided up among so many individuals no one is responsible and chaos ensues." It finally decided to put a single individual in charge each afternoon after school and two people were made responsible for the weekends. Things were immediately better for the children with the new system.

In rural communes in particular the birth of a baby tends to be an occasion for celebration. It is a part of nature, beautiful. Commune mothers are more apt than others to choose natural childbirth, and they breast-feed longer than average. Alice Rossi concludes it is when infants start to become youngsters that problems start. Rearing a child, she said, involves obligations and future planning for which commune members are not prepared. In at least one of the communes visited by Rothchild and Wolf, children had their own sleeping quarters in a bunkhouse some distance away from where their mothers slept.

Children are more exposed to nudity in communes than in the average household but little importance seems to be attached to it. In some communes there is sexual intrigue among adults, but the more normal pattern is to observe a sexual taboo among housemates.

At the doorless Cosmic Circle, Rothchild and Wolf noted an incident where an angry young son kept pulling the quilt off the bed where his unattached mother was sleeping with some man from outside the commune.

How well the various novel experiments in alternate life-styles of families living together work out for the children seems to depend mainly on:

- How much interested respect is shown toward children.
- How much stability is provided in the children's environment.
- How much the children's own parents are involved in the rearing.

THE FARM

Probably the commune that has given the most thoughtful attention to its children is The Farm near Summertown, Tennessee.

A remarkable man, Steve Gaskin, is the founder and the spiritual and practical leader of his commune of about thirteen hundred persons. He was a student of S. I. Hayakawa, semanticist at San Francisco State who became a U.S. Senator. Gaskin became the leader of a large group of hippies, took them on caravans in about thirty buses around the country, and finally, more than a decade ago, settled the group on the thousand-acre farm in Tennessee. Neighbors call them "Technicolor Amish." There are real Amish in the area. Gaskin's group has for the most part gotten along fine with its neighbors. Members not only work the farmland, mainly for high-protein soy beans, their staple, but they have construction crews that work outside the farm. They were partners in a sawmill but got out because they didn't like to destroy nature. They have developed cottage industries such as designing and building radiation detectors and fetal heart monitors. And they run a small publishing house. One of its publications is an authoritative quarterly, *The Practicing Midwife*. People at the farm are vegetarians. They do not use money among themselves. Food is served communally. Clusters of people live in old farmhouses or several dozen newly built dwellings. The Farm has its own accredited school system, bakery, and well-equipped medical center with two doctors and many midwives.

These mostly long-haired people are friendly, disciplined, and fairly young men and women. They have a Sunday morning inspirational service which Gaskin conducts.

In my chat with him Gaskin said his people were "religious but have no name for it." Their religion seems to be a reverence for nature, good will among people, and procreation. People's behavior, they believe, is controlled by "life force energy." Gaskin stressed to me that they scorn extramarital sex. The people at The Farm rarely use acid anymore but rely on good human relations for their heavy charges.

Gaskin is a slim, ascetic man in blue jeans, who has a happy face, a whispy beard, stringy hair, rimless steel glasses. He is in his forties, is eloquent, still talks at times in counterculture slang of experiences being "trips." Gaskin seems to be very much in charge, with the other adults his apparently willing disciples.

Whatever its shortcomings. The Farm exults in its children — about a third of the population — and prides itself in its child-support activities. The Farm is not one of those free-living communes where people hesitate to say no to a child. Gaskin told me:

"We found that children accept correction from their natural parents that they won't accept from anyone else. Most of the physical discipline is done by the mother, not the father." It is done without anger.

Marriages at The Farm are till death do ye part. Gaskin does most of the marrying on Sunday morning after all the legal papers have been obtained. A few group marriages have been attempted. Birth is a sacrament at The Farm, natural childbirth the norm.

The children seem healthy, sunny but disciplined. Parents are urged to raise them to be honest and hardworking. They rarely cry or whine. They never run in packs as at the Ranch. Some say they act more like smiling, well-behaved Chinese children than typical American children.

Children at The Farm are included in most social activities. And many child-adult games are organized, such as broad-jumping. Mothers placidly hold their babies at parties and in lunch line-ups.

Gaskin tells his disciples that children are a part of "your own immortality — another chance for you to do it right." Here are some of his precepts:

"We believe that working it out with our kids and raising them to be sane and honest is a heavy yoga. If you can turn out a kid that's pretty sane, that's heavier than writing a poem."

"What you are trying to do is to teach a kid not to be a rip-off."

"If a kid has just gone outlaw and says, 'I want it all' don't get emotional, and don't get mad. Pick him up and carry him away from the energy source." (At The Farm there is a lot of talk about life-energy sources.) Carrying a child away usually means taking it to its bedroom. "You can't just walk into the bedroom and say 'You be good.' You've got to be willing to walk in and out of that room and open and close the door a whole lot of times."

"When the kid is out of order, look for a chance to put a teaching down. If you put the same teaching down a lot of times in a row the same way, the kid will learn."

"In general your kid ought to have access to you every time he comes to you."

When parents are working during the day on group activities there are schools and care centers on The Farm for the child. However, Gaskin says, "We don't go along with the idea that kids are supposed to be raised by a whole bunch of other folks. That makes for crazy kids."

CHILDREN OF THE SEXUAL EXPERIMENTERS

Sexual experimentation is another aspect of what Etzioni called the current social trend toward *de-intensifying* the husband-wife relationship.

Sex outside marriage used to be an extremely serious offense against the social norm, for women in particular. Assured contraception, the emergence of a new freedom for women, the growing tenuousness of marriage, the near-breakdown of social mechanisms for maintaining scrutiny in cities, and a wide embracing of a do-your-own-thing philosophy have greatly diminished the social offense. Often only the possibility of an angry spouse has to be calculated. And he or she may say, "It's only okay if we both do it."

Some married women look upon extramarital sex now as a novel form of game-playing. And often they are encouraged in this by their own game-playing husbands who want to be relieved of guilt.

Hence the recent upsurge in our society of married swingers or "consensual adultery." Some couples swing in groups, others work out deals with other mate-swapping couples.

Connecticut College psychologist Bernard I. Murstein, after investigating swinging, concluded that perhaps a million U.S. couples have been involved.

Who are the swingers? They are not as glamorous as their ads in magazines and newsletters make them sound. (Some of the ads even include the wife's dimensions.) They tend to be mechanical in their relations. While they are not necessarily near divorce, they do tend to be a bit bored with their marriage, particularly the sexual aspect of it. The wives are more likely to be housewives than career women. Many of the couples have few interests beyond TV viewing. Most do not go to church more than occasionally, but send their children to Sunday School or its equivalent.

There have been numerous academic studies of the swingers. The best study of who they are, as far as I can find, was made by sociologist Brian G. Gilmartin.[5] He compared the lives of one hundred swingers with one hundred conventional couples. Swingers, he found, are significantly more likely:

- to have had cool, often strained relations with their own parents as youngsters, and not to have gotten much affection from them;
- to have experienced psychotherapy while growing up;
- to have relatively few contacts today with relatives, even when they live in the same metropolitan area;
- to have high geographical mobility;
- to have formed fewer contacts with their present neighbors.

In short, swingers come from the kind of people our times have been producing in large numbers. Author Walker Percy in his novel *Lancelot* used an amusingly exaggerated but acerbic comment by one of his characters to suggest a tendency if not a trend. His Lancelot Lamar in talking of the drift of modern society, termed it: "A generation stoned and . . . devalued. Pricks after pussy, pricks after pricks, pussy after pussy. But most of all pussy after pricks. Christ, what a country."

Some group sex encounters involving couples indeed are mass frolics, but more commonly everything is rather demure at first. The gathering may seem like a cocktail or bridge party. But at a certain time, say ten o'clock, a man and woman will slip into a bedroom. And people generally may start undressing. Usually there is soft music.

Typically, the men are not matches for the women, who, once sexually aroused, are capable of far more orgasms per evening than men. Hence, as a number of on-the-spot observers have reported, many of the women turn to homosexuality while the men rest to regather their sexual forces.

The great majority of swingers have children. And each swinging group seems to have its own norms on what to do about the children. The older, middle-class Midwestern swingers in particular seem extremely anxious that their children know nothing of the extracurricular sex. They hide their swinger magazines and correspondence, send the children away while hosting, or lock the children's doors. Some report that when children discovered their parents' swinging activities, "family function was seriously disturbed."[6]

Gilmartin found that about three-quarters of the swinging couples in his sample who were parents reported their children already knew of their spouse-sharing recreations. In some swinging groups it is felt to be all right to have toddlers trotting about or napping in various action rooms, but that children from five to twelve shouldn't be exposed to swinging. Some young, hard-pressed swingers who are loathe to pay for baby-sitters bring their small children along to the evening event.

Anthropologist Gilbert Bagley, who did an eyewitness study of sexual swinging by married couples, reports a case in which a man mounting the hostess happened to notice that the hostess's seven-year-old daughter was standing quietly in the bedroom doorway watching. The unflustered mother simply suggested to the girl, "You shouldn't be up, darling. Why don't you go back to bed?"

The daughter dutifully trotted off, but the man involved was sufficiently unnerved to be incapable of sexual arousal the rest of the evening.

Gilmartin found from his sample of swinging adults — apparently most in California — that six of the families actively encouraged their own teenage children to form their own "love groups." He asked all his hundred swinging couples what they thought of the idea of having teenagers stage love groups at a neighboring house, under the supervision of one of the swinger wives who happened to be menstruating. One-third liked the idea, two-thirds did not. The teenager swingers seem to enjoy fondling indiscriminately — and often are encouraged by their parents to get some practice in same-sex fondling — but the kids tend to be conservative and reserve coitus for "sweethearts." Some of the parents justified the "love group" for teenagers as helping the youngsters gain genuine self-confidence.

In the homes of swingers there tend to be far fewer rules for children regarding how they should behave themselves in everyday life than in nonswinger homes. If rules are needed, swingers and their children tend to make them up — amid shouting — when a situation calls for a rule. Gilmartin found swingers and their children get along in relative harmony, perhaps because the swingers pay relatively little attention to their children. The swingers are preoccupied with living their own lives. The one common complaint of swingers' children was that their parents did not pay enough attention to them.

Most of the teenage children of the swinging couples were also sexually active. In fact they engaged in sexual intercourse several times a week, typically in their own bedrooms. Gilmartin got the impression that the younger preteen daughters of swingers tended to be more aggressive and tomboyish than such daughters of nonswingers. The younger sons tended to have an above-average interest in having girls in their play groups.

OPEN-ENDED MARRIAGES

Many couples become annoyed by the complications of arranging swinging get-togethers and with the swingers' taboo against emotional involvements, so they drift into "open marriages." The husband-wife bond remains primary, but both are free to maintain sexual liaisons with other partners. This freedom is said to fulfill better the personal and emotional needs of the partners and adds the excitement of new romantic involvements.

The Journal of Sex Research carried a six-thousand-word report on seventeen sexually open marriages.[7] The wives had had an average of 4.8 outside affairs. Most of the couples had children, yet the report carried only a paragraph about children — to the effect that the "open" affairs were kept secret from the children because they were not old enough to understand the complexities of the situations.

Open marriages came in for considerable public discussion and some approbation in the early 1970s when the husband-wife team of Nena and George O'Neill wrote their widely read book *Open Marriage*. They contended that sexual fidelity was becoming an antiquated concept. The subject of children was barely mentioned.

Now Mrs. O'Neill at least has revised her opinion in a later book, *The Marriage Premise*. After noting the high rate of marital disruptions among the extramarital sex crowd, she concluded: "Sexual fidelity is not just a vow in marriage or a moral or religious belief but a need associated with our deepest emotions and our quest for emotional security. Infidelity is an extremely threatening situation."

She might have added that when an "extremely threatening situation" exists between married people who have children, the tension almost inevitably is communicated to the children. Also, threatened people are likely to have a hard time concentrating on their parental roles.

SERIAL MONOGAMY

Mrs. O'Neill predicted that the marriage of the future would be "more intense but shorter." This concept got a lot of support from the widely read book *Passages: The Predictable Crises of Adult Life*, by Gail Sheehy. She contended that individual adults go through stages of change (somewhat like the Erikson stages of growth from infancy to maturity) so that "the odds are minimal that any couple can enjoy matched development." The marital ideal of "till death do you part" was to her a static notion that interferes with individual growth. She, like the O'Neills, didn't dwell much on children. But what are the implications of a revolving-door approach to marriage for the children who are created by it?

Meredith Ringler-White, who has run the monitored parent-child visitation center in Denver, has seen many children who have gone through two or more divorces and their accompanying shifts of parental affiliation. It is her impression that such multiple divorces are particularly destabilizing for children, but she stresses that few good systematic studies of the impact of multiple-divorce on children have been made at this writing.

GROUP MARRIAGES

These have attracted the wistful interest of many sexual liberals in the United States and Europe. In fact, however, group marriages are so complicated to manage successfully because of prohibitions, ground rules, and multiple relationships, that the ongoing ones in the U.S. at least apparently number in the low thousands.

The sexual liberals refer to any ordinary married couple consisting of two partners as a dyad. A group marriage, entered into informally, can be a triad (three partners), a tetrad (four partners), a pentad (five partners), or a hexad (six partners). Whatever the size of the group, each person considered himself married to at least two other persons.

The most common is the tetrad in which two married couples join together into what they regard as a married unit. Virtually all group marriages involve sexual relations with more than one person.

An adult has co-wives or co-husbands. A very large proportion of the groups involve children who, hence, have co-daddies and/or co-mommies.

Co-daddies and co-mommies of the children usually sleep with each other on a fixed rotation basis to reduce the possibility of jealousy, according to Larry and Joan Constantine, who contacted about a hundred groups marriages around the U.S. and studied a dozen extensively. Larry Constantine is a family therapist in the Boston area. But even on a rotation basis of sharing beds, a partner may become more enthusiastic about one sexual partner than another. Jealousy becomes a major disrupting factor.

Children in group marriages tend to think of themselves as living in a family within a family. Less than half of the group marriages studied by the Constantines lasted as long as a year, so that few solid conclusions about the impact on children could reasonably be reached.

Group marriages seem to fall apart mainly because of the overload of decision-making and because of jealousy (even among old friends).

Children identify primarily with a biological parent, especially the woman from whom they were born. The Constantines tell, in *Group Marriage,* of an interview they had with one child invited to draw pictures of people he knew. When asked who one figure was the child replied "Dad." When asked who another male figure was the child said: "Umm, Jim."

"Who is Jim to you?"

"Well, he's kind like a daddy. . . . He is a daddy, but sorta."

Advocates of group marriage say it is fine for children because it gives them an enriched environment of adults to relate to. Also the children, as one proponent put it, are given more "freedom to be themselves" (i.e., they tend to get below-average attention from their natural parents). Some children in these settings feel self-conscious because their friends tell them they have a weird or strange family setup. The Constantines referred to one badly behaving boy, who kept interrupting the Constantines' talk with one of his parents, as "the nexus of unarticulated tension."

Younger children may not be particularly aware of family structure. What seems critical is the nature and quality of their own parents' interaction with them. The fast falling apart of most group marriages presumably creates puzzlement and uneasiness for many of the children involved.

UNMARRIED PARENTS

Movie stars such as Vanessa Redgrave made it glamorous — to many — to have "love children" outside of marriage.

Some young women who have children simply cohabit with the father they love; others want to do the child thing all by themselves. They want a child without the bother of a husband.

The counterculture inspired a surge of both types of unmarried parenting, particularly cohabiting. The U.S. Census Bureau recently was aware of 272,000 nonmarital households with children. The cohabitors with children have often expressed a belief that their own relationship would remain more viable without that "silly piece of paper," as one actor put it. There seems to be little concern about the children because the stigma of bastardy has receded, at least in big cities.

Henry Foster, past president of the Family Law Section of the American Bar Association, suggests that such unwed parents create seriously blurred legal rights for their children.[8]

If the unwed parents part, the child has no sure right to child support from the father unless the father has signed an official statement of paternity (an order of filiation). Simply letting his name be on the birth certificate is not enough. Such children also miss out on inheritance from the father unless the father during his lifetime prepares a specific court order. And collection of government benefits in adult life may be complicated. Foster added:

"There are all kinds of future embarrassments and penalties that may be inflicted on the perfectly innocent child who happens to be illegitimate.'' He thought it very selfish of such parents to leave the child in jeopardy simply because they don't want to get caught up in the legal involvements of being married.

As for the woman who does her own thing (with the benefit of the best sperm available to her), her self-satisfaction should be balanced against the probable short-changing of the child. There is a greater likelihood the child may be stigmatized at school for bastardy than the child of cohabitation. There is a fifty percent loss for the child in sense of roots when he or she grows up. But most important, we have seen that the presence of an adult male as a model and mentor in the child's life is a very real asset.

THE NEW INTEREST IN INCEST

In our folklore incest is committed mainly by lusting hillbilly daddies who haul their daughters behind the henhouse and ravish them. Incest has been probably the most profound of taboos.

Today a whole flock of sex researchers, academic sexual radicals, and other influential individuals and groups have been pushing the idea that incest can be either positive or abusive depending on the circumstances.[9] The taboo against intimacy, they contend, puts a child beyond real intimacy within the family at a time when our world is becoming increasingly depersonalized. Incest is being opposed, they say, by uptight people. Sex researchers tend to enjoy exploring new frontiers of sexual contacts. Among sex investigators who have been speaking mildly or benignly about incest are John Money of Johns Hopkins and Wardell Pomeroy, co-author of the original Kinsey reports.

The influential report of the Sex Information and Education Council of the U.S. (SIECUS) aimed at sex education carried an article by sex researcher James Ramey. He contended that antiquated ideas about incest today are comparable to the fears of masturbation a century ago.

Whereas a decade ago incest was virtually taboo not only as an act but as a topic of discussion, it is now openly explored in most forms of media. Motion picture films such as *Luna,* featuring Jill Clayburgh, depict an incestual relationship between mother and son. In real life incest overwhelmingly involves father-daughter, with the latter typically age eight to eleven at first assault. A woman author recalling her incestuous relation with her father (*Father's Day*) got on the big TV talk shows.

The columnist Ann Landers has returned again and again to incestuous situations.

A psychologist at the Nazareth Child Care Center in Boston estimates that there are at least a quarter million cases of incest every year involving Americans.

One of the arguments advanced by sexual liberals to ease the taboo is that it violates children's rights to have the same consensual sex experiences as adults have. But at what age really does a youngster have the ability to give informed consent to the sexual advances of an authority figure in its own family?

To conclude we have noted an array of experiments in parented relationships and activities where child-rearing is involved. Throughout history good parents have served not merely to preserve the species but to improve it. When two adults of the opposite sex try to raise children with devotion, sacrifice, and the best ideals they can muster, humanity prospers.

Any massive move to a more casual, less personalized, less respectful, less protective mode of child-rearing seems to pose a clear threat to our children.

I was impressed particularly by a statement made by Carlfred Broderick while he was editor of *The Journal of Marriage and the Family*. He said:

"It is precisely the exclusivity and the durability of marriage that gives it its competitive advantage. Every study of personality development has shown that being reared in a stable and unthreatening emotional environment is most conducive to developing ego strength and social competence in children."

5

Some Concluding Thoughts

Nine Adult Skills
That Help Children Thrive

"Few things speak more fully and plainly about who a person really is than the way he or she relates with and raises children."

— *Larry and Joan Constantine, family-life consultants*

About twenty years ago I had the interesting, if a bit weird, experience of being a judge of the All-American Family contest. A family from each state was selected by family-life specialists in those states. The families assembled, all expenses paid, at a vacation spot near Fort Myers, Florida.

Criteria for the final judging were drawn up primarily by Emily Mudd, the highly respected authority on family living at the University of Pennsylvania. We five judges did a lot of conferring and observing parent-child relations. I was the only non-pro. I gather I was invited because I had written extensively about family life. As I recall, I spent an hour with each of twelve different families. One thing I did at such individual sessions was to present the family members with a family emergency and watch how they handled it in terms of communication and cooperative skills.

In the two decades since that curious "contest," developmental psychologists and other specialists on growing up have added vastly to our knowledge of what constitutes expertise in helping children develop. The findings apply particularly to parents, but most of them also apply to other people who work a lot with children. I inevitably came across many of their conclusions while researching this book. I have sifted through the views and will present here nine skills that seem to me to loom as particularly important.

I should say that I am not impressed with any particular recipe or vogue for raising children. The feelings that the parents themselves, for example, bring to the role — their pleasure in parenting, their great patience, their respect for each child — seem to be more important than specific lines of action (or positions one takes on the permissiveness scale). Good parenting is not done by formula. Jerome Kagan of Harvard says that how many times a parent kisses a child or how and when one feeds it are less important than "the melody those actions comprise." He would include in the "melody" such patterns as consistency, variety, and regularity.

Obviously there is no model youngster that families should be striving to turn out as with cookie cutters. The dynamics of personal growth are intricate. Many high achievers, for example, would seem to come from unlikely family backgrounds. Noted actors and actresses tend to come from stormy homes. Many eminent people come from homes where there was trouble or adversity of some sort. Historian Arnold Toynbee's concept that civilizations rise in large part as a response to the challenge of adversity may well carry over to individual achievers. And there are probably born geniuses. Albert Einstein, as is well known, was a puzzle and perhaps an embarrassment to his parents. He seemed backward, a poor student, neurotic, had virtually no early friends. Apparently he marched to his own distant drummer.

The Goertzels found in their study *Cradles of Eminence* a few common denominators: "In almost all the homes there is love for learning in one or both parents, often accompanied by a physical exuberance and a persistent drive toward goals."[1] In my own study (pre-dating the Goertzel study) of the characteristics of people reaching the presidency of substantial corporations I found that the number-one trait was "the ability to maintain a high level of thrust toward goals."[2] The thrust came not just from energy. If often appeared in surprisingly frail people as a compulsion of psychic origin. Many top executives are not particularly contented or appealing people.

Personal development also often does not move in a straight line. The dynamics of growth create surprises. Also events and encounters alter life courses and personal growth. Successful youths don't necessarily make successful adults. That long-term study of infants followed to adulthood at the University of California, Berkeley, uncovered many seeming reversals.[3] Some boys who had been rebels emerged in adulthood as well-integrated, competent, or creative adults, clear about their values and with good feelings about themselves. Some attractive children raised in atmospheres seemingly free of strain became the male athletic heroes and the good-looking, popular girls. By age thirty, the study found, many of these were "brittle, discontented and puzzled adults."

Most of us are not trying to raise future tycoons or beauty queens. As parents, what most of us hope for are offspring who will produce a pleasing amalgam of the better traits of their two parents plus a bonus of some inculcated improvements. We want children we can be proud of. We hope also they will be effective in their chosen life courses. We hope they will be affectionate and can laugh as well as cry.

Regarding specific traits desired in one's children as they grow up, in 1980 *Parents* magazine reported that its polling of readers showed that "intelligence" was the trait most desired in both sons and daughters. The second most important quality hoped for was "personality," particularly in girls. "Creativity and imagination" came next. "Appearance" was rated fourth for girls, sixth for boys (behind mechanical and athletic ability). The parents wanted their children to be ambitious but not unreasonably competitive. They placed a substantial value on cooperativeness.

These are sensible, reasonable hopes. They can usually be realized by parents skilled in helping their offspring thrive.

First a few basics. The Children's Defense Fund neatly summed up four elementary needs of *all* children in these words:

- a need to feel wanted and accepted;
- a need for continuity in relationships with biological or psychological parents;
- a need to have some sense that there is a regular, dependable quality to the world in which they live;
- a need for thoughtful guidance in coping with the demands of growing up.

As we have seen, in the modern world some of these most elementary needs of children frequently are not met.

In child-raising there are also some fairly elementary goals toward which all parents should work. A well-raised youngster should be:

- capable of being affectionate;
- capable of trusting others;
- capable of feeling self-worth;
- capable of being effective;
- capable of being socially competent;
- capable of accepting responsibility.

In that long-term California study, four principal tests that were used in gauging infancy-to-adulthood development were:

1. Have they become well-integrated?
2. Are they clearly competent or creative?
3. Are they clear about their values?
4. Do they have an understanding and acceptance of themselves and others?

Parents are forcing an extra challenge upon themselves if they space their children less than two and a half years apart. Under the age of two and a half, Burton White found, a toddler is still so absorbed with mother and home that the appearance of a new rival for attention often comes as a shock the toddler is ill-equipped to handle.

So let's get to what was promised: nine skills of expert parents which I feel particularly help create the melodious kind of environment in which growing children will thrive. (Most of these skills are also very useful for parent substitutes and others engaged in guiding children.)

1. A skillful child-developer makes it clear that he or she is indeed crazy about that particular child.   Urie Bronfenbrenner of Cornell put it best in these words: "The child needs at least one person who has an irrational involvement with him, someone who thinks the kid is more important than other people's kids."

New York child psychologist Charles E. Schaefer asked fifty parents whose grown offspring seemed well launched in life for the best advice they could give young parents. The number-one recommendation was: "Love abundantly." This parental love should be constant and unconditional — which means it is *always* present, "even when the child is acting in a most unlovable manner."

The former head of the American Psychoanalytical Association, Heiz Kohut, has put as the child's number-one need, "mirroring, the gleam in the mother's eye that says 'you are here and you are fabulous.' "

As a child learns to talk, a parent can assure the child of unconditional *love* and still make clear the parent does not *like* specific bad behavior. One mother of a four-year-old daughter, who seems to have done a fine job of mothering, says she and her daughter have a litany when the mother reprimands her severely. The child will say anxiously:

"You don't like me?"

"I don't like the way you are behaving."

"But you do love me, right?"

"Right."

The mother says, "That seems to steady her in her anxiety."

2. A skillful child developer does a lot of interacting with the child, especially verbal interacting. The expert child raiser stimulates infants and toddlers by giving them a lot of talk and laughter, rocking and smiling. And the expert parent gives older children a lot of conversational exchange every day.

Some parents think it is pointless to talk to a baby because it doesn't seem to understand, and besides it can't talk back, only babble. The typical father, as noted, spends less than a minute a day in verbal interaction with his infant. The egalitarian fathers with job-holding wives do talk quite a bit more as they feed, rock the infant, and change its diapers. The infant who is only occasionally talked or sung to is a deprived infant. Human speech is achieved largely through interacting.

The infants of expert parents are literally bathed by the sound of voices addressing them personally. Burton White has suggested that you not only talk to the older toddlers as often as possible but use words to provide a related idea. For example: If your child shows you a ball, urge him to "throw the ball" to you. Talk about whatever the baby is doing at the moment.

An infant may only get the general drift of what you are communicating, but the verbalizing is important for a number of reasons. It is reassuring and usually pleasurable to the infant. It can help in assuring an intensity of attachment between infant and mother. It contributes significantly to the child's ease in learning how to talk. Human development investigator Alison Clarke-Stewart of the University of Chicago made an extensive review of research on child development and concluded: "The amount, richness (variety) and complexity of adult speech in face-to-face interaction with the child is related to when, how early, and how well the child talks and understands speech." (Some say this assumes both are enjoying the interaction.)

Even the child's intelligence level probably will be affected by lots of verbalizing from parent figures while it is young. Clarke-Stewart further concluded: "In general the more the parent looks, talks, plays or otherwise interacts with the young child in a stimulating way, the more likely is the child to do well in IQ tests . . . to be creative, to do well in school — to excel in overall competence."[4] Child psychologist Lee Salk has observed that early stimulation seems to foster greater learning.

In the young human brain there seems to be a neural predisposition that facilitates the acquisition of language. In most cases, the ability to think seems to rise in parallel to a rise in language ability. The occasionally discovered wild children who have lived in isolation from humans turn out to be children with greatly diminished thinking ability. Some may have been retarded from birth. Deaf-mutes indicate thinking skills. They may develop an internal language.

One reason middle-class children tend to have a built-in advantage over lower-class children, according to Stanford psychologist Robert D. Hess, is that the middle-class mothers tend to elaborate on what they say. They use more explanatory sentences.

Fathers who are more available to their children than average, who are nurturant, accepting, and serve as active teachers, tend to have children who excel in school. If they have been supportive and interactive with daughters you get another surprising long-term benefit. The girls' degree of orgasmic satisfaction as they develop sexual relationships has been associated with the excellence of their relationship with their father.

A particularly useful way to interact verbally with a young child is to read illustrated stories to him or her every day. The child will comment and exclaim as he listens and looks. The look-listen combination is particularly important in creating for the child an enriched environment. Small animal studies at the University of California, conducted initially under the leadership of the late David Krech, found that the animals subjected to an enriched environment of play, interaction and challenging tests actually underwent physical changes in the brain to cause the brain to function more efficiently. The best way to create an enriched environment for young humans is by plenty of exposure to language.

3. The person skilled in developing children works in many ways to help the youngster develop a high sense of self-esteem. This is sometimes called ego strength. To thrive in life a youngster needs to know he is valued by people important to him, particularly his parents. It is the low-esteem youngsters who get into trouble, either by venting their resentful feelings, or by being extra conforming and pliable.

If circumstances of life for a family are relatively harsh compared to those of surrounding families or if the youngsters are victims of discrimination, then helping children achieve self-esteem may be especially challenging. It helps considerably if the parents themselves are prideful people, if they are respected for their community activities and if they are good at parenting.

An interesting study centered at Lehigh University was made of ninety-eight white middle-class youngsters from stable, two-parent families.[5] They had been divided (by testing and teacher evaluations) into high self-esteem youngsters and low self-esteem youngsters. Studies were then made of their home situations. The investigators' conclusion: "The family climate associated with high self-esteem appears to be one in which both mother and father are supportive of their child and of each other." "Directive behavior in parents (issuing lots of commands) was generally associated with low self-esteem in children."

Parents should encourage their youngsters' efforts to achieve proficiencies that they can feel good about, especially proficiencies in interacting easily with other children and with adults.

Here are some specific suggestions for promoting self-esteem in children:

- Start right in the first year to instill a sense of trust in the infant by providing him/her with loving attention and knowledgeable caretaking. This sense of trust not only helps the infant develop its own identity but also, when older, helps the youngster reach out readily to be sociable with other people, and to think of the world as a positive place.
- Be a good active listener when the growing child has problems, and demonstrate your genuine interest in them.

- Always treat the child with respect, whatever his or her behavior, and expect respect in return. Encourage the child to know you have high expectations for him. Don't talk baby talk to a baby old enough to comprehend you. Sally Knisely, Connecticut psychotherapist, says: "For a child, being respected is quite an experience. . . . Its effect never fails, for it allows the beginning and strengthening of an honest relationship."

- Encourage the preschool child's attempts to take the initiative, to move out from the family nest, to be self-directing and to set reasonable goals.

4. The skillful child developer conditions children to do well.   Doing well not only contributes again to children's self-esteem but gets them started in habit patterns such as persistence and planning and ways of thinking about themselves that will increase their chances of being effective, productive adults. For healthy growth, children need a chance to sense achievement. This does not mean, however, that parents push the child beyond potential or show disappointment if the child has difficulty meeting their expectations.

The child should be encouraged to save. (Few youngsters today are so encouraged according to a Rand Survey.) They should be encouraged to undertake projects that require planning and projects where there is delay in gratification of reward. One of the characteristics of "very well developed" children, according to Burton White, is that they have reason to be proud of personal accomplishment.

I have before me a fascinating account of a remarkable young man of Puerto Rican background named Luis Velez.[6] He grew up on welfare in a broken home in a burned-out slum in the South Bronx, New York. His uneducated father, a chronic gambler, left home when he was two and showed up occasionally. An exuberant, friendly youth, Luis had a brilliant scholastic and extracurricular career, on scholarship, at the elite Collegiate School in New York. The teachers called him "unbelievable." Then he went on to Princeton University, and a university spokesman in 1982 advised me he would shortly be graduated as a political science major.

His older sister Nelida taught him to write before school age by using the kitchen stove as a blackboard. His mother continually urged him on. Even his father, on his visits, talked with him at length about how he was doing and the importance of striving. Luis explained:

"We've been conditioned to do well in my family. Some people are conditioned to be oppressed. Oppression becomes a style of life."

5. Experts in child development encourage children to be explorers. One of Burton White's more interesting conclusions from child-watching is that parents should reduce where feasible the use of restrictive devices in the home such as playpens and jumpseats. He acknowledges that such devices simplify child care. They keep small siblings from beating up on each other. They reduce breakage. They reduce hazards. "Nevertheless," he says, "we have found that in families where children are developing very well, restrictive devices are rarely used. In families where children are developing rather poorly, restrictive devices play a relatively prominent role."[7]

The more time a toddler spends in idleness the higher he rates on an "index of emptiness" and the greater the hazard of slow development. When devices are necessary, others point out, they should be used creatively with parent-child interaction kept as a goal.

A four-month-old baby still ga-gaing will be more stimulated in perceptual development by discovering novel objects he or she can explore by hand, mouth and eyes than to be given the same old rattle-type toys. (If a playpen is felt really to be necessary, it can be moved around regularly with new objects frequently introduced.)

After the eighth month the crawling infant is incredibly curious and should be encouraged to take off on all fours to explore his small universe. He or she loves to come upon and manipulate anything with hinges, even a door or book or a box with a hinged lid. Just give this crawler a clean floor and remove obvious hazards such as an ironing board that can be knocked over. Electric sockets can be plugged.

As the crawler becomes a toddler, his horizons for exploration should broaden, again with a minimum of restrictive devices and "No" warnings. The good parent, White says, designs the main living area to nurture the curiosity of the one to three-year-old. Tidiness should give way to kid attractiveness. The house should have plenty of small, manipulable, visually detailed objects and safe places to climb.

As youngsters become older there should be expeditions to farms, sawmills, museums, zoos, woodlands. I am pleased to recall that as my sons were growing up we spent every birthday journeying to a different mountain to explore. It was their idea, not mine. The more a youngster is encouraged to follow through on his curiosity, the more likely he or she will be an imaginative, creative person.

6. Skillful parents try to give their children a strong sense of family solidarity.   (This also applies in the one-parent home.)

Some months ago, I was a guest in the home of Mr. and Mrs. Robert Alto of Ukiah, California. He is a college official; she has a couple of part-time jobs involving writing and public relations that interest her very much. The Altos have three sons, ages (when I saw them) three, five, and seven.

The sons were delightful. Each without any prompting came and chatted curiously with me. Hayward, the second-grader, happened to have a sheet of homework he had just finished in his hand. I asked to see it. It was a three-paragraph description of a trip he had taken. For clarity, spelling, neatness, and sentence structure it was superior to the classwork handed in by millions of college freshmen.

Early the next morning Mrs. Alto spent an hour driving me to the nearest airport. I commented on how deeply her sons impressed me. She said:

"Garrett came and got in bed with us for about a half hour this morning. That's permitted after dawn. All three sons come in at least once during a week. If we don't want them we put them on the floor beside the bed. We keep a pad and blanket there." The Alto boys each have their own bedroom but all sleep in one room on the bed or curled up in sleeping bags.

We talked about child-rearing. She mentioned that every Monday night the Altos have a "family home evening" for about an hour and that the boys love it. They sing songs. Each boy takes turns deciding what will be sung. Sometimes they compose their own brief tunes. One that Garrett composed was "The Motorcycle Comes Roaring By." But mostly they sing folk songs. Mrs. Alto said:

"We work out our problems at these sessions. Each has a chance to say what is worrying or bugging him. We, the parents, hand out allowances with admonitions that they put some in savings. Some nights we call on an ailing friend. By talk and actions Bob and I try to convey some of our beliefs about ethics and decent moral behavior."

All the family members have a chance to tell a story or give a little talk. The older boys are pretty good little public speakers. At the end of the session they have snacks. The three boys take turns choosing what the snacks will be. Mrs. Alto seemed surprised when I mentioned that such a weekly family session was unusual these days. She said:

"We're Mormons. Ukiah has a lot of Mormons and almost all have family nights on Monday. Teachers at the schools go easy on assigning homework Monday nights; and many civic organizations deliberately don't schedule meetings on Monday nights.'' Among the hundreds of Mormon families in Ukiah, she said, the rate of marital breakup is very low. Few of the kids get into trouble and ''those that do almost all are strong enough to pull out of it.''

The Altos, incidentally, have a television set. As a family they watch four shows a week. Otherwise the set is ignored. The parents decide the four choices of the week after receiving suggestions from the boys.

Youngsters tend to thrive if their parents seem to be pleased to play games with them daily, to take them on outings, to take them to athletic, social, or religious events, to dine together.

I once encountered in Western Nebraska a wonderful large farm family in which every member played an instrument in a family band. The band was often invited to give concerts at villages and towns in the area. I know a family that spends two weeks every summer on an exploratory trip. They confer for weeks about where they will go. They have explored the lakes, rivers, or shorelines of Ontario, the Maritime Provinces, and New England.

The benefits for the youngsters of having a sense of family unity are considerable. In the study of children of low and high self-esteem cited a few paragraphs back, the investigators reported this finding: ''Self-esteem in children was associated with a warm and involved style of family interaction.''

Family-life researchers Boyd C. Rollins and Darwin L. Thomas have concluded from a review of the literature that social competence in children is clearly associated with the degree of support they get from their parents.

The three-decade study at the University of California following infants to adulthood noted that the closeness of the family's affectional relationships during the second year of life correlates significantly with IQ scores even at early middle age!

Family closeness promotes pride and a basic trust that enables the youngster to press out on his own, take risks. And it assures that the youngster will not be overinfluenced by peer group pressure. Family closeness with lots of interaction also gives the youngster a head start in developing social competence. He or she finds it easier to relate confidently with others, both adults and peers. This is particularly true if the small child has had pleasant aunts, uncles, cousins.

The warmer the family interplay and hilarity, the more likely the child will develop a good-natured disposition, which can be a formidable asset in the long haul of life.

Burton White lists among the important traits of a "very well developed" three-year-old the social abilities of getting and holding the attention of adults and expressing mild annoyance to both adults and peers.[8] A good interplay with the family promotes such skills.

Nick Stinnett, chairman of the Department of Human Development and the Family, University of Nebraska, has been involved in two major studies of strong families and their characteristics. He gave me these six qualities as ones that stood out in the hundreds of strong families studied.

1.   Family members express a good deal of appreciation for each other and build each other up psychologically.

2.   They spend a lot of time together, and genuinely enjoy being together.

3.   They do a lot of direct talking with each other, so they are not thrown off by rumor.

4.   They are deeply committed to promoting each other's happiness and welfare.

5.   They tend to be committed to a spiritual life-style. This seems to help them have a sense of purpose and helps them to be more patient and forgiving with each other.

6.   They draw upon the trust they have in each other to unite in coping with a crisis rather than to be fragmented by it.

7. Expert parents are adept at moving their children from parent discipline to self-discipline.   I came from a rural area where it was customary for fathers to use a strap to the behind of sons who had seriously misbehaved. We on the receiving end did not take it personally and hate our fathers. We knew it was a prevailing community custom. My father was normally an amiable man much interested in my welfare.

A couple decades ago sociologist Arnold Green reported an interesting finding about discipline. He studied life in a New England industrial town where there were many Polish-Americans. Fathers frequently thrashed their wailing sons. But the thrashing did not get to the youngster's "core of the self." They took it in stride. Green pointed in contrast to the incidence of neuroses among youngsters reared in "Protestant, urban, college-educated middle class" homes where a disciplinary hand might never be laid on the children. Such neurotic children often found their personality absorbed by their parents. In cases where the child actually is a bother to a man and wife because he interferes with their dominant values, withdrawal of love may occur for days or weeks. The child is thrown into a panic. Parents of the major white-collar classes often seek to arouse in the child a fear of losing parental love as a technique in training the child.

"In such a child," Green pointed out, "a disapproving glance may produce more terror than a twenty-minute lashing in little Stanislaus Wojcik."

The above examples are noted not to put me on the side of the thrashers. (I definitely am not.) The point I wish to make is that the way parental disapproval is perceived by the recipient child is relevant.

We all abhor the kind of child abuse that occurs when the unstable parent vents his own anger or frustration on the defenseless child. Punishment of any kind in fact is a concept rarely thought of by skillful parents. They think rather in terms of discipline. In their parenting role they have the obligation of socializing their children for entry into mature living. In this function they know that rules are important.

If a child places himself in physical danger (i.e., wandering into a street in violation of a rule) a sharp reprimand may be a more reliable deterrent against future wanderings than a reasoned lecture. For violations of less critical rules, the form of disciplining used is not particularly important — withdrawal of privileges, verbal admonishment, extra work, restriction to an area.

The expert parents are careful to be consistent in enforcing rules. They are careful to set clear rules and to make sure they are understood. When discipline is required the parent explains — when the child has stopped wailing — specifically what the infraction was. And the parents are always careful to back each other up on disciplinary matters in the presence of the rule-breaking child.

As the child moves into nursery school age, the expert parents will be helping him or her gradually to learn self-discipline. The child is encouraged to take pride in achieving responsibility for his or her behavior. Children are praised when they show evidence of controlling their impulses for self-gratification or for destructiveness. Positive reinforcement through praise has consistently been found to be more effective than punishment in shaping constructive behavior. The self-restraint that the child sees in his own parents is also extremely important in promoting self-discipline. Modeling is a powerful motivator for a child who loves his/her parents.

Sometimes the self-restraint comes from sheer parental inspiration. The tale of the boyhood of actor James Cagney is pertinent. He grew up under desperate and ominous conditions in a very tough section of New York. His father was a heavy drinker. He and his brothers worked at odd jobs and brought every cent home so that the family would have enough to eat. Some of his school and street chums ended up in penitentiaries, one in the electric chair.

How did James escape their fate of unrestrained behavior? He explained:

"We had a mother to answer to. . . . We loved her profoundly, and our driving force was to do what she wanted because we knew how much it meant to her."[9]

Gradually, too, self-discipline is enhanced during the early school years as the youngster develops a conscience. Some studies indicate that conscience is promoted by the nurturing warmth of the mother, the degree to which the child identifies with the father, and the way parent-child discussions are handled after a child breaks a rule.

Self-discipline, along with impulse control, also is strenthened for the youngster as he is guided toward feeling a sense of competence. With recognized competence, the youngster starts taking a more thoughtful view of life, instead of operating out of fear.

8. The skillful parents guide their children toward a clear system of values. As the primary socializing agents of society, parents have responsibilities that go beyond care and nurture. They are building for the future. Good parents, as a matter of desire, muster the very best that is in themselves to see that their progeny become assets of society.

In this they inculcate their youngsters with beliefs about living — ethics and morals — that will help them promote a good and just society. Stable democracies can only exist where you have a large majority of the people trained in responsible citizenship.

Responsible citizens have a clear idea of what is appropriate behavior for themselves and also a sense of responsibility for the well-being of others in their community and society.

Alas, greatly increasing numbers of children are growing up with fuzzy notions about values. Values that are widely agreed upon are in sharp decline among adults. Children are often ill-prepared to cherish any values beyond pleasure and self-enhancement.

The decline in shared values springs from the growing impersonality of urban life, the fragmenting of families and communities, the bigness of institutions which makes impersonal acts acceptable (for example, ripping off an insurance company). Then there is the constant exposure to dishonest acts through the media, and the decline in child-adult contacts.

Merritt Low, ex-president of the American Academy of Pediatrics, put the situation harshly: "The value problem is essentially that many people don't have any values and therefore have none to hand on to their children."

Living in a presently value-deficient society makes more challenging the raising of children with a clear personal system of pro-social values. If the situation is to be improved, it has to begin at home. Actress Lauren Bacall, in recalling her early life with her divorced mother, recalls:

"She always taught me character. That was the most important thing in life. There was right and wrong. You did not steal. You did not cheat. You worked for a living and you worked hard. . . . Being the best you could be was something to be proud of."

Harvard child specialist Nathan B. Talbot stated that for the child to develop values, "it is essential that the child sees himself as a member of a coherent group. Otherwise he cannot understand the basis for moral thought." There are various possible groups available to the child but "we know of no satisfactory substitute for having a decent family at the core."

A great amount of research points to the critical role of the family in the character development of children. Largely, character is learned by firsthand example. Month after month the youngster sees what his parents stand for and work for. Altruism in children is clearly related to altruism in parents, particularly the same-sex parent.[10] Values are most likely to be absorbed and reinforced in the family where there is a strong sense of solidarity.

9. Skillful parents help their children experience plenty of responsibility. The thrusting of responsibilities they can handle upon children teaches them early to respond to challenges. Meeting the challenge contributes to their sense of self worth and accomplishment. It helps them sense that they are growing up.

The environment in which families function today often does not encourage youngsters to thrive, due in large part to the changes in our society and institutions I have been describing. Some families overcome this by insightful planning.

Take the case of the John Lama family. There are five youngsters all over eight years old. The Lamas were materially successful, lived in a prosperous Detroit suburb. He was director of a professional association. But he and his wife were dissatisfied. Everyone seemed to be on a different schedule of coming and going. Most of the youngsters didn't have anything really important to do. The father worried about the fact that they spent too much time loafing around town or sitting around the house, looking out the window, watching TV, or listening to rock. The parents were called repeatedly into conferences with teachers because one daughter, who seemed bright enough, was a poor student. The only jobs the youngsters had to do were unproductive chores such as taking out the garbage and making their beds, and sometimes they didn't do that.

John Lama, like Mrs. Robert Alto, was another chance encounter for me, this time at a conference where we both had some time to kill. We got to talking about his home life. He said:

"I wanted my five kids to be doing something vital."

What the Lamas did was fairly drastic. They sold their nice suburban home and moved fifty miles south to a farm near a small town close to the Michigan–Ohio border. John Lama got himself another job in a completely different field, working as a consultant in a municipality. about twenty-five miles from the farm so he had a long daily commute.

At the farm, when I talked with him, they had ten head of cattle, twelve hogs, twenty-one chickens. Each Lama youngster had definite responsibilities. He said:

"Each youngster has income from a hog. They all follow the price of pork in the newspapers with interest. They also get income from eggs. Lots of kids today have no real idea where eggs come from. The youngsters grind their own corn, from corn we have raised, to make hog feed.

"The kids," he continued, "wanted horses. So I said okay, make the hay. There is no place today where the average kid can see the one-to-one ratio between work put into something and the benefits you get. My kids know if you don't feed the chickens you don't get the eggs."

Now the Lamas eat their dinner together every night. The kids talk over problems without being asked. The daughter who was having trouble in school is now doing great at a local public school and "smashed" the Iowa test scores in her examinations. She is also active in the local 4-H club for farm youngsters. Mr. Lama said:

"I believe the move is making them better kids. My eight-year-old boy drives the John Deere tractor and feels like a man."

In other families in urban areas children are learning in less dramatic ways how to achieve a "vital" feeling. Parents encourage them to remodel rooms, raise and sell guinea pigs for pets, escort younger kids across the street before and after school.

The Goertzels found in their study of the early life of eminent people that two-thirds of the doctors, lawyers and scientists of eminence had had both lots of opportunities for exploration and a lot of early responsibilities thrust upon them. A study of adolescents in Israel indicates that those with the more stable personalities had learned early to participate and take responsibilities.

Such youngsters are not the type of young people we so often hear referred to as "alienated."

The problem today in highly urbanized societies is finding responsibilities that can plausibly be thrust on youngsters. There are of course household maintenance chores such as washing the dishes, making beds, taking out the garbage. But those are not likely to be felt as vital or productive activities with any challenge to them. They may in fact seem like makework.

There are, however, home maintenance tasks that are vital, challenging, and very helpful to the family. Sons and daughters can with a little guidance or study save money for the family by repairing chairs, repairing ailing plumbing fixtures, painting rooms, installing insulation to save on energy, or helping build an extra room for the dwelling.

They can save the family a lot of money by knowing how to maintain the family cars, by cleaning filters or repairing carburetors. They can help the family budget by growing vegetables in a nearby plot.

Also they can become early entrepreneurs by getting into weaving or pottery, raising white mice for laboratories, running a neighborhood car-polishing business, a paper delivery service, a lawn-mowing service, or building model boats for sale.

Then there are the people-related services that can contribute greatly to the development of important skills and to a sense of compassion. Children can be very good at taking care of elderly people or invalids. They can, if they are good at it, be in demand as baby-sitters.

In general, however, our society and institutions can do far more than they have to make it natural for youngsters to take on responsibilities that contribute to their development and to their society as they grow up. We'll note some of these in the next chapter.

23

A More Congenial
Environment for Children

"Our greatest challenge may be to increase public
responsibility for children without destroying . . . the
decision-making power of parents."

— *Alison Clarke-Stewart, analyst of child care research*

Upon returning from China, Yale's William Kessen observed that he
was particularly struck by the degree and variety of social support given
to the Chinese family. He mentioned as an example the place given the
elderly as overseers of children. Every Chinese child also is expected to
contribute to the welfare of society while in school and to engage in
productive work, even if it is packing crayons for export.

The United States has been called the only modern society that doesn't
have a coherent family policy. The people of Sweden and France, for
example, have devoted a lot of thought to developing such coherent
policies. What policies and processes there are in America add up, as
we have seen, to a largely anti-child picture.

There seems little chance of any coherent federal policy emerging in
the U.S. at the moment for improving our treatment of children or for
supporting the presently beleaguered family. Currently the federal government seems in a mood to slash any program with a human resources
label on it. Further to complicate the problem there is the strong ideo-

logical split between the so-called pro-family coalition and the women's movement on such issues as the Equal Rights Amendment, day-care, and abortion. However, I believe a great deal indeed can be done to create a more congenial environment for child-raising. I have already noted improvements needed in the practices of apartment developers, child support agencies, hospitals, custody courts, playground officials, and corporations in their transfer policies.

Here as final thoughts will be some proposals on what institutions can do:

- to improve the preparation of youngsters for adult living;
- to assist the parents who are starting families;
- to make it easier for parents in need of good substitute care for children to obtain it;
- to bring employment policies into harmony with the new realities of family life;
- to arrange community life in ways that will help children thrive.

IMPROVING THE PREPARATION OF YOUNGSTERS FOR ADULT LIVING

All people, including youngsters, feel better about themselves if they are doing something useful. American public schools are not only characterized all too frequently by pandemonium but by keeping youngsters in a prolonged state of dependence isolated from the adult world.

Youngsters march in lockstep up through the grades. What follows are some ways in which most schools could do a better job in preparing the young for adult living.

Real-life experiences inside the school world   A school outside Copenhagen has a facility where any youngster can do welding.[1] It is enormously popular. Some ten-year-olds have attained such proficiency that they already have one adult job skill.

In many schools in Iceland every youngster is assigned a plot of land on which he or she competes in raising vegetables. In American cities students could have plots on school rooftops, or they could be bused to their plots in vacant lots or fields outside the city.

A few U.S. schools are setting up, on a microcosm basis, projects that provide real-life experience such as operating savings banks, dry cleaning establishments, and greeting card companies.

Experience in community service   Every pupil should be required to earn credit from a wide range of opportunities to perform valued public service. These should be genuine needs providing real challenges that help create a sense of maturity and contribution.

At a school in Kirkwood, Missouri, students can get credit in existing classes such as math, social studies, science or English by assisting in nonprofit day-care centers and community projects. They can work at serving at blood donor centers or in animal shelters or by making tapes for the blind or working in the local botanical garden or helping at a recycling facility.

In Darien, Connecticut, about fifty students have been given advanced first aid training such as mouth-to-mouth resuscitation and are on call after school hours to man an ambulance. They are even qualified to aid in the home delivery of babies. In Sacramento, school-age youngsters serve on work crews to rehabilitate condemned homes of welfare recipients. There should be more such programs.

Experience in helping people   Schools should require every student to gain specific experience in helping others. Today most youngsters can reach middle adolescence without ever having felt they had been important to someone.

Older youngsters should be encouraged to earn credit and cash by working as aides in elementary school programs that provide after-school care for children whose mothers have jobs. Urie Bronfenbrenner, one of the nation's top authorities on child development, calls for a *Curriculum for Caring* from the earliest grades onward. In Adams, a rural Minnesota community, there is a class for aiding the handicapped. After teenagers receive training in physical therapy at the Mayo Clinic, they spend an hour a day helping the handicapped to stretch, strengthen, and loosen their muscles. They are not only serving but learning. One student was overheard to say: "He needs his hip adductor muscles stretched, but his quadricep muscles seem stronger." [2]

Youngsters can gain a sense of competence as well as service by tutoring younger students who are having trouble with schoolwork. In Philadelphia 120 young tutors increased their own mean reading age by one year simply by helping younger students with their reading! Bright black pupils with possible inferiority feelings can greatly ease those feelings — and improve their competence — by tutoring one-year-younger white pupils.

In a few areas elementary school classes develop ties with homes for the elderly. The pupils visit at least once a week and learn to know — often as a friend — every older person there.

Work-study programs for adolescents   Starting at the ninth or tenth grades, students should have the opportunity to explore and engage in the world of serious grown-up work that interests them. Two or three such programs will help them greatly in setting their career goals. And the programs will give them a sense of real-life competence. Further, it will put them fairly closely into contact with the adult world.

By the eleventh grade they should be gaining significant experience in real-life jobs, with the school serving as broker. In Oakland, California, many skilled adults are volunteering to take on students from the Far West School on a one-to-one basis for in-depth career exploration in the volunteer's specialty. The students in some instances receive pay as well as class credit. Supervisory employees in addition take small groups of students on a complete exploration of how the company functions.

At the Mariner High School in Everett, Washington, there is a program where students spend the last six weeks of the school year off campus working in settings related to school courses. Students in human biology work in local hospitals and clinics. Some on-the-job experience is required for graduation.

In Hinesburg, Vermont, the local high school has a program in which students work full-time for at least eight weeks with adult experts such as parole officers, veterinarians, librarians, and officials of the police department, mental health centers, and hospitals. They may receive pay for their work as well as class credit. Oak Ridge High School in Tennessee has a program in which skilled craftsmen from the Atomic Energy Commission and Union Carbide take on students as aides in such challenging areas as electronics, machine processing operations, and physical testing. Students receive both credit and pay.

High school students in Atlanta, Georgia, can spend three months of independent study away from school on archeological digs. They locate fragments of Indian life up to ten thousand years old, seek to calculate the size, age, and use of the artifacts they uncover.

All these programs listed are of a pioneering nature. Comparable programs should be widely available to students.

Working after school   In recent years there has been a sizable increase in the number of older teenagers who hold jobs after school.

Partly this has occurred because of the decline in homework. Partly it is due to the wide cutting back on extracurricular activities as economy moves. Also, there is a widespread uneasiness among young people who already are physiologically adults that they are still in a dependent state doing little that is useful. Finally, it is due to a desire to be independent from their parents for spending money.

The jobs mostly are in fast-food stores and supermarkets, or are office odd jobs. Some pump gas. Two studies of working youngsters concur in finding that such youngsters: [3]

- acquire practical knowledge that may help them later;
- gain useful knowledge on how the world of business functions;
- gain useful knowledge on how to find and hold a job;
- gain information on how to manage money and how to assess their goals;
- gain skill in handling their emotions so as to get along effectively with people;
- take pride in accomplishment.

Studies also show that many part-time jobs available to these older teenagers are essentially boring, nonproductive chores. And they show that most youths work not for some future goal such as college, but rather to have immediate spending money. Estimates are that youngsters sixteen or over can properly handle jobs requiring fourteen hours a week but that twenty-hour-a-week jobs (common) definitely threaten to hurt schoolwork.

Many schools now have bulletin boards where after school job opportunities are posted. Several schools in Fairfield County, Connecticut, have a better method. They assign a professional counselor to receive and assess job offers and to interview students who might want the jobs. This helps the employer by some pre-screening and it helps the students by protecting them from exploitive jobs, or jobs that will be too much of a drain on their time, unless the home economic situation is desperate.

Schools as moral communities   The reports of violence, pot smoking, and theft in schools have led the majority of Americans, polls show, to believe schools should take over a share of the responsibility for the moral development of youth.

Educators have split into at least four schools of thought on how value clarification studies can be added to school programs. Some efforts have seemed rather vapid or loosely conceived or heavy on a specific indoctrination. The State Board of Education in Georgia mandated sixteen goals to be taught to all children, values ranging from respect for God and authority and property to concepts of right and wrong and an appreciation of proper manners.

Some U.S. and Canadian school systems still teach values by the "lifeboat" experience, which can give a youngster nightmares. Ten youngsters sit in a circle. They are told they are on a ship that is sinking. The lifeboat only holds nine. Each is asked to examine his life and then state why he as a person of value deserves a seat on the boat. The class then votes on those who most deserve and least deserve a seat on the boat.

When school programs get down to specifics on moral dilemmas, parents often become uneasy out of fear children will be encouraged to discuss events occurring in the privacy of the home. Fundamentalist and liberal parents also often have conflicting ideas about what constitutes moral behavior and how it should be inculcated.

However, it certainly is valid for students in secondary schools to be encouraged to feel they are part of a just and decent community. They should be reminded, at the outset of school years, that their school, like any democratic institution, can function well for all only if the great majority of students exercise responsible citizenship. . . . The students, as responsible citizens of that school community, should express their disapproval of antisocial or indecent behavior.

Student governments should be encouraged to set up forums for discussions on what constitutes seriously objectionable behavior. They should establish a judicial body whose function is to pass judgment on students caught cheating, stealing, bullying, using or selling drugs, or having sex in the stockrooms. A school counselor skilled in value clarification should be available as a consultant to these judicial bodies. Violators of agreed standards of decent behavior might well be inhibited from future offenses by knowledge that they face the judgment of their peers. The judicial body would post any findings of guilt after reviewing the evidence and giving the offender a chance to explain. School administrators would continue to make their own decisions regarding discipline.

Possible improvements in regulations regarding attendance   Decade by decade the length of schooling has increased. Some noted U.S. educators have become skeptical of society's expectation that all self-respecting youngsters should finish high school by age eighteen. At present those students who fail are stigmatized as "dropouts" or "push-outs." Many are simply bored and want to get real-life experience. Many with below-average intelligence see little to gain from further exposure to the kind of schooling commonly provided by high schools. For all such students school, at that point at least, has little more of a practical nature to help them beyond a diploma. Young people in such a mood have become a very heavy burden on the public school system of the U.S.A.

James Coleman supervised a Report on Youth to the President's Science Advisory Committee, which proposed that at age sixteen any student could leave school to get work experience. The student would receive a voucher entitling him or her to return for two more years of free schooling whenever the student felt it would be helpful. The noted educator Harold Shane of Indiana University has gone further. He proposed modifying the present compulsory education laws so that by the age of fourteen or fifteen, students could enter a "paracurriculum" in which they would hold down a real job with educational content. Such individual arrangements would be made with socially conscious employers and would be monitored by the school. The student would have infinite school exit and reentry privileges.

Both compulsory attendance and the child labor laws are coming under increasing scrutiny. Do they fit our times and needs, especially in view of the evidence that hundreds of thousands of high school graduates are awarded their diplomas for attendance, not competence as literate, well educated persons? A report of the National Association of Secondary School principals stated:

"Keeping young people in school up to an arbitrary age apparently inhibits reforms [in the schools]." In a few states, such as California and Connecticut, under recent reforms, students can leave school at the age of sixteen and get the legal equivalent of a high school diploma whenever they can pass a proficiency examination.

The noted sociologist Amitai Etzioni in his new book on rebuilding America proposes to rebuild the schools. In view of modern conditions he would put children in school starting at age four. And he would let students between sixteen and eighteen move in and out. They would combine their studies with work under supervision in the real world.

Two of the nation's top experts on family law, Henry H. Foster and Doris Jonas Freed, have questioned whether compulsory school attendance and child labor laws are now in the best interests of minors. They wrote in *The New York Law Journal:*

We are doing an inadequate job of providing a bridge between school and life work for many of our young people. Whatever the causes or the blame, the fact remains that the primary function of some schools is a warehousing or custodial one to keep kids off the streets. Many of these youngsters might be better off on job training or apprenticeship work but due to compulsory attendance and child labor laws they are frozen into meaningless routine.

The usual pattern in the American states is to bar any kind of wage employment to children under fourteen, and to bar any employment of people under sixteen during school hours. (Hence no one under sixteen can hold down a normal full-time job during most of the year.)

Even the long-hallowed federal minimum wage law is being reexamined as far as its impact on youngsters seeking to get a job. To allow young people under eighteen to start full-time work at a pay level 10 percent below the federal minimum wage would cause employers to look with new interest at the young end of the labor market where unemployment now is so appallingly high. In 1982 when this was being considered it became a controversial issue between some union leaders and spokesmen for the unemployed young.

ASSISTING PARENTS WHO ARE STARTING FAMILIES

We have noted that people in the U.S. who elect to have and raise children today are making a major financial commitment. For many it is comparable to buying a home. The first two years of a new child's life involve particular sacrifice in terms of money and time demand, and consequent unusual strains on the marriage.

The air is full of exhortations on the need to strengthen family life. Meanwhile the federal government subsidizes just about every growing crop except children. (Help for children is spotty and indirect: aid based on proof of poverty, a nominal tax exemption for dependents, a small tax credit for substitute child care expenses, discounts on school lunches, etc.). Sheila Kamerman, professor of social planning at Columbia University, finds it astonishing that the U.S. is the only advanced industrial society that has no statutory provision assuring a female employee about to have a baby of a paid leave and job protection.

When our society gets its priorities straight it will start making a direct allowance to every married couple with a newborn child if the husband's income is under $20,000 (in 1983 dollars). The allowance should be at least $4,000, to be paid during the child's first two years of life, in quarterly installments of $500. This would apply only to the family's first two children.

The total cost would be only 1 or 2 percent of the presently projected cost of a B-1 bomber fleet. In those cases where one parent of a marriage is already absent because of death or divorce after the child is born, the same $4,000 allowance should be available for either of the family's first two children if the remaining parent's income from all sources does not exceed $10,000 a year.

This $4,000 for each of a family's first two children would help relieve the present intense pressure that hundreds of thousands of new mothers feel each year to obtain or return to jobs almost immediately after a child's birth. Society will be better served if new mothers have the luxury of some choice about when they will start holding down a job if they have an infant or crawler in the home.

Organizations with more than three hundred employees should be required to grant a leave without pay to any married female employee who is about to have a baby. The leave should be for a maximum of fourteen months. It would *begin* when the company's regular paid leaves for maternity, vacation, etc. have expired. Thus if a new mother chose to request the full paid and unpaid leave available, she would have a job waiting for her for at least sixteen months after the birth of her baby. Those critical months should help her get her new child well-launched in life.

However, to protect the employer in its personnel planning, the expectant mother, to qualify, would be required to sign a leave of absence agreement. It would specify the date she would be back. There would be penalties for breach of contract. Also, there should be an option in the agreement that she could return to work on a part-time basis at a specified date before the leave expired, say one year after birth of the baby. This should appeal to many companies. Part-timers give them more flexibility in scheduling work.

The leave of absence agreement should bring a big difference in corporate attitudes toward pregnant employees. Currently nearly half the women who take a paid maternity leave from an employer fail to return to work with that employer.

Today, companies which allow a leave of even six months without pay, such as American Telephone and Telegraph and Procter and Gamble, are considered very generous. These leaves are in addition to paid medical leaves. A survey of 142 company policies in the New York area found that only sixteen of these companies granted indefinite leaves. Companies in service industries tended to be more generous than manufacturing companies. *Marriage and Divorce Today* reports that a survey of 815 two-career couples revealed that the median time taken by the women for maternity leaves was three months.

East European countries tend to have the world's most generous policies in permitting long maternity leaves. Most grant a year's unpaid leave with uninterrupted credit toward retirement. In Hungary a new mother can stay home for three years if she wishes, and receives a small monthly payment sufficient to cover the child's basic costs. In Czechoslovakia new mothers get a half year of leave at 90 percent of their regular salary, and have the opportunity to take unpaid leave until their child is two years old.

MAKING IT EASIER TO OBTAIN GOOD SUBSTITUTE CARE

I have before me a number of statements calling for "universal day care," "free twenty-four-hour service," "free excellent day-care facilities," etc. Federal officials have forecast a big rise in this decade in the need for day-care. Yet the federal government shows extreme reluctance to provide more than nominal support for day-care, except to help the very poor. For others, aid for substitute care when both parents work is modest and indirect. A typical two-paycheck couple can deduct as a business expense about $500 a year for money spent on substitute care for a child. That is perhaps one-seventh the cost of good full-time care for a child. The deduction improves somewhat at lower income levels. In fairness, the tax credit should be doubled at all levels for working *single* parents (if they are not benefiting from the Aid to Families with Dependent Children program).

The reluctance of the government is partly based on expenses. A truly universal program for free day-care could cost tens of billions of dollars. The reluctance is also based on reservations about the wisdom of shifting the care of the very young children out of the home and away from their parents. I have indicated that I have developed my own reservations about turning to organized day-care for infants and the younger toddlers except in situations where there is no realistic alternative. For hundreds of thousands of mothers there presently is no alternative. Perhaps the best alternative was missed: a decision not to have the child until circumstances were more favorable. One of the finest federal child programs, now under attack by the budget cutters, is the family-oriented Head Start program for children age three and four from deprived backgrounds. This should be expanded. However, it is more of an enrichment than a care program.

While the prospects of significant federal involvement in child care are not high at present, there are many things that can be done within communities to reduce the stress and anxiety and inconvenience of those needing organized care.

Much of the strain upon the mother with a job comes from anguish. Sample source of anguish: landing a job and then not being able to find substitute care . . . or trying to find care in case of an emergency because a sitter is sick or gets a job . . . discovering that the care her child is getting is slapdash. These strains can be eliminated if concerned groups set up local centers for information such as the one in Cambridge, Massachusetts, and the Women's Resource Center at the University of California, Los Angeles. These centers for day-care consumers — which finally are starting to appear in many areas of the U.S.A. — can put mothers in contact with sitters or centers or adult sitters with indicators of qualifications. State licensing officials tend to be wary of classifying day-care centers beyond "conforming" and "nonconforming." A qualified day-care expert could at least provide a factual description of facilities, staff ratios, total number of children, and costs, etc.

Anxieties about emergencies would fade if American cities adopted services such as those available in several West German cities. There "granny" emergency services are springing up to help people with child crises. Just call a number and a retiree with parenting experience will be dispatched to take over for you. The cost is nominal. In Hamburg, such an emergency service has a staff on call of nearly one hundred older people.

Town and city zoning commissions could contribute significantly by requiring that all apartment complexes with more than two hundred multiroom units provide a free ground floor space for a child care center. Any resident with small children could use the center at a big discount from normal costs while off to work or just off to shop.

Child care centers for preschoolers could be opened by paying nominal rent at local elementary schools which have empty rooms because of the current shortage of early-school-age children.

An Indiana University educator, Sandra M. Long, has advanced the very interesting proposal that high schools add classes in parenting and child development. The students would gain practical experience at a nursery school run within the high school building.

Something like this already has been established at the Reuther Alternate High School in Kenosha, Wisconsin, where a nursery was set up for a different purpose — for teenage mothers who needed someplace to leave their children while finishing high school. All students can get credit in a home economics class by caring for these infants two hours a week.

A little search would also turn up good child care sites in areas of buildings rarely used in the average weekday, such as Sunday School rooms, lodge halls, union halls.

Local, socially-conscious employers could be urged to provide vouchers that cover some of the fee at any local accredited center for a female employee's child. Any employers seeking to employ a substantial number of married women might readily be persuaded to see the wisdom of helping underwrite the building of a day-care center in a residential area from which it hopes to draw many of its female employees. One survey showed half the companies queried were willing at least to consider this.

BRINGING EMPLOYMENT POLICIES INTO HARMONY
WITH THE NEW REALITIES OF FAMILY LIFE

This to my mind is where the greatest gains can be made in easing the child care problems of working wives. Changes in work patterns would greatly reduce the need for substitute care, at no cost in productivity.

Employers eager to attract employees, or to keep them contented, are starting to show a willingness to be innovative. More than a hundred of the largest U.S. corporations have been studying changes to help employees with small children. In Massachusetts, Governor Edward King in 1980 called on business and labor leaders to devise ways to help single-parent families and parents in two-income households spend more time with their families.

Employee groups too should be rethinking traditional goals. The main drive of unions has been toward shortening the work week to four days and, with long hours, three days. Married employees with young children should be calling instead for shorter workdays within the five-day week. This would permit the working father and mother to adjust their working hours each day so that one of them would be able to be at home with young children most of each day.

The most encouraging development on the horizon for parents of small children is flexitime, or flexible hours for doing one's job. One of the major sources of stress to mothers of young children who have jobs is the inflexibility of their nine-to-five jobs.

In 1965 a female economist in West Germany, Christel Kammerer, touched off what is becoming a worldwide revolution. She was trying to figure how to bring more mothers into the job market to ease the labor shortages. Her big idea: let people work when it was most convenient for them. The idea was adopted, cautiously, in 1967 by Messerschmitt-Borkow Richmer, primarily to cope with traffic congestion at the plant gates. Within seven years, sixteen thousand West German companies and government offices were turning to flexitime. The basic idea was that all employees were expected to be at work during certain "core" hours in the middle of the day but otherwise they could set their own pattern as to when they began and when they stopped work. The only requirement was that they got their assigned work done. Usually the employees worked out with the supervisor an agreed schedule when they would be on the job each week.

The idea swept across Western Europe at a time when the push in America was toward an inflexible but shorter number of work days per week. (Since then a few German firms have also been experimenting with totally "variable" working hours. The employee can come and go as he wishes and has a key in case no one else is working.)

A few years ago some agencies of the U.S. federal government began experimenting with flexitime. Again the interest was inspired less by concern for parents than to ease the horrendous traffic jams around mammoth offices. The idea has spread now to several hundred U.S. companies such as Hewlett-Packard and Pitney Bowes, and many large banks and insurance companies heavily staffed by women. About one full-time worker in eighteen in the U.S. now is on some sort of flexitime.

It was feared that such an arrangement, where everyone set his own schedule, would produce chaos and hurt productivity. Flexitime is indeed not practical at some rigidly structured assembly-line plants. But in general it is a success. The American Management Association has reported that flexitime helps morale and cuts down lateness. A study by a Georgetown University professor of 445 organizations using flexitime found wide satisfaction and about half the companies reported productivity gains averaging twelve percent.

The big gainers have been working parents, who have become considerably less dependent on substitute child care arrangements. And there is much less worry about getting an ailing child to the doctor. Single mothers whose children are in day care have a much better chance of being able to drop off and pick up their children when it is convenient.

Fathers on flexitime see a lot more of their children.

Any company flexible enough to thrive on flexitime can also introduce part-time jobs for parents of young children.

At first some feminists were wary of any movement toward part-time jobs on the grounds that they were not ''real'' jobs. Now part-time jobs are generally accepted by feminists as a ''good temporary solution'' for women who want to resume their career later on.

Fortunately for mothers of young children there has been a great surge of part-time jobs available. The entire work force of a bindery in St. Paul, Minnesota, consists of part-time employees. *The Wall Street Journal* reports that ''more and more companies'' are discovering that part-timers provide benefits such as increased flexibility on work scheduling.

A Labor Department study found that part-time employees are more productive, more loyal, and less tardy than full-time employees. After studying sixty-eight major corporations now turning extensively to part-time help, the Department study concluded: ''Employers are going to be moving ahead using part-timers.'' Part-time jobs seem to work particularly well for women in department stores, insurance companies, hotels, and hospitals. Such employees now are being given, on a prorata basis, such benefits as vacations, sick leaves, pensions and insurance.

A variant of the part-time job is job sharing. Two people agree to share equally a full-time job. Two mothers of young children now handle a single teaching job, a single computer programming job, a single city planning job, a single librarian job, a single probation worker job, a single hospital receptionist job. There are hundreds of possibilities.

RESTORING COMMUNITY LIFE AND ARRANGING IT IN WAYS
THAT WILL HELP OUR CHILDREN THRIVE

We have noted the anti-child framework for living that has been building up in the U.S. For example, American society has become:

- more and more thoughtlessly compacted into urban sprawls;
- more fragmented by the breakdown of community life, generational ties, and uprooted families;

- more wildly out of scale for children as a result of the giantism of educational and residential systems;
- more hazardous to children because of the alienation of young people who lack real ties to the adult world;
- more hostile to permitting families with children to live near non-childed people.

We need to begin at the neighborhood level to shape more congenial environments for child-raising. A great deal can be done if concerned parents begin pressing the need for a greater sense of community.

First let us note what an authentic human community is.

The authentic human community is one in which the social groupings are small so that a sense of belonging is almost automatic.

It provides a natural way for people to come together if they wish to do so and imbues them with a feeling that they have control over important events that affect their lives. They can take pride in that control.

This authentic human community also provides a natural setting for people to achieve a sense of well-being. This well-being is achieved by having some opportunities for intimacy . . . a chance to be able to gain recognition for one's competence, for example in child-raising . . . a chance to know people who share your concerns . . . a chance to be near people you can depend on in a pinch. (These four primary sources of well-being were developed by Robert Weiss.)

An authentic community enjoys children as evidence of the wonder of creation and the continuity of life. It provides many ways for natural interaction between people of all ages, and would be appalled by "no children" signs on residential buildings.

Two points should be made. People with a will can create congenial communities in unlikely places. Consider the residents of the Park Slope area of Brooklyn, near Prospect Park. For many years this area of brownstone row houses deteriorated from its turn-of-the century affluence. These old houses with pinnacles, stained-glass windows, gas lights and coal-burning stoves were falling apart, abandoned. There were almost no children. The area was considered too dangerous because of bums and gangs. Mostly poor elderly people were hanging on there in what was now widely considered to be a slum.

A few young couples, native to the area, set out to try to save Park

Slope as a place that could be an appealing community for energetic couples with children, such as themselves. After all, the houses were cheap and roomy; and a park, a museum, and a zoo were not far away.

Gradually they attracted cautious young "settlers" with families who rolled up their sleeves and, with their children, plunged into renovations. They did much of the work themselves, such as stripping walls, painting, and staining beams. In the renovations the couples sought counsel from each other on problems of plumbing, electricity, and wallpaper. The conferring and helping each other led to coffee parties and later supper parties. These led to many discussions over larger community-type problems. Since many of the wives had careers, there was an urgently felt need for day-care for younger children. No acceptable nursery was nearby, so the parents set up a cooperative one in two rooms in a neighborhood church.

Another problem was that in that area streets were typically littered. They began forming block associations which brought newcomers and old residents together. On many Saturdays the block officials arranged for the streets to be closed off, first for cleaning the litter. So many people seemed to enjoy the participation that later they began closing off the blocks for planting trees and holding carnivals, run mainly by children.

Also on Saturday at the nearby area of Prospect Park, which had been considered too dangerous for children to play in because of roving bands of tough kids, the fathers and children began playing touch football games and softball, with no bother from anyone.

More and more dozens of blocks were renovated, each block with its own association. Thousands of close friendships have emerged. Everywhere, in the stores, on the streets, in the park, you now see people chatting where people rarely chatted before.

And everywhere there are children playing.

MAKING HIGH-RISE ENVIRONMENTS MORE CONGENIAL FOR YOUNGSTERS

With considerable thought and a drive to community even urban life in high-rise glass towers can be made viable.

One of my surprises, during my research, was a trip I made to Co-op City on the edge of the Bronx, New York. Frequently I had driven past its dozens of stark apartment towers, many more than twenty-five stories high. The complex houses more than sixty thousand humans. I assumed that if high-rise living is indeed hard on children, it should be epitomized here.

Not at all. Co-op City, which is off by itself, teems with youngsters and adults — many on bicylces — mingling in reasonable harmony. Two things seem to have protected Co-op City from the major problems cited earlier for children in high-rise living.

First, Co-op City was planned to be a total community, not just a group of high-rises. Child experts were consulted. It was planned to make it easy for people to know each other readily through mutual interests and physical design. The first floors of several high-rise buildings have public facilities such as art galleries, nurseries, and public libraries. There are schools and shops within easy walking distance of every building. The shops are almost all of the small neighborhood type, run by such merchants as butchers and bakers that everyone seems to know personally. Six-year-old children can often run errands for their mothers without crossing the street.

Second, the pioneers in settling Co-op City came somewhat like the wagon train settlers of the West. As the Bronx apartment buildings, walk-ups, and row houses deteriorated, whole neighborhoods moved to Co-op City almost en masse. A group of old neighbors would often arrange in advance to take over one, two, or three whole floors. Thus most of the newcomers already had friends next door. I found that Co-op City had lots of extended families living there. A kid can visit a grandma or an aunt without getting on a bus. One mother told me: "It's totally different from New York City" (of which it is a peripheral part).

The bicycle paths are widely used by young and old for both transport and exercise. Many of the children from four to seven years old who have trouble balancing on a bicycle ride "hot wheels," high-speed big-wheeled tricycles. And there are attractive play areas within easy walking distance. Most can be reached without crossing a road.

At Co-op City there are many community centers with heavy schedules of activities. If you want to start a ballet class for young children, all you have to do is post a notice and get a half-dozen parents to join you. Myrna Weinstein, who supervised a Co-op Consultation Center for people with problems, showed me the Co-op City Community Services Directory available to everyone. It ran to eighty pages.

Peer group culture among teenagers is pretty strong, but at the time of my visit there were no known gangs of the destructive to delinquent type. The crime rate is considerably lower than in the rest of the Bronx, and there is little trouble with vandalism or graffiti.

Fran Gordon, who has raised her son there and who headed one of the nurseries, said: "Compared to Manhattan we have a protected environment. There is a considerable sense of trust." Many of the older children attending her nursery (which starts at age two and three-quarters) came and left without being accompanied by parents.

At the time of my visit there were no day-care centers for infants and toddlers in Co-op City. This was not so much a matter of neglect as a lack of consensus among residents. I was told there was a "lot of ambivalence" among residents about when it was appropriate for mothers of small children to go back to work. A "toddler" becomes a "pre-schooler" qualified for nursery school at age two and three-quarters at Co-op City. (There are centers that will take toddlers within a half mile of Co-op City.)

Co-op City, however, did have several excellent cooperative nurseries for children over two and three-quarters years old. The Aldrich Nursery which Fran Gordon directed is open from 7:30 A.M. to 6:00 P.M. It is on the ground floor of one of the high-rise buildings and is run by a parent board. Rates are relatively low because the Co-op City management considers the nursery a community asset. Therefore it charges only a nominal rental fee. Immediately outside the nursery are two different play areas with wading pools, mounds of sand, wheelbarrows for moving the sand, etc.

One volunteer attendant was a ninety-four-year-old woman from the building, whom all the children seemed to love and called "Jennie." The children got still another dimension of real life from the fact that every day a local security officer in uniform brought his own child to the center. Ms. Gordon said: "Our children are learning that a cop is not someone to be afraid of."

Co-op City is not a paradise. Far from it. But it has done much to bring the high-rise down to human scale for children.

If we must live in high-rises, then more imaginative thinking must be done to the structure itself to encourage neighborliness and provide play areas. For example:

1. Soundproofing should be written into city codes as mandatory for housing developers catering to the general public. In apartment buildings where insulation is adequate, studies show, there are few worries about children annoying neighbors.

2. Parents should try to avoid apartment buildings with long, narrow, scary inside corridors with their solid metal doors on each side.

These corridors almost inevitably make people who are passing wary of each other. They provide little inducement for neighbors to get to know each other.

Parents should seek out those new or existing structures that by their layouts permit some sense of interaction of neighbors and sense of community. Public demand and pressure could soon bring change. Consider how rapidly, within a decade, the design of the Hyatt's Regency Hotel in Atlanta spread in response to public delight. Its novel concept was to have wide inner balconies circling an open inner court for all its dozens of floors. That was a posh hotel, but the same general idea using inexpensive materials would make even more sense for apartment buildings catering to families. The first five feet in front of each apartment could be considered a private "front yard," indicated by two-foot high dividers. The remainder would be public accessway to elevators or stairs.

In such a setting parents could sit in their front yards and chat with neighbors while the children played either in their own "front yards" or in the yard of a neighbor who had children. If a parent had to shop, the neighbor would watch both sets of children.

This setting would provide both more intimacy *and* more security than the typical narrow corridor.

Thieves would be extremely wary of a situation where they could be seen by people sitting in their "yards" from many directions. Apartments with outer balcony access — not uncommon — are less intimate but still have considerable appeal.

One of the early British investigators of high-rises, W. F. R. Stewart, found that only 9 percent of high-risers with balcony access to their apartments professed loneliness, whereas more than half the dwellers with access only from inside corridors professed loneliness.[4]

Even the conventionally shaped high-rise slab of say twenty-four stories could be made far more congenial to children and parents if every fifth floor, or a part of it, was left open as a kind of park and play area with benches where parents could chat while the children played. This open public area could have a small shop for staple foods and snacks, card tables, Ping-Pong tables, etc. This public area could be enclosed or open-air.

If we are to live in the sky, let's do it in a civilized way, and a way congenial to children.

THE PHYSICAL FRAMEWORK ITSELF OF A NEIGHBORHOOD
CAN PROMOTE OR INHIBIT COMMUNITY SPIRIT

A free and easy sense of community can develop in apartment communities if the design promotes a sense of neighborhood. Two- or three-story garden apartment complexes with the buildings built around a common area for strolling, chatting, recreation, and children's play will promote neighborliness. Even in high-rise complexes neighborliness can be promoted if the builder avoids long, narrow inside corridors, and provides a common lounge or open area with a small shop for staples and snacks every few stories, and has the buildings oriented inward to a commons.

Some of the large New Towns built from scratch in Europe and the U.S. have been successful in going far beyond the typical large developers in creating developments that promote a community spirit. An outstanding example is Columbia, Maryland, near the Baltimore–Washington corridor. It is the creation of developer James Rouse who has gained fame from transforming run-down sections of inner cities into exciting areas that give the whole city a greater sense of community. Rouse bet hundreds of millions of dollars on the idea he could, starting from scratch, build a substantial city called Columbia based on neighborhoods. He sought to combine the advantages of small-town life and the excitement and amenities of city living.

The master plan called for the center of the city to be on a lake with a vast enclosed mall, theater, symphony hall, etc. This City Center was to be separated by open greenery and water from at least five villages. And each village consists of three or four clearly defined neighborhoods, again separated by greenery.

Today Columbia is a thriving city of sixty thousand people, widely hailed for its school system as well as its livability. It has five branches of colleges and a hospital. Also it has created jobs for thirty thousand people. In a region of racial tension it has won acclaim for its relaxed integration of twelve thousand blacks into the neighborhoods throughout the city.

The neighborhood was Rouse's basic building block at Columbia. It consists of eight hundred to twelve hundred families whose townhouses, detached houses, or apartments are oriented to a neighborhood center.

At each neighborhood center is an elementary school. It is within easy walking distance of all children in the neighborhood. Older children go to village schools also within walking or easy biking distance.

At the neighborhood center is a convenience store, a park, a play-ground, a swimming pool, and a meeting room. Many neighborhoods have a child-care center where a child can be left for an hour or a day.

A pathway system and winding roads lead to the village centers. The paths usually cross under roadway overpasses. A nine-year-old girl told me she not only walks to school but to her ballet classes, her religious class, and her flute lessons. "Mom doesn't have to drive me anywhere," she said.

Most of the villages have centers designed for teenage enjoyment and also have supervised play areas for children while mother shops.

Every neighborhood has a multitude of projects going. Newcomers are called upon immediately by at least a couple people in the neighborhood as well as by a city employee. People are on call if any neighbor has an emergency.

I chatted with a mother who had been in Columbia only a year. Her family had lived the seven preceding years in a typical housing development in Pikesville, outside Baltimore. At Pikesville she got to know only two families who were near neighbors. Her children were lonely. Here in Columbia the family's circle of friends is "tremendous." There is no special pressure, she said, "but if you want to you can enjoy a real sense of community."

The change that has come into their daily life, she said, was extraordinary. Yet, she said as if in amazement, "we are the same people."

A congenial environment helps any child to thrive. And if the children are thriving they are free of many of the growing pains that afflict so many millions of youngsters in the Western World today.

In these pages we have examined a number of areas of modern life where we have been giving our children a hard time. We have seen how the various troubles we have been causing them — some long-lasting — can be eased. Substantial overall improvement will come only as we restore community life and start functioning as a more thoughtful, more human, more cohesive, more forward-looking society.

Notes

Introduction

1. Robert H. Bremner (ed.), *Childhood and Youth in America,* Volume 1 — 1600–1865 (Cambridge: Harvard University Press, 1970), p. 601.

2. William Kessen, *The Child* (New York: John Wiley & Sons, 1965), pp. 45–56.

3. Jerome Kagan, "The Parental Love Trap," *Psychology Today* (August 1978), p. 54.

Chapter 1

1. "National Survey of Children," Summary of Preliminary Results, Foundation for Child Development (345 East 46th Street, New York), September–December 1976.

Chapter 2

1. Blair Justice and David F. Duncan, "Running Away: An Epidemic Problem of Adolescence," *Adolescence,* vol. 11, no. 43 (Fall 1976).

2. Edward Zigler, "Who Will Speak for Children and Families? A Case for Strengthening OCD," *The American Journal of Orthopsychiatry,* vol. 47, no. 4 (October 1977).

3. Jerry E. Bishop, "Age of Anxiety," *The Wall Street Journal* (April 2, 1979).

4. Robert J. Trotter, "East Side, West Side: Growing Up in Manhattan," *Science News,* vol. 109, no. 20 (May 15, 1976).

5. Urie Bronfenbrenner, "The Changing American Family," *AFL-CIO American Federationalist* (February 1977).

6. "The Games Teen-Agers Play," *Newsweek* (September 1, 1980).

7. Dick Soderlund, "Swedish Ban on Child Beating Sets Precedence," *Irish Times* (May 28, 1979).

8. Richard J. Gelles, "Violence Toward Children in the United States," *The American Journal of Orthopsychiatry,* vol. 48, no. 4 (October 1978).

9. Graham B. Blaine, Jr., *Are Parents Bad For Children?* (New York: Coward, McCann & Geoghegan, Inc., 1973), pp. 84–88.

Chapter 3

1. Comment made in a survey by Caroline Bird. See her book *The Two Paycheck Family* (New York: Rawson, Wade, 1979).

2. J. E. Veevers, "Voluntary Childlessness: A Review of Issues and Evidence," *Marriage & Family Review,* vol. 2, no. 2 (1979).

3. Ibid. See also "Childlessness Among Professional Women: A Trend?" *Marriage and Family Review* (September 15, 1980).

4. See J. E. Veevers, "Voluntary Childless Wives: An Exploratory Study," In *Family in Transition,* edited by Arlene and Jerome Skolnick, summarized in *Marriage & Family Review* (Summer 1979).

5. Michael Novak, "The Family Out of Favor," *Harper's* (April 1976), p. 37.

6. Judith Lorber, "Beyond Equality of the Sexes: The Question of Children," *The Family Co-ordinator* (October 1975).

7. Sandra Toll Goodbody, "The Psychosocial Implications of Voluntary Childlessness," *Social Casework* (July 1977).

8. See "Raising Children in a Changing Society," The General Mills American Family Report, 1976–77, conducted by Yankelovich, Skelly and White, Inc., 575 Madison Ave., New York.

9. "Middle Class Kids Are the New Delinquents," *Today's Child* (May 1979).

10. Betty Friedan, "Feminism Takes a New Turn," *The New York Times Magazine* (November 18, 1979).

11. "Employment and Training Report of the President," report by the U.S. Department of Labor and the U.S. Department of Health, Education and Welfare, transmitted to the Congress 1978, p. 75.

12. Angus Campbell, Philip E. Converse, and Willard L. Rodgers, *The Quality of American Life* (N.Y.: Russell Sage Foundation, 1976), see especially pp. 325, 343, 398, 438.

13. Mary Jo Bane, *Here to Stay: American Families in the Twentieth Century* (New York: Basic Books, 1976 and Harper Colophon Books). See especially the analysis on p. 162 in the latter.

14. Jean Walker Macfarlane, "Perspectives on Personality Consistency and Change From the Guidance Study," *Vita Humana,* vol. 7 (1964). See especially pp. 123–124.

15. Terry Martin Hekker, "The Satisfactions of Housewifery and Motherhood in 'An Age of Do-Your-Own-Thing,' " *The New York Times* (December 20, 1977).

Chapter 4

1. Two studies are of particular interest because of their scope: the British Perinatal Mortality Study, which checked back on virtually all youngsters born in Great Britain in a single week in 1958; and the Collaborative Perinatal Project sponsored by the U.S. National Institute of Child Health and Human Development. It has been studying 50,000 pregnancies at twelve U.S. medical centers.

2. Harold W. Demone and Henry Weschler, "Changing Drinking Patterns of Adolescents Since the 1960s," in *Alcoholism Problems in Women and Children,* edited by Milton Greenblatt and Marc A. Schuckit (New York: Grune and Stratton, 1976).

3. Ann P. Streissguth, "Maternal Drinking and the Outcome of Pregnancy," *American Journal of Orthopsychiatry,* vol. 47, no. 3 (July 1977).

4. Personal communication from Ms. Terry Bellicha as Director of the National Clearinghouse for Alcohol Information, National Institute on Alcohol Abuse and Alcoholism, Rockville, Maryland.

5. Mark Gerzon, *A Childhood for Every Child* (New York: Outbridge and Lazard, 1973), p. 86.

6. "Childbirth Painkillers Affect Child for Years," *Children Today* (February 1979).

7. Sarah H. Broman of the National Institute of Neurological and Communicative Disorders and Stroke and Yvonne Brackbill, University of Florida. From abstract: "Obstetric Medication and Early Development," presented at annual meeting of The American Association for the Advancement of Science, San Francisco, January 4, 1980.

8. Muriel Sugarman, "Paranatal Influences on Maternal-Infant Attachment," *American Journal of Orthopsychiatry,* vol. 47, no. 3 (July 1977).

9. "Childbirth Sitting Up," *Newsweek* (March 2, 1981).

Chapter 5

1. For an analysis of state laws see "Children and Families — The Latest Victims of Exclusionary Land Use Practice," staff report to the U.S. Department of Housing and Urban Development, written by Special Assistant to the Secretary, Rita A. Calvan.

Chapter 6

1. Tim Gerstmann, "Transfer Policies, Career and Family: Are They Compatible?" paper presented to the National Council on Family Relations Annual Meeting, Philadelphia, October 19–22, 1978. See also *A Nation of Strangers* by Vance Packard (New York: David McKay, 1972), particularly Chapter 18, "Impact on the Children."

2. "Violent Schools — Safe Schools," The Safe School Study Report of the National Institute of Education to the Congress. HEW Document EA 010 281, p. 19.

3. D. M. Fanning, "Families in Flats," *British Medical Journal,* vol. 4 (1967).

4. Pearl Jephcott, *Homes in High Flats* (Edinburgh: Oliver & Boyd, 1971), pp. 83–84.

5. Franklin D. Becker, "Design for Living: The Residents' View of Multi-Family Housing," (Ithaca, N.Y.: Cornell University Press, 1974, mimeograph.)

6. P. Crawford and A. Virgin, "The Effects of High Rise Living on School Behavior," Toronto: a brochure by the Board of Education of the Borough of North York, 1971.

7. Oscar Newman, *Defensible Space* (New York: Macmillan, 1972), pp. 29–33.

8. D. Geoffrey Hayward et al., "Children's Play and Urban Playground Environments," *Environment and Behavior,* vol. 6, no. 2 (June 1974).

9. K. Polk, "Teenage Delinquency in Small Town America," Research Report 5, Center for Studies of Crime and Delinquency, National Institute of Mental Health, 1974.

10. Dean V. Babst et al , "The Relationship Between Friends' Marijuana Use, Family Cohesion, School Interest and Drug Abuse Prevention," *Journal of Drug Education,* vol. 6, no. 1 (1976).

11. Thomas J. Abernathy et al., "A Comparison of the Sexual Attitudes and Behavior of Rural, Suburban and Urban Adolescents," *Adolescence* (Spring 1979).

12. *Toward a National Policy for Children and Families.* Advisory Committee on Child Development, Assembly of Behavioral and Social Sciences, National Research Council, National Academy of Sciences, Washington, D.C., 1976, p. 36.

13. Freda Rebelsky and Cheryl Hanks, "Fathers' Verbal Interaction With Infants in the First Three Months of Life," in F. Rebelsky and L. Dorman, *Child Development and Behavior* (New York: Knopf, 1974), p. 145.

14. Dean V. Babst, et al., "A Study of Family Affinity and Substance Use," *Journal of Drug Education,* vol. 8, no. 1 (1978).

15. "Erratic and 'Distressing' Contact With a Natural Parent Found Better Than None . . ." *Behavior Today* (February 20, 1978).

Chapter 7

1. "Help! Teacher Can't Teach," *Time* (June 16, 1980).
2. Gene Lyons, "Why Teachers Can't Teach," *Texas Monthly* (September 1979).
3. National Institute of Education, op cit., Chapter 6, note 2, p. 18.
4. Robert J. Rubel, "Trends in School Violence and Crime in Secondary Schools from 1950–1975: A Historical View," HEW Document EA 010 760.
5. James S. Coleman et al., *Youth: Transition to Adulthood*. Report of the Panel on Youth of the President's Science Advisory Committee (Chicago: University of Chicago Press, 1974), p. 146.
6. Saied Jacob, "We Are Wonder-Full." In "Guided Wonderment: How People Learn," *The Forum* (Fall–Winter 1980), published by the J.C. Penney Company.
7. "Hope for the Schools," *Newsweek* (May 4, 1981).
8. "Back to Basics in Values," *Newsweek* (May 4, 1981).
9. "Trying the Old-Fashioned Way," *Time* (March 9, 1981).

Chapter 8

1. Marie Winn, *The Plug-In Drug* (New York: Viking Press, 1977, and Bantam edition 1978). Citation from latter, p. 197.
2. David Fleiss and Lillian Ambrosino, "An International Comparison of Children's Television," prepared by the National Citizens Committee for Broadcasting, Washington, D.C., July 1971.
3. T. G. Bever et al., "Young Viewers' Troubling Response to TV Ads," *Harvard Business Review* (November–December 1975).
4. According to a "Violence Index" on level of violence in television programming maintained by the School of Communications, University of Pennsylvania.
5. Winn, op. cit., note 1 above, quoting an FBI study, p. 73.
6. Howard Muson, "Teenage Violence and the Telly," *Psychology Today* (March 1978).
7. Shirley L. O'Bryant and Charles R. Corder-Bolz, "Tackling 'The Tube' With Family Teamwork," *Children Today* (May–June 1978).
8. See article on teenagers as advertising target in *Media Decisions* (October 1976).
9. "They're Not Dancing, They're Falling Apart," *Today's Child* (February 1978).
10. Hugh Powers, M.D., and James Presley, *Food Power: Nutrition and Your Child's Behavior* (New York: St. Martin's Press, 1978), pp. 60–61.

Chapter 9

1. "Families At Work: The General Mills American Family Report 1980–81," Survey conducted by Louis Harris and Associates (Minneapolis: General Mills, 1981).
2. "The Latchkey Children," *Newsweek* (February 16, 1981).
3. Brian G. Gilmartin, *The Gilmartin Report* (Seacaucus, N.J.: The Citadel Press, 1978) p. 345.
4. Joann S. Lublin, "Women at Work: Life In Morton Grove Hasn't Been the Same Since Wives Took Jobs," *The Wall Street Journal* (September 22, 1978).
5. Harriet Engel Gross, "Dual-Career Couples Who Live Apart: Two Types," *Journal of Marriage and the Family* (August 1980).
6. Betty Frankle Kirschner and Laurel R. Walum, "Two Location Families," *Alternative Lifestyles* vol. 1, no. 4 (November 1978).
7. Nadine Brozan, "Children, A Job, and No Time," *The New York Times* (August 13, 1981).

Chapter 10

1. Douglas B. Sawin and Ross D. Parke, "Father's Affectionate Stimulation and Caregiving Behavior with Newborn Infants," *The Family Coordinator* (October 1979).

2. Selma Fraiberg, *Every Child's Birthright* (New York: Basic Books, 1977), p. 27.

3. Berry Campbell and W. E. Petersen, "Milk 'Let-Down' and the Orgasm in the Human Female," *Human Biology,* vol. 25, no. 3 (September 1953).

4. Henry N. Massie, "Patterns of Mother-Infant Behavior and Subsequent Childhood Psychosis," *Child Psychiatry and Human Development,* vol. 7, no. 4 (Summer 1977).

5. Princeton Center for Infancy, *The Parenting Advisor,* general editor, Frank Caplan (Garden City, N.Y.: Anchor Press/Doubleday, 1978), pp. 364–365.

6. T. G. R. Bower, *A Primer of Infant Development* (San Francisco: W. H. Freeman & Co., 1977), pp. 50–58.

7. Fraiberg, op. cit., note 2 above, pp. 45–62.

8. Burton L. White, *The First Three Years of Life* (Englewood Cliffs, N.J.: Prentice-Hall, 1975), see particularly pp. 4, 110, 113, 130.

Chapter 11

1. Urie Bronfenbrenner's overviews can be found in an appendix on the effects of day-care on child development in *Toward a National Policy for Children and Families* (Washington: National Research Council, National Academy of Sciences, 1976). A later overview by Bronfenbrenner appears in Chapter 8 of his book *The Ecology of Human Development* (Cambridge: Harvard University Press, 1979). Michael Rutter's overview of ninety-two studies appeared in January 1981 in an analysis entitled "Social-Emotional Consequences of Day Care of Preschool Children," in *The American Journal of Orthopsychiatry.*

2. Jerome Kagan, Richard B. Kearsley, and Philip R. Zelazo, "The Effects of Infant Day Care on Psychological Development," from Jerome Kagan's *The Growth of the Child* (New York: W. W. Norton & Company, 1978), p. 78. For a more extensive report of the Kagan group's study of day-care, see their book *Infancy: Its Place in Human Development* (Cambridge: Harvard University Press, 1978).

3. Jay Belsky and Laurence D. Steinberg, "What Does Research Teach Us About Day Care," *Children Today* (July–August 1979).

4. Sally Provence, Audrey Naylor and June Patterson, *The Challenge of Daycare* (New Haven: Yale University Press, 1977), pp. 227–228.

5. J. Conrad Schwarz, Robert G. Strickland, and George Krolick, "Infant Day Care: Behavior Effects at Preschool Age," *Developmental Psychiatry,* vol. 10, no. 4 (1974).

6. "Parenting Study Finds America an 'Unresponsive' Society," *Behavior Today* (May 7, 1979).

7. Beatrice Marden Glickman and Nesha Bass Springer, *Who Cares for the Baby?* (New York: Schocken Books, 1978), pp. 204–205.

8. Ellen Galinsky and William H. Hooks, *The New Extended Family: Day Care That Works* (Boston: Houghton Mifflin, 1977), pp. 35–48.

9. Cited by Robert Metz in "Life Insurance for Toddlers," *The New York Times* (July 5, 1978).

10. Alice H. Cook, "The Working Mother: A Survey of Problems and Programs in Nine Countries," issued by the New York State School of Industrial and Labor Relations, Cornell University, 1978.

11. Princeton Center for Infancy, op. cit., chapter 10, note 5.

12. "National Day Care Study," *Children Today* (May–June 1979). This study was made for the Administration for Children, Youth and Families, U.S. Department of Health, Education and Welfare by Abt Associates of Cambridge, under the direction of Richard Ruopp.

13. Sally Provence, Audrey Naylor, June Patterson, op. cit., note 4 above. See particularly p.

197. The study was made at "Children's House," sponsored by directors of the Yale Child Study Center and funded by the U.S. Children's Bureau.

14.   Ellen Galinsky and William Hooks, op. cit., note 8 above, pp. 15–20.

Chapter 12

1.   J. A. Fulton, "Parental Reports of Children: Post-Divorce Adjustment," *The Journal of Social Issues,* vol. 35, no. 4 (1979).

2.   *Newsweek,* op. cit., chapter 9, note 2.

3.   To obtain, write for "A Parent's Guide to Day Care," DHHS Publication Number (OHDS) 80-30254, U.S. Government Printing Office, Washington, D.C. 20402.

4.   James A. Levine and Michelle Seltzer, "Why Are These Children Staying After School?" *Redbook* (September 1980).

5.   Catherine Clusen, "Schools Experiment with Extended Day as a Response to Childcare Needs of Working Families," *Education Times* (November 30, 1981).

6.   Michelle Seligson Seltzer, "The Experience of a Parent-Run Program in the Public Schools," from *School-Age Child Care: Programs & Issues,* edited by Andrea Genser and Clifford Baden (Urbana, Ill.: College of Education, 1980, Catalogue No. 189).

7.   Levine and Seltzer, op. cit., note 4 above.

Chapter 13

1.   Ira Victor and Win Ann Winkler, *Fathers and Custody* (New York: Hawthorn Books, 1976), pp. 101–102.

2.   Doris S. Jacobson, "The Impact of Marital Separation/Divorce on Children: II Interparent Hostility and Child Adjustment," *Journal of Divorce,* vol. 2, no. 1 (Fall 1978).

3.   Deborah A. Luepnitz, "Which Aspect of Divorce Affects Children?" *The Family Coordinator* (January 1979).

4.   Rubin Todres, "Runaway Wives: An Increasing North American Phenomenon," *The Family Coordinator* (January 1978).

5.   Morton Hunt and Bernice Hunt, *The Divorce Experience* (New York: McGraw-Hill, 1977), p. 159.

6.   Neil Kalter, "Children of Divorce in an Outpatient Psychiatric Population," *The American Journal of Orthopsychiatry,* vol. 47, no. 1 (January 1977).

7.   E. Mavis Hetherington, Martha Cox, and Roger Cox, "The Aftermath of Divorce," a paper presented at a meeting of the American Psychological Association in Washington, September 1976.

8.   E. Mavis Hetherington, Martha Cox, and Roger Cox, "Family Interaction and the Social, Emotional and Cognitive Development of Children Following Divorce." Presented at the symposium on "The Family: Setting Priorities," sponsored by the Institute for Pediatric Service of Johnson and Johnson in Washington, D.C., May 17–20, 1978. A version reprinted in *The Journal of Social Issues,* vol. 35, no. 4 (1979).

9.   E. Mavis Hetherington, Martha Cox, and Roger Cox, "Play and Social Interaction in Children Following Divorce," paper presented at the National Institute of Mental Health Conference on Divorce, Washington, D.C., February 1978.

10.   John F. McDermott, "Parental Divorce in Early Childhood," *American Journal of Psychiatry* vol. 124, no. 10 (April 1968).

11.   Judith S. Wallerstein and Joan B. Kelly, "The Effects of Parental Divorce: Experiences of the Pre-School Child," *Journal of the American Academy of Child Psychology* (Autumn 1975).

12.   Joan B. Kelly and Judith S. Wallerstein, "The Effects of Parental Divorce: Experiences of the Child in Early Latency," *The American Journal of Orthopsychiatry,* vol. 46, no. 1 (January 1976).

13. Judith S. Wallerstein and Joan B. Kelly, "The Effects of Parental Divorce: Experiences of the Child in Later Latency," *The American Journal of Orthopsychiatry,* vol. 46, no. 2 (April 1976).

14. Judith Wallerstein and Joan Berlin Kelly, "The Effects of Parental Divorce: The Adolescent Experience," in *The Child in His Family: Children at Psychiatric Risk,* vol. 3. Edited by E. J. Anthony and C. Koupernik (1974), pp. 479–505.

15. Lora Heims Tessman, *Children of Parting Parents* (New York: Jason Aronson, 1978), p. 515.

16. Richard A. Gardner, *The Parents Book about Divorce* (Garden City, N.Y.: Doubleday, 1977), p. 356.

Chapter 14

1. Berthold Berg and Robert Kelley, "The Measured Self Esteem of Children From Broken, Rejected and Accepted Families," *Journal of Divorce,* vol. 2, no. 1 (1979).

2. Andrew S. Watson, "The Children of Armageddon: Problems of Custody Following Divorce," *Syracuse Law Review,* vol. 21, no. 1 (Fall 1969).

3. Deborah Rankin, "Taxes and Accounting: Which Divorced Parent Gets Exemptions?" *The New York Times* (March 14, 1978).

4. Donald N. Bersoff, "Representation for Children in Custody Decision: All That Glitters Is Not Guilt," *Journal of Family Law,* vol. 15 (1976–1977).

5. *Marcus v. Marcus,* 248 N.E.2d 800 (Ill. 1969).

6. David M. Siegel and Suzanne Hurley, "The Role of the Child's Preference in Custody Proceedings," *Family Law Quarterly,* vol. 9, no. 1 (Spring 1977), 1–58.

7. Katherine Tasios Dominic and Benjamin Schlesinger, "Weekend Fathers: Family Shadows," *Journal of Divorce* (Spring 1980).

8. "Mediation Couples More Often Opt for Joint Custody Arrangements," *Marriage and Divorce Today* (May 4, 1981).

Chapter 15

1. Victor and Winkler, op. cit., chapter 13, note 1, pp. 80–81.

2. Constance R. Ahrons, "Joint Custody Arrangements in Post-Divorce Family," *Journal of Divorce* (Spring 1980).

3. Susan Steinman, "The Experience of Children in a Joint Custody Arrangement: A Report of a Study," *American Journal of Orthopsychiatry* vol. 51, no. 3 (July 1981).

4. Judy Klemesrud, "Child Custody: Separate But Equal," *The New York Times* (February 2, 1978).

5. Alice S. Rossi, "A Biosocial Perspective on Parenting," *Daedalus,* vol. 106, no. 2 (Spring 1977).

6. Glenn Collins, "A New Look at Life with Father," *The New York Times Magazine* (June 17, 1979).

7. Harry Finkelstein Keshet and Kristine M. Rosenthal, "Single Parent Fathers: A New Study," *Children Today* (May–June 1978).

Chapter 17

1. Louise Guerney and Lucy Jordon, "Children of Divorce — A Community Support Group," presented at the annual conference of the National Council on Family Relations, San Diego, October 1977.

2. Thomas L. Hozman and Donald J. Froiland, "Families in Divorce: A Proposed Model for Counseling the Children," *The Family Coordinator* (July 1976).

3. Marybeth Shinn, "Father Absence and Children's Cognitive Development," *Psychological Bulletin,* vol. 85, no. 2 (1978).

Chapter 18

1. J. W. Santrock, "The Relation of Type and Onset of Father Absence to Cognitive Development," *Child Development,* vol. 43 (1972), pp. 455–469.

2. Mel Krantzler, *Creative Divorce: A New Opportunity for Personal Growth* (New York: Signet, 1975), p. 75.

3. Michael J. Smith, "The Social Consequences of Single Parenthood: A Longitudinal Perspective," *Family Relations* (January 1980).

4. See Mary Jo Bane, "Marital Disruption and the Lives of Children," *Journal of Social Issues,* vol. 32, no. 1 (1976), pp. 103–117.

5. Alvin Toffler, *The Third Wave* (New York: William Morrow, 1980), p. 230.

6. Michael E. Lamb and Jamie E. Lamb, "The Nature and Importance of the Father–Infant Relationship," *The Family Coordinator* (October 1976).

7. Harold Feldman, "Why We Need a Family Policy," *Journal of Marriage and the Family* (August 1979).

8. For a short presentation of Weiss's findings, see "Growing Up a Little Faster: Children in Single-Parent Households," *Children Today* (June 1981). An extensive treatment of his research into a single-parent living appeared in his *Going It Alone* (New York: Basic Books, 1979).

9. Carin Rubenstein, "The Children of Divorce as Adults," *Psychology Today* (January 1980).

10. Julius Segal and Herbert Yahraes, *A Child's Journey* (New York: McGraw-Hill, 1979), pp. 128–129.

11. E. Mavis Hetherington, "Effects of Father Absence on Personality Development in Adolescent Daughters," *Developmental Psychology,* vol. 7, no. 3 (1972), pp. 313–321.

12. "Teens With Single Parents More Likely to be Sexually Active," *Marriage and Divorce Today* (October 23, 1978).

13. Henry B. Biller, "Father Absence and the Personality Development of the Male Child," *Developmental Psychology,* vol. 2, no. 2 (1970). See also Jack C. Westman's "Effect of Divorce on a Child's Personality Development," *Medical Aspects of Human Sexuality* (January 1972).

14. Michael E. Lamb, in *The Role of the Father in Child Development,* edited by Lamb (New York: John Wiley & Sons, 1976), p. 23.

15. Judith S. Wallerstein and Joan B. Kelly, "California's Children of Divorce — after five years," *Psychology Today* (January 1980). For an overall report of their massive study of children of different age levels and different periods after divorce, see their book *Surviving the Breakup: How Children and Parents Cope with Divorce* (New York: Basic Books, 1980).

16. John F. McDermott, "Divorce and Its Psychiatric Sequelae in Children," *Archives of General Psychiatry* (November 1970). See also Michael Rutter, "Parent–Child Separation: Psychological Effects on the Children," *Journal of Child Psychology and Psychiatry,* vol. 12 (1971), p. 241.

17. J. W. B. Douglas, "Broken Families and Child Behavior," *Journal of The Royal College of Physicians, London,* vol. 4 (1970).

18. Elizabeth Herzog and Cecelia E. Sudia, "Children in Fatherless Families," in *Review of Child Development Research,* Bettye Caldwell and Henry N. Riccuti, eds., vol. 3 (Chicago: University of Chicago Press, 1973), p. 149.

19. Helen Mendes, "Single Fathers," *The Family Coordinator* (October 1976).

20. John W. Santrock and Richard A. Warshak, "Father Custody and Social Development in Boys and Girls," *Journal of Social Issues,* vol. 35, no. 4 (1979).

21. "In California: Unswinging Singles," *Time* (June 15, 1981).

Chapter 19

1. Marybeth Shinn, op. cit., chapter 17, note 3.

2. R. B. Zajonc, "Family Configuration and Intelligence," *Science* (April 1976).

3. "One Parent Families and Their Children: The Schools' Most Significant Minority," a staff report in *The Principal* (September 1980), published by The National Association of Elementary School Principals.

4. John Touliatos and Byron W. Lindholm, "Relationships of Traditional and Non-Traditional Family Types to Child Mental Health," presented before the annual meeting of the National Council on Family Relations, Boston, August 1979.

Chapter 20

1. "The Family in Transition: Challenges From Within," *The New York Times* (November 27, 1977).

2. Kristine M. Rosenthal and Harry F. Keshet, "The Impact of Childcare Responsibilities on Part-Time or Single Fathers," *Alternative Lifestyles* (November 1978).

3. Judith S. Wallerstein, "The Effect of Divorce on the Parent Child Relationship." Notes from an address presented to the Wheelock College Symposium on Children and Divorce, November 3–4, 1978. Transcripts now available at college.

4. Lora Heims Tessman, "Working With Children of Parting Parents." Notes from an address presented to the Symposium on Children and Divorce, Wheelock College, November 3–4, 1978. Transcripts now available at college.

5. Emily B. Visher and John S. Visher, *Step-Families* (New York: Brunner/Mazel, 1979), p. 163.

6. Nan Robertson, "Stepparents: Many Endure Frustration," *The New York Times* (March 1, 1980).

7. Kenneth M. Walker and Lillian Messinger, "Remarriage After Divorce Dissolution and Reconstruction of Family Boundaries," *Family Process* (June 1979).

8. Jane W. Ranson et al., "A Stepfamily in Formation," *American Journal of Orthopsychiatry* (January 1979).

9. Lucile Duberman, "Step-Kin Relationships," *Journal of Marriage and the Family* (May 1973).

10. Neil Kalter, op. cit., chapter 13, note 6.

11. Irene Fast and Albert Cain, "The Step-Parent Role: Potential for Disturbance in Family Functioning," *The American Journal of Orthopsychiatry,* April 1966.

12. Emily and John Visher, op. cit., note 5 above, p. 177.

13. John Leonard, "Private Lives," *The New York Times* (May 28, 1980).

Chapter 21

1. (New York: Doubleday & Co., 1976).

2. Rosabeth Moss Kanter, Dennis Jaffe, and D. Kelly Weisberg, "Coupling, Parenting, and the Presence of Others: Intimate Relationships in Communal Households," *The Family Coordinator* (October 1975), pp. 433–452.

3. Sterling E. Alam, "Middle-Class Communes: The New Surrogate Extended Family," in *Exploring Intimate Life Styles,* edited by Bernard I. Murstein (New York: Springer, 1978).

4. Virginia Rankin, "Children in Communes," in *The Child Care Book,* edited by Vicki Breithart (New York: Alfred A. Knopf, 1974).

5. Brian G. Gilmartin, *The Gilmartin Report* (Seacaucus, N.J.: The Citadel Press, 1978).

6. Duane Dedfeld and Michael Gordon, "The Sociology of Mate Swapping: Or the Family that Swings Together Clings Together," in *Beyond Monogamy,* edited by James R. Smith and Lynn G. Smith (Baltimore: Johns Hopkins University Press, 1974).

7. Jacquelyn J. Knapp, "An Exploratory Study of Seventeen Sexually Open Marriages," *The Journal of Sex Research* (August 1976), pp. 206–219.

8. Leslie Bennetts, "Unwed Parents: The Arrangement Seems Legitimate to Them," *The New York Times* (March 24, 1978).

9. See "The Pro-Incest Lobby" by Benjamin DeMott in *Psychology Today* (March 1980), and "Attacking the Last Taboo," *Time* (April 14, 1980).

Chapter 22

1. Victor and Mildred Goertzel, *Cradles of Eminence* (Boston: Little, Brown, 1978), p. 272.

2. Vance Packard, *The Pyramid Climbers* (New York: McGraw-Hill, 1962). See chapter "Seven Abilities That Seem to Count Greatly."

3. Macfarlane, op. cit., chapter 3, note 14.

4. Alison Clarke-Stewart, *Child Care in the Family* (A review of research and some proposals for policy) (New York: Harcourt Brace Jovanovich, 1977). See pp. 20–79.

5. From a paper entitled, "Family Interaction Patterns Associated with Self-Esteem in Preadolescent Girls and Boys," prepared by Roger C. Loeb, Leslie Horst, and Patricia J. Horton.

6. Richard Flaste, "One Who Broke Down the Barriers Formed by Poverty and Isolation," *The New York Times* (July 22, 1977).

7. White, op. cit., chapter 10, note 8, p. 146.

8. Ibid., p. 168.

9. Segal and Yahraes, op. cit., chapter 18, note 10, p. 287.

10. Paul Mussen and Nancy Eisenberg-Berg, *Roots of Caring, Sharing and Helping* (San Francisco: W. H. Freeman, 1977), pp. 86–87.

Chapter 23

1. John Holt, *Escape from Childhood: The Needs and Rights of Children* (New York: E. P. Dutton, 1974), p. 183.

2. "Community Service One Path to Learning," Curriculum Report of the National Association of Secondary School Principals, vol. 4, no. 5 (May 1975).

3. Sheila Cole, "Send Our Children to Work?" *Psychology Today* (July 1980).

4. W. F. R. Stewart, "Children in Flats: A Family Study," published by the Developments Department of the National Society for the Prevention of Cruelty to Children, 1 Riding House Street, London, September 1970.

Index